A Place Apart

A Place Apart

A Cape Cod Reader

Edited by Robert Finch

W. W. Norton & Company

New York   London

Copyright © 1993 by Robert Finch

Printed in the United States of America

First Edition

The text of this book is composed in 10/12 Galliard with the display set in Galliard Bold Italic.
Composition and manufacturing by the Maple-Vail Book Manufacturing Group.
Book design by Susan Hood.

Library of Congress Cataloging-in-Publication Data

A Place apart : a Cape Cod reader / edited by Robert Finch.
    p.   cm.
    Includes index.
    1. American literature—Massachusetts—Cape Cod.   2. Cape Cod (Mass.)—Literary collections.   I. Finch, Robert, 1943–
PS548.M4P53   1993
810'.8'0974492—dc20   92-39867

ISBN 0-393-03480-1

W. W. Norton & Company, Inc., 500 Fifth Avenue
New York, N.Y. 10110
W. W. Norton & Company Ltd., 10 Coptic Street
London WC1A 1PU

1 2 3 4 5 6 7 8 9 0

To John and Kristi Hay

who made our lives here possible

Contents

Contents

Contents

Contents

Acknowledgments

Anyone who puts together an anthology embarks on a voyage of self-discovery of his own ignorance of a field he thought he knew well. I am happy to acknowledge here the many individuals and institutions who helped me discover, and partially reduce, the depths of mine.

First and foremost, of course, this anthology would not have been possible without the resources and cooperation of the various, and often unique, Cape Cod libraries and their staffs. I am most especially grateful to the invaluable assistance and personal interest of Charlotte Price, curator of the Cape Cod History Collection at the Cape Cod Community College, the essential research center for any aspect of life on this peninsula. I would also like to acknowledge the generous assistance of Susan Raidy Klein of the Sturgis Library in Barnstable, Cheryl Bryan and Chris Lord at the Brewster Ladies Library, Jane Eldridge at the Eastham Public Library, Elaine McIlroy at the Wellfleet Public Library, the staff of the Cobb Memorial Library in Truro, the Truro Historical Society, the Fine Arts Work Center in Provincetown, and the Nantucket Athenaeum. I am particularly indebted to Ann Tanneyhill and Ernestine Gray at the Mashpee Archives for helping me locate the Wampanoag texts in this collection, and to the Chatham Historical Society for their generosity in allowing me to reprint the selections from Elizabeth Reynard's *The Narrow Land*. I would also like to thank the Boston Athenaeum and the Massachusetts Historical Society, two venerable institutions whose long and ongoing dedication to public service is as rare as it is invaluable. To all these institutions and their staffs I owe not only the discovery of much of the material included here, but the historical context in which I have tried to place it. Any errors or inadequacies in the latter are, of course, my own.

In addition, there are many individuals whose interest and assistance have greatly enriched this collection. Mrs. Donald Considine of Brewster first introduced me to the remarkable correspondence between Captain Joseph and Emily Lincoln, then in her late husband's collection of Lincoln memorabilia and now housed in the Sturgis Library in Barnstable. To Kathy Shorr I owe special thanks for her extensive efforts in discovering for me many of the contemporary Provincetown selections herein and for her valuable critical acumen. Other individuals who contributed their time, effort, and happy suggestions include Meadow Dibble, Janine and Richard Perry, Beth Finch, Deanne Urmy, Marian Wylie, and Louise Kelley.

One of the great pleasures of compiling this collection was making the acquaintance of and working with so many of the writers themselves. Their enthusiasm for the project, personal generosity, and, in many cases, efforts on my behalf with their publishers, have made this collection immeasurably richer. Above all, it seems, writers wish to be read. It was my aim to further that wish, and I only ask them to forgive any unintended interpretations I may have put on their work.

This book would not have been possible without two stalwart friends and editors at W. W. Norton: Jim Mairs, who makes good books happen, and Eve Picower, whose intelligent suggestions, rare patience, and unflagging competence in dealing with the daunting task of permissions and the thousand other details that come with an anthology of this size, allowed me to concentrate on the fun stuff.

Finally, if this book owes its origin anywhere, it is to Ann Boardman Sherry, who thirty years ago first introduced me to the magic that is Cape Cod and gave me her copy of *The Outermost House*. She did not know what treasures she opened.

The effulgence of this sun-blasted, blue-burning, ragged Cape Cod landscape, invisibly but passionately ablaze between the cruel reflectors of sun and sea, as if set on fire by a vast magnifying glass . . . he found himself suddenly seeing the whole Cape Cod landscape as one immense and beautiful thing, from Buzzard's Bay to Provincetown, from shoulder to sea tip, every detail clear, still, translucent, as in a God's-eye view. The salt marshes rotting in powerful sunlight; the red cranberry bogs; the sand-rutted roads through forests of scrub pine and scrub oak, and the secret ponds that existed on no map; thickets of wild grape and bull-briar; fields of blueberry and hot goldenrod; grass-grown wind-carved dunes, inlets and lagoons, mudflats bedded with eelgrass, bare at low tide, haunt of the eel, the bluecrab, the horseshoe crab, the fiddlers; and the blown moors, too, with high headlands and dwarfed cedars and junipers, the dry moss and the poverty grass crumbling underfoot, the wild-cherry trees glistening with the white tents of the tent caterpillar under the dome of August blue: he saw it all at a glance, sun-washed and sea-washed, alive, tangled, and everywhere haunted by the somehow so sunlit ghost of the vanished Indian. The Indian names—and the English names— these, too, were a vital part of it—Cataumet, Manomet, Poppennessett, Cotuit, Monomoy—Truro, Brewster, Yarmouth, Barnstable, Shoot-Flying Hill, the King's Highway—they ran through it like a river, ran gleaming into the past, ran too into the future. And the houses; the cottages of the sea captains—a mile of them in Dennis, the sea captains who had known St. Petersburg and Canton as well as Boston—or the porticoed and pagodaed mansions of the China traders; and the ruined farmhouses and barns, silver-gray ghosts, the sad shingles and clapboards smokelessly consuming, among wild apples and wild lilacs back into the burning earth from which they had risen—yes, it was all of a piece, all in one vision.

—*from* Conversation; or, Pilgrim's Progress *by Conrad Aiken (1940)*

Introduction

One Vision: Four Centuries of Cape Cod in Literature

I

Thoreau, that inland dweller, once observed that the seashore was "a most advantageous point from which to view this world." The history of literature on Cape Cod seems to have borne him out. Over the past four hundred years the Cape's landscape and its people have probably inspired more memorable writing than any other nonurban area of comparable size. The sheer *amount* of books on the subject is impressive enough, as a glance at the Cape Cod shelves in any of the local libraries will attest. At the Cape Cod Community College Library in West Barnstable, the Nickerson Memorial Room houses a collection of some six thousand books, articles, pamphlets, papers, manuscripts, and other documents about Cape Cod.

It is, of course, not primarily the amount of writing about this place but the extraordinary quality and wide appeal of so much of it that is remarkable. Anyone who reads very far into the wealth of stories, poems, legends, histories, plays, folklore, travel books, nature writing, personal essays, and biographies that the Cape has spawned cannot fail to be pleased, somewhat amazed, and eventually curious as to what has produced such an abundance. From the Wampanoag creation myths to the latest *New Yorker* piece on "the Cape scene," this slim arc of glacial leavings seems to have been more generously touched than most places by the muses.

Why has the Cape's sandy soil been such fertile ground for the literary imagination? And why does writing about Cape Cod seem to appeal to such a wide audience?

Cape Cod has always held an undeniably special place in the American imagination, though the reasons for this are not always easy to pin down. Some are historical, of course, having to do with such things as the *Mayflower's* first landing in Provincetown Harbor in 1620, or the general exportation of certain cultural and natural products, such as the Cape Cod house, cranberries, and Wellfleet oysters. More, no doubt, are rooted in the Cape's long standing as one of the country's premier vacation resorts. For well over a century it has served, for millions of Americans, as one of those magical destinations, a place apart from the ordinariness and stress of daily existence. Thus any writing about it has something of a mythic appeal. This symbolic pull has been two-edged, however, for, as many a "washashore" lured here by his or her own illusions about the Cape has discovered, existence is not necessarily any easier here than anywhere else.

The broad appeal of so much Cape literature, however, is due to the fact that the best of it is not provincial in character, but grapples with universal human concerns and behavior. As Thoreau said at the beginning of his own classic account, "I did not see why I might not make a book on Cape Cod, as well as my neighbor on 'Human Culture.' It is but another name for the same thing, and hardly a sandier phase of it." Cape historian Henry C. Kittredge echoed this claim when he insisted that Cape Codders were not the "quaint eternal types" limned in more popular literature, but "ordinary samples of our race," from whose lives we might learn about ourselves.

Yet just as the Cape is an uncommon landscape, there has also been something undeniably distinctive about its traditional culture and history that seems to have drawn more than its share of chroniclers. Truro historian Shebnah Rich, ahead of his time, recognized the shaping effect of environment on human culture when he said:

The laws of physical geography . . . have an overruling agency in the development of mankind. From certain climate and soil, we may as surely expect a certain crop of men, as of corn and potatoes.

Moreover, as Kittredge also observes, Cape Codders were distinguished by being "ordinary men placed in extraordinary circumstances." Those extraordinary circumstances, of course, have much to do with the Cape's maritime history and culture, in which the people of Cape Cod participated and by which they were shaped to a remarkable degree. Impressed by the nonchalance with which the local inhabitants went to sea, Thoreau commented:

In ancient times the adventures of these two or three men and boys would have been made the basis of a myth, but now such tales are crowded into a line of shorthand signs, like an algebraic formula in the shipping news.

Just why Cape Cod has attracted so many *writers* of note is again a question that has both obvious and not so obvious answers. The early Pilgrim and Puritan settlers, for instance, brought with them a strong intellectual tradition, one that accounts for such distinguished early works as Bradford's *Of Plimoth Plantation* and Mourt's *Relation*. No doubt its proximity to Boston and New York has made it a natural destination and vacation spot for many writers, including such distinguished academics as Timothy Dwight of Yale and Elizabeth Reynard of Barnard. Harvard College (founded in 1636, only one year before Sandwich, the Cape's first town), in particular, seems to have had an unusually long and fruitful relationship with Cape Cod and its people. A remarkable proportion of the writers who have produced Cape-based literature attended that university: they include Timothy Alden, Emerson, Thoreau, Henry James, Henry Beston, Eugene O'Neill, Conrad Aiken, Henry Kittredge, Wyman Richardson, Robert Nathan, E. J. Kahn, Jr., Stanley Kunitz, Howard Nemerov, Norman Mailer, John Hay, Richard Wilbur, James D. Lazell, William Martin, and Robert Finch.

On the other hand, the Cape itself was no cultural backwater, though it was often painted as such by many of the earlier urban writers. It is an old saying that during the heyday of the clipper ship, many a Cape Codder had been to China who had never gone to Boston by land. Wives and children often sailed with the shipmasters, and several of Cape Cod's small villages boasted a cosmopolitan culture that was unusual among mid-nineteenth-century New England towns. As Kittredge put it, "Narrow-mindedness found barren soil in a district where two houses out of every three belonged to men who knew half the seaports of the world and had lived ashore for months at a time in foreign countries." No doubt it was this comparatively sophisticated rural culture that helped produce such exceptional local historians as Amos Otis and Shebnah Rich.

At the turn of the century a happenstance of individuals at the tip of Cape Cod initiated a movement that eventually turned Provincetown (and eventually, by spillover, Truro and Wellfleet) into a mecca for artists and writers. The formation of the Provincetown Players in 1916 brought together writers like Mary Heaton Vorse, Eugene O'Neill, Susan Glaspell, Wilbur Daniel Steele, and Edna St. Vincent Millay. Numerous literary figures have continued to flock to the Cape End over the decades, often taking up seasonal or permanent residence. Province-town's status as a writing colony of national importance was further enhanced with the establishment in 1968 of the Provincetown Fine Arts Work Center, an institution which has enlisted and encouraged the talents of such writers as Stanley Kunitz, Alan Dugan, Mary Oliver, Roger Skillings, Cynthia Huntington, Susan Mitchell, David Wojahn, and Mark Doty.

Writers, like other people, like to vacation in pleasant surroundings with like-minded people. But vacationing, living, or even working in a place does not necessarily mean you will write about it. Why have so many off-Cape writers who come to the Cape written about the Cape? That is perhaps the most interesting question of all, and one to which I will offer only a speculative answer.

Just as so many Cape artists have remarked on the unique sea-reflected quality of the Cape's light, so I think there is a special appeal to the writer's imagination in the Cape's landscape. For nature writers, this appeal is fairly obvious, and is discussed in the introduction to the section titled "Natural Mystery." But poets, essayists, and fiction writers, too, seem to have been entranced by its peculiar character. This attraction seems to me to have something to do with its pervasive sense of change and exposure, a sense that this peninsula, thrust thirty miles out into the sea, is one of the world's great edges.

Edges, as every birdwatcher knows, are particularly rich habitats, producing more species than most areas. So this edge, where land meets sea, has proved to be a fruitful site for illuminating the human condition. On one side we have the implacable ocean, a presence that dwarfs our own and helps to give us what Kittredge calls "a true perspective." On the other side is the peculiarly human character of the Cape landscape, at once cosmic and classical, open to the broad sky and the vast sea, yet built on a human scale, molded as if for our particular use, seemingly designed—in its miniature hills, hollows, lakes, rivers, and forests—for a fabulous race destined to enact parables, rituals, and myths. And so we have.

One of the more interesting characteristics of Cape writers as a whole is the intense, long-term, intimate, and ongoing dialogue, or conversation, that they have sustained among themselves over the centuries. It is one of the things, I think, that make our literature a real "tradition." Many of them, of course, knew or have known one another personally. But these authors not only tend to be very much aware of their contemporaries and predecessors, they also extensively comment on them, criticize them, quote from them, allude to them, parody them, reimagine them, and steal from them shamelessly. *Everybody,* for instance, seems to have stolen or borrowed material from old Shebnah Rich, paraphrasing or retelling his marvelous stories, more often than not without acknowledgment. Poet Conrad Aiken manages to incorporate into a poem a line taken verbatim from the Pilgrims' account of their landing in Provincetown Harbor—and makes it rhyme, to boot. Thoreau, of course, has frequently been the subject of later writers; but he himself was not above using other Cape scribes to pad his own work. In his chapter "The Plains of Nauset," there are long, seemingly endless stretches of passages lifted from early church histories and sermons of old Eastham ministers. At the end of the chapter Thoreau offers the following justification (which is *almost,* but not quite, clever enough to excuse him):

There was no better way to make the reader realize how wide and peculiar that plain was, and how long it took to traverse it, than by inserting these extracts in the midst of my narrative.

The breadth of Cape Cod's literature is certainly striking for a place so small, not only for the many forms and voices it has taken, but for the extraordinary variety of environments and cultures it has reflected over its long history. Yet despite its rich diversity, there appear to be certain elements of both the landscape and the people of Cape Cod to which its best writers have recurred again and again. Just as the painter in Aiken's *Conversation,* looking at the varied and "burning" landscape of Cape Cod from Bourne to Provincetown, saw it "all of a piece, all of one vision," so it seems to me that the literature of the Cape, varied as it is, nonetheless forms one vision, one testament to a continuing entity that is embodied, informed, and sustained by the land and the sea that created it.

II

This book owes much of its origin and inspiration to Edith and Frank Shay's fine 1951 anthology *Sand in Their Shoes,* the first comprehensive compilation of Cape Cod literature. For one thing, it introduced me to many of the older Cape writers, whose works I subsequently tracked down and read in their entirety. It has long been a fixture on my Cape bookshelf, and I was pleased when it was recently reprinted. But that event also made me realize that the Shays had, by necessity, left out many wonderful pieces. And in any case, it seemed that in the past forty years enough new and interesting Cape writing had appeared to warrant a new anthology.

Every anthology is personal, but perhaps this one is more, or more overtly, personal than most. I have not necessarily tried for any kind of literary balance, and I certainly make no claim that the selections represent all of the historical periods, geographical areas, or cultural groups of the Cape. Art is never democratic or all-inclusive; rather, it illuminates, and by illuminating touches places beyond its subject or origin. Primarily I have chosen to include those authors and selections for which I have held a long affection and those recently discovered ones that I most wanted to share with others. For that reason, certain well-known Cape writers or passages may not be found here. In some cases, to have more room for new material, I have not reprinted some of the classic pieces that can be found in the Shays' collection. In others, some once very popular works seem to have lost much of their appeal for today's readers, and at any rate they can still easily be found on the shelves of almost any Cape Cod library.

A few distinguished writers with strong Cape connections—Norman Mailer and Arturo Vivante, for instance—have not been included. While I admire much of their work, it seemed to me that, in these cases, their best work has not been set on the Cape. In a few other instances—such as Eugene O'Neill's *Ile,* his one-act play about a Provincetown whaler—the works were simply too long to include.

The arrangement of the selections, too, is personal. I could have presented them all chronologically, or strictly by period, but it seemed to me that they fell naturally into groups of common subject matter, and that it might be more interesting, say, to compare descriptions of a Cape Cod house by four different writers from different eras, or to read two very different accounts of the same shipwreck, or to see how the remarkable community of Provincetown has changed over the centuries. In other words, I have tried to juxtapose the selections so as to reveal how they resonate with one another, and also so as to reflect that on-going "conversation" that Cape writers have held with one another over the centuries. Also not without some trepidation, I have provided some titles of my own for those selections that do not have them in the original text. These appear without quotation marks in the table of contents and at the head of the selections.

Despite the unabashedly subjective choice of the selections here, I eventually found myself with the inevitable dilemma that all anthologists face, for, in a field so rich, including one selection inevitably means leaving out something else. There are, after all, certain books one would like to include in their entirety, wonderful works like Thoreau's *Cape Cod,* Vorse's *Of Time and the Town,* Kittredge's *Cape Cod,* Rich's *Truro: Cape Cod,* Beston's *The Outermost House,* Reynard's *The Narrow Land,* Berger's *Cape Cod Pilot,* Hay's *The Run,* and virtually all of the Cape poems by Mary Oliver or Marge Piercy. Fortunately, almost all of these works are currently available in new or reprint editions.

Moreover, once I began actively looking for new material, it was hard to know where to stop. After a while, in fact, I began to wonder if there was any writer of note who *hadn't* written about the Cape. After all, who would expect to find a marvelous child's view of a train ride to Provincetown in Thomas Merton's *The Seven Story Mountain?* Finally I began to feel as I often do after scratching for quahogs on the tidal flats, when the sun has gone down and the tide is rising, and my bucket is full above the rim and I am lugging it back toward shore. Inevitably it is then I stumble on several "honey holes," full of as many littlenecks or cherrystones as I could wish. But there is a point at which, no matter how carefully you balance them, the bucket will just not hold any more clams. And so it was with this anthology: at some point, I just stopped scratching.

At the end of his introduction to *Sand in Their Shoes,* Frank Shay says, "Cape Cod has been, still is, and will always be good for America." This was the disarming and affectionate boast of an adopted Cape Codder in a more innocent and culturally distinct age. Today Cape Cod has less to offer that is separate from the rest of America. A burgeoning and at times overwhelming human presence has made it much harder to stand here, as Thoreau did, and "put all America behind him." Yet in the four decades since the Shays' anthology appeared, the flow of new voices and new visions of this land has not abated. If anything it has grown stronger; over half of the works represented here have been published since World War II. Whatever Cape Cod may offer the country at large today, there seems little question that it has been, still is, and for some time to come will continue to be good for American writers and readers.

Robert Finch
Brewster, Massachusetts
January 1993

A Place Apart

Loomings

~~~~~~

W HEN BARTHOLOMEW GOSNOLD "discovered" Cape Cod in 1602, it had, of course, been inhabited for millennia by native peoples. Recent archaeological discoveries have pushed the first human settlement of Cape Cod back at least eight thousand years.

There is also no question that the original Cape Codders—the various Wampanoag Indian tribes—had developed a considerable body of other oral literature at the time of European contact. A number of their legends and myths, many of which concern the benevolent giant Maushop, have survived the centuries. Some were recorded first or second hand from the original tellers by early historians. Some continue to be told today by their descendants, such as the Mashpee Wampanoag, Nosapocket. Still others, such as the tales in "The Death of the Giant" section of Elizabeth Reynard's *The Narrow Land,* have been collected and "rendered" by non-Indian writers.

Besides the native presence, earlier European eyes than Gosnold's had beheld Cape Cod, and earlier feet may have trodden it. John and Sebastian Cabot likely observed its shores when they sailed from Labrador to Virginia in 1498. Giovanni da Verrazzano rounded its bold headland on his way north to Maine in 1524. French and Basque fishermen are known to have fished off New England throughout the sixteenth century, and, as Kittredge suggests, they may have taken refuge from storms and even established seasonal habitation in Provincetown Harbor.

Over the years, numerous assertions have been made that various Scandinavian voyagers—notably Leif Ericsson, Thorwald, and Thorfinn—landed, and even settled, on Cape Cod around A.D. 1000. It is not my intention to get into the long-standing controversy over the Vikings on Cape Cod. This is a literary anthology, and whether or not the Vikings ever visited these shores may be of historic interest, but it is of little literary interest. The descriptions of "Vinland" in the Icelandic sagas are too vague to embody any definite sense of place, and, except for providing the occasion for some really bad punning by Thoreau on his own name and the various Viking "Thor-s," the putative Viking presence on the Cape has not inspired much memorable writing in later authors.

By the same reasoning, however, despite prior sightings and perhaps even landings, Gosnold's voyage in the bark *Concord* in May 1602 can legitimately represent the literary discovery of Cape Cod. In the first place, he gave it its permanent name, one so rooted in its character that not even an attempt by Captain John Smith in 1614 to change it to Cape James, in honor of his monarch, succeeded in prying it loose.

More significantly, Gosnold's voyage provided the first detailed descriptions of the Cape landscape and its native inhabitants. The two principal accounts were written by Gabriel Archer and John Brereton, gentlemen members of Gosnold's crew. Both published their accounts in England. Brereton's, considered the more lively narrative, is generally the one reprinted. But his temperament seems to have been primarily that of a public-relations man, and his account (rushed into print the same year as the voyage) seems intended to encourage speculation and the settlement of "plantations" in "Northern Virginia," as New England was then known. It is remarkably free of the navigational dangers of the coast, or of attacks and threats from the Indians, that other explorers noted. By the same token, his description of the fertility, abundance, and variety of the local flora, fauna, and soil is hyperbolic: the Cape is presented as a natural cornucopia, "in comparison whereof the most fertile part of England is (of itself) but barren."

Archer, by comparison, seems more candid about the dangers encountered and more tempered, though still laudatory, in his description of the Cape's natural abundance. What is true of both accounts, in fact of all the early explorers' reports, is that this coast was "very full of people."

Unfortunately, we have no surviving accounts by the native Indians of their original way of life. Like most Native American peoples of the Northeast, the Wampanoags and their culture were largely wiped out in the early seventeenth century, first by various "plagues" (probably typhus or smallpox, brought by earlier European expeditions), and later by "legal" appropriations of their lands. The surviving Cape Indians were eventually given title to what is now the Town of Mashpee in

1682, but by then their traditional culture had already been profoundly and permanently altered.

For a portrait of the early Cape Indians, then, we have only the accounts of the European explorers and first settlers. Their interpretations of the character of the Indians are certainly suspect, often telling us more about the writer than the Indians. Also, the great variation in the Indians' behavior recorded in different encounters no doubt reflects the difference in various Europeans' behavior toward *them*. Nonetheless, these first descriptions of the physical appearance, clothing and adornments, habitations and settlements of the natives are vivid, detailed, and often highly complimentary.

It may have been that the largely enthusiastic accounts of Archer, Brereton, and other English explorers encouraged the Pilgrim band from Leyden, Holland, to consider the Cape as a possible settlement site, though we know from their own account that their intended destination was the Hudson River and that it was only "contrary winds" and the "dangerous shoals and roaring breakers" off Chatham that changed their course and that of American history.

William Bradford's *Of Plymoth Plantation* is generally considered the first significant work of English prose written in this country. Few books of such stature and importance have had such a curious history. Bradford, an elder of the Pilgrim company and afterward governor of the Plymouth Colony for nearly thirty years, completed his history about 1650, but it was not published until more than two hundred years later. The manuscript was stolen by British soldiers during the Revolution and remained lost until the middle of the next century later, when it showed up in the possession of the Bishop of London. The text was finally published by the Massachusetts Historical Society in 1856, and the original manuscript was eventually returned, with great pomp and legislative ceremony, to the Commonwealth of Massachusetts in 1897.

Bradford's account is, of course, invaluable to historians, but his narrative also contains many memorable passages, none more so than his meditation on the position of the Pilgrim band after the *Mayflower* first landed in Provincetown Harbor in November 1620. Despite being what seems to us now a biased view of the Cape's Native Americans, this passage remains a powerful expression of the enormous isolation the Pilgrims faced and the trials they were to endure over the next several years in Plymouth. It also stands, 370 years later, as an enduring benchmark from which we may gauge and sense the incredible transformations this land has undergone.

Bradford's history draws much of its strength from the unflagging conviction of its author of the divine purpose of the Pilgrims' settlement in the New World: the creation of a new spiritual "City on the Hill." *Mourt's Relation* tells the same story in a noticeably more objective and accessible manner. Its style is vivid and straightforward, less solemn than Bradford's and free of the latter's Scriptural baggage. Published in London in 1622, this misleadingly named narrative is generally considered the work of several hands, most notably Bradford and Edward Winslow, a colleague of Bradford's and also an early governor of Plymouth Colony. "Mourt" was probably George Morton, an agent of the Pilgrims in England who acted as publisher of the work.

Many later writers have gotten considerable mileage out of its lively incidents and descriptions: the Cape woods that "tore our armor to pieces"; the mysterious skull in the Indian grave with "fine yellow hair still on it"; and the famous "First Encounter" fight with the Indians at Eastham. The story of Bradford's being caught in the Indian leg trap is told with such thinly veiled delight that I have always suspected that it is Winslow's, secretly relishing the upending of his colleague's magisterial dignity. The touching incident of the retrieval of the "lost boy," young John Billington, demonstrates a promising sympathy and cooperation between the Plymouth colonists and the Cummiquid Indians under Chief Iyanough, but it seems to have had an unfortunate sequel. A few years later these same Indians, according to Josef Berger, were "driven by the guns of the English into the swamps, there to die of pestilence."

To later writers the Pilgrims themselves have proved a rich subject for literary treatment. (The drowning of Bradford's wife, Dorothea, in Provincetown Harbor, for instance, has given rise to much imaginative speculation about "the Cape's first suicide.") They have also been taken to task, especially by contemporary historians, for their blatant "hypocrisy," especially toward the native Indians. Despite the fact that the Pilgrims had generally peaceful and beneficial relationships with the local Wampanoags, and despite the fact that they themselves repeatedly ransacked the Indians' corn caches, snitched their kettles, violated their graves, and "legally" stole their land, Bradford, Mourt, and other early writers repeatedly refer to the Indians as "thievish," and there is even a harbor at Plymouth named Thievish Harbor, after a perceived act of Indian theft.

On the other hand, it is hard to call this hypocrisy, in the ordinary sense, since the Pilgrim fathers recorded all of their own (to our eyes) reprehensible actions with such remarkable candor. Nor, I think, can we as modern readers totally regret these actions, since we have subsequently derived so much pleasurable moral outrage from them.

One of the first to do so was Thoreau, in his classic work *Cape Cod,* published in 1864. One notable element of this book is its revisionist view of what was then the accepted view of the Pilgrims' "right" to Indian lands. The passage about "Not Any" reprinted here, couched in Thoreau's caustically ironic style, is one of the first defenses of Indian land rights by a major literary figure.

Finally, Reynard's portrait of the "praying Indians"—those converted, at least outwardly, to Christianity by such early Pilgrim preachers as Richard Bourne and Samuel Treat—is a wry indictment of how, with the most noble intentions, the early Cape settlers destroyed the indigenous culture in order to "save" its people.

"Mirage on the Dunes"

By Elizabeth Reynard

A SLIM PENINSULA of white lies like a silver key thrust in the portals of a continent, a key that has, long since, unlocked a nation. Tall dunes cast shadows like the prows of ships whose moving figureheads are silhouetted from the bowing crests of dunes. Fluctuant sands wear occult veils of mirage. Winds are the voices of Indian giants, of shrill *Pukwudgees,* of *Whistlin' Whales,* of the *Screechin' Hannah.* The moon is a witch familiar, and the stars are the *Chart o' God.* Once paradise of twenty thousand sailors, once rendez-vous of half a thousand pirates, this port of whalers was, itself, born of a great ice whale. The vast Moby Dick of glaciers, pushing dark silt before it, ploughed homeward to the sea to die. With transparent lips it sucked the ocean, while its gaunt sides withered inward, leaving around them a narrow shroud rimmed by tallow-white beaches, plumed with blue fire of waves and flanged by the smoky sea.

—from *The Narrow Land* (1934)

Maushop's Smoke

By Timothy Alden

IN FORMER TIMES, a great many moons ago, a bird, extraordinary for its size, used often to visit the south shore of Cape Cod, and carry from thence to the southward, a vast number of small children.

Maushop, who was an Indian giant, as fame reports, resided in these parts. Enraged at the havock among the children, he, on a certain time, waded into the sea in pursuit of the bird, till he had crossed the sound and reached Nantucket. Before Maushop forded the sound, the island was unknown to the aborigines of America.

Tradition says, that Maushop found the bones of the children in a heap under a large tree. He then wishing to smoke a pipe, ransacked the island for tobacco; but, finding none, filled his pipe with poke, a weed which the Indians sometimes used as its substitute. Ever since the above memorable event, fogs have been frequent at Nantucket and on the Cape. In allusion to this tradition, when the aborigines observed a fog rising, they would say, "There comes old Maushop's smoke."

—from *Memorabilia of Yarmouth*
(1797)

———

The Benevolent Trout

BEFORE THE EXISTENCE of Coatuit Brook,* a benevolent trout, intending to furnish the Indians with a stream of fresh water, forced his way from the sea into the land; but finding the effort too great for his strength, he expired, when another fish took up the work where he left it, and completed the brook to Sanctuit Pond. The reader may believe as much of this story as he pleases. He probably would regard the whole as a fiction, if he was not assured, that thousands of persons have seen the mound of earth, which covers the grave of the benevolent trout. It is on the grounds of Mr. Hawley, and not far from his house; and is twenty-seven feet over, and fifty-four feet in length.

—from *A Description of Mashpee, in the County of Barnstable* (1802)

———

* Now the Santuit River in Mashpee.

"The Formation of the Islands"

By Elizabeth Reynard

YEARS AGO, IN the days before the first white people came across the sea, a young giant named Maushop lived in the Narrow Land. He was so large that no wigwam nor Council House could hold him, so he slept under the stars. Sometimes he lay on one part of the Cape, sometimes on another. To him snowdrifts were like handfuls of beach-sand and wrapped in his robe of many hundred bearskins, the heat from his body kept him warm in the cold winter weather. If he awakened on an icy night, and found that the chill had crept under his robe, he warmed himself by jumping back and forth across-Cape.

In summer he could not sleep when the heat of the land grew oppressive. On such nights he made a bed of the lower Cape; of the cool lands that lie narrowly between ocean and bay. There his body twisted and turned, changing position, seeking repose, until he shifted the level sand into dunes and hollows.

Once, on a night when the wind ceased blowing and stars hung heavy with unshed lightning, Maushop became more than usually restless. He tossed. He flung himself about, till his moccasins unfastened themselves and burrowed into the ground. When Geesukquand, the Sun Spirit, lighted the tepee fires of dawn, Maushop awoke, missed his moccasins, and felt about for them. He found them and holding them tightly he raised his arm and flung the sand from them far to the south. This sand became the South Sea Islands, *Nantucket* and *Martha's Vineyard*.

—from *The Narrow Land* (1934)

—

The Legend of Maushop

By Nosapocket

HE USED TO come to the Cape, and Mashpee was one of the village sites for the Wampanoags. But he used to swim here and fetch wood for the Aquinnah Wampanoags, the Gay Head (people). And turns out that it was our feeling as well as the creator's that he was spoiling those people by doing many of their labors (so) that they themselves became more lazy. And from the tale that I hear—one of my favorites—is a reminder not to become lazy, because the creator had counsel with Maushop and reminded him that he was spoiling the people from being what they could be, what their capacities were. (He) pampered them like little children. Therefore the Creator informed Maushop that he was to be changed into another type of medicine being, a white whale. And so he was given time to say goodby to the Aquinnah people as well as us, the Mashpee people, and we went to see him at the Gay Head cliffs to say farewell. And his companion, a very huge toad was overtook with sorrow, seeing his friend was going to leave him and never be with him any more. And in his grief and sorrow the Creator saw that it wasn't good, and so changed him into a stone. So to this day there is a stone on the Gay Head cliffs that resembles a huge frog, a reminder to us not to be sorrowful about our Creator's decisions, that they are the best for all living things. Maushop was later through the centuries referred to and called Moby Dick. I met a fellow named Amos Smalley when I was younger, and he told me that he was the one who killed Moby Dick. He was a very old gentleman when I met him. He was an Aquinnah Wampanoag, Gay Head. He was of the very people that Maushop loved so dearly and pampered as if they were his own children. And it could only have been a Wampanoag, in my mind, that could have killed a Moby Dick, sought after by so many whalers.

—from *Spirit of the New England Tribes* (1986) by William S. Simmons

from *The Relation of Captain Gosnold's Voyage to the North Part of Virginia* (1602)

By Gabriel Archer

THE FIFTEENTH DAY we had again sight of the land, which made ahead, being as we thought an island, by reason of a large sound that appeared westward between it and the main, for coming to the west end thereof, we did perceive a large opening, we called it Shoal Hope. Near this cape we came to anchor in fifteen fathoms, where we took great store of cod-fish, for which we altered the name, and called it Cape Cod.* Here we saw sculls of herring, mackerel and other small fish, in great abundance. This is a low sandy shoal, but without danger, also we came to anchor again in sixteen fathoms, fair by the land in the latitude of 42 degrees. This cape is well near a mile broad, and lieth north-east by east. The captain went here ashore and found the ground to be full of pease, strawberries, whortleberries, &c., as then unripe, the sand also by the shore somewhat deep, the firewood there by us taken in was of cypress, birch, witch-hazel and beech. A young Indian came here to the captain, armed with his bow and arrows, and had certain plates of copper hanging at his ears; he showed a willingness to help us in our occasions.

The sixteenth, we trended the coast southerly, which was all champaign and full of grass, but the island somewhat woody. Twelve leagues from Cape Cod, we descried a point with some breach, a good distance off, and keeping our luff to double it, we came on the sudden into shoal water, yet well quitted ourselves thereof. This breach we called Tucker's Terror, upon his expressed fear. The point we named Point Care; having passed it we bore up again with the land, and in the night came with it anchoring in eight fathoms, the ground good.

The seventeenth, appeared many breaches round about us, so as we continued that day without remove.

---

*Here and elsewhere in the early texts, the terms "Cape Cod" and "Cape Cod Harbor" were applied to Provincetown and Provincetown Harbor respectively. Not until the early 1800s did "the Cape" come to refer to the entire peninsula.

The eighteenth, being fair we sent forth the boat, to sound over a breach, that in our course lay of another point, by us called Gilbert's Point, who returned us four, five, six and seven fathoms over. Also, a discovery of divers islands which after proved to be hills and hammocks, distinct within the land. This day there came unto the ship's side divers canoes, the Indians apparelled as aforesaid, with tobacco and pipes steeled with copper, skins, artificial strings and other trifles to barter; one had hanging about his neck a plate of rich copper, in length a foot, in breadth half a foot for a breastplate, the ears of all the rest had pendants of copper. Also, one of them had his face painted over, and head stuck with feathers in manner of a turkey-cock's train. These are more timorous than those of the Savage Rock, yet very thievish. . . .

This coast is very full of people, for that as we trended the same savages still run along the shore, as men much admiring at us. . . . The one-and-thirtieth, Captain Gosnold, desirous to see the main because of the distance, he set sail over; where coming to anchor, went ashore with certain of his company, and immediately there presented unto him men women and children, who, with all courteous kindness entertained him, giving him certain skins of wild beasts, which may be rich furs, tobacco, turtles, hemp, artificial strings colored, chains, and such like things as at the instant they had about them. These are a fair-conditioned people. On all the seacoast along we found mussel shells that in color did represent mother-of-pearl, but not having means to dredge, could not apprehend further knowledge thereof. This main is the goodliest continent that ever we saw, promising more by far than we any way did expect: for it is replenished with fair fields, and in them fragrant flowers, also meadows, and hedged in with stately groves, being furnished also with pleasant brooks, and beautified with two main rivers that (as we judge) may haply become good harbors, and conduct us to the hopes men so greedily do thirst after. . . .

———

from *A Brief and True Relation of the Discovery of the North Part of Virginia* (1602)

By John Brereton

THESE PEOPLE,* AS they are exceeding courteous, gentle of disposition, and well conditioned, excelling all others that we have seen; so for shape of body and lovely favor, I think they excel all the people of America; of stature much higher than we; of complexion or color, much like a dark olive; their eyebrows and hair black, which they wear long, tied up behind in knots, whereon they prick feathers of fowls, in fashion of a coronet; some of them are black thin bearded; they make beards of the hair of beasts: and one of them offered a beard of their making to one of our sailors, for his what grew on his face, which because it was of a red color, they judged to be none of his own. They are quick-eyed, and steadfast in their looks, fearless of others' harms, as intending none themselves; some of the meaner sort given to filching, which the very name of savages (not weighing their ignorance in good or evil,) may easily excuse: their garments are of deer skins, and some of them wear furs round and close about their necks. They pronounce our language with great facility; for one of them one day sitting by me, upon occasion I spake smiling to him these words: How now (sirrah) are you so saucy with my tobacco? which words (without any further repetition,) he suddenly spake so plain and distinctly, as if he had been a long scholar in the language. Many other such trials we had, which are here needless to repeat. Their women (such as we saw) which were but three in all, were but low of stature, their eyebrows, hair, apparel, and manner of wearing, like to the men, fat, and very well favored, and much delighted in our company; the men are very dutiful towards them. And truly, the wholesomeness and temperature of this climate, doth not only argue this people to be answerable to this description, but also of a perfect constitution of body, active, strong, healthful, and very witty, as the sundry toys of theirs cunningly wrought, may easily witness.

*The native Wampanoags

12

A Nauset Indian's Dream of the Black Man*

By Thomas Shepard

FOURTHLY, A FOURTH and last observation wee took, was the story of an *Indian* in those parts, telling us of his dreame many yeers since, which he told us of openly before many witnesses when we sate at meat: the dreame is this, hee said "That about two yeers before the *English* came over into those parts there was a great mortality among the *Indians,* and one night he could not sleep above half the night, after which hee fell into a dream, in which he did think he saw a great many men come to those parts in cloths, just as the *English* now are apparelled, and among them there arose up a man all in black, with a thing in his hand which hee now sees was all one *English* mans book; this black man he said stood upon a higher place then all the rest, and on the one side of him were the *English,* on the other a great number of *Indians:* this man told all the *Indians* that God was *moosquantum* or angry with them, and that he would kill them for their sinnes, whereupon he said himself stood up, and desired to know of the black man what God would do with him and his *Squaw and Papooses,* but the black man would not answer him a first time, nor yet a second time, untill he desired the third time, and then he smil'd upon him, and told him that he and his *Papooses* should be safe, and that God would give unto them *Mitcheu,* (i.e.) victualls and other good things, and so hee awakened."

—from *The Clear Sun-Shine of the Gospel Breaking Forth upon the Indians in New England* (1648)

———

*This prophetic vision was told to Shepard by a Nauset Indian from Yarmouth who dreamed it during the great plague of 1617–1619, a few years before the coming of the Pilgrims.

from "Mayflower"

By Conrad Aiken

Listen: the ancient voices hail us from the farther shore:
now, more than ever, in the New England spring,
we hear from the sea once more
the ghostly leavetakings, the hawser falling, the anchor weighing,
cries and farewells, the weeping on the quayside, and the praying:
and the devout fathers, with no thought to fail,
westward to unknown waters set joyless sail,
and at length, 'by God's providence,' 'by break of day espied
land, which we deemed to be Cape Cod.'
'It caused us to rejoice together and praise God,
seeing so goodly a land, and wooded to the brink of the sea.'
And still we share that providential tide,
the pleasant bay, wooded on every side
with 'oaks, pines, juniper, sassafras,' and the wild fowl rising
in clouds and numbers past surmising.

———

from *Of Plymouth Plantation*

By William Bradford

Chapter IX: Of their Voyage, and how they Passed the Sea; and of their Safe Arrival at Cape Cod

SEPTEMBER 6 [1620]. These troubles being blown over, and now all being compact together in one ship, they put to sea again with a prosperous wind, which continued divers days together, which was some

14

encouragement unto them; yet, according to the usual manner, many were afflicted with seasickness. And I may not omit here a special work of God's providence. There was a proud and very profane young man, one of the seamen, of a lusty, able body, which made him the more haughty; he would alway be contemning the poor people in their sickness and cursing them daily with grievous execrations; and did not let to tell them that he hoped to help to cast half of them overboard before they came to their journey's end, and to make merry with what they had; and if he were by any gently reproved, he would curse and swear most bitterly. But it pleased God before they came half seas over, to smite this young man with a grievous disease, of which he died in a desperate manner, and so was himself the first that was thrown overboard. Thus his curses light on his own head, and it was an astonishment to all his fellows for they noted it to be the just hand of God upon him.

After they had enjoyed fair winds and weather for a season, they were encountered many times with cross winds and met with many fierce storms with which the ship was shroudly shaken, and her upper works made very leaky; and one of the main beams in the midships was bowed and cracked, which put them in some fear that the ship could not be able to perform the voyage. So some of the chief of the company, perceiving the mariners to fear the sufficiency of the ship as appeared by their mutterings, they entered into serious consultation with the master and other officers of the ship, to consider in time of the danger, and rather to return than to cast themselves into a desperate and inevitable peril. And truly there was great distraction and difference of opinion amongst the mariners themselves; fain would they do what could be done for their wages' sake (being now near half the seas over) and on the other hand they were loath to hazard their lives too desperately. But in examining of all opinions, the master and others affirmed they knew the ship to be strong and firm under water; and for the buckling of the main beam, there was a great iron screw the passengers brought out of Holland, which would raise the beam into his place; the which being done, the carpenter and master affirmed that with a post put under it, set firm in the lower deck and otherways bound, he would make it sufficient. And as for the decks and upper works, they would caulk them as well as they could, and though with the working of the ship they would not long keep staunch, yet there would otherwise be no great danger, if they did not overpress her with sails. So they committed themselves to the will of God and resolved to proceed. . . .

But to omit other things (that I may be brief) after long beating at sea they fell with that land which is called Cape Cod, the which being made and certainly known to be it, they were not a little joyful. After some deliberation had amongst themselves and with the master of the ship, they tacked about and resolved to stand for the southward (the wind and weather being fair) to find some place about Hudson's River for their habitation. But after they had sailed that course about half the day, they fell amongst dangerous shoals and roaring breakers, and they were so far entangled therewith as they conceived themselves in great danger; and the wind shrinking upon them withal, they resolved to bear up again for the Cape and thought themselves happy to get out of those dangers before night overtook them, as by God's good providence they did. And the next day they got into the Cape Harbor where they rid in safety. . . .

Being thus arrived in a good harbor, and brought safe to land, they fell upon their knees and blessed the God of Heaven who had brought them over the vast and furious ocean, and delivered them from all the perils and miseries thereof, again to set their feet on the firm and stable earth, their proper element. . . .

But here I cannot but stay and make a pause, and stand half amazed at this poor people's present condition; and so I think will the reader, too, when he well considers the same. Being thus passed the vast ocean, and a sea of troubles before in their preparation (as may be remembered by that which went before), they had now no friends to welcome them nor inns to entertain or refresh their weatherbeaten bodies; no houses or much less towns to repair to, to seek for succour. It is recorded in Scripture as a mercy to the Apostle and his shipwrecked company, that the barbarians showed them no small kindness in refreshing them, but these savage barbarians, when they met with them (as after will appear) were readier to fill their sides full of arrows than otherwise. And for the season it was winter, and they that know the winters of that country know them to be sharp and violent, and subject to cruel and fierce storms, dangerous to travel to known places, much more to search an unknown coast. Besides, what could they see but a hideous and desolate wilderness, full of wild beasts and wild men—and what multitudes there might be of them they knew not. Neither could they, as it were, go up to the top of Pisgah to view from this wilderness a more goodly country to feed their hopes; for which way soever they turned their eyes (save upward to the heavens) they could have little solace or content in respect of any outward objects. For summer being done, all things stand upon them with a weatherbeaten face, and the whole country, full of woods and thickets, represented a wild and savage hue. If they looked behind them, there was the mighty ocean which they had passed and was now as a main bar and gulf to separate them from all the civil parts of the world. . . .

What could now sustain them but the Spirit of God and His grace?

———

from *Mourt's Relation* (1622)

By G. Mourt

A Relation or Journal of the Proceedings of the Plantation settled at Plymouth in New England

WEDNESDAY, THE SIXTH of September [1620], the wind coming east-north-east, a fine small gale, we loosed from Plymouth, having been kindly entertained and courteously used by divers friends there dwelling, and after many difficulties in boisterous storms, at length, by God's providence, upon the ninth of November following, by break of the day we espied land which we deemed to be Cape Cod, and so afterward it proved. And the appearance of it much comforted us, especially seeing so goodly a land, and wooded to the brink of the sea. It caused us to rejoice together, and praise God that had given us once again to see land. And thus we made our course south-south-west, purposing to go to a river ten leagues to the south of the Cape, but at night the wind being contrary, we put round again for the bay of Cape Cod. And upon the 11th of November we came to an anchor in the bay,* which is a good harbor and pleasant bay, circled round, except in the entrance which is about four miles over from land to land, compassed about to the very sea with oaks, pines, juniper, sassafras, and other sweet wood. It is a harbor wherein a thousand sail of ships may safely ride. There we relieved ourselves with wood and water, and refreshed our people, while our shallop was fitted to coast the bay, to search for a habitation. There was the greatest store of fowl that ever we saw.

* Provincetown Harbor

And every day we saw whales playing hard by us, of which in that place, if we had instruments and means to take them, we might have made a very rich return, which to our great grief we wanted. Our master and his mate, and others experienced in fishing, professed we might have made three or four thousand pounds' worth of oil. They preferred it before Greenland whale-fishing, and purpose the next winter to fish for whale here. For cod we assayed, but found none; there is good store, no doubt, in their season. Neither got we any fish all the time we lay there, but some few little ones on the shore. We found great mussels, and very fat and full of sea-pearl, but we could not eat them, for they made us all sick that did eat, as well sailors as passengers. They caused to cast and scour, but they were soon well again.

The bay is so round and circling that before we could come to anchor we went round all the points of the compass. We could not come near the shore by three quarters of an English mile, because of shallow water, which was a great prejudice to us, for our people going on shore were forced to wade a bow shot or two in going a land, which caused many to get colds and coughs, for it was nigh times freezing cold weather.

This day before we came to harbor, observing some not well affected to unity and concord, but gave some appearance of faction, it was thought good there should be an association and agreement that we should combine together in one body, and to submit to such government and governors as we should by common consent agree to make and choose, and set our hands to this that follows word for word.

In the name of God, Amen. We whose names are underwritten, the loyal subjects of our dread sovereign lord King James, by the grace of God, of Great Britain, France, and Ireland King, Defender of the Faith, etc.

Having undertaken, for the glory of God, and advancement of the Christian faith, and honor of our king and country, a voyage to plant the first colony in the northern parts of Virginia, do by these presents solemnly and mutually in the presence of God and one of another, covenant, and combine ourselves together into a civil body politic, for our better ordering and preservation, and furtherance of the ends aforesaid; and by virtue hereof to enact, constitute, and frame such just and equal laws, ordinances, acts, constitutions, offices from time to time, as shall be thought most meet and convenient for the general good of the colony: unto which we promise all due submission and obedience. In witness whereof we have hereunder subscribed our names; Cape Cod, the 11th of November, in the year of the reign of our sovereign lord King

James, of England, France and Ireland eighteenth and of Scotland fifty-fourth, Anno Domini 1620.*

The same day, so soon as we could we set ashore fifteen or sixteen men, well armed, with some to fetch wood, for we had none left; as also to see what the land was, and what inhabitants they could meet with. They found it to be a small neck of land, on this side where we lay is the bay, and the further side the sea; the ground or earth, sand hills, much like the downs in Holland, but much better; the crust of the earth a spit's depth excellent black earth; all wooded with oaks, pines, sassafras, juniper, birch, holly, vines, some ash, walnut; the wood for the most part open and without underwood, fit either to go or ride in. At night our people returned, but found not any person, nor habitation, and laded their boat with juniper, which smelled very sweet and strong and of which we burnt the most part of the time we lay there.

Monday, the 13th of November, we unshipped our shallop and drew her on land, to mend and repair her, having been forced to cut her down in bestowing her betwixt the decks, and she was much opened with the people's lying in her, which kept us long there, for it was sixteen or seventeen days before the carpenter had finished her. Our people went on shore to refresh themselves, and our women to wash, as they had great need. But whilst we lay thus still, hoping our shallop would be ready in five or six days at the furthest, but our carpenter made slow work of it, so that some of our people, impatient of delay, desired for our better furtherance to travel by land into the country, which was not without appearance of danger, not having the shallop with them, nor means to carry provision, but on their backs, to see whether it might be fit for us to seat in or no, and the rather because as we sailed into the harbor there seemed to be a river opening itself into the main land. The willingness of the persons was liked, but the thing itself, in regard of the danger, was rather permitted than approved, and so with cautions, directions, and instructions, sixteen men were set out with every man his musket, sword, and corslet, under the conduct of Captain Miles Standish, unto whom was adjoined, for counsel and advice, William Bradford, Stephen Hopkins, and Edward Tilley.

Wednesday, the 15th of November, they were set ashore, and when

---

*This is the earliest known text of the famous "Mayflower Compact," traditionally described as the first document of self-government in this country. Though the government established by the Pilgrims at Plymouth was far from a pure democracy, this is still a seminal document in American history.

they had ordered themselves in the order of a single file and marched about the space of a mile, by the sea they espied five or six people with a dog, coming towards them, who were savages, who when they saw them, ran into the wood and whistled the dog after them, etc. First they supposed them to be Master Jones, the master, and some of his men, for they were ashore and knew of their coming, but after they knew them to be Indians they marched after them into the woods, lest other of the Indians should lie in ambush. But when the Indians saw our men following them, they ran away with might and main and our men turned out of the wood after them, for it was the way they intended to go, but they could not come near them. They followed them that night about ten miles by the trace of their footings, and saw how they had come the same way they went, and at a turning perceived how they ran up a hill, to see whether they followed them. At length night came upon them, and they were constrained to take up their lodging, so they set forth three sentinels, and the rest, some kindled a fire, and others fetched wood, and there held our rendezvous that night.

In the morning so soon as we could see the trace, we proceeded on our journey, and had the track until we had compassed the head of a long creek, and there they took into another wood, and we after them, supposing to find some of their dwellings, but we marched through boughs and bushes, and under hills and valleys, which tore our very armor in pieces, and yet could meet with none of them, nor their houses, nor find any fresh water, which we greatly desired, and stood in need of, for we brought neither beer nor water with us, and our victuals was only biscuit and Holland cheese, and a little bottle of aquavitae, so as we were sore athirst. About ten o'clock we came into a deep valley, full of brush, wood-gaile, and long grass, through which we found little paths or tracks, and there we saw a deer, and found springs of fresh water, of which we were heartily glad, and sat us down and drunk our first New England water with as much delight as ever we drunk drink in all our lives.*

When we had refreshed ourselves, we directed our course full south, that we might come to the shore, which within a short while after we did, and there made a fire, that they in the ship might see where we were (as we had direction) and so marched on towards this supposed river. And as we went in another valley we found a fine clear pond of

---

*Pilgrim Springs, a site within the Cape Cod National Seashore in North Truro, has been identified as the source of this water.

fresh water, being about a musket shot broad and twice as long. There grew also many fine vines, and fowl and deer haunted there; there grew much sassafras. From thence we went on, and found much plain ground, about fifty acres, fit for the plow, and some signs where the Indians had formerly planted their corn. After this, some thought it best, for nearness of the river, to go down and travel on the sea sands, by which means some of our men were tired, and lagged behind. So we stayed and gathered them up, and struck into the land again, where we found a little path to certain heaps of sand, one whereof was covered with old mats, and had a wooden thing like a mortar whelmed on the top of it, and an earthen pot laid in a little hole at the end thereof. We, musing what it might be, digged and found a bow, and, as we thought, arrows, but they were rotten. We supposed there were many other things, but because we deemed them graves, we put in the bow again and made it up as it was, and left the rest untouched, because we thought it would be odious unto them to ransack their sepulchres.

We went on further and found new stubble, of which they had gotten corn this year, and many walnut trees full of nuts, and great store of strawberries, and some vines. Passing thus a field or two, which were not great, we came to another which had also been new gotten, and there we found where a house had been, and four or five old planks laid together; also we found a great kettle which had been some ship's kettle and brought out of Europe. There was also a heap of sand, made like the former—but it was newly done, we might see how they had paddled it with their hands—which we digged up, and in it we found a little old basket full of fair Indian corn, and digged further and found a fine great new basket full of very fair corn of this year, with some thirty-six goodly ears of corn, some yellow, and some red, and others mixed with blue, which was a very goodly sight. The basket was round, and narrow at the top; it held about three or four bushels, which was as much as two of us could lift up from the ground, and was very handsomely and cunningly made. But whilst we were busy about these things, we set our men sentinel in a round ring, all but two or three which digged up the corn. We were in suspense what to do with it and the kettle, and at length, after much consultation, we concluded to take the kettle and as much of the corn as we could carry away with us; and when our shallop came, if we could find any of the people, and come to parley with them, we would give them the kettle again, and satisfy them for their corn. So we took all the ears, and put a good deal of the loose corn in the kettle for two men to bring away on a staff; besides, they that could put any into their pockets filled the same. The rest we buried again for we were so laden with armor that we could carry no more.*. . .

In the morning we took our kettle and sunk it in the pond, and trimmed our muskets, for few of them would go off because of the wet, and so coasted the wood again to come home, in which we were shrewdly puzzled, and lost our way. As we wandered we came to a tree, where a young sprit was bowed down over a bow, and some acorns strewed underneath. Stephen Hopkins said it had been to catch some deer. So as we were looking at it, William Bradford being in the rear, when he came looked also upon it, and as he went about, it gave a sudden jerk up, and he was immediately caught by the leg. It was a very pretty device, made with a rope of their own making and having a noose as artificially made as any roper in England can make, and as like ours as can be, which we brought away with us. In the end we got out of the wood, and were fallen about a mile too high above the creek, where we saw three bucks, but we had rather have had one of them. We also did spring three couple of partridges, and as we came along by the creek we saw great flocks of wild geese and ducks, but they were very fearful of us. So we marched some while in the woods, some while on the sands, and other while in the water up to the knees, till at length we came near the ship, and then we shot off our pieces, and the long boat came to fetch us. Master Jones and Master Carver being on the shore, with many of our people, came to meet us. And thus we came both weary and welcome home, and delivered in our corn into the store, to be kept for seed, for we knew not how to come by any, and therefore were very glad, purposing, so soon as we could meet with any of the inhabitants of that place, to make them large satisfaction. This was our first discovery, whilst our shallop was in repairing. . . .

The next morning we followed certain beaten paths and tracks of the Indians into the woods, supposing they would have led us into some town, or houses. After we had gone a while, we light upon a very broad beaten path, well nigh two feet broad. Then we lighted all our matches and prepared ourselves, concluding that we were near their dwellings, but in the end we found it to be only a path made to drive deer in, when the Indians hunt, as we supposed.

When we had marched five or six miles into the woods and could find no signs of any people, we returned again another way, and as we came into the plain ground we found a place like a grave, but it was

---

*The site of this pilfering of the Indians' corn cache, known as Corn Hill, is commemorated by a plaque at the mouth of the Little Pamet River in Truro. One has to wonder if this act was a factor in the hostility of the Indians subsequently described at First Encounter Beach.

much bigger and longer than any we had yet seen. It was also covered with boards, so as we mused what it should be, and resolved to dig it up, where we found, first a mat, and under that a fair bow, and there another mat, and under that a board about three quarters long, finely carved and painted, with three tines, or broaches, on the top, like a crown. Also between the mats we found bowls, trays, dishes, and such like trinkets. At length we came to a fair new mat, and under that two bundles, the one bigger, the other less. We opened the greater and found in it a great quantity of fine and perfect red powder, and in it the bones and skull of a man. The skull had fine yellow hair still on it, and some of the flesh unconsumed; there was bound up with it a knife, a packneedle, and two or three old iron things. It was bound up in a sailor's canvas cassock, and a pair of cloth breeches. The red powder was a kind of embalment, and yielded a strong, but no offensive smell; it was as fine as any flour. We opened the less bundle likewise, and found of the same powder in it, and the bones and head of a little child. About the legs and other parts of it was bound strings and bracelets of fine white beads; there was also by it a little bow, about three quarters long, and some other odd knacks. We brought sundry of the prettiest things away with us, and covered the corpse up again. After this, we digged in sundry like places, but found no more corn, nor any thing else but graves.

There was variety of opinions amongst us about the embalmed person. Some thought it was an Indian lord and king. Others said the Indians have all black hair, and never any was seen with brown or yellow hair. Some thought it was a Christian of some special note, which had died amongst them, and they thus buried him to honor him. Others thought they had killed him, and did it in triumph over him.

Whilst we were thus ranging and searching, two of the sailors, which were newly come on the shore, by chance espied two houses which had been lately dwelt in, but the people were gone. They, having their pieces and hearing nobody, entered the houses and took out some things, and durst not stay but came again and told us. So some seven or eight of us went with them, and found how we had gone within a flight shot of them before. The houses were made with long young sapling trees, bended and both ends stuck into the ground. They were made round, like unto an arbor, and covered down to the ground with thick and well wrought mats, and the door was not over a yard high, made of a mat to open. The chimney was a wide open hole in the top, for which they had a mat to cover it close when they pleased. One might stand and go upright in them. In the midst of them were four little trunches knocked into the ground, and small sticks laid over, on which they hung their pots, and what they had to seethe. Round about the fire they lay on mats, which are their beds. The houses were double matted, for as they were matted without, so were they within, with newer and fairer mats. In the houses we found wooden bowls, trays and dishes, earthen pots, handbaskets made of crabshells wrought together, also an English pail or bucket; it wanted a bail, but it had two iron ears. There was also baskets of sundry sorts, bigger and some lesser, finer and some coarser; some were curiously wrought with black and white in pretty works, and sundry other of their household stuff. We found also two or three deer's heads, one whereof had been newly killed, for it was still fresh. There was also a company of deer's feet stuck up in the houses, harts' horns, and eagles' claws, and sundry such like things there was, also two or three baskets full of parched acorns, pieces of fish, and a piece of a broiled herring. We found also a little silk grass, and a little tobacco seed, with some other seeds which we knew not. Without was sundy bundles of flags, and sedge, bulrushes, and other stuff to make mats. There was thrust into a hollow tree two or three pieces of venison, but we thought it fitter for the dogs than for us. Some of the best things we took away with us, and left the houses standing still as they were.

So it growing towards night, and the tide almost spent, we hasted with our things down to the shallop, and got aboard that night, intending to have brought some beads and other things to have left in the houses, in sign of peace and that we meant to truck with them, but it was not done, by means of our hasty coming away from Cape Cod. But so soon as we can meet conveniently with them, we will give them full satisfaction. Thus much of our second discovery.

Having thus discovered this place, it was controversial amongst us what to do touching our abode and settling there; some thought it best, for many reasons, to abide there. . . . But to omit many reasons and replies used hereabouts, it was in the end concluded to make some discovery within the bay, but in no case so far as Anguum. Besides, Robert Coppin, our pilot, made relation of a great navigable river and good harbor in the other headland of this bay, almost right over against Cape Cod, being in a right line not much above eight leagues distant, in which he had been once; and because that one of the wild men with whom they had some trucking stole a harping iron from them, they called it Thievish Harbor. And beyond that place they were enjoined not to go, whereupon, a company was chosen to go out upon a third discovery. Whilst some were employed in this discovery, it pleased God that Mistress White was brought a-bed of a son, which was called Peregrine.

Wednesday, the 6th of December, we set out, being very cold and hard weather. We were a long while after we launched from the ship before we could get clear of a sandy point which lay within less than a furlong of the same. . . .

. . . As we drew near to the shore, we espied some ten or twelve Indians very busy about a black thing—what it was we could not tell— till afterwards they saw us, and ran to and fro as if they had been carrying something away. We landed a league or two from them, and had much ado to put ashore anywhere, it lay so full of flat sands. When we came to shore, we made us a barricade, and got firewood, and set out our sentinels, and betook us to our lodging, such as it was. We saw the smoke of the fire which the savages made that night, about four or five miles from us.

In the morning we divided our company, some eight in the shallop, and the rest on the shore went to discover this place, but we found it only to be a bay, without either river or creek coming into it. Yet we deemed it to be as good a harbor as Cape Cod, for they that sounded it found a ship might ride in five fathom water.* . . .

We went ranging up and down till the sun began to draw low, and then we hasted out of the woods, that we might come to our shallop, which when we were out of the woods, we espied a great way off, and called them to come unto us, the which they did as soon as they could, for it was not yet high water. They were exceeding glad to see us (for they feared because they had not seen us in so long a time), thinking we would have kept by the shore side. So being both weary and faint, for we had eaten nothing all that day, we fell to make our rendezvous and get firewood, which always costs us a great deal of labor. By that time we had done, and our shallop come to us, it was within night, and we fed upon such victuals as we had, and betook us to our rest, after we had set out our watch. About midnight we heard a great and hideous cry, and our sentinels called, "Arm! Arm!" So we bestirred ourselves and shot off a couple of muskets, and the noise ceased; we concluded that it was a company of wolves or foxes, for one told us he had heard such a noise in Newfoundland.

About five o'clock in the morning we began to be stirring, and two or three which doubted whether their pieces would go off or no made trial of them, and shot them off, but thought nothing at all. After prayer we prepared ourselves for breakfast and for a journey, and it being now the twilight in the morning, it was thought meet to carry the things down to the shallop. Some said it was not best to carry the armor down; others said they would be readier; two or three said they would not

---

*Most likely Wellfleet Harbor.

carry theirs till they went themselves, but mistrusting nothing at all. As it fell out, the water not being high enough, they laid the things down upon the shore and came up to breakfast. Anon, all upon a sudden, we heard a great and strange cry, which we knew to be the same voices, though they varied their notes. One of our company, being abroad, came running in and cried, "They are men! Indians! Indians!" and withal, their arrows came flying amongst us. Our men ran out with all speed to recover their arms, as by the good providence of God they did. In the meantime, Captain Miles Standish, having a snaphance ready, made a shot, and after him another. After they two had shot, other two of us were ready, but he wished us not to shoot till we could take aim, for we knew not what need we should have, and there were four only of us which had their arms there ready, and stood before the open side of our barricade, which was first assaulted. They thought it best to defend it, lest the enemy should take it and our stuff, and so have the more vantage against us. Our care was no less for the shallop, but we hoped all the rest would defend it; we called unto them to know how it was with them, and they answered, "Well! Well!" every one and, "Be of good courage!" We heard three of their pieces go off, and the rest called for a firebrand to light their matches. One took a log out of the fire on his shoulder and went and carried it unto them, which was thought did not a little discourage our enemies. The cry of our enemies was dreadful, especially when our men ran out to recover their arms; their note was after this manner, *"Woach woach ha ha hach woach."* Our men were no sooner come to their arms, but the enemy was ready to assault them.

There was a lusty man and no whit less valiant, who was thought to be their captain, stood behind a tree within half a musket shot of us, and there let his arrows fly at us. He was seen to shoot three arrows, which were all avoided, for he at whom the first arrow was aimed, saw it, and stooped down and it flew over him; the rest were avoided also. He stood three shots of a musket. At length one took, as he said, full aim at him, after which he gave an extra-ordinary cry and away they went all. We followed them about a quarter of a mile, but we left six to keep our shallop, for we were careful of our business. Then we shouted all together two several times, and shot off a couple of muskets and so returned; this we did that they might see we were not afraid of them nor discouraged.

Thus it pleased God to vanquish our enemies and give us deliverance. By their noise we could not guess that they were less than thirty or forty, though some thought that they were many more. Yet in the dark of the morning we could not so well discern them among the trees, as they could see us by our fireside. We took up eighteen of their arrows which we have sent to England by Master Jones, some whereof were headed with brass, others with harts' horn, and others with eagles' claws. Many more no doubt were shot, for these we found were almost covered with leaves; yet, by the especial providence of God, none of them either hit or hurt us though many came close by us and on every side of us, and some coats which hung up in our baricade were shot through and through.

So after we had given God thanks for our deliverance, we took our shallop and went on our journey, and called this place, The First Encounter.* . . .

* * *

A Voyage Made By Ten of our men to the Kingdom of Nauset, to seek a boy that had lost himself in the woods; with such accidents as befell us in that voyage.

The 11th of June [1621] we set forth [from Plymouth], the weather being very fair. But ere we had been long at sea, there arose a storm of wind and rain, with much lightning and thunder, insomuch that a spout arose not far from us, but, God be praised, it dured not long, and we put in that night for harbor at a place called Cummaquid, where we had some hope to find the boy. Two savages were in the boat with us, the one was Squanto, our interpreter, the other Tokamahamon, a special friend. It being night before we came in, we anchored in the midst of the bay, where we were dry at alow water. In the morning we espied savages seeking lobsters, and sent our two interpreters to speak with them, the channel being between them; where they told them what we were, and for what we were come, willing them not at all to fear us, for we would not hurt them. Their answer was, that the boy was well, but he was at Nauset; yet since we were there they desired us to come ashore and eat with them; which, as soon as our boat floated, we did, and went six ashore, having four pledges for them in the boat. They brought us to their sachem or governor, whom they call Iyanough,† a man not exceeding twenty-six years of age, but very personable, gentle, courteous, and fair conditioned, indeed not like a savage, save for his attire. His entertainment was answerable to his parts, and his cheer plentiful and various.

One thing was very grievous unto us at this place. There was an old woman, whom we judged to be no less than a hundred years old, which

---

* First Encounter Beach, on the Bay side of Eastham, is named after this event.
† This Wampanoag leader has given his name, in different variations, to several places on the Cape, including Hyannis and Wianno.

came to see us because she never saw English, yet could not behold us without breaking forth into great passion, weeping and crying excessively. We demanding the reason of it, they told us she had three sons who, when Master Hunt was in these parts, went aboard his ship to trade with him, and he carried them captives into Spain (for Squanto at that time was carried away also) by which means she was deprived of the comfort of her children in her old age. We told them we were sorry that any Englishman should give them that offense, that Hunt was a bad man, and that all the English that heard of it condemned him for the same; but for us, we would not offer them any such injury though it would gain us all the skins in the country. So we gave her some small trifles, which somewhat appeased her.

After dinner we took boat for Nauset, Iyanough and two of his men accompanying us. Ere we came to Nauset, the day and tide were almost spent, insomuch as we could not go in with our shallop, but the sachem or governor of Cummaquid went ashore and his men with him. We also sent Squanto to tell Aspinet, the sachem of Nauset, wherefore we came. The savages here came very thick amongst us, and were earnest with us to bring in our boat. But we neither well could, nor yet desired to do it, because we had least cause to trust them, being they only had formerly made an assault upon us in the same place, in time of our winter discovery for habitation. And indeed it was no marvel they did so, for howsoever, through snow or otherwise, we saw no houses, yet we were in the midst of them.

When our boat was aground they came very thick, but we stood therein upon our guard, not suffering any to enter except two, the one being of Manomoyik, and one of those whose corn we had formerly found; we promised him restitution, and desired him either to come to Patuxet for satisfaction, or else we would bring them so much corn again. He promised to come; we used him very kindly for the present. Some few skins we got there but not many.

After sunset, Aspinet came with a great train, and brought the boy with him, one bearing him through the water. He had not less than a hundred with him, the half whereof came to the shallop side unarmed with him, the other stood aloof with their bows and arrows. There he delivered us the boy, behung with beads, and made peace with us, we bestowing a knife on him, and likewise on another that first entertained the boy and brought him thither. So they departed from us.

Here we understood that the Narragansets had spoiled some of Massasoit's men, and taken him. This struck some fear in us, because the colony was so weakly guarded, the strength thereof being abroad. But we set forth with resolution to make the best haste home we could;

yet the wind being contrary, having scarce any fresh water left, and at least sixteen leagues home, we put in again for the shore. There we met again with Iyanough, the sachem of Cummaquid, and the most of his town, both men, women, and children with him. He, being still willing to gratify us, took a runlet and led our men in the dark a great way for water, but could find none good, yet brought such as there was on his neck with him. In the meantime the women joined hand in hand, singing and dancing before the shallop, the men also showing all the kindness they could, Iyanough himself taking a bracelet from about his neck and hanging it upon one of us.

Again we set out, but to small purpose, for we gat but little homeward.

Our water also was very brackish, and not to be drunk. The next morning. Iyanough espied us again and ran after us; we, being resolved to go to Cummaquid again to water, took him into the shallop, whose entertainment was not inferior unto the former.

The soil at Nauset and here is alike, even and sandy, not so good for corn as where we are. Ships may safely ride in either harbor. In the summer they abound with fish. Being now watered we put forth again, and, by God's providence, came safely home that night.

"Not Any's" Representatives

By Henry David Thoreau

WHEN THE COMMITTEE from Plymouth had purchased the territory of Eastham of the Indians, "it was demanded, who laid claim to Billingsgate?" which was understood to be all that part of the Cape north of what they had purchased. "The answer was, there was not any who owned it. 'Then,' said the committee, 'that land is ours.' The Indians answered, that it was." This was a remarkable assertion and admission. The Pilgrims appear to have regarded themselves as Not Any's representatives. Perhaps this was the first instance of that quiet way of "speaking for" a place not yet occupied, or at least not improved as much as it may be, which their descendants have practiced, and are still practicing so extensively. Not Any seems to have been the sole proprietor of all America before the Yankees. But history says, that when the Pilgrims had held the lands of Billingsgate many years, at length, "appeared an Indian, who styled himself Lieutenant Anthony," who laid claim to them, and of him they bought them. Who knows but a Lieutenant Anthony may be knocking at the door of the White House some day? At any rate, I know that if you hold a thing unjustly, there will surely be the devil to pay at last.

—from *Cape Cod* (1865)

———

"Tales of the Praying Indians"

By Elizabeth Reynard

ON SABBATH MORNINGS, standing in sunshine on the quiet hills of Mashpee, John Eliot, or John Cotton, or Richard Bourne,* told to the People of the Place of Bays stories of a Squaw who bit Wisdom out of an Apple, of a Great Chief nailed to crossed Wood, of a medicine-man named Jonah who worked Canoe-magic inside a whale, of Red Water that divided into two sections like a clamshell, and of a Sagamore named Samson whose Strength-secret lay in his hair. In turn, the medicine-men and chiefs offered accounts of Kiehtan, of Weetucks, of Mahtah-dou the Devil-Bird; but the three white men, who spoke the language of the Wampanoag, refused to hear. Old Maushop, they declared, was an instrument of the White Devil. That was difficult news to a man who loved Maushop as a friend and knew him to be a hero. Better keep the old tales within the tribe, not attempt to share them with intruders. The Long Land bore witness, every lake, hill, and river of it, to the truth of the stories. The contours of islands and bays explained themselves, if a spirit-being looked on them with wisdom.

Beside new, stone hearthfires, discussion centered on problems of war, rum, windmills, and ministers. Converts, especially Indian children, imbued with Christian tenets, looked over their shoulders fear-

---

* Seventeenth-century ministers and missionaries among the Cape's Indian tribes.

fully, for instead of a Gentle Giant one might now expect to encounter the White Lucifer in the forest, or alongshore. Stories of the friendly Giant-being were transferred to Satan, who was obviously of great stature, since he managed to perform mischief now in one part of the land, now in another, and all while the eyelid of the tame cat moved across its moon-green eye.

—from *The Narrow Land* (1934)

How They Lived

≈≈≈≈≈

O NE OF THE perennial attractions of this peninsula for writers has
been the "Cape Codder," a protean figure that has changed significantly over the centuries, but that, until quite recently, was part of a
distinct and continuous maritime culture. In the following selections,
the author might be a native-born writer trying to bring to life one of
his own great-greats, or a traveler fascinated with the strange human
apparitions often met with on its beaches, or a modern Wampanoag
Indian retelling a historical legend, or a historian wrestling with the
complexities and contradictions of past events, or a contemporary poet
brooding on the figures and artifacts of a vanished age. But whatever
the perspective, these descriptions of the old Cape Codders and how
they lived are, like all good portraits, colored in part by the varied pal-
ettes and temperaments of the writers who painted them.

Amos Otis's account of the first settlers in Barnstable, for instance, is
a vivid example of a nineteenth-century native historian trying to reconcile the unquestioned virtues and fortitude of the First Comers with
some undeniable evidence of their inhumanity to one another. In the
various descriptions of the traditional Cape Cod house, too, one hears
the personalities and perspectives of the individual writers. Thoreau's
classic sketch of such a Wellfleet house reflects the novel impression
such structures made on "outsiders." By contrast, Shebnah Rich's recollection of a similar house is tinged with the unmistakable affection
and detailed, tactile sense of an individual who actually grew up in one.
Josef Berger, taking the social critic's view, sees little to recommend
such nostalgia, condemning the ill effects the huge open fireplaces had
on their young inhabitants.

In a country that has as one of its founding principles the separation of Church and State, we often forget that in the early days of the New England theocracy, governments temporal and eternal were, in most important respects, one and the same. That this had some invidious results is clear from such incidents as the Salem Witch Trials of 1692 and the persecution of the Quakers on the Upper Cape in the late 1650s; but it is also the source of some of our most treasured democratic traditions. The New England town meeting, that last bastion of grassroots democracy, and the concept of local "home rule" both had their roots in the Congregational parish form of self-government. The intellectual and scholarly traditions of many of the early Cape settlers, which made them initially such poor farmers and inept fishermen, are responsible for the remarkably thorough and candid nature of their public, as well as private, records. Morally strict they may have been, but prudishness was not a Puritan trait. One cannot help notice, however, in reading the accounts of punishments handed out by local officials and zealots, how often they were visited upon women, frequently—as in the cases of Reynard's scandalous Abigail or Otis's outspoken Widow Nabby—for "unwomanly" behavior.

To Shebnah Rich we owe one of the earliest accounts of a subject still largely avoided even in contemporary histories: slavery in New England. Rich, on the other hand, confronts the ugly fact head on and reminds us that each age has its own moral darkness to confront. Though Rich himself did not completely escape all the racial biases of his age (which of us can?), his unusually humane and compassionate nature is evident in his narrative of the Truro slave Pomp.

In their accounts of ministers and their churches, the historians also reveal their personalities. Kittredge tells his stories with wit and appreciation. Nosapocket of Mashpee gives a vivid account of an incident said to have occurred when her tribe regained possession of the old Indian Meeting House in the mid-nineteenth century. The modern ironic view of local ecclesiastical history is expressed in Scott Corbett's anecdote about a nationally famous, but locally infamous, minister.

From the beginning, off-Cape travelers and visitors have been fascinated by the Cape Cod character in its various incarnations. Two of the earliest, Augustus Kendell, an English visitor, and Timothy Dwight, the indefatigable president of Yale College, have roughly contemporary but widely divergent views of the quality of life at the tip of the Cape in the early 1800s. In fact, one might think Kendell's bleak account was a conscious retort to Dwight's sentimental picture, were it not that Kendell's was published thirteen years earlier. On the other hand it seems almost certain that Josef Berger had read Kittredge's uncritical and hyperbolic praise of clipper ships and their Cape Cod captains, and that it had rankled his proletarian spirit. In Berger's skewering of the "heroic" treatments of this subject, one almost feels Kittredge's eulogy on the spit.

In his sketches of colorful local figures, Thoreau often saw Cape Codders as parts of the landscape rather than as flesh-and-blood human beings. The outstanding exception to this in *Cape Cod* is the "Wellfleet Oysterman" John Young Newcomb. Though one critic described him as Thoreau's "Specimen Cape Cod Man," he is without a doubt Henry David's most fully realized portrait, drawn with affection, an ear for real speech, and an appreciation of a lifetime of earnest labor and local knowledge. True, some of the description approaches slapstick (the "tobacco juice" episode is said to have made Thoreau's Concord audience laugh till they cried—surely a rare event at Thoreau's lectures), but his satire is gentle and good-natured, and his barbs are pointed at himself as much as at his hosts.

Joseph C. Lincoln, son of a Brewster sea captain, was Cape Cod's most popular writer of fiction and perhaps did more than any other author to make the Cape part of the imaginative consciousness of the nation. His dozens of highly successful novels were based on stories he heard in his youth, and his characters—dry-witted, slightly comical, good-hearted, and spouting a dialect fraught with nautical metaphors—created perhaps the most enduring image of the Cape Codder in the popular mind. Today his most enduring work seems to me to be a handful of lyrics and *Cape Cod Yesterdays,* a collection of reminiscences of his Brewster boyhood. Besides Lincoln's characteristic wit these essays contain a wealth of information on a life now vanished and some memorable portraits of the real Cape Codders he knew.

John Hay and Scott Corbett were both part of the new wave of off-Cape immigrants who arrived in numbers after World War II. Much of their writing describes a traditional culture that was already fast disappearing but was still a strong presence in the landscape. Hay's Nate Black and his "Black Hills Emporium" are no more, though his barber's chair and instruments are on display in the Brewster Historical Society Museum. Corbett's charming account of the unusual system of local nomenclature used in the village of East Dennis has an interesting footnote. Presumably to protect the privacy of his neighbors, he created fictional names for most of them. Shortly after moving to the Cape, I paid a visit to the East Dennis library, housed in the wonderfully turreted Jacob D. Sears Memorial Hall building. Browsing through the shelves, I came upon the library's copy of Corbett's book. Taped to the inside front cover was a carefully typed key, arranged like a cast list, giving the names of the book's major characters and their real-life counterparts, apparently in order to ensure that the local residents could tell who was who in the book!

The final selections in this section are examples of how contemporary writers have reimagined a past that no longer exists, and in some cases never existed. Conrad Aiken's meditation on old West Brewster graveyards is, to my mind, one of the most evocative elegies in the language. David Wojahn's imagined tableau crystallizes a turn-of-the-century moment in which the rise of a genteel, artificial culture on the Cape remains bracketed by the older, mortal struggles with the sea. In a different way, Charles Philbrick's involuntary visit to a Wellfleet museum attests to the latent power of dusty artifacts to evoke past lives vividly. So do we all here on Cape Cod find, at one time or another, ways to borrow a sense of history to deepen our own lives.

My own contribution to this section is an example of a historical "legend," that is, a story which purports to have a basis in historical fact, but in reality does not. I first heard this tale in 1962 when I was a counselor at Camp Viking, one of a half-dozen now-vanished sailing camps that were then strung along the shores of Pleasant Bay. It was told by the senior counselors to campers on overnight sails to Nauset Beach, or, on occasion, around a campfire on Little Sipson Island itself. Later many of the campers in turn became counselors themselves and told it to their campers. Thus, in the compressed genealogies of summer camps, it persisted over several generations.

The First Settlers in Barnstable

By Amos Otis

MR. LOTHROP AND the large company arrived in Barnstable Oct. 11, 1639, O. S., Oct. 21, new, bringing with them the crops which they had raised in Scituate.

Though they had much to do to prepare for the winter, yet they did not forget their duty to God. Oct. 31, 1639, O. S., was set apart as a day of fasting, humiliation and prayer. It was the first fast day observed in Barnstable, the special object whereof was, "For the grace of our God to settle us here in church estate, and to unite us together in holy walking, and make us faithful in keeping Covenaunt w'th God and one to another."

The Rev. Joseph Hull and the Rev. John Mayo were both residents in Barnstable when Mr. Lothrop came, but there is no record that a church had been organized. Mr. Hull was the leading man in the plantation—the lands had been granted to him and Mr. Dimmock as a committee in behalf of themselves and their associates; he had procured an act of incorporation, had established a civil community, and had exercised his gifts as a preacher before any of Mr. Lothrop's church came. Very soon after we find him an exile, a wanderer, a persecuted man. In my account of Mr. Hull the details are given. However great may be our veneration for Mr. Lothrop and his followers, our sympathies are irresistibly enlisted on the side of poor Mr. Hull. The historian finds it a difficult matter to explain; he cannot "make bricks without straw." . . .

During the first winter they had no lack of food. Fish were abundant in the waters, wild game visited the coast in immense flocks, and the woods were filled with deer and other animals that tested the sportman's skill. Of the forty-five families then in Barnstable not more than ten, probably not more than eight, had comfortable two story frame houses. Three-fourths of the families occupied tenements that poorly sheltered them from the storms. . . .

1640. During the winter of 1639–40, there was little sickness in the plantation and no death occurred. The bills of mortality kept by Mr. Lothrop show that Barnstable was one of the most healthy towns in the Colony. During the year 1639 there was no deaths; in 1640, 3; '41, 10; '42, 2; '43, 1; '44, 4; '45, 1; '46, 4; '47, 0; '48, 3; '49, 5; '50, 3;

'51, 1; '52, 1; and to Nov. 1653, 1, making 38 in all. Of these 8 were still-born, 23 children, and 7 of mature age. Two of the latter were drowned at Nauset. In the spring of 1640 there were 45 families, and taking the usual average of 5, it gives 225 as the number of inhabitants. In 1653 the number of families had increased, and three hundred is not a high estimate of the number of inhabitants. If the average number of inhabitants be called only 250 during the whole period, it shows that the average annual mortality was only one in each one hundred. For so long a period it is doubtful whether a parallel case can be found.

The greatest mortality was in 1641. The spring was unusually cold and wet, the whooping cough prevailed, and several children died of that disease. In 1647 there was sickness in every family, scarce an individual escaped, yet no death occurred in the plantation that year. In 1649 the chin cough and the whooping cough prevailed among children and there were some cases of small pox. Though the deaths amounted to five that year, most of them appear to have died of other diseases. Mr. Lothrop was confined to his house, and unable to attend to the duties of the ministry for seven weeks by a cough and "a stitch in his side."

The statistics show that the first settlers of Barnstable had an abundance of nutritious food, were comfortably clothed, and lodged, during the first period of fifteen years.

Of the cereals, they had rye, barley, and some wheat, and an abundance of Indian corn; all the vegetables now generally cultivated, excepting the potato; pork, poultry, and venison; and of fish and grain they had a great abundance. They were not able to add much to the stock of clothing which they brought over. They raised flax, and manufactured some linen cloth. . . . It was many years before wool was raised in sufficient quantities to supply the domestic demand. Deer and other skins, which the natives understood the art of dressing in a superior manner, they substituted for woollen cloths in making their outside garments. Many of the first settlers were tanners and shoemakers, and none suffered for want of covering for the feet.

In the course of three years all had comfortable, though not elegant houses. The poorer kinds were one story, and the walls and floors were of hand-sawed boards. The favorite locality was the southeastern declivity of a hill, near to wood and water. They dug into the hill-side, and the bank was a support to the stone chimney and oven. The seams between the boards were "daubed" with mortar or clay, and the walls were banked up as high as the windows in winter, with drift from the sea-shore which kept out the cold winds. Many of the better class of houses were built on side-hills. The Nathaniel Bacon house was so built, the timber of which was as sound after two centuries as on the day it was hewn. Not being covered, it became thoroughly seasoned, and impervious to rot.

The first settlers of Barnstable had little whereof to complain. None but the idle and improvident lacked the conveniences of life. They were happy and contented—a law unto themselves—vice did not obtain a foothold in their little community.

—from *Genealogical Notes of Barnstable Families* (1888)

———

Blackbirds and Bachelors

By Henry David Thoreau

"IN 1667 THE town [of Eastham] voted that every housekeeper should kill twelve blackbirds, or three crows, which did great damage to the corn, and this vote was repeated for many years." In 1695 an additional order was passed, namely, that "every unmarried man in the township shall kill six blackbirds, or three crows, while he remains single; as a penalty for not doing it, shall not be married until he obey this order."

The blackbirds, however, still molest the corn. I saw them at it the next summer, and there were many scarecrows, if not scare-blackbirds, in the fields, which I often mistook for men. From which I concluded, that either many men were not married, or many blackbirds were.

—from *Cape Cod* (1865)

———

A Cape Cod House

By Henry David Thoreau

HAVING WALKED ABOUT eight miles since we struck the beach, and passed the boundary between Wellfleet and Truro, a stone post in the sand,—for even this sand comes under the jurisdiction of one town or another,—we turned inland over barren hills and valleys, whither the sea, for some reason, did not follow us, and, tracing up a Hollow, discovered two or three sober-looking houses within half a mile, uncommonly near the eastern coast. Their garrets were apparently so full of chambers, that their roofs could hardly lie down straight, and we did not doubt that there was room for us there. Houses near the sea are generally low and broad. These were a story and a half high; but if you merely counted the windows in their gable ends, you would think that there were many stories more, or, at any rate, that the half-story was the only one thought worthy of being illustrated.

The great number of windows in the ends of the houses, and their irregularity in size and position, here and elsewhere on the Cape, struck us agreeably,—as if each of the various occupants who had their *cunabula* behind had punched a hole where his necessities required it, and according to his size and stature, without regard to outside effect. There were windows for the grown folks, and windows for the children,—three or four apiece; as a certain man had a large hole cut in his barn-door for the cat, and another smaller one for the kitten. Sometimes they were so low under the eaves that I thought they must have perforated the plate beam for another apartment, and I noticed some which were triangular, to fit that part more exactly. The ends of the houses had thus as many muzzles as a revolver, and, if the inhabitants have the same habit of staring out the windows that some of our neighbors have, a traveler must stand a small chance with them.

Generally, the old-fashioned and unpainted houses on the Cape looked more comfortable, as well as picturesque, than the modern and more pretending ones, which were less in harmony with the scenery, and less firmly planted.

—from *Cape Cod* (1865)

The First Houses

By Shebnah Rich

THE FIRST HOUSES were usually built two story in front, with long slanting roofs reaching within a few feet of the ground in the rear. Later, the rule was one low story still lower in the rear, with two liberal-sized front rooms, an immense kitchen, with two bedrooms and a buttery, or pantry, on the lower floor, and a "square chamber" up-stairs. The construction and general arrangement were substantially the same as in the now so well-known, "old-fashioned double house," which Thoreau describes as looking so fast anchored to the soil, and which, considering the cost and adaptation to the then style of living, the comfort for winter and summer, was a success, and could not be much bettered to-day. . . .

All the houses fronted the south and told twelve o'clock meridian with the accuracy of a chronometer. Every window was a sun dial, and often the only time-keeper. The front of the house was always sunny, and sometime during the day the long kitchen was sure to catch the broad sunbeams. The two front rooms were usually known as the "east room," where the family lived with the sunshine, say from November till April or May; and the west room, known as the "great room," which was for guests and especial occasions. The spacious kitchens, always fresh and cool, were open to all work in summer, and used for storage and common work in winter. How altogether homelike and hospitable were these roomy, unrestricted old kitchens; whitewashed, floor-sanded and wide fireplaced. What a sense of long-day comfort floated in the air. How a cool current drifting through the open north windows, invited a siesta on the old settle or red chest.

For many years, the houses as a rule, were innocent of paint or paper, and some of plastering, particularly the kitchen, though kept light and clean with frequent whitewashing. The open beams, girders and walls were festooned with flowering herbs, stock-bearing seeds, and various home products for ornament and use, varying with the season. From the roots, herbs, berries, wild flowers, and a little New England rum, the mothers could prepare remedies to cure all the ills of body and soul.

—from *Truro—Cape Cod* (1883)

The Cape Cod Cottage

By Josef Berger (Jeremiah Digges)

CAPE COD'S MAIN contribution to the architecture of homes is simplicity. The principle seems to be, roughly, that the looks of a house are not enhanced by any "gadget" or trick which does not in some way add to its function as a shelter; and conversely, if the need for shelter is perfectly fulfilled, and the structure best designed to meet the elements where it stands, its looks will take care of themselves—will be good looks. There is nothing new, of course, about the principle; but there is plenty of evidence that it is not always followed. The Cape Cod cottage adheres faithfully.

The type is the "story and a half," with a large chimney in the center. This generous piece of masonry is important not only for the draught, but as a mainstay for the entire structure. A large chimney, a well shaped mass around it, and a few carefully placed windows, are main requisites. The windows are small-paned, and they go up near the eaves. Any form of dormer is incongruous. The ceilings are kept low, and the usual design places one square room on each side of the front door, a large kitchen across the rear, with a "buttery" at one end and a small bedroom at the other. From the entrance hall in front, a narrow stairway, which is sometimes called the "chicken ladder," goes steeply to the attic, slanting towards the front of the chimney. Upstairs there are usually two rooms and a bath. With this design as a base, ells can be built on, and were built to keep up with the expanding family. Piazzas go poorly.

The foundation of stone, set dry, provides for plenty of ventilation. In the fall, many old Cape Codders "banked up" for the winter, filling a trough around the base of the house with seaweed to stop the draughts. The salt air of the Cape will very soon bring the shingles of a new house around to a beautiful silver gray. Inland, they turn brown or dark gray, but here, if a house is shingled with white cedar, it will lose its schoolgirl complexion in a couple of years and weather to the color of its century-old companions.

A trellis or two and the conventional white picket fence, from eighteen to twenty-four inches high, are the only bits of "running rigging" your craft needs out of doors. Even the fences had one function to perform, suggested by the woman who "could count the missing pickets in her neighbor's fence quicker than she could mend her own." The condition of the fence, on the Cape, is as important as the state of a flight of white steps in Baltimore.

The earmarks of an old house are several. If the door to her brick oven is wooden, she probably was built before 1800. If her window panes are twenty-four, she is older than if they are twelve. If her shingles are of white pine, add a century earlier than cedar. If they are split or "rived," instead of sawn, do the same. If any of her floor-planks are more than two feet wide, she has heard talk of the British on our shores, and her timbers may have been to sea. If she has a round-cellar, she deserves respect, or has succeeded to the site of one that did; but for such veneration, she should also have a "summer beam" in her kitchen, she should face south, and there should be a mark upon her floor under one of the windows, for the telling of time on sunny days; under her attic steps there should be a cat-hole; there should be a little grooved rain-trough on her threshold, and she may have a millstone, perhaps, as her doorstep. She is at her best if her fireplace in the kitchen is large enough for her mistress to walk in and do the cooking, and for the children to sit at the ends and look up through the chimney at the stars. The high child mortality rate that attracts the notice of wanderers in Cape cemeteries probably owes much to the colds caught in the fireplace.

—from *Cape Cod Pilot* (1937)

———

Puritan Justice

By Josef Berger (Jeremiah Digges)

THE CONGREGATIONAL CHURCH of Barnstable, which can be reached by turning right at the stoplight just beyond the graveyard, is one of the oldest buildings on the Cape, dating from 1717. The church society traces its existence back to the formation of the Congregational Church of Southwalk, London, in 1616, and asserts that it is therefore the oldest such unit in America.

There was considerable persecution of the founders, and the Reverend John Lothrop, Cambridge graduate who was the society's second pastor, spent two years in a London jail. In 1634 he brought thirty followers with him to Boston, and they went to Scituate to settle; but five years later Pastor Lothrop led his flock, now twenty-five families, down the Cape trail to Barnstable.

To its church the old village confided its life-and-death secrets; and these, ghost-secrets now, peer out from between the sedate lines of the clerical record where they were tucked away.

On June 4, 1649, Mrs. Judith Shelley is excommunicated for calling the pastor dirty names. "Wee had long patience towards her, and used all courteous intreatyes and persuations; but the longer wee waited, the worse she was. She is wondrous perremptorye in all her carriages."

Mrs. Shelley has a daughter, Hannah, 12 years.

March 9, 1652—Hannah Shelley, 15, is married to David Linnel, 25.

May 30, 1652—David Linnel and his young wife Hannah, "children of the Barnstable church," are summoned and attend a meeting of the church and there, before the congregation, confess their fault ("fornication in unlawful accompanying," before their marriage). They are both, by the sentence and joint consent of the church, "pronounced to be cutt off from that relation which they hadd formerlye to the church by virtue of their parents covenaunt."

Plymouth, June 3, 1652—Mr. Thomas Dexter and John Chipman, grand jurors from Barnstable, make complaint of the "publique fame" in the Barnstable church. The Court condemns both David Linnel and Hannah Linnel "to be publicly whipt at Barnstable where they live."

June 8, 1652—Sentence is executed upon David and Hannah Linnel.

—from *Cape Cod Pilot* (1937)

———

"The Double Trial of Abigail"

By Elizabeth Reynard

MISTRESS ABIGAIL MUXOM entered Old Wareham church. She paused, once inside the building, and looked toward the high pulpit. Over it towered a dome-shaped sounding board, behind it shone a great window. Lost in the pulpit's cavernous depths stood Rowland Thacher, the minister. He could not see out, and she could not see him, for the pulpit was built on an heroic scale and Rowland Thacher was not.

The deacons, ready to condemn Mistress Abigail, sat forward on the Deacon Seats at the foot of the pulpit, facing the congregation. Near them, the pew of the minister's wife gaped, so lately empty, so soon to be occupied by pretty Hannah Fearing, widow of the Squire's son. As goodmen and their goodwives rose to peer over the tops of pews, seats snapped upward in the square stall-pews around the walls; noisily, if the hand of caution failed to ease their progress; squeakily where hinges were stiff or wood had warped in fog. Alone, on the narrow pulpit stairs, sat the son of the grave-digger, waiting to turn the minister's hourglass, watching to give the deacons word of improprieties.

In the centre of this church stood two sections of benches, the forward bench reserved for sinners; behind them the deaf and the old; on the rear benches children, carefully guarded from slumber or activity by the vigilance of tidy-men (tithing men) who bore rods with a rabbit's foot on one end and a copper ship's nail on the other. For a first offence one was touched with the rabbit's foot; for a second one encountered the nail.

Abigail Muxom seated herself on the forward bench. Her head was high, her cheeks flushed, and she 'wore no garment of humility.' When the time came for her condemnation, Rowland Thacher, from his impenetrable stronghold, read three depositions against her:

Elisha Benson Saith That he was at Edmund Muxom's house sometime since & saw sd Muxoms wife very familiar with Joseph Benson by talking of balderdash stuff & kissing and hugging one another in the absence of her husband. At another time I saw them coming out of the house together & discovered none but they two. Middleborough, Octr. 1750.

Abigail rose from the forward bench. So far as we know she had come alone, had no friend, no attorney to represent her, and her husband was not present to defend her though he had not put her by. The man who might have demanded justice for the erring as well as for the righteous read the indictment. Mercifully hidden from the sharp eyes of the congregation, and from her ironic gaze, he waited, alone in that high pulpit, for her answer. Abigail formally denied the charge.

The second statement was then read aloud:

Caleb Cushman & his wife do Testify & say That we some time since have seen Joseph Benson & Abigail Muxom at our house & their behaviour was uncommon for married people; she was fawning about him & sometimes in his lap or upon his knee & he haleing of her, running his face up to hers, & as we suppose kissing of her or aiming to do so & talking & joacking like young people.

Plymton, Octr. 1750.

There was a stir of consternation in the church, the queer, dead rustling, like autumn leaves, made by gossipy bodies in gossipy clothes. In the House of God, the tidy-men watched the squirming children, but the deacons and peeping townsmen watched Mistress Abigail as the minister read words that he had delayed three years to read. Every man wondered why the examiner of souls had held back such damning evidence and had administered communion to the sinner, and called her 'Sister.' She was very beautiful, men said, and of the minister they thought what righteous minds have always thought when scandal and sin are condoned in the young and gay: Rowland had an eye for a lady. But now that his wife was dead and he was in love with the Squire's daughter, he complied with the will of his parishioners, and read aloud the unsworn statements that would condemn the goodwife with whom his name had been linked in gossip. Abigail rose from the forward bench and denied the second charge.

The minister read the final deposition:

Jedidah Swift wife to Eben[r] Swift Junr Saith that she was at the house of Edmund Muxom four times the summer past & his wife Abigail Muxom did several times call her child to her & ask the child who its father was, & the child would answer Doctor Jo's at which she would laugh & make sport of.

Wareham, Decem[r]. 3. 1750.

The two first statements were sauce for the goose; the third was sauce for the gander. With any luck on the side of righteousness, Abigail was destined to wear the letter A, as Mary Eaton of the Cape had worn it, as other women had been branded in Plymouth and Massachusetts Colonies. The two first charges were pleasant scandal; the third was matter for grave action. If she had repudiated the lighter accusations, it was obvious that she would deny this one. But Abigail was not obvious. She stated that the last charge was true.

Rowland Thacher, from his cavernous pedestal, asked for the vote of the townsmen. Women were allowed no vote, and without more ado the men convicted the accused, pronouncing her 'guilty of immoral Conduct.' The congregation waited for the word of their minister; it was his duty to determine her punishment. But Rowland Thacher seemed to lose the thunder that in his sermons inspired men with fear of retribution for sin. He suspended Abigail Muxom from the 'communion table' till she 'give a Christian satisfaction.' The congregation, taken aback, resented this unwonted clemency.

She went out of the Meeting House and walked beside the sabrelike waves that curved along the shore. Hers was a happy disposition; so she nodded as she passed Deacon Swift's tavern, and there the farmers, bartering mutton and hay for rum, and the tavern roisterers lifted their glasses and toasted first the King, then Mistress Abigail, prettiest, naughtiest, gayest housewife in Agawame.

Rowland married the Widow Fearing, and rapidly increased his family. His salary remained always in arrears. Twelve days before his death, in 1774, it was voted not to allow him anything 'for the year past more than his stated salary.' As the town had failed to pay his 'stated salary,' this precaution against generous impulse was unnecessary.

Meanwhile Abigail lived happily in Agawame. Her son grew up and became a likeable sailor. Her husband continued to live with her. Joseph Benson continued to visit her. But the scandal never died. She had not paid the penalty of sin; and the townspeople held it against her. They determined, after Mr. Thacher's death, that the new minister should 'sweep clean.' They chose a spiritual leader who was at the clean-sweeping age. His name was Noble Everitt, and he came directly from Yale College. One of his first actions, as minister, was to appoint a committee 'to converse with brethren and sisters who are or may be guilty of public offense according to the rule given in Mat. 18.' That committee knew exactly what it wanted: Abigail Muxom was at last to receive punishment overdue some thirty years.

She was an old woman in 1783, with nothing against her save a memory of a minister's baffling leniency, and three dust-worn depositions in the church records. The committee found that John Benson was ready to testify again. After thirty years his memory had improved and he was able to add new details in his remembrance of incidents that had occurred before 1750. His testimony was more damning than it had been in 1753, more circumstantial—for in this world important memories increase their data as one grows old. Hannah 'Bessee,' of the 'garrulous Besse women' was also ready with testimony concerning Abigail's youthful philandering. The old depositions were clearly in the records and could be re-read from the pulpit. So in 1783 Abigail Muxom was again summoned to the Meeting House. No longer beautiful, she had the hardy open-air look of a Cape woman. Steady work at heavy tasks had left its imprint on her shoulders. The goodmen did not have to rise so often to peer over their pews; they found it easier to remember what she looked like.

As for Abigail, she had lost her sense of the dramatic. Neither she nor the English King were toasted now in the taverns of a new-born nation still bleeding from its birth wound. There was no money to meet taxes; her son, 'Lem,' was ill; the farm was not providing food for sustenance. This fanatic revival of a long buried scandal seemed to her futile, childish, 'trawlin' fer minnews.' The nobility of Noble Everitt bored her. He was young; Yale College might not be responsible for him; still, she was glad that her son had not gone there, though it did not matter much as he was like to be drowned at sea. From the mist of thirty years she recalled another voice exhorting her from this same pulpit, a voice more hesitant, a voice that gossip had called 'guilty.'

No such irksome conscience hampered Noble Everitt, who thundered the new deposition in his 'sou'wester' voice:

John Benson of Middleborough testifieth that upwards of 20 years ago he was at the house of Edmund Muxom the husband of said Abigail, sometime in the afternoon before sunset, he saw said Abigail on bed with Joseph Benson, in the easterly part of the house. He also saith that at another time he was at work near Edmund Muxom's house and heard him repeatedly bid his son Lem. go and fetch the horse and on refusal corrected him. Abigail came to the door and said—What do you whip that child for? it is none of yours, upon which John Benson said I always thought so, at which she went into the house and said no more.

April II. 1783.

Hannah Besse testifieth that sometimes about 20 years ago or upward she went to Edmund Muxom's house late in the evening and there saw Abigail his wife on bed by the fire with Joseph Benson.

April II. 1783.

With increasing indignation Abigail listened to the charges. What right had John Benson to make false testimony against his brother Joseph? Why traduce old memories? Life was sufficiently difficult without that. In the presence of the 'assembled church' Abigail declared that 'the evidences of John Benson and Hannah Besse are false.' Again no attorney represented her; no friend spoke for her; there was no cross-examining of the unsworn witness. The church voted that she was 'guilty of the charge.'

Definite punishment was deferred in the hope that she could be induced to 'make a penitent and public confession of her sin.' The deacons, who had voted her guilty, laboured with her zealously. The women pleaded with her to confess and be forgiven. Abigail continually lost her temper. She called the witnesses 'liars'; she described Noble Everitt and the ladies of the parish as 'wet-foot turkeys'; the deacons she appears to have regarded as beneath contumely. After some weeks she was summoned for a third time before the assembled church and was publicly 'admonished' in a long exhortation by the minister. She sat, proud and defiant, on the forward bench. Steadily she refused to confess her guilt, refused to be drawn into any orgy of the emotions. Day after day she worked in the fields, or washed the clothes, and did her household chores.

Then, from the neighbouring towns, six ministers were summoned. They came mounted on six ministerial horses, sleek, fat animals, cemetery nourished, for the ecclesiastics of the early Cape had the privilege of foddering their steeds on graveyard turf. So these mounts were reputed to be familiar with ghosts, to be 'fey' horses, and their presence in the graveyards gave rise to many tales of heavily breathing 'sperrits,' of moving 'nottomies' (skeletons) in white, of ghostly Indian giants encountered near the Burying Acre.

The ministers, invited to this inquest upon the defunct romance of Abigail, were royally entertained at the homes of goodmen. Then, on a day when no man worked, the curious gathered from miles around, and the floor and galleries of the Meeting House were packed. Abigail Muxom stood in the presence of the six visiting ministers, while the evidences were read aloud. She denied their truth. In a dramatic appeal, Noble Everitt requested the ministers 'to give their opinion what particular immodest conduct our sister is guilty of, and how this church ought to proceed with her.' The ministers were prompt and unanimous. Her conduct was 'forbidden by the 7th commandment' and it was her duty 'to make a penitent and public confession of her sin' She refused. Parson Everitt then pronounced her excommunicate. The custom of the wearing of the letter *A* had passed; but the minister branded her with unforgettable words, described her publicly, in the presence of the large assembly, as 'visibly a hardened and impenitent sinner out of the visible Kingdom of Christ, one who ought to be viewed and treated by all good people as a heathen and a publican in imminent danger of eternal perdition.'

Abigail, quite alone, went out of the Meeting House, and walked beside the thin, curving lips of the sea. She was old and no longer nodded to the roisterers of the town tavern, and they no longer toasted either the King or Abigail's smile. At dusk she went home to Agawame and there, day after day she worked in the fields, or washed the clothes, and did her household chores.

—from *The Narrow Land* (1934)

"Tar and Feathering"

By Amos Otis

ABIGAIL FREEMAN,* BAPTIZED in the East Church Sept. 21, 1729, was a daughter of Thomas Davis of Barnstable. The few among the aged who remember her, call her the Widow Nabby Freeman. April 8, 1753, at the tender age of fifteen, she married David Freeman of Fairfield, Conn. His mother, who was a Sturgis, had married for her second husband, Job Gorham, and it appears that some of her children came with her to Barnstable. Abigail had a son born March 25, 1757, named Thomas Davis Freeman, and she became a widow soon after that date. She united with the East Church March 26, 1758, and continued to be a member, of good standing, till the close of her life in November, 1788.

She resided in the ancient dwelling house probably built by Joseph Lothrop, Esq., that stood next east of the new Court House, where Judge Day now resides. Early in life she became a widow and had to rely on her own unaided exertions to procure the means of subsistence. She kept a small grocery store, and being an outspoken tory, refused to surrender her small stock of tea, to be destroyed by the Vigilance Committee. She was talkative, a fault not exclusively confined to her sex, was a frequent visitor at the house of Otis Loring, made no attempt to conceal her tory principles, and was sometimes severe in her denunciation of the acts of leading whigs. Her course was not patriotic and not to be commended. Even at the present day (1863) there are persons who condemn, with more severity, the acts of our government and the leading politicians, than did Abigail Freeman during the Revolutionary struggle; yet no sane man would consider it wise or expedient to enact laws, restraining the freedom of speech in regard to the policy of measures, or the motives of individuals. Some of our Revolutionary fathers in Barnstable, thought differently and acted differently. Abigail Freeman was an eye sore to them. She kept a little grocery store, saw many persons, and would keep her tongue in motion whenever and wherever she could find a listener. Doctors Freeman and Smith, for whom she

---

*Interesting dramatized portraits of both Abigail Freeman and Aunt Rebecca Blush (see Otis's story of "Aunt Beck," p. 81) are given in Reynard's *The Narrow Land*.

had a strong antipathy, some of the Crockers with whom she had a private quarrel, and some of the radical whigs, resolved that a bridle should be put upon her tongue. Ducking stools, for the cure of scolds and unquiet women, had then gone out of use, and the then modern invention of tarring and feathering, and riding on a rail, were in vogue. Perhaps it is well that the names of the individuals who took part in this courteous ceremony were not recorded. They were all young men, and acting in the shade of night, perhaps were not recognized in the disguises which they assumed.

When they came to the house of Mrs. Freeman she had retired for the night. They obtained an entrance, took her from her bed to the Green, besmeared her with tar and covered her with feathers. A rail was procured from a fence in the vicinity, across which she was set astride, and either end thereof was placed on the shoulder of a stout youth. She was held in her position by a man who walked at her side, holding her by the hand. When they were tired of the sport, and after they had exacted from her a promise that she would no more meddle in politics, they released her, and the gallant band soon after sneaked homeward.

Though some who took an active part in this demonstration—this visible argument for personal liberty and the freedom of speech—disliked to be known as participators: yet a strong party in Sandwich and Barnstable justified the act.

No apologist for this can now be found: but before condemning the participators, we must take into consideration the mitigating circumstances. Its respectability and influence, if not actual participators, countenanced and supported those that were. Allowance must also be made for the excitement of the times, and that men acting under the influence of such excitement, often do things which they afterwards regret. The Widow Freeman was a thorn in their sides—she could out-talk any of them, was fascinating in her manners, and had an influence which she exerted, openly and definantly, against the patriotic men who were then hazzarding their fortunes and their lives in the struggle for American independence. Sitting quietly at our firesides we may condemn such acts, and, as moralists say, the end does not justify the means. Perhaps if we were placed in the same circumstance that our fathers were, we should do as they did. These considerations are not presented as a justification of the gross and shameless violation of the personal rights of Widow Abigail Freeman, but as mitigating circumstances which should temper the verdict of public opinion.

—from *Genealogical Notes of Barnstable Families* (1888)

" 'Widdows at Vandue' "

By Elizabeth Reynard

NO POORHOUSES EXISTED in the early days of the Colony. When goodmen died leaving widows and half-cleared acres, the land, if not self-sustaining, was disposed of by order of the General Court, and the 'relicts' were 'farmed out.' The annual process of selling bereaved wives became known as the 'Widow's Vandue.' Prices varied yearly, but in 1770 their average value to the towns was £3 per widow, taken as they ran. As a woman grew old and feeble, often she was not profitable in services rendered. Sometimes at the auctions the towns had difficulty in disposing of such widows at all.

Fortunately for exchequers, 'Towne Widdows' seldom attained a ripe old age. They worked too hard; they suffered too constantly from the strain of knowing that as their faculties declined they might be moved from comfortable homes to farms whose owners could only afford to pay the town a small sum for their services. Occasionally the old women were reduced as low as ninepence per annum; whereas a young comely widow brought over £10.

The expenses of a widow's illness always occasioned a 'bickerfest.' Should the community be required to pay the doctor if the family overworked and underfed their charge? Often such expenses were determined in advance, and when a widow exceeded in her needs the amount that the town had voted for possible illness, she was forced to continue without further medical attention, unless bestowed gratuitously, until the completion of her 'Widow's yeare.'

The evils of this system, horrible in theory, proved less appalling in practice. Throughout colonial New England many wives died young, victims of too frequent child-bearing, of overwork at household tasks, or stricken by the prevalent diseases. A comely widow had a good chance of re-marriage within the year to an attractive widower, for both men and women believed it wise to console themselves as promptly as possible after a marital loss. Older widows were blessed with sons to care for them, and run their farms. Rich widows provided money to hire labour. Others had kind relatives willing to give them homes.

Nevertheless, even fine women were forced to undergo the humiliations of auction. Mistress Lovell appeared at the annual 'vandue' in

1776, was 'set up by the Selectmen . . . and struck of (f) to Josiah Stevens for to keep one year for the Sum of nine pounds Six shillings & if She did not live the Year in he to have in that proportion.' She lived to appear at eight annual auctions. Her clothes grew shabby with time; but there were no new bonnets and cloaks in the yearly contracts, and the people with whom she worked were unwilling to provide fresh garments. In 1782 Mistress Lovell was officially in need of a shirt. The town voted to buy her a cheap one, expense sixpence; then sold her again. This sale was a 'bargain,' for the Widow was not thriving. Born of gentle English stock, she had not been able to assume the heavy household tasks, the stock-tending required of her. Seven years of servitude broke her in spirit and health.

'Set up' again in 1783, she was transferred to a new home, and in the following September the town elders were summoned to a stormy meeting. The Widow Lovell lay dead in her 'poverty box,' under the pine trees in the churchyard since her clothes were not considered suitable for a last entrance into the Meeting House. Over the coffin a sailcloth was thrown while the selectmen estimated and bickered. Finally they voted 'a winding sheet and a shift for the Widow Lovell, eight shillings.'

—from *The Narrow Land* (1934)

"Pomp's Lot"

By Shebnah Rich

NORTHEASTERLY FROM THE house of Leonard P. Rich is a wood-lot that keeps alive the memory of "Pomp," who was an African of the pure Congo species, purchased or stolen according to the gospel of the times, by the captain of a whaleman from Truro, and on arrival sold to Jonathan Paine. Pomp performed his duties as a slave faithfully, but he was never fairly happy or content. He indulged in the homesick passion which the negro feels, and with his countrymen, believed in metempsychosis, or transmigration of soul.

One day when the longing for kith and kin and home was deep in his heart, he took a jug of water, a loaf of bread and a rope, and went into a thick wood-lot belonging to his master. Selecting a high tree, the stump of which may yet be seen, he placed his jug of water and loaf of bread at the foot of the tree, to sustain him over the journey, and placing the rope around his neck, took his departure for Afric's sunny fountains. Many days after, his body was found hanging to the tree; his soul had gone to the God who gave it, in whose merciful hands we leave him.

It may seem unaccountable and unreconcilable in our day, that the settlers of New England, with their positive conscience, and honest convictions, should have planted such dragon's teeth as slavery. We must, however, remember the moral condition of the world, the wrongs and cruelties of society, and how much had been done, rather than how much remained undone. Not thirty years are yet passed since slavery was defended by the press, the pulpit, the platform, and the sword of this Christian nation. The villainous traffic in African slaves was prosecuted with great energy and profit, and regarded a fair field for enterprise, for more than a hundred years after the settlement of Plymouth.

—from *Truro—Cape Cod* (1883)

———

Methodist Ministers

By Henry C. Kittredge

IT IS NOT hard to see why Methodism made so strong an appeal to the whalemen and cod-fishermen of the lower Cape. A modified form of itineracy which the new denomination practiced provided that no minister should preach in the same town for more than two years and sometimes only for one. There was, therefore, no danger that a congregation should suffer long from the harangues of a dull preacher. But variety of another sort is what made most converts. The Methodist preachers were often men of little education and no religious training. Zeal and 'a call' with them took the place of theological schools. The consequence was a breezy informality in their discourses. They never hesitated to employ startling tricks to keep their hearers awake. On one occasion a Methodist minister in Truro interrupted his sermon by the remark, 'Brethren, your stove pipe is so confoundedly crooked, that I can't preach a straight sermon.' Another whose subject was 'the World, the Flesh, and the Devil,' prefaced his remarks by saying, 'I shall touch lightly upon the World, hasten to the Flesh, and pass on to the Devil, when I will give it to you hot as you can sup it.' It is a consolation, if we are to get the Devil, to be given him in a language that we can understand. There was, in fact, little danger that a Methodist preacher would shoot over the heads of his hearers. This—with a pleasant smattering of rugged wit—went far toward making Methodism popular, for no men appreciate wit more keenly than Cape-Codders. The Reverend Edgar Clark, one of the early Methodist ministers in Provincetown, showed adroitness and much sense when a pharisaic whaleman of his congregation asked him what to do if, after cruising for months without filling a cask, he sighted a hundred-barrel whale on Sunday. 'I think,' said Mr. Clark, 'I should call all hands together and ask the Lord to bless us. Then I would go and get the whale.' . . .

These early men of God had to be men of fine parts to get their positions in the first place; before they were officially called to a church, they were often required to prove their mettle by a long series of sermons before congregations as critical and as potentially hostile as school boys. Timothy Alden preached sixteen times to the Yarmouth Parish before they were satisfied that he would do; and Mr. Joseph Green, who antedated him by a few years, worked for fifty-two Sundays to earn the same position. Sandwich was still more candid. Unable to decide whether Thomas Tupper or Richard Bourne was the better man, the congregation asked them to preach in competition, and he who had the fuller house was named 'minister for the day.'

The ministers needed ready tact and large sympathies, if they were to cope successfully with such troublesome parishioners as Sunday fishermen, many of whom were for nine months of the year exemplary Christians. What, for example, was the Truro parson to say to a certain noted skipper who used to assert with commendable candor that 'there was no hope for him if he died during the fishing season, but in winter he was all right?' Such questions wanted nice handling. Lack of tact cost the Reverend Charles Boyter his pulpit in Truro. He arrived there about a hundred years ago and decided one day to swell the numbers of his congregation by announcing that his next discourse would be a sermon on Luck. Sunday morning found the church filled with interested fishermen, who knew more about luck than any other class of men in the world. But Mr. Boyter proclaimed that there was no such thing as luck; industry and hard work, not luck, were what brought full fares of fish.

'Bait your hooks with red flannel,' he told them; 'then if you don't catch codfish, it will be because you don't try.' And he compared the rigors of the Grand Banks to 'trouting in the brooks of Vermont with a fly and pole.' Shortly after this sermon, Mr. Boyter left Truro to try his luck in Orange, New Jersey.

—from *Cape Cod, Its People and Their History* (1930)

———

The Weasel in the Church

By Nosapocket

WE HAVE A meeting house in Mashpee. The old Indian church as some call it, built in around 1680 I believe, and it was in around, I'd have to say around 1880 that this story took place because when we regained control of the meeting house there was a gathering held on Sunday afternoon and the native people were assembled in the building which has a balcony and there's a male entrance and a female entrance like an old style longhouse would have. And in through the male door swung open with quite a bash comes running a weasel. It ran right up into the front of the congregation, spun around, and stopped. And after it had gathered everyone's attention started up into the balcony and stood on the bannister and transformed itself into a male, a man, just brief enough not for anyone to know and recognize him as what family he came from or anything. Just that it was an Indian man, he just, poof, and then he collapsed back into the weasel form and darted out the door never to be seen again.

—from *Spirit of the New England Tribes* (1986) by William S. Simmons

———

The Reverend Horatio Alger, Jr.

By Scott Corbett

THOSE MID-CENTURY YEARS were the great years in Brewster, but the era was already waning by the time of the Civil War. . . .

However, the greatest town repercussions during those years were caused not by the war itself but by the brief stay in Brewster of a young minister who was destined to become one of America's most famous authors. Horatio Alger, Jr., is still known today as the immortal creator of a hundred rags-to-riches dime novels, but in Brewster he won a different sort of notoriety.

In November of 1864 it was voted to engage Mr. Alger for a year at a salary of eight hundred dollars, and for fifteen months all went well. Then, on March 6, 1866, at a town meeting, three successive votes were taken which show the upset state of minds at that gathering:

"7th. Voted not to engage the Rev. Mr. Alger for the ensuing year.

"8th. Voted to reconsider the foregoing vote.

"9th. Voted to adjourn to Tuesday, March 13th at two O'clock P.M."

The following Tuesday an investigating committee was chosen "to investigate Parish affairs and report" to a meeting six days later. At that time the words "to investigate certain reports in relation to Mr. Alger" were substituted for the more ambiguous "parish affairs" and a letter was written to the secretary of the American Unitarian Association in Boston.

The letter announced that Mr. Alger had "recently been charged with gross immorality and a most henious . . . abbommible and revolting crime of unnatural familiarity with *boys.*" The letter said that Alger made no denial or excuses but heard the charges and evidence with "the apparent calmness of an old offender—and hastily left town in the very next train for parts unknown—probably Boston."

That being a day when moral indignation was inclined to override prudishness, the whole of this succession of events was doggedly and frankly recorded in the town records.*

—from *Cape Cod's Way* (1955)

*And, true to the Puritan tradition of candid acknowledgment, Alger's name is boldly cast on the brass plaque listing all of the church's ministers in the foyer of Brewster's First Parish Unitarian Church.

"Sesuit"

By Conrad Aiken

A giddy young lass of Sesuit
fell in love with a lad from Cotuit;
   said the preacher from Wareham
   who proceeded to pair 'em,
Sesuit, cotuit, go to it.

———

The Happy Lot of Province Town's Inhabitants

By Timothy Dwight

A STRANGER, BORN and educated in the interiour of New-England, amid the varied beauties of its surface, and the luxuriant succession of its produce, naturally concludes, when he visits Province Town, that the inhabitants, and the neighbours also, must possess a very limited share of enjoyment. Facts, however, refute this conclusion. For aught, that we could discern, they were as cheerful, and appeared to enjoy life as well, as any equal number of their countrymen. This, indeed, is easily explicable. Food, and clothing, houses, lodging, and fuel, they possess of such a quality, and with so much ease in the acquisition, as to satisfy all the demands of that middle state in life, which wise men of every age have dignified by the name of *golden*. Nature and habit endear to them the place, in which they were born, and live; and prevent them from feeling what would be serious inconveniences to a stranger. Their mode of life is naturally not less pleasing, than that of the farmer or mechanic: for no people are more attached to their employment than seamen. The enterprise, which this life requires, and the energy which it supplies, render it less even and dull, and are probably as well suited to the natural taste of man, as arts or agriculture. The situations of others they rarely see, and are therefore rarely led to make irksome comparisons. The lawn, the meadow, the orchard, and the harvest, excite in their minds, neither wishes nor thoughts. The draught of herrings, the fare of codfish, the conquest of a shark, and the capture of a whale, prompt their ambition, engross their care, and furnish pleasures, as entirely unknown to the farmer, as the joy of harvest is to them. To solitude they are strangers. An active, enterprising life is scarcely molested by *ennui*. Almost every day strangers visit Province Town from different parts of the world: for there is hardly any spot, except great trading cities, which is more frequented by vessels of all descriptions, than this. By these they are furnished with business and intelligence; and with not a few of those little varieties in thought and feeling, which contribute so much to the cheerfulness of life. Nor do they fail of enjoying a conscious, uninterrupted superiority over mere landsmen. While most of their countrymen have been chained to a small spot of earth, they have traversed the Ocean. While the husbandman has followed the plough, or brandished the sickle, the inhabitant of Province Town has coasted the shores of Greenland, swept the Brazilian seas, or crossed the Pacific Ocean, in chase of the whale. Who, that has circumnavigated the globe, will not look down on him, who has scarcely travelled out of his native county, or spent life on his own farm?

—from *Travels in New England and New York* (1822)

———

The Hard Lot of Cape Codders

By Edward Augustus Kendell

ONE OF THOSE visionary writers, of whom we are acquainted with so many, might easily give to Truro and its vicinity the most inviting description. He might say, that the youth and strength of the country are employed, for two-thirds of the year, in obtaining, by hardy and audacious toil, the wealth of seas beyond the line, and even on the further side of Cape Horn; and while these (in the phrase of a New England writer) are thus *cultivating* the ocean, their blooming wives and daughters might be exhibited as deriving an easy subsistence from the bounteous hand of nature, that fills every bay and creek with fish: nay, even the decrepitude of age, and the feebleness of infancy, might be drawn as capable of finding, at the common table, a daily, luscious, and abundant food. The truth is, that early habits of life, and the lure of voyages occasionally prosperous, induce the male population to devote themselves to the fisheries. They begin destitute of every thing, and engage *upon shares* with the ship-owner and merchant. Before they embark, they must have an *outfit* of clothes and necessaries, all which the merchant retails at a profit; and next their wives must have credit given them at a *store,* on the credit of the merchant or holder of a share in the ship, unless such holder be in her neighbourhood, and be himself the keeper of this *store,* or country-shop. Here, they obtain rum, molosses, wares and clothing, all at a high price. Meanwhile, their daily subsistence, and the subsistence of all the family, young and old, depends almost exclusively on fish taken with a line, or on shell-fish, raked out of the sand. In such an employ, in angling for hours from a punt, paddled out from shore, or in raking in the sand of the beach, the weakest, the oldest, and the youngest, may indeed employ themselves; and their prey, when they have caught it, they may eat. But, in this pursuit of food passes their hours; except, when by the light of lamps of fish-oil, they sit down to the wheel or loom. Their persons are frequently squalid; their hair hangs often in dirt over their eyes; and their dress is marked by poverty. And how can it be otherwise, among a race that depends for its subsistence upon a search after food, directed almost by the immediate cravings of the stomach; and whom a stormy day may deprive of a dinner, or send shivering, when the tide is out, to prowl upon the beach for food? The land that they possess, and which might be manured both with sea-weed and with fish, is but negligently cultivated; and indeed nothing, the fish for food excepted, is seriously their care. It is certainly in their power to do better; but, for the poor and destitute, the temptation is strong to seek food at free cost to-day, and, having found it, to seek it so again to-morrow. The facility encourages the practice, and encourages indolence; and, indolence once become habitual, it is easier to suffer than to labour. Life is protracted and spent amid small expectations, and expectations that are often not smaller than they are vain.

The whaling-voyage is terminated, and the men and boys return to their cottages. Do they come laden with the profits of the voyage? Do they come to close a period of privation, and to open one of plenty? Do they come—to speak of plain life, and of plain facts—do they come to wipe off the debt at the *store,* and at least to begin a new account upon even terms? Far from it! I was assured by practical men, by dealers or merchants, and by farmers who have spent many years of their lives in these voyages, that it does not happen, oftener than once in ten years, that the shares amount to enough to relieve a whaler from his debts. In all the intermediate period, the close of every voyage leaves him on the books of the ship-owner, whose summons for the next voyage he must obey, or answer for the debt in gaol. While at home, he digs for sand-clams, and warms himself in the smoke of his hovel. For a new voyage, he must have a new outfit, and his wife new credit; and the result of every voyage is almost certainly an addition to his debts:—he lives, however, and his wife and children live; and this is all. Nay, we have thrown out of the account all the subtractions from human welfare, incident to misfortune and to folly. No allowance is here made for hurts, for sickness, for thoughtless extravagance, nor for intemperance; but each of these occasionally adds shade to the picture, and, in its effects on the resources of the fisherman, commonly counter-balances the luck that may reward his perseverance, one year in ten.

—from *Travels Through Part of the United States* (1809)

———

The Wrecker

By Henry David Thoreau

THERE WAS NOT a sail in sight, and we saw none that day,—for they had all sought harbors in the late storm, and had not been able to get out again; and the only human beings whom we saw on the beach for several days were one or two wreckers looking for drift-wood, and fragments of wrecked vessels. After an easterly storm in the spring, this beach is sometimes strewn with eastern wood from one end to the other, which, as it belongs to him who saves it, and the Cape is nearly destitute of wood, is a godsend to the inhabitants.

We soon met one of these wreckers,—a regular Cape Cod man, with whom we parleyed, with a bleached and weatherbeaten face, within whose wrinkles I distinguished no particular feature. It was like an old sail endowed with life,—a hanging-cliff of weather-beaten flesh,—like one of the clay boulders which occurred in that sand-bank. He had on a hat which had seen salt water, and a coat of many pieces and colors, though it was mainly the color of the beach, as if it had been sanded. His variegated back—for his coat had many patches, even between the shoulders—was a rich study to us when we had passed him and looked around. It might have been dishonorable for him to have so many scars behind, it is true, if he had not had many more and more serious ones in front. He looked as if he sometimes saw a doughnut, but never descended to comfort; too grave to laugh, too tough to cry; as indifferent as a clam,—like a sea-clam with hat on and legs, that was out walking the strand. He may have been one of the Pilgrims,—Peregrine White,* at least,—who has kept on the back side of the Cape, and let the centuries go by.

He was looking for wrecks, old logs, water-logged and covered with barnacles, or bits of boards and joists, even chips which he drew out of the reach of the tide, and stacked up to dry. When the log was too large to carry far, he cut it up where the last wave had left it, or rolling it a few feet, appropriated it by sticking two sticks into the ground crosswise above it. Some rotten trunk, which in Maine cumbers the ground, and is, perchance, thrown into the water on purpose, is here thus carefully picked up, split and dried, and husbanded. Before winter the wrecker painfully carries these things up the bank on his shoulders by a long diagonal slanting path made with a hoe in the sand, if there is no hollow at hand. You may see his hooked pike-staff always lying on the bank, ready for use. He is the true monarch of the beach, whose "right there is none to dispute," and he is as much identified with it as a beach-bird.†

—from *Cape Cod* (1865)

———

* Peregrine White (1620–1704), born during the Pilgrims' stay in Provincetown Harbor, was the first child of English parents in New England.
† In *Mooncussers of Cape Cod,* Kittredge playfully takes Thoreau to task here for "so quickly . . . sounding the depths of a man whose life had been spent beside the sea," and shows how Thoreau himself would soon succumb to the universal beachcombing instinct with "rank enthusiasm."

A Talk with a Lighthouse Keeper

By Ralph Waldo Emerson

SEPT. *5, 1853 Cape Cod*

Went to Yarmouth Sunday 5; to Orleans Monday , 6th; to Nauset Light on the back side of Cape Cod. Collins, the keeper, told us he found obstinate resistance on Cape Cod to the project of building a light house on this coast, as it would injure the wrecking business. He had to go to Boston, & obtain the strong recommendation of the Port Society. From the high hill in the rear of Higgins's, in Orleans, I had a good view of the whole cape & the sea on both sides. The Cape looks like one of the Newfoundland Banks just emerged, a huge tract of sand half-covered with poverty grass, & beach grass & for trees abele & locust & plantations of pitchpine. Some good oak, & in Dennis & Brewster were lately good trees for shiptimber & still are well wooded on the east side. But the view I speak of looked like emaciated orkneys—Mull, Islay, & so forth, made of salt dust, gravel, & fishbones. They say the Wind makes the roads, &, as at Nantucket, a large part of the real estate was freely moving back & forth in the air. I heard much of the coming railroad which is about to reach Yarmouth & Hyannis, &, they hope, will come to Provincetown. I fancied the people were only waiting for the railroad to reach them in order to evacuate the country. For the starknakedness of the country could not be exaggerated. But no, nothing was less true. They are all attached to what they call *the soil*. Mr Collins had been as far as Indiana; but, he said, hill on hill—he felt stifled, & longed for the Cape, "where he could see out." And whilst I was fancying that they would gladly give away land to anybody that would come & live there, & be a neighbor: no, they said, all real estate had risen, all over the Cape, & you could not buy land at less than 50 dollars per acre. And, in Provincetown, a lot on the Front street of forty feet square would cost 5 or 600 dollars.

Still I saw at the Cape, as at Nantucket, they are a little tender about your good opinion: for if a gentleman at breakfast, says, he don't like Yarmouth, all real estate seems to them at once depreciated 2 or 3 per cent.

—from *Journals* (1909–1914)

"The Wellfleet Oysterman"

By Henry David Thoreau

WE KNOCKED AT the door of the first house, but its inhabitants were all gone away. In the mean while, we saw the occupants of the next one looking out the window at us, and before we reached it an old woman came out and fastened the door of her bulkhead, and went in again. Nevertheless, we did not hesitate to knock at her door, when a grizzly-looking man appeared, whom we took to be sixty or seventy years old. He asked us, at first, suspiciously, where we were from, and what our business was; to which we returned plain answers.

"How far is Concord from Boston?" he inquired.

"Twenty miles by railroad."

"Twenty miles by railroad," he repeated.

"Didn't you ever hear of Concord of Revolutionary fame?"

"Didn't I ever hear of Concord? Why, I heard guns fire at the battle of Bunker Hill. [They hear the sound of heavy cannon across the Bay.] I am almost ninety; I am eighty-eight year old. I was fourteen year old at the time of Concord Fight,—and where were you then?"

We were obliged to confess that we were not in the fight.

"Well, walk in, we'll leave it to the women," said he.

So we walked in, surprised, and sat down, an old woman taking our hats and bundles, and the old man continued, drawing up to the large, old-fashioned fire-place,—

"I am a poor, good-for-nothing crittur, as Isaiah says; I am all broken down this year. I am under petticoat government here."

The family consisted of the old man, his wife, and his daughter, who appeared nearly as old as her mother, a fool, her son (a brutish-looking, middle-aged man, with a prominent lower face, who was standing by the hearth when we entered, but immediately went out), and a little boy of ten.

While my companion talked with the women, I talked with the old man. They said that he was old and foolish, but he was evidently too knowing for them.

"These women," said he to me, "are both of them poor good-for-nothing critturs. This one is my wife. I married her sixty-four years ago.

She is eighty-four years old, and as deaf as an adder, and the other is not much better."

He thought well of the Bible, or at least he *spoke* well, and did not *think* ill, of it, for that would not have been prudent for a man of his age. He said that he had read it attentively for many years, and he had much of it at his tongue's end. He seemed deeply impressed with a sense of his own nothingness, and would repeatedly exclaim,—

"I am a nothing. What I gather from my Bible is just this; that man is a poor good-for-nothing crittur, and everything is just as God sees fit and disposes."

"May I ask your name?" I said.

"Yes," he answered, "I am not ashamed to tell my name. My name is [John Newcomb] My great-grandfather came over from England and settled here."

He was an old Wellfleet oysterman, who had acquired a competency in that business, and had sons still engaged in it. . . .

The old man said that the great clams were good to eat, but that they always took out a certain part which was poisonous, before they cooked them. "People said it would kill a cat." I did not tell him that I had eaten a large one entire that afternoon, but began to think I was tougher than a cat. He stated that pedlars came round there, and sometimes tried to sell the women folks a skimmer, but he told them that their women had got a better skimmer than *they* could make, in the shell of their clams; it was shaped just right for this purpose.—They call them "skim-alls" in some places. He also said that the sun-squawl was poisonous to handle, and when the sailors came across it, they did not meddle with it, but heaved it out of their way. I told him that I had handled it that afternoon, and had felt no ill effects as yet. But he said it made the hands itch, especially if they had previously been scratched, or if I put it into my bosom, I should find out what it was.

He informed us that no ice ever formed on the back side of the Cape, or not more than once in a century, and but little snow lay there, it being either absorbed or blown or washed away. Sometimes in winter, when the tide was down, the beach was frozen, and afforded a hard road up the back side for some thirty miles, as smooth as a floor. One winter when he was a boy, he and his father "took right out into the back side before daylight, and walked to Provincetown and back to dinner."

When I asked what they did with all that barren-looking land, where I saw so few cultivated fields,—

"Nothing," he said.

"Then why fence your fields?"

"To keep the sand from blowing and covering up the whole."

"The yellow sand," said he, "has some life in it, but the white little or none." . . .

At length the fool, whom my companion called the wizard, came in, muttering between his teeth,

"Damn book-pedlars,—all the time talking about books. Better do something. Damn 'em. I'll shoot 'em. Got a doctor down here. Damn him, I'll get a gun and shoot him;" never once holding up his head.

Where at the old man stood up and said in a loud voice, as if he was accustomed to command, and this was not the first time he had been obliged to exert his authority there:

"John, go sit down, mind your business,—we've heard you talk before,—precious little you'll do,—your bark is worse than your bite."

But, without minding, John muttered the same gibberish over again, and then sat down at the table which the old folks had left. He ate all there was on it, and then turned to the apples, which his aged mother was paring, that she might give her guests some apple-sauce for breakfast, but she drew them away and sent him off. When I approached this house the next summer, over the desolate hills between it and the shore, which are worthy to have been the birthplace of Ossian, I saw the wizard in the midst of a cornfield on the hillside, but, as usual, he loomed so strangely, that I mistook him for a scarecrow.

This was the merriest old man that we had ever seen, and one of the best preserved. His style of conversation was coarse and plain enough to have suited Rabelais. He would have made a good Panurge. Or rather he was a sober Silenus, and we were the boys Chromis and Mnasilus, who listened to his story.

> Not by Hæmonian hills the Thracian bard,
> Nor awful Phœbus was on Pindus heard
> With deeper silence or with more regard.

There was a strange mingling of past and present in his conversation, for he had lived under King George, and might have remembered when Napoleon and the moderns generally were born.

He said that one day, when the troubles between the Colonies and the mother country first broke out, as he, a boy of fifteen, was pitching hay out of a cart, one Doane, an old Tory, who was talking with his father, a good Whig, said to him:

"Why, Uncle Bill, you might as well undertake to pitch that pond into the ocean with a pitchfork, as for the Colonies to undertake to gain their independence."

He remembered well General Washington, and how he rode his horse along the streets of Boston, and he stood up to show us how he looked.

"He was a r—a—ther large and portly-looking man, a manly and resolute-looking officer, with a pretty good leg as he sat on his horse."— "There, I'll tell you, this was the way with Washington."

Then he jumped up again, and bowed gracefully to right and left, making show as if he were waving his hat.

Said he, *"That* was Washington."

He told us many anecdotes of the Revolution, and was much pleased when we told him that we had read the same in history, and that his account agreed with the written.

"Oh," he said, "I know, I know! I was a young fellow of sixteen, with my ears wide open; and a fellow of that age, you know, is pretty wide awake, and likes to know everything that's going on. Oh, I know!" . . .

In the course of the evening I began to feel the potency of the clam which I had eaten, and I was obliged to confess to our host that I was no tougher than the cat he told of; but he answered, that he was a plain-spoken man, and he could tell me that it was all imagination. At any rate, it proved an emetic in my case, and I was made quite sick by it for a short time, while he laughed at my expense. I was pleased to read afterward, in Mourt's Relation of the landing of the Pilgrims in Provincetown Harbor, these words:

"We found great muscles (the old editor says that they were undoubtedly sea-clams) and very fat and full of seapearl; but we could not eat them, for they made us all sick that did eat, as well sailors as passengers, . . . but they were soon well again."

It brought me nearer to the Pilgrims to be thus reminded by a similar experience that I was so like them. Moreover, it was a valuable confirmation of their story, and I am prepared now to believe every word of Mourt's Relation. I was also pleased to find that man and the clam lay still at the same angle to one another. But I did not notice sea-pearl. Like Cleopatra, I must have swallowed it. I have since dug these clams on a flat in the Bay and observed them. They could squirt full ten feet before the wind, as appeared by the marks of the drops on the sand.

"Now I am going to ask you a question," said the old man, "and I don't know as you can tell me; but you are a learned man, and I never had any learning, only what I got by natur."—It was in vain that we reminded him that he could quote Josephus to our confusion.—"I've thought, if I ever met a learned man I should like to ask him this question. Can you tell me how *Axy* is spelt, and what it means? *Axy,"* says he; "there's a girl over here is named *Axy*. Now what is it? What does it mean? Is it Scripture? I've read my Bible twenty-five years over and over, and I never came across it."

"Did you read it twenty-five years for this object?" I asked.

"Well, *how* is it spelt? Wife, how is it spelt?"

She said, "It is in the Bible; I've seen it."

"Well, how do you spell it?"

"I don't know. A c h, ach, s e h, seh,—Achseh."

"Does that spell Axy? Well, do *you* know what it means?" asked he, turning to me.

"No," I replied, "I never heard the sound before."

"There was a schoolmaster down here once, and they asked him what it meant, and he said it had no more meaning than a bean-pole."

I told him that I held the same opinion with the schoolmaster. I had been a schoolmaster myself, and had had strange names to deal with. I also heard of such names as Zoheth, Beriah, Amaziah, Bethuel, and Shearjashub, hereabouts.

At length the little boy, who had a seat quite in the chimney-corner, took off his stockings and shoes, warmed his feet, and having had his sore leg freshly salved, went off to bed; then the fool made bare his knotty-looking feet and legs, and followed him; and finally the old man exposed his calves also to our gaze. We had never had the good fortune to see an old man's legs before, and were surprised to find them fair and plump as an infant's, and we thought that he took a pride in exhibiting them. He then proceeded to make preparations for retiring, discoursing meanwhile with Panurgic plainness of speech on the ills to which old humanity is subject. We were a rare haul for him. He could commonly get none but ministers to talk to, though sometimes ten of them at once, and he was glad to meet some of the laity at leisure. The evening was not long enough for him. As I had been sick, the old lady asked if I would not go to bed,—it was getting late for old people; but the old man, who had not yet done his stories, said:

"You ain't particular, are you?"

"Oh, no," said I, "I am in no hurry. I believe I have weathered the Clam cape."

"They are good," said he; "I wish I had some of them now."

"They never hurt me," said the old lady.

"But then you took out the part that killed a cat," said I.

At last we cut him short in the midst of his stories, which he promised to resume in the morning. Yet, after all, one of the old ladies who came into our room in the night to fasten the fire-board, which rattled, as she went out took the precaution to fasten us in. Old women are by nature more suspicious than old men. However, the winds howled around the house, and made the fire-boards as well as the casements rattle well that night. It was probably a windy night for any locality, but we could not distinguish the roar which was proper to the ocean from that which was due to the wind alone.

Before sunrise the next morning they let us out again, and I ran over to the beach to see the sun come out of the ocean. The old woman of eighty-four winters was already out in the cold morning wind, bare-headed, tripping about like a young girl, and driving up the cow to milk. She got the breakfast with dispatch, and without noise or bustle; and meanwhile the old man resumed his stories, standing before us, who were sitting, with his back to the chimney, and ejecting his tobacco-juice right and left into the fire behind him, without regard to the various dishes which were there preparing. At breakfast we had eels, buttermilk cake, cold bread, green beans, doughnuts, and tea. The old man talked a steady stream; and when his wife told him he had better eat his breakfast, he said:

"Don't hurry me; I have lived too long to be hurried."

I ate of the apple-sauce and the doughnuts, which I thought had sustained the least detriment from the old man's shots, but my companion refused the apple-sauce, and ate of the hot cake and green beans, which had appeared to him to occupy the safest part of the hearth. But on comparing notes afterward, I told him that the buttermilk cake was particularly exposed, and I saw how it suffered repeatedly, and therefore I avoided it; but he declared that, however that might be, he witnessed that the apple-sauce was seriously injured, and had therefore declined that. After breakfast we looked at his clock, which was out of order, and oiled it with some "hen's grease," for want of sweet oil, for he scarcely could believe that we were not tinkers or pedlars; meanwhile, he told a story about visions, which had reference to a crack in the clock-case made by frost one night.

He was curious to know to what religious sect we belonged. He said that he had been to hear thirteen kinds of preaching in one month, when he was young, but he did not join any of them,—he stuck to his Bible. There was nothing like any of them in his Bible. While I was shaving in the next room, I heard him ask my companion to what sect he belonged, to which he answered,—

"Oh, I belong to the Universal Brotherhood."

"What's that?" he asked, "Sons o' Temperance?"

Finally, filling our pockets with doughnuts, which he was pleased to find that we called by the same name that he did, and paying for our entertainment, we took our departure; but he followed us out of doors, and made us tell him the names of the vegetables which he had raised from seeds that came out of the Franklin. They were cabbage, broccoli, and parsley. As I had asked him the names of so many things, he tried me in turn with all the plants which grew in his garden, both wild and cultivated. It was about half an acre, which he cultivated wholly himself. Besides the common garden vegetables, there were yellow-dock, lemon balm, hyssop, Gill-go-over-the-ground, mouse-ear, chick-weed, Roman wormwood, elecampane, and other plants. As we stood there, I saw a fishhawk stoop to pick a fish out of his pond.

"There," said I, "he has got a fish."

"Well," said the old man, who was looking all the while, but could see nothing, "he didn't dive, he just wet his claws."

And, sure enough, he did not this time, though it is said that they often do, but he merely stooped low enough to pick him out with his talons; but as he bore his shining prey over the bushes, it fell to the ground, and we did not see that he recovered it. That is not their practice.

Thus, having had another crack with the old man, he standing bareheaded under the eaves, he directed us "athwart the fields," and we took to the beach again for another day, it being now late in the morning. It was but a day or two after this that the safe of the Provincetown Bank was broken open and robbed by two men from the interior, and we learned that our hospitable entertainers did at least transiently harbor the suspicion that we were the men.*

—from *Cape Cod* (1865)

———

*On his 1857 trip to the Cape, Thoreau passed by John Newcomb's house and learned that the old man had died the previous winter, at age ninety-five. The house, still sporting its collection of little windows that so intrigued Thoreau, stands on a knoll on the east side of Williams Pond near Newcomb Hollow.

A Gloss on Thoreau

By Josef Berger (Jermiah Digges)

"I'VE THOUGHT, IF I ever met a learned man I should like to ask him this question. Can you tell me how Axy is spelt, and what it means? Axy," says he; "there's a girl over here is named Axy. Now, what is it? What does it mean? Is it Scripture? I've read my Bible twenty-five years, over and over, and I never come across it."

"Did you read it twenty-five years for this object?" I asked.

"Well, how is it spelt? Wife, how is it spelt?"

She said, "It is in the Bible; I've seen it."

"Well, how do you spell it?"

"I don't know. A-c-h, ach; s-e-h, seh—Achseh."

"Does that spell Axy? Well, do you know what it means?" he asked, turning to me.

"No," I replied, "I've never heard the sound before."

This passage occurs in the chapter of Thoreau's *Cape Cod* entitled "The Wellfleet Oysterman." I have an old second-hand copy of this work, which I bought of a down-Cape dealer, and in the margin along-side the passage, I find, in a faint and trembling hand:

"Judges, I, 13, the old fool."

—from *Cape Cod Pilot* (1937)

Windmills

By Henry David Thoreau

THE MOST FOREIGN and picturesque structures on the Cape, to an inlander, not excepting the salt-works, are the windmills,—gray-looking, octagonal towers, with long timbers slanting to the ground in the rear, and there resting on a cartwheel, by which their fans are turned round to face the wind. These appeared also to serve in some measure for props against its force. A great circular rut was worn around the building by the wheel. The neighbors who assemble to turn the mill to the wind are likely to know which way it blows, without a weathercock. They looked loose and slightly locomotive, like huge wounded birds, trailing a wing or a leg, and reminded one of pictures of the Netherlands.

—from *Cape Cod* (1865)

———

Henry Hall, the Miller

By Henry C. Kittredge

CLOSE BEHIND THE builder in prestige, came the miller. His task was no sinecure, and was so essential to the prosperity of the towns that great inducements were held out to any man who would undertake it. Just as the mill itself went untaxed, so was the miller exempt from military duty, and he was a privileged character in other ways besides; he need not hold office, his social position was assured, and he was often given a good-sized piece of land adjacent to the mill. His pay was in kind; from every bushel of corn he ground he was authorized to take a stated quantity, known as the miller's 'pottle'; and it was well earned. At the beginning of each day he had to mount to the top of the mill and scale the long arms to set the sails, which were rigged in nautical fashion with halliards; at night he must climb out again and furl them. If it blew hard, he had to shorten sail by twisting up the lower part of each sail. In a gale the mill scudded under bare poles, the surface of the slats across the arm offering sufficient resistance to the wind. Unlike the master of a ship, however, the miller had no crew of nimble acrobats to carry out his orders aloft. He was his own crew, and was perpetually short-handed. The clumsy rigging and primitive mechanism of his command made the work not only hard but dangerous. But for the fact that many of the millers were retired seamen who had learned agility at the mastheads of fishing schooners, casualties would have been more frequent than they were. If Henry Hall, for example, who at the age of seventy operated a mill in Dennis, had not been a sailor in his early days, he never could have extricated himself from the very ticklish position in which he once found himself. He had stopped his mill to shorten sail, but had neglected to make the arms fast with the huge iron chain which was used for that purpose. When he was halfway out on one of the arms, a free flaw caught the sails, and the arms began to turn. With amazing activity Hall worked his way back along the revolving arm until he reached the shaft, which, of course, was also revolving. Here he perched, three stories above the ground, straddling the shaft and maintaining an upright position by hitching himself clear of his seat as it turned under him. Luckily assistance arrived before the old mariner was exhausted.

—from *Cape Cod, Its People and Their History* (1930)

———

73

"The Old Miller"

By Shebnah Rich

HE IT WAS who climbed the slender latticed arms and set the sails; he it was who hitched the oxen, waiting grist, to the little wheel, and with the boys pushing, turned the white wings to the wind's eye; he it was who touched the magical spring, and presto! the long wings beat the air, the great shaft began to turn, cog played to its fellow cog, and the mammoth stones began to revolve. He it was who mounted like Jove upon his Olympian seat, and with one hand on the little regulator, that, better than the mills of the gods that ground only slow, could grind fast or slow, coarse or fine, with the other hand caught the first golden meal.

—from *Truro—Cape Cod* (1883)

———

The Boston Packet

By Shebnah Rich

GOING TO BOSTON by land was less common than a voyage to China. It must be the king's business that demanded such an outlay of time and capital. Excepting the mails, carriage by water was the only recognized connection with Boston. Hence the "packet" early became almost a personality. My history would be imperfect without some reference thereto. I cannot learn that any one vessel was engaged in this traffic till after the War of 1812. Yet I have no reasonable doubt that there was some periodical connection many years before. The first regularly-established packet of which I have authentic information, was the pinkey *Comet,* Captain Zoheth Rich. In about 1830, Captain Rich and his friends determined to build a first-class packet. The result was the schooner *Post-boy,* the finest specimen of naval architecture, and of passenger accommodation, in the Bay waters. Her cabin and furniture were finished in solid mahogany and bird's-eye, and silk draperies. She was the admiration of the travelling public; all that had been promised in a first-class packet, and was often crowded to overflowing with passengers. Captain Rich, better known at home as Captain Zoheth, knew the way to Boston in the darkest night, and could keep his passengers good-natured with a head wind. He could laugh as heartily at an old story as a new one, and was always a good listener. Good listeners have many secrets. One of the most popular women in Europe could not communicate a perfectly finished sentence, but she could keep a secret, and was consulted more on important interests than all the rest. The captain of the *Post-boy* was not a fluent man, nor of a vivid imagination. His vocabulary was limited to the fewest monosyllabic words, which he used with miserly economy, cutting them short in a quick, hurried, inimical style; then as if impressed that he had not done full justice to his subject, he would repeat his first words still quicker, and with more marked emphasis.

The first day from Boston was always a busy one, and the captain was on the alert. People would soon begin to inquire, "Captain Zoheth, when do you go to Boston again?" "I think we'll go Wens'dy, wind and weather permit'n; yes, go to Bost'n about Wens'dy," They knew well enough that the *Post-boy* never went to Boston on that declaration; none expected it. The next day the same question would be asked, with this answer, "Goin' to-morrer, if can get out the harbor; go to-morrer." "To-morrer" was sure to bring a scant tide, and scant wind, and the packet would not move.

Somebody was now sure to say, "Why, Capt'n, you didn't go to Boston to-day." "No, didn't get out; *divlish* low tide, and head wind." "Well, when *are* you going?" The last said, perhaps, with a slight impatience. "The *Piz-by* will go Bost'n to-morrer; yes, *sir,* the *Piz-by* will go Bost'n to-morrer, wind or no wind, tide or no tide, by gracious!" Now it was well understood the packet would go to Boston to-morrow. Early the next morning the captain would be seen coming with his little black-leather trunk that always meant business; long before highwater the colors floated at the topmast head, the signal for Boston; and the *Post-boy* went to Boston, just about the time the captain intended, and when from the first it was understood she would go. I do not mean to say this was the captain's rule, by no means; when business was good, he made quick trips, and never stood on the order of going or coming;

but there are scores now living, who well remember the *Post-boy,* Captain Zoheth, and his nervous Anglo-Saxon.

—from *Truro—Cape Cod* (1883)

———

A Cape Cod Man

By Herman Melville

STUBB WAS THE second mate. He was a native of Cape Cod; and hence, according to local usage, was called a Cape-Codman. A happy-go-lucky; neither craven nor valiant; taking perils as they came with an indifferent air; and while engaged in the most imminent crisis of the chase, toiling away, calm and collected as a journeyman joiner engaged for the year. Good-humored, easy, and careless, he presided over his whale-boat as if the most deadly encounter were but a dinner, and his crew all invited guests. He was as particular about the comfortable arrangement of his part of the boat, as an old stage-driver is about the snugness of his box. When close to the whale, in the very death-lock of the fight, he handled his unpitying lance coolly and off-handedly, as a whistling tinker his hammer. He would hum over his old rigadig tunes while flank and flank with the most exasperated monster. Long usage had, for this Stubb, converted the jaws of death into an easy chair. What he thought of death itself, there is no telling. Whether he ever thought of it at all, might be a question; but, if he ever did chance to cast his mind that way after a comfortable dinner, no doubt like a good sailor, he took it to be a sort of call of the watch to tumble aloft, and bestir themselves there, about something which he would find out when he obeyed the order, and not sooner.

What, perhaps with other things, made Stubb such an easy-going, unfearing man, so cheerily trudging off with the burden of life in a world full of grave peddlers, all bowed to the ground with their packs; what helped to bring about that almost impious good-humor of his; that thing must have been his pipe. For, like his nose, his short, black little pipe was one of the regular features of his face. You would almost as soon have expected him to turn out of his bunk without his nose as without his pipe. He kept a whole row of pipes there ready loaded, stuck in a rack, within easy reach of his hand; and, whenever he turned in, he smoked them all out in succession, lighting one from the other to the end of the chapter; then loading them again to be in readiness anew. For, when Stubb dressed, instead of first putting his legs into his trowsers, he put his pipe into his mouth.

I say this continual smoking must have been one cause, at least, of his peculiar disposition; for every one knows that this earthly air, whether ashore or afloat, is terribly infected with the nameless miseries of the numberless mortals who have died exhaling it; and as in time of the cholera, some people go about with a camphorated handkerchief to their mouths; so, likewise, against all mortal tribulations, Stubb's tobacco smoke might have operated as a sort of disinfecting agent.

—from *Moby-Dick* (1851)

Captain Peleg's Promise

By Josef Berger (Jeremiah Digges)

THE TOWN OF Barnstable, like a mackerel seiner with a full trip of fish, carries the biggest part of her story "below water line." From the wealth that is stowed in her hold I have pitched up only a few items here. But better this than to dismiss the centuries in the manner of old Captain Peleg Hawes on a voyage to China.

"Now then, Arathusy," Captain Peleg told his wife, "it's twenty minutes to sailing-hour. Better start your crying and get it over with, so's I won't be holding up the vessel."

As he pursed his lips and began tidying up his ditty-box, an obedient sob escaped his wife.

"Oh, Peleg, 'twouldn't be so hard, if you'd only write me a letter while you're away on these eternal long v'yages! Promise me, Peleg, you'll write this time—just one letter!"

The Captain groaned and promised. And eighteen months later, Arathusy, all a-tremble, tore open an envelope and read:

Hong Kong, China,
May 21, 1854.

Dear Arathusy:
I am here and you are there.

P. Hawes.

—from *Cape Cod Pilot* (1937)

———

Clipper Ships and Their Captains

By Henry C. Kittredge

A FULL ACCOUNT of the merchant marine of Cape Cod would require
not a chapter but a volume. Its tentative beginnings, its gradual rise to
the glory of the forties and fifties, and its inevitable decline, comprise
too vast and varied a subject for a condensed narrative. So in this chapter no mention can be made of many names that in their day were great,
or of many ships that spread their masters' greatness from sea to sea.
No foreign voyage is insignificant; every captain is in a very real sense
his country's ambassador. Especially was this true in the early days of
our nation, when we were yet a people unknown and untested, with
the world before us to antagonize or conciliate, and no one but our
shipmasters to represent us. These men neither antagonized nor concil-
iated. Instead, by their shrewdness, resourcefulness, and vigor, they won
for their country the reluctant and sometimes acidulated respect of the
world. . . .

Mighty as they were, these Cape-Codders were to become yet migh-
tier before they died. They were still unsatisfied and kept looking ahead
for new worlds to conquer. They had long to wait, for the dawn of the
clipper-ship era was at hand. Space is lacking to discuss the evolution
of these wonderful vessels. Suffice it to say that they revolutionized the
naval architecture of two nations, ourselves and the British, and became
at once the envy and the despair of the other maritime countries of the
world. The bows of the clippers, instead of being the bluff, apple-cheeked
affairs of the earlier type, were sharp, tapering, and concave, and cut

deep into the waves instead of beating flat against them. Then the flare of the hull at the fore-rigging lifted them over the waves and prevented them from being flooded too often. The sterns, too, tapered gracefully and no longer squatted flat in the water. The alterations in the design of the hull were hardly greater than the changes in rigging and top-hamper. The masts of the clippers towered to a height hitherto undreamed of, and spread one and in some cases two more courses of sails. These sails fitted as sails had never fitted before, with the result that the clippers, when it came to windward work, sailed like yachts, and would lie closer to the wind than anything of their size afloat. Supplied with such ships from the yards of New York and Boston by such builders as Webb and Westervelt, Hall, Curtis, and McKay, the American captains sailed forth in the fifties and in a year or two had captured the commerce of the world.

The clippers were the most beautifully finished and expensive vessels that had ever been built and were the pride of their owners' hearts—a pride nicely blended with anxiety when they considered the investment that each ship represented. Handling these wild beauties was ticklish business, requiring far more dexterity, nerve, and experience than was needful for the old-style barrel-bottomed craft that bobbed along comfortably under stumpy masts and seldom came to grief. Even the stalwart packets were eclipsed by these glorious vessels. The owners wanted the best men in the business for commanders, and they got them. Hence the clipper-ship captains became the aristocrats of an already aristocratic profession—the conquerors of the conquerors of the world—and scores of Cape men strode proudly in their ranks.

There was Baker, of the Flying Dragon and Shooting Star; Burgess, of the Whirlwind and Challenger; Kelly, of the Fleetwing; Sears, of the Wild Hunter; Jenkins, of the Raven; Crowell, of the Robin Hood; Sprague, of the Gravina; Dillingham, of the Snow Squall; Stevens, of the Southern Cross; Bearse, of the Winged Arrow; Hallett, of the Phantom; Baxter, of the Flying Scud; Hatch, of the Northern Light. The list might be doubled and trebled, and every name, whether of ship or master, would be of the first magnitude. And it must be emphasized once more that the first magnitude in this case means not merely first among Cape captains nor even among American masters. It means of first magnitude in the world—men who commanded the finest ships afloat—extreme clippers that could leave any other vessel of any other type hull down in half a day.

—from *Cape Cod, Its People and Their History* (1930)

"Gawd-Damned Historic"

By Josef Berger (Jeremiah Digges)

THIS STORY COMES out of books. Like Aphrodite, it springs full-rigged from the foam—the foam raised by historians, with which I became just a little fed up by the time they had done with the subject of clipper ships.

Clipper ships *were* noble. They *were* beautiful, graceful, proud, fast, matchless, etc., etc. And clipper ship captains *did* reach the heights of glory in the great days of sail, they *did* race over the banging course around the Horn to set up new speed records in the middle of the last century, records which no windjammers have equaled since. But about all this business, there is something that lures the unwary scribe into superlatives; and beyond a certain dosage, superlatives begin to cloy. I don't think any venture of mankind on land or sea has been set down for posterity with so much verbal fancywork, so many "ests" to the adjectives, as the story of the clipper ships; and neither do I think that story has ever been told any other way. Every clipper ship was the finest ever built, if not for this, then for that. Everyone, it seems to the casual reader, held a record for something. Every captain was the first to do something, or did something which has never been done since.

But one wonders if, in the enthusiasm for these tall ships, certain phases of the business have been slighted. After hearing of the hazards that attended even the average Boston–to–San Francisco voyage around the Horn, one wonders whether some of these famed clipper ship captains were not more foolhardy than heroic, careless of their own lives and the lives of their crews, in the race for freights.

And while we are on the subject of heroism, it may be as well to make one little point, for what it's worth. The skipper was not risking his neck for nothing, for in a rough sort of parallel, his earning power piled up with his speed records. The crew, on the other hand, did risk their necks for nothing, or for the next thing to it; for there was no sharing of profits here, and the fixed wage of an able seaman on the California clippers averaged between eight and twelve dollars a month. After buying out of the "slopchest" enough clothes to keep himself from freezing, he often ended the voyage in debt. If he had the price of a Boston newspaper, he could read about the glorious feat of the skip-

per who had ordered him aloft to the to'gallant yards while the ship
was rolling like a leaf in a millrace.

—from *Bowleg Bill* (1938)

———

" 'Aunt Beck' and Her Museum"

By Amos Otis

ELISHA BLUSH MARRIED for his first wife June 2, 1790, Rebecca Linnell—familiarly known as "Aunt Beck,"—the third wife and widow of
John Linnell, deceased. . . .

When young I had often heard of Aunt Beck's Museum, and there
are very few in Barnstable who have not. In the winter of 1825, I resided
in her neighborhood, and made several calls to examine her curiosities.
Her house, yet remaining, is an old-fashioned, low double-house, facing due South, with two front-rooms, a kitchen, bedroom and pantry
on the lower floor. The east front-room, which was her sitting-room,
is about fourteen feet square. The west room is smaller. Around the
house and out-buildings every thing was remarkably neat. The wood
and fencing stuff was carefully piled, the chips at the wood-pile were
raked up, and there was no straw or litter to be seen about the barn or
fences. It was an estate that the stranger would notice for its neat and
tidy appearance.

In my visits to her house the east front-room was the only portion I
was permitted to see, though I occasionally caught a glimpse of the
curiosities in the adjoining rooms through the half-opened doors. I was
accompanied in my visits by a young lady who was a neighbor, and on
excellent terms with Aunt Beck. She charged me not to look around
the room when I entered, but keep my eye on the lady of the house, or
on the fire-place. To observe such precautions was absolutely necessary,
for the stranger who, on entering, should stare around the room, would
soon feel the weight of Aunt Beck's ire, or her broom-stick. I followed
my instructions, and was invited to take one of the two chairs in the

room. It was a cool evening, and all being seated close to the fire, we were soon engaged in a friendly chat, and I soon had an opportunity to examine the curiosities. In the northeast corner of the room stood a bedstead with a few ragged, dirty bed-clothes spread thereon. The space under the bed was occupied partly as a pantry. Several pans of milk were set there for cream to rise, (for Aunt Beck made her own butter); but when she made more than she used in her family, she would complain of the dullness of the market. In front of the bed and near the centre of the room stood a common table about three feet square. Respecting this table a neighbor, Captain Elisha Hall, assured me that to his certain knowledge it had stood in the same place twenty years, how much longer he could not say. On this table, for very many successive years, she had laid whatever she thought curious or worth preserving. When an article was laid thereon it was rarely removed, for no one would dare meddle with Aunt Beck's curiosities. Feathers were her delight; but many were perishable articles, and in the process of time had rotted and changed into a black mould, covering the table with a stratum of about an inch in thickness.

In front of the larger table stood a smaller one near the fire-place, from which the family partook of their meals. This table was permanently located, and I was informed by the neighbors that no perceptible change had been made in the ORDER, or more properly DISORDERLY, arrangements of the furniture and curiosities for the ten years next preceding my visit. The evening was cool, and though my hostess was the owner of extensive tracts of woodland, covered with a heavy growth, she could not afford herself a comfortable fire. A few brands and two or three dead sticks, added after we came in, cast a flickering light over the room; but, fortunately for our olfactories, did not increase its temperature.

The floor, excepting narrow paths between the doors, fire-place and bed, was entirely with broken crockery, old pots, kettles, pails, tubs, &c., &c., and the walls were completely festooned with old clothing, useless articles of furniture, bunches of dried herbs, &c., &c., in fact every article named in the humorous will of Father Abby, excepting a "tub of soap." The other articles named in the same stanza were conspicuous:

> A long cart rope,
> A frying-pan and kettle,
> An old sword blade, a garden spade,
> A pruning-hook and sickle.

But in justice to Aunt Beck, I should state that she did for many long years contemplate making "a tub of soap." For thirty years she saved all her beef-bones for that purpose, depositing the same in her large kitchen fire-place and in other places about the room. During the warm summer of 1820, these bones became so offensive that Aunt Beck reluctantly consented to have them removed, and Captain Elisha Hall, who saw them carted away, says there was more than an ox-cart load.

Of the other rooms in the house I cannot speak from personal knowledge; but the lady who went with me and who is now living, informed me that in the west room there was a bed, a shoemaker's bench, flour barrels, chests containing valuable bedding, too good to use, and a nameless variety of other articles scattered over the bed and chairs; from the walls were suspended a saddle and pillion, and many other things preserved as rare curiosities. In time the room became so completely filled that it was difficult to enter it. The kitchen, bedroom, pantry and chambers were filled with vile trash and trumpery, covered with dirt and litter.

This description may seem imaginary or improbable to the stranger; but there are hundreds now living in Barnstable who can testify that the picture is not drawn in too strong colors. Truth is sometimes stranger than fiction, and this maxim applies in all its force to Rebecca Blush. That she was a monomaniac is true; but that she was insane on all subjects is not true. Early in life she was neat, industrious and very economical, but her prudent habits soon degenerated into parsimony. Economy is a virtue to be inculcated, but when the love of money becomes the ruling passion, and a man saves that he may hoard and accumulate, he becomes a miser, and as such, is despised. The miser accumulates money, or that which can be converted into money. Aunt Beck saved not only money, but useless articles that others threw away. These she would pick up in the fields, and by the roadside, and store away in her house. During the latter part of her life she seldom went from home. During more than twenty years she thus gathered up useless trash, and as she did not allow any thing (except the bones) to be carried out for more than forty years, it requires no great stretch of the imagination to form a correct picture of the condition and appearance of the place, she called her home.

Her estate, if she had allowed her husband to have managed it, would have been much larger at her death. Her wood she would not be allowed to be cut and sold, and the proceeds invested. She lost by investing her money in mortgages on old houses and worn-out lands, and loaning to persons who never paid their notes. She also had a habit of hiding parcels of coin among the rubbish in her house, and sometimes she would forget not only where she had placed the treasure, but how many such deposits she had made. It is said that some of her visitors, who were not over-much honest, often carried away these deposits, unknown and unsuspected by her.

On one subject, saving, Rebecca Blush was not of sound mind. She was, however, a woman naturally of strong mind—no one could be captain over her. She knew more or less of almost every family in town, and was always very particular in her inquiries respecting the health of the families of her visitors. She delighted in repeating ancient ballads and nursery tales. In her religious opinions she was Orthodox; and she hated the Methodists, not because they were innovators, but because the preachers called at her house, and because her husband contributed something to their support.

Not a dollar of the money saved and accumulated by her, during a long life of toil and self-denial, now remains. In a few short years it took to itself wings and flew away. Her curiosities, which she had spent so many years in collecting and preserving, were ruthlessly destroyed before her remains were deposited in the grave. She died on Sunday. On the Thursday preceding, her attendants commenced removing. She overheard them, and asked if it thundered. They satisfied the dying woman with an evasive answer. Before her burial, all her curiosities were either burnt, or scattered to the four winds of heaven.

The old house soon lost all its charms, and its doors ceased to attract visitors. Its interior was cleansed and painted; paper-hangings adorned the walls, and handsome furniture the rooms. Forty-five days after her death there was a wedding-party at the house. Mr. Blush endeavored to correct the sad mistake which he made when a young man, by taking in his old age a young woman for his second wife, forty-three years younger than himself, and fifty-seven years younger than his first wife.

During the closing period of his life, a term of nearly six years, Elisha Blush enjoyed all those comforts and conveniences of life of which he had been deprived for forty years, and to which a man having a competent estate is entitled. This great change in his mode of living did not, however, afford him unalloyed happiness. One remark which he made at this period is worth preserving: it shows the effect which habits of forty years growth have on the human mind. Some one congratulated him on the happy change which had taken place. "Yes," said he, "I live more comfortably than I did," but he added with a sigh, "my present wife is not so economical as my first."

—from *Genealogical Notes of Barnstable Families* (1888)

"Fish Weirs"

By Joseph C. Lincoln

ALONG THE NEW Jersey coast they call them "traps" but throughout that section of Cape Cod with which the writer is acquainted they are always "weirs." In the season there are hundreds of them, big and little. Vineyard Sound and Nantucket Sound, with all their inlets and coves and bays, are edged with them, and Cape Cod Bay without its fringe of fish weirs would be strangely bare and unfamiliar.

In general plan they are all pretty much alike. The old-fashioned fly trap, which used to be placed on the kitchen tables before the days of window screens, was constructed on the same general principle. There was a small opening through which the fly was expected to enter but which he was counted upon to overlook, when trying to escape. The eel trap and the lobster pot of today are so made. Of course, if the fish or the fly or the eel or the lobster were not stupid, if he had intelligence worth mentioning, he could get out easily enough and before it was too late; but, for the matter of that, if he had possessed a teaspoonful of intelligence, he would never have gone in.

It is comforting to realize that a human being is superior to this sort of idiocy. *He* never rushes blindly into something he knows nothing about. No, indeed! When *he* explores a new country, he blazes the trail as he travels it. When he enters the limestone cave, he strings clews behind him. When he buys shares in a "get-rich-quick" scheme, or borrows money from the bank in order to profit by margin trading on an "inside" stock-market tip, he—he—well, you see—

But why bring *that* up?

There are deep-water weirs and low-water weirs, but their construction and layout differ only slightly. The deep-water weir is most common. It has a long "leader", a high fence constructed of poles driven into the sand at equal distances apart, the spaces between the poles closed with nets hung on ropes. The upper edges of these ropes are buoyed with wooden floats and the lower edges are weighted with lead. The leader extends from the shallower water near shore out to the deep water of the channel.

A mackerel, swimming along about his business, which is presumably chasing a sand eel or a whitebait or some other edible creature smaller than he is, suddenly finds his progress interfered with by the long row of nets. He cannot get through, so he turns to the right or left. If he goes to the left, he finds the water becoming more and more shallow. Shoal water, so his reason or instinct or experience—whatever it is that prompts a fish to do anything—has warned him that shoal water usually means trouble, so he turns once more and swims in the opposite direction. Got to get through or around this blessed thing somehow.

If he swims long enough, he reaches the outer end of the leader. Ah! Everything is all right now. Here is open water at last. But it isn't. Instead of one fence of nets there are now two. They are set a good way apart but the provoking things are there, behind as well as before him. He follows one set until he reaches a narrow opening. Here is the real exit, of course. He darts through. Yes, here we are. The fact that there are now so many other mackerel beside him proves it; only, why are they milling around in frantic circles? Why don't they go somewhere? There is plenty of water, deep water. Why—

And then he makes another terrifying discovery. He is not free at all. Not only are those nets on every side, but beneath. He dashes hither and thither, but to no avail. That narrow opening by which he entered—he has forgotten it altogether. Panic-stricken, he joins the rest of the school and swims in circles, getting nowhere. He is in the "pound", and the pound of a weir is, to a fish, the condemned cell. "All hope abandon, ye who enter here."

And, the next morning, when the tide is high, men in boats come out from the beach and proceed to draw the net covering the bottom of the pound, draw it from the water, foot by foot and yard by yard, until this particular mackerel and his thousands of fellow prisoners are thrown together,—a flapping, silvery mass in a bulging pouch of netting. That pouch is lifted over the side of one of the boats and emptied inboard. That is, for our mackerel, the end of the story. What happens afterward does not interest him. . . .

That is how a deep-water weir is operated on both sides of the Cape and, so far as I know, everywhere else alongshore. . . .

As a boy, I never refused an invitation to ride out to a fish weir with its owner. Sometimes we boys did not wait for an invitation, but went afoot—barefoot, of course; but we rode when we had the chance.

Always we rode in a blue truck-wagon, behind a plodding horse or a yoke of oxen. An ox team was an everyday sight along the Cape roads at that time, but I cannot remember seeing one within Barnstable County limits for years and years. Oxen were particularly fitted for hauling a load of fish over the wet flats and through the shallow channels. They were slow movers but they were strong and, after all, time was a minor consideration in a trip to and from a fish weir. You started out when the tide was ebbing and if, homeward bound, you forded the inshore channel before the water was up to the wheel hubs, that was all that was necessary.

On a summer afternoon, perched on the boxed seat of a smelly truck-wagon, with old Beriah Hallett beside you, his whiskered jaws moving as he chewed his tobacco, and the feet of the oxen "plop-plopping" or "splash-splashing" as they moved across the flats or waded the channels—that was good enough fun for a couple of bare-footed freckle-faced youngsters.

We reached the inshore end of the leader and followed it. The leader of a low-water weir was, in our day, not netted but lathed, the narrow strips set an inch or so apart. It was strongly constructed, too; we little chaps used to stick our bare toes between the slats and climb to the top and roost there, like the gulls. When these weirs were taken down in the fall, the slatted sections were brought ashore and the poles left standing. At least, that, according to my recollection, was the usual procedure.

Beriah Hallett's weir was, like the rest, erected on the outer bar itself, the pound just at the farther edge where, even at the lowest tide, there were always two feet or more of water. Beriah would back the truck-wagon into the pound, climb out and, wading thigh deep amid the fish, select the marketable kinds from the "culch" and, with a dip-net, toss them into the cart. If he had a lucky day there would be mackerel there and tautog—"black fish" they call them elsewhere, I understand—and plaice and flounders and an occasional cod and haddock.

They were interesting, but we boys were quite as much interested in the despised "culch", the varieties that Mr. Hallett ignored and did not trouble himself to dip out. Sculpin and skate and blowfish—tickle a blowfish's "tummy" and he swells up like balloon—and horsefoot crabs—king crabs, if you must be correct—and sea robins and squid—always plenty of squid.

Squid, in the deep-water weirs, and perhaps in the low-water ones now, are saved and sold to cod fishermen for bait, but Beriah did not save his. He chased them out of his way and swore at them, but that was all. We boys had a good time with them, however. Strike the water before a school of them, or throw a stone among them, and they would vanish in a smoke screen of their own creating. "Squid ink" we used to call the black liquid they squirted when alarmed. It was good for something—we juveniles were sure of that—but there was some difference of opinion among us as to what that something was. Good for rheumatism or to write letters with, or—or—well, it does not matter now. It did not matter then, for, so far as I ever heard, no boy ever collected any for experimental purposes.

The ride home was not so much fun as the ride out, for we were wet through by that time, and chilly and hungry. Incidentally, it was edging on to the supper hour and we had all been warned what might happen if we were late for supper again. But, no matter what did or did not happen, the next time Mr. Hallett invited any of us to go "weiring" with him, we went. . . .

There were several deep-water weirs in the bay opposite our town. They were, of course, set farther out than the low-water weirs and, as I remember, were owned, not by individuals, but by several persons in partnership. Occasionally a horse mackerel or a sturgeon got into the pound of one of those weirs and then there was a scrimmage. The amount of damage a six-foot sturgeon or a five-hundred-pound horse mackerel can do to a weir is considerably more than a little.

To get him into a boat alive is out of the question. He must be clubbed and hacked to death, and that is a long and dangerous job when you are fenced in by a wall of netting which you are anxious to keep from being torn to rags. And then, when at last he is killed and rolled inboard, he is good for nothing. Bring him ashore, throw him out on the beach and let him rot in the sun—that is, or was, the procedure. One of our most fragrant recollections is that of a dead horse mackerel and a sturgeon or two lying on the shore to windward of the weir shanties at Quivet Neck.

But that was as it used to be. That was when a horse mackerel was just a horse mackerel and no one would have dreamed of eating him, any more than they would have dreamed of eating a horse. It is very different now. He is not a horse mackerel any more; he is a tuna. One of the great shocks of my life came with the discovery that the "leaping tuna", the great game fish that sportsmen travel away out to the Pacific Coast to catch on a hook, that fishing clubs are named for, that is served in restaurants and canned for home consumption—that he is, after all, nothing but the horse mackerel we used to hear sworn at and see thrown away to rot—ah, that was a shock!

I am not very fond of tuna—even a boarding-house tuna-fish salad does not stir my appetite. No, the memory of that beach and its aroma comes between me and the salad plate.

But that, of course, is just a prejudice and prejudices formed in boyhood are hard to get rid of. One day, at the fish wharf, I watched a weir boat unload. Different kinds of fish went into different barrels—cod in one, plaice in another, etc. There was, however, one barrel into which almost anything seemed to go. A fair-sized skate was pitched into it. Now the idea of a skate being worth saving was, to my Cape Cod mind, beyond comprehension. I asked about it. The man with the pitchfork shook his head.

"Huh!" he grunted. "That's one of the New York barrels. They eat anything over there."

Well, a skate is a ray and, in France—or, no doubt, to a French cook anywhere—the ray is a delicacy. If we Cape Codders met him during the course of a banquet at a New York hotel, we probably should have no fault to find with him. Unless he were labelled "skate." Then we would scornfully pass him by.

We do not care to eat skates, or to catch them, either.

—from *Cape Cod Yesterdays* (1935)

"An Old Place, an Old Man"

By John Hay

WHEN THE FEEL of winter comes, in November or early December—though by astronomical calculation winter does not start until December twenty-second—when the first hard seal is set on the ground, and we are settled in with a new plainness, then it is not difficult to bring back yesterday and its country living. Winter's role in the year's wheel is an arresting, for the sake of renewal, a sleep, or half sleep, for later waking. It has its own suspense and violence, its roars and silences, like the other seasons, but in general its order is of a different quality, having an inwardness and resistance, a bare, gray need to keep things inside and hidden down. This is the time of year that shows a plain connection between human beings and their land.

I see last leaves whipping around the hollows off an old Cape road, or walk through the now more oblique rays of the sun that yellow the sandy ground held by thin, waving grasses, gray beach plum or bayberry bushes, and I recognize what has been left behind.

Here, surrounded by open slopes, is an abandoned house site, now a cellar hole, walled by square blocks of glacial granite. Orchard grass, timothy, and redtop still engage the old domesticity. Inside their circle you can see where children played, water was fetched and carried, chickens fed, and voices raised. There are yucca plants close to the foundations, and a rose or two. I transplanted such a rose a few years ago, and with added nourishment it turned from a slight, single-petaled flower to a great bunch of pinkish-purple fragrance.

Unlike some abandoned farm sites in other parts of New England, there is nothing left here to show what the inhabitants did. There are no harrows, stone bolts, yokes, or farm implements, not even any pots and pans. The stones are left, and the faithful grasses, and beyond them the crunchy, gray deer moss, and beard grass of indigenous fields. It was a small place, of bare subsistence. Whatever the qualities of the people who lived there, they left simplicity behind them. Not too far away, a bulldozer is making a desert with giant scoops, high-tension wires are marching by, and a plane rips the air overhead. We are encroaching in our oblivious fashion, without delay. The new domesticities may occupy only a tenth of an acre each, but they engage all lands. The old domestic wildness cannot be replaced. It was a lodgment limited by need, gray outside and dark within, perhaps unbearably close and confined at times, but with a knowledge of its earth.

It seems to me that as the world has grown outward in recent years, even I, a comparative newcomer to Cape Cod, have lost some local life to memory. When you live in a place for the first time you see behind it to its roots and grain, before the storms of circumstance blow you away from it. I remember a few old men who seemed so representative of the old Cape that it will never be the same now that they are gone. The loss is of a country speech, the flavor of a flesh and blood nurtured on locality. What has replaced them can be defined in terms of California as well as Cape Cod, which means no detriment to either, for what we are now obliged to consider is locality in a wider field. But those old men were born as we may not yet be born, sturdily, in custom and resignation.

Nathan Black died in October 1957, at the age of ninety-two. He was born in 1865, the year Abraham Lincoln was assassinated. He was a near neighbor. His land abutted mine, and since he was the proprietor of the Black Hills Barber Shop, I could walk down through the woods to get my hair cut, for the price, in a trillion-dollar world, of fifty cents. He was a heavy man, with bright brown eyes, and a head of curly white hair. He fitted the open Cape Cod weather, or the weather fitted him. I am not sure of the distinction. Nearly ninety years of change, of natural cataclysm, of both peace and abysmal war in the human world, had left him in the same place, with the same measure, outwardly at least, of stability.

When he left his place, or the customary orbit of work and old friends that constituted his life, perhaps to drive out on a new highway or to the chain store, he may never have stopped being surprised. I remember his looking at me with a kind of amused questioning—but no alarm— and saying something about no one belonging here any more. The new population didn't quite make sense to him.

In the way of old countrymen who knew their boundaries, he was tough and unforgiving in his role of landowner. He had his rights, "By gawly!" and he would know when someone did him wrong. He held on hard, and I suspect there were neighbors who felt the possessiveness too strongly, but this being none of my business, I will go in and get my hair cut.

The shop, with a tool shed under the same roof, where "Nate" used to grind knives and axes, stood, and still stands, across the yard from the house where he was born. There are some other gray-shingled, out-lying buildings on both sides of a dirt road that runs through scrubby woods and hollows, dry hills sloping down to marshy bottom land . . . wood-lot country. One December day I rapped at the door, and he put his jacket on and walked across the yard with me, where two white ducks were parading and some red chickens giving the frozen ground a going over. The old man bent down a little and spoke to his dog Bonnie, a cream-colored spaniel, which had just wagged up to him: "Did you get it?"

Then, to me: "I lost an egg. Picked up five eggs, out of the hen yard this mornin', and came back with four. Maybe there was a hole in these old pants of mine."

The barber shop was small, long and narrow, but he had a stove in there that kept it warm. There were some old magazines on a bench against the wall, with a black Homburg hat hanging on a peg. It had been given him by an old customer, a wealthy man who had lived on the Cape during the summer and had come in to have his hair cut for many years before he died. There was a photograph on the wall of the two of them with an inscription underneath that read: "Established 1884. A satisfied customer is our best advertisement." They were stand-ing out in front of the shop, smiling in the sun.

"Feller came here yesterday and I had to clip him in the kitchen. Shop was too cold," Nate said.

The calm of the place was comforting. It came, I suppose, from an acceptance that emanated from him, and brought in many old friends, who would sit down to say: "Nate, just thought I'd come over and pass the time of day."

Whatever he had to say about other people never left them without the honor of human circumstances. "Pretty close, he is," he would say with a little laugh, or "I guess he had a shade on" (a Cape Cod expression for being drunk). "Guess you can't hold on to nothin'," he said about some local theft, in a way that insisted on not being roused beyond necessity.

His origins were out of a kind of history of which there was very little left intact except himself. He once showed me a tintype of his mother, a handsome girl named Bridget Malady, who had emigrated from Ireland in 1862. His father, Timothy Black, was born in Yarmouth, on the Cape. At the age of ten he signed on as a cook aboard the packet which sailed between East Dennis and Boston, and seems to have spent a good deal of his life on intermittent voyages at sea. He was also in the butchering and slaughtering business with his two sons. In the autumn they used to butcher eighty-five hogs or more, at the rate of three a day. And in some rough but related way, Timothy Black started his son in the barbering business. Nate remembered how his father used to cut his hair in the kitchen, long before the Black Hills emporium was established: "I used to sit there while he was sort of pummeling at me on the back of the neck. By gol! I sure did cringe when he was chopping me with those women's scissors."

While I, seventy or eighty years later, was sitting in the barber's chair, getting more expert and calmer work done on me, I assembled a little of the past. In the nineteenth and early twentieth centuries an expedition to the post office or the store took up a large part of the day. That was the time when you could hitch the horse up to a post and stop for a long chat, "having the capacity to waste time" as I heard a Texan phrase it about some of his countrymen in the western part of the state. People walked between their houses—there are foot paths still showing—on barren hills. They had small herds of cows that foraged on the sloping fields. Families used to picnic together by the ponds, and there were barn dances on Saturday nights, which were sometimes the occasion for a rip-roaring fight. I have heard it said that Nate Black was the strongest fighter in the region, when outraged beyond his normal patience, but he would reveal none of this prowess to me.

The Black family also held dances in their kitchen. The father of the house played the violin. On such occasions they would have plum porridge suppers, or they served crackers, milk, and raisins, and sometimes hulled corn.

He was of a piece with his surroundings. I think of many things he talked about while I was having my hair cut and they all meant the gray, sea-girded land, and a human closeness to it. I think of the deer that ate his beans, of his duck that was carried off by a fox, of foxes being reduced in population by the mange, of a watering place for horses by Cedar Pond in East Dennis (a beautiful pond with ranks of dark cedars backing it up, and now being encroached upon by house lots); and he talked about the big eels waiting to eat young herrin' (or alewives) at the mouth of a pond, and of sounding the depths of Round Pond here in West Brewster.

And then there was his dog which had to be chained up because it got so wildly excited chasing rabbits through the woods that it was constantly lost, having once been picked up nearly ten miles away; and the coon that climbed a tree after a hen; and his little granddaughter wanting to shine a flashlight through the window one night and take a picture of a coon she saw outdoors, because it was "such a pretty-looking animal."

There also come to mind the fishing boats all-over white with screaming gulls, that he once spoke about with real excitement, and, of course, the yearly work on his cranberry bogs . . . he and his tart and lively wife used to pick them together; and the shifting price of cranberries, and his wood lots, and who was after him to buy some of his land.

"Yes yes" he would say, in the Cape Cod fashion, and always, when a customer was leaving the shop: "Come again."

His wife Emily died two years before him. Some time before that I stopped to talk with him when he was scything the family plot in Red Top Cemetery, which lies at the junction of two country roads, on a little hill or high knoll up in the sky and the ocean winds. He told me two women had come up one day while he was there and said: "What a nice place!" He and his wife are buried there, in a place which has no more permanence than any other, but for them and by them had the simple power of acquaintance.

—from *Nature's Year* (1961)

———

Sears Village

By Scott Corbett

CAPE COD POST offices are not what they used to be, according to old-timers. They used to be full of retired sea captains yarning all day long. They were the local clubhouse, news center, and forum.

Maybe they aren't what they used to be, but they are still a good deal more than just a place to pick up mail.

Our post office was about the size one might expect in a place where there were less than a hundred boxholders in winter. It was in a nice little white building with a real-estate office next door, and when I looked at it the first time all I could think of was the many times I had walked up Eighth Avenue to a post office so big there was room enough for "Neither rain, nor snow, nor heat, nor gloom of night stays these couriers from the swift completion of their appointed rounds" to be engraved across its front in letters as tall as I was. On our post office there would have been just about room enough for "No Loitering and No Spitting" in headline size.

The postmistress, Mrs. Nora Larkins, welcomed us to town and explained the workings of the local postal system. There was no house delivery. Boxholders paid a box rental of twenty-five cents every three months, and if a person objected to that he could get his mail % General Delivery and not have a box.

As for Mrs. Larkins, oddly enough she was not a native. It may have been that the appointment was made under a Democratic administration and the only way they could find a Democrat in East Dennis was to import one, I don't know, but anyway there she was.

While we were talking to Mrs. Larkins, a small, gray-haired lady came in for her mail and the postmistress introduced us. Her name was Mrs. Sears, but she did not particularly resemble Mrs. Luella Sears. She was pleasant and said it was nice to have somebody in the Landry house again, and that they had all liked the Landrys very much and knew Mr. Landry would never have sold the house to anybody who wasn't nice.

A moment later another small, gray-haired lady came in and was introduced to us as Mrs. Sears. She had scarcely left when the first small, gray-haired lady came in again.

"Have you met Mrs. Sears?" asked Mrs. Larkins.

"Yes, two Mrs. Searses ago," I said, and both women laughed.

"No, this is *another* Mrs. Sears," said Mrs. Larkins, and I apologized for having mistaken her for the first one. . . .

. . . I remarked to Elizabeth on the way home, "Say, wasn't that a funny coincidence having three Mrs. Searses come in one after the other?"

"Yes, especially when they all looked exactly alike."

"It seemed so to me. Now that I try to think back, not only did the third one look like the first one, but the second one looked like both of them!"

"Maybe they were triplets. You know, one of those things where three sisters marry brothers."

"That's the kind of stuff that's supposed to go on in New England," I agreed. "We'll have to ask somebody about it. Do you suppose they're part of Mrs. Luella Sears' family? They must be related, having the same name and all." . . .

When we went to the post office next day we met two more Mrs. Searses, and while we could have sworn they were the same ones we had met before, Mrs. Larkins assured us they were not.

"I notice the local store is run by a Sears, too, and one of the roads running off the highway up the hill there is Sears Road. Is everybody in this town named Sears except you and the Underhills and us?"

"No, there are a few named Crowell," said Mrs. Larkins. "You know, this used to be nicknamed Sears Village years ago, because then it was practically all Searses."

"Are they all related?"

"Well, sort of. Some of them don't claim some of the others that claim *them*. They like to pick and choose their branches, but I guess back a ways they're all connected somehow." . . .

. . . We joked about the confusion of Searses, of course—a standard joke in East Dennis these past two hundred years or so—and [Mrs. Asa Sears] explained the local system used to avoid first-name confusion among the womenfolk.

Needless to say, in a place where there were three Gertrude and four Esther Searses, for example, something had to be done, so each woman's first name was combined with her husband's first name. Thus Esther, wife of Dean Sears, was called Esther Dean to avoid confusion with Esther Howard, wife of Howard Bailey Sears, who was called Howard Bailey to avoid confusion with Everett Howard Sears.

She herself was called Ruth Asa, to differentiate her from Ruth Daniel. As for the men, most of them were referred to by their two given names, even formally—'Mr. Joe Homer,' for example, with the 'Sears' understood. (We later met a lady who was a Sears herself, who grew up in East Dennis, and who was fifteen years old before she knew that the last name of 'Mr. Isaac Berry' was not Berry. Not once in fifteen years had she heard anyone refer to him as Mr. Sears.)

—from *We Chose Cape Cod* (1953)

———

from "Mayflower"

By Conrad Aiken

God's Acres once were plenty, the harvest good:
five churchyards, six, in this sparse neighborhood,
each with its huddled parish of straight stones,
green rows of sod above neat rows of bones.
The weeping-willow grieves above the urn,
the hour-glass with wings awaits its immortal turn:
on every slab a story and a glory,
the death's head grinning his *memento mori*.
All face the sunset, too: all face the west.
What dream was this of a more perfect rest—?
One would have thought the east, that the first ray
might touch them out of darkness into day.
Or were they sceptics, and perforce, in doubt,
wistful to watch the last of light go out?

And in the sunset the names look westward, names like eyes:
the sweet-sounding and still watchful names. Here lies
Mercy or Thankful, here Amanda Clark,*
the wife of Rufus; nor do they dread the dark,
but gaily now step down the road past Stony Brook,
call from the pasture as from the pages of a book,

---

*The Clark family were the original inhabitants of the three-hundred-year-old West Brewster farmhouse that Aiken bought in 1940 and christened, with literal poetry, "41 doors."

their own book, by their own lives written,
each look and laugh and heartache, nothing forgotten.
Rufus it was who cleared of bullbriar the Long Field,
walled it with fieldstone, and brought to fabulous yield
the clay-damp corner plot, where wild grape twines.
Amanda planted the cedars, the trumpet-vines,
mint-beds, and matrimony vine, and columbines.
Each child set out and tended his own tree,
to each his name was given. Thus, they still live, still see:
Mercy, Deborah, Thankful, Rufus and Amanda Clark,
trees that praise sunlight, voices that praise the dark.

The houses are gone, the little shops are gone,
squirrels preach in the chapel. A row of stone
all now that's left of the cobbler's, or in tall grass
a scrap of harness where once the tannery was.
And the blue lilacs, the grey laylocks, take possession
round every haunted cellar-hole, like an obsession:
keep watch in the dead houses, on vanished stairs,
where Ephraim or Ahira mended chairs:
sneak up the slope where once the smoke-house stood
and herrings bronzed in smoke of sweet fernwood.
Lost, lost, lost, lost—the bells from Quivett Neck
sing through the Sabbath fog over ruin and wreck,
roofs sinking, walls falling, ploughland grown up to wood.
Five churchyards, six, in this sparse neighborhood:
God's Acres once were plenty, the harvest good.

———

"At the Wellfleet Historical Society, During a Moderate Tempest"

By Charles H. Philbrick

We slammed in out of the summer storm,
Shook, dripped, squeezed hair and hushed the children;
Then started to circle the past, and peer in its corners.

There were sadirons sheer and solid as dreadnaughts,
Capstan-bars, quadrants, quilts and tin churns;
Daguerreotypes of the righteous buttonhooked tight
To the collar in beady-black strings of no nonsense,
Square wooden pattens for hoofs of obedient horses
Who hauled off the marshes the salt hay they lived on; the scoop
Of sloths' claws well fitted and polished, wood into wood,
That has outlived the cranberries here; the sparse-
Starred flags, the pillows patched and plumped for homing men,
Potato-mashers unchanged from my childhood, the gothic-backed potty-
    chair;
And the worn, humbling school-desk for midget seamen-to-be.

There were schoolbooks, paperknives slivered from transoms
Of famous wrecks; and scrimshawed tusks on which the boys
From Wellfleet School improved each idle and continent hour,
Scoring their fathers' votes, the whales and other objects of desire,
As they lolled in the doldrums of middle-Pacific, stinking
After the slaughters from which money rose like the soot.
Here a local gulliver's surgical kit for probing the whale
To deep death and grand transfigurations into corsets
And Bible-reading light; here models of four-finned schooners
That drew a full fathom through the yellowing charts and past
Lighthouses marking a land that has not survived its surveying.

And there was in the last upstairs corner the immaculate skull
Of the richly flinted and full-ribbed Pamet brave, a skull
Of such incised and settled shape, so right as to alert

All sculptors to the hopelessness of flesh-blurred heads.
This tenant of the land we buy and bully, tax, looks now
As though he'd smelled us coming, and it ate his nose away.

Down from his clean presence, past the stove-blacked safe
That housed a grandfather's haul and a few crisp clippings,
Back we came through all the dried produce of attics owned
By good granddaughters who thus outstripped the auctioneers,
Past the rusty flare-headed hatchets that hacked off disasters,

And out in this gale to the ocean at exercise under stiff skies.
Why am I so much involved with things I have never used,
Or seen except in the vast museums of memory?

Perhaps old notions like identity hide under dust,
And continuity's refreshed by swipes of spray;
History and the world's working brushed me with rust
Near both shores of Wellfleet, that loud and quiet day.

———

"Game of Croquet"

By David Wojahn

—after Eakins

The boats pull out
though many will be lost to
the storm unleashed tonight, hurricane winds
of the century's first autumn, but for now
the world is strict bright
colors on a lawn,

a girl singing
the advanced songs of Mahler
at a window where the curtains stir only

to the notes cascading from her lips,
the stricken fall only
with the *clack*

of maple globes
against one another, moribund
planets in collision, though I suppose
these minute deaths mean something beyond
themselves, Katherine in her
pink gingham dress,

gathered at the waist,
Mavis in simple white; and their
suitor, Captain Shuttleworth, returned last
month from Havana, peers from the gazebo's
botched minaret to a thundercloud
simmering above

Hyannisport, the bay
a gunmetal blue, the wind now rising
as Dottie the maid gathers picnic baskets,
overturned goblets, the ladies' magazines from
London, calling the airedales
home; and the game

is won by Mavis
who takes Captain Shuttleworth's
arm in triumph, as though she has now proven
he will choose her, leaving Katherine to sulk
her afternoons along the paths
of the salt marsh

where gulls wheel
down to the brackish water.
Accompany her, please. Touch her forehead
that glistens with fever, the trembling, girlish
shoulders. She feels as though
she will never die.

———

"The Legend of Screaming Island"

By Robert Finch

THIS IS A story that is dying. It is dying where they tell it along the inlets of Pleasant Bay, along the soft slopes and tall pines that overlook the long wide islands resting in the waters off South Orleans and Chatham. As a legend it is fairly new and uncommonly localized in its telling, and yet, perhaps because it has no moral to speak of, it is dying fast and lives even now only in the minds of the very young and the very old. And when the old tell it or the young listen, it is as though it were a piece of strange flotsam that has come in with the tide, that is not pleasant or instructive to look at, but which owns a certain fascinating grotesqueness which is now perhaps all that holds it against the final ebb into oblivion.

This is the story they tell:

They say that even as a small boy he had white hair. They say that he was one of the sad, fragile ones whom the wind may pick up and twist into permanent strangeness, and whose only protection is the constant protection of love. And it was early in his years that his protection fell into the sea and into the dust and he was left naked.

The records show that Walter Nathan Eldredge came into the world in a small sea-captain's house set in Chatham Harbor on the 18th of November, 1843. He was the only son of Captain Josiah and Sarah Eldredge and survived the normal childhood diseases. When he was three days short of seven years old, his father's ship was torn apart by a storm 150 miles southeast of his home, and eight months later his mother died of a brain concussion after being kicked in the head by a plowhorse she was steering across their back field.

They say that in the months after his father was taken by the sea the boy could be seen standing on the dark beaches, small and white, or moving like a spirit through the bending yellow grass of the marshes. They say that he stood on the sand, looking out, and that the looking took the love of the sea from him, that the long waves reached up at him and stole his tears, and that the marsh winds pierced his blue eyes and turned them yellow.

They say that his spirit walked on a fragile stick and that the stick broke with his mother's head. At the funeral he did not cry but stood as though listening for something from a long distance. In the days that followed he stood, abstractedly, in the long afternoon sun of the hot field, and they say the sun burnt the love of the green leaves from his eyes and turned them dark, and that when the wind passed above him he would look up and sometimes laugh hollowly as the gray gulls sailed by.

At the age of seven and a half, Walter Nathan Eldredge was given into the guardianship of his maiden aunt, Jennifer Hopkins of South Orleans, on the 20th day of June, 1851, there to be raised until adoption should be arranged. The records show that at the end of two years Miss Hopkins filed a petition to the town selectmen declaring her inability to maintain the child and requesting that he be made a ward of the state. The requests were complied with, and on New Year's Day, 1854, Walter was placed in a local orphan's home to be cared for by state and town funds until such time as he could support himself.

They say he always walked alone and that no one, that nothing, could touch him. They tried to teach him carpentry, but at a sudden moment he would seem to hear something far off, and his arm would stop and he would walk off, leaving the hammer hanging in a tree. They say he would wander the beaches and stand listening to the wind with his white hair blowing and his twisted blank eyes sometimes coming alive with a gleam as he watched the birds fly in from the sea.

One day Walter was seen to pick up a pebble from the sand and hurl it at a small bird dancing on the beach. The bird fell and lay flopping. Walter walked slowly over to it, bent down and picked it gently up, and carefully tore off both its wings before flinging the still wriggling, wingless body into the waves. A terrified and delighted boy ran home breathlessly after witnessing the incident, reporting that "that wicked Walter looked awful funny, as though he'd been wantin' to do it for an awful long time!" This was the first, but not the last time that Walter Eldredge would give cause to be known as Wicked Walter.*

---

* Years after I first heard this story, I discovered that the name "Wicked Walter" had been borrowed from a real person living in Chatham earlier in this century. There were, in fact, two Walter Eldredges living in town at that time, and both kept an account at the local store run by Andrew Harding, which caused some confusion for Mr. Harding. One day, when he had them both in the store, he pointed to one and said, "Now *you,* you go to church regular, so you'll be 'Good Walter.'" Then, pointing to the other, "And you, you *don't* go to church much, so you'll be 'Wicked Walter.'" The names stuck to both men for the rest of their lives. Needless to say,

Horrible things were said of Wicked Walter. They say he roamed the beaches more and more, that his listlessness became a desperate hunt, and that the blankness in his dark eyes became a twisted searching that descended upon the life of the Great Beach. They say that he grabbed small toads with his hands and broke their legs. That he forked snakes and nailed them to pine trees by their tails. That he trapped rabbits alive and peeled off their skin with his fingers. But his passion was the great gray gulls that flew in from the east. Once in a long while he would bring one down with a rock—and then they would not say what he did.

But they say that in the doing of it his fragile hands became large and twisted like his eyes, that his eyes became as unfeeling as the gull's, and that he did what he did with the dark calmness of the sea and the slow inevitability of fate. Only afterwards was there a dark shining on his face that surpassed the satisfaction of revenge.

And so the child Walter, Walter Nathan Eldredge, Wicked Walter, grew into a kind of manhood.

On the 14th day of March, 1865, Walter Nathan Eldredge, aged twenty-one, without provocation took an ax and chopped off the left hind foot of a horse belonging to Joe Newton, hardware store proprietor. The following week a special meeting of the Orleans selectmen was called "to take resolutory action on the prolonged and unhealthy misconduct of the local ward," who had now reached an independent age. He was adjudged an unfit member of the community, and in a closed and unrecorded session the following resolution was unanimously passed:

". . . that Walter Nathan Eldredge should be transported to Little Sipson's Island in Pleasant Bay, there to be left with tools and materials sufficient to build himself a shelter; that he should be supplied by the town with living necessities and that twice a month food should be delivered by boat and a report on his condition furnished by a welfare agent of the town."

They say that he was taken quietly, with no resistance. After the first two weeks the wood and tools had disappeared, but no shelter had been raised. After the second two weeks the provided food had not been touched, but they say that the bones of seagulls lay scattered in profusion around the entrance of a rude cave that had been hollowed out in the southern side of the island.

---

no resemblance between the protagonist of this story and the real "Wicked Walter" is intended.

The records show that, provision of food being found unnecessary, inspections of the island and its inhabitant were gradually decreased to once every month, then every two months, and by 1867 to once every six months.

They say that the people of Orleans breathed easier, that children who had been kept in after supper were let out to play, that the town moved cleanly again, as though it had cut out of itself some dark and ugly growth.

They say that his hair grew wild and his face shaggy and his clothes sand-colored, and that he still stood for hours staring out across the bay and the Great Beach towards the ocean. They say he began to grow into the life of the island, that it twisted his body into its own small humpy shape, that his hands grew to resemble the small scraggly bushes that gripped the soft soil, that his eyes became as white and lost as the sinking sand.

The records show that Walter Nathan Eldredge was last seen alive on the 17th of October, 1868. Inspections of the island the next spring disclosed no sign of human habitation—only the gulls remained. The ward of the town was presumed accidentally drowned and inspections of the island were terminated. A small memorial marker was placed by the town in the family plot of the local cemetery.

But when the great gray clouds of gulls that have long nested on the island rose, weaved above it like vast screaming choirs of violins; people remembered how the voice of Walter Nathan Eldredge could sometimes be heard to rise unconsciously with them, in a scream of its own that was equally cold, impersonal, and lost. And in time a new name was given to the place of Walter's disappearance. Along the quiet inlets of Pleasant Bay began to spread the strange legend of the sole inhabitant of Screaming Island.

Leviathan

❧❧❧❧❧

G IVEN THAT NANTUCKET and New Bedford were the preeminent American whaling ports during the nineteenth century, it is somewhat surprising to find such an abundance of exceptional accounts— poems, fiction, essays, descriptions, even plays—about whales on Cape Cod, and the men who pursued them. Yet it was on the Cape that the New England whaling industry began, and in 1690 it was Captain Ichapod Paddock of Yarmouth that Nantucket sent for "to instruct the people in the art of killing whales."

Accounts of whales and whaling begin with such fabulous early descriptions of leviathans as the 1719 account of the "sea monster" in Provincetown Harbor by Benjamin Franklin, the English uncle of the famous inventor and statesman. Despite the contemporary change in attitudes toward whaling, Melville's fictional account of his "Cape Cod Man" Stubbs killing a sperm whale can still move us with its narrative power. Kittredge's scathing indictment of the harsh and dehumanizing conditions aboard most whalers, with its strong insinuations of sexual depravity, was still unusual criticism in 1930, but we must not read Kittredge backward as some sort of proto-environmentalist. His concern was not for the whales but for the whalers, much as the Puritans condemned such cruel practices as bearbaiting not from sympathy for the animals but from disapproval of the coarsening effects these spectacles had on the spectators' morals. Nor were men the only ones abused by the rigors of long whaling voyages, as Berger's sad anecdote of Viola Cook illustrates. Still, whaling remained an accepted fact of life for most Cape Codders well into this century, and Thornton Burgess's reminiscence of one whale's arrival in Sandwich is a marvelous example of how certain natural experiences in childhood can indelibly shape the adult's vision of the world.

One Cape whale species has spawned an entire subgenre of cetacean literature. Blackfish, or pilot whales, are toothed whales that are fifteen to twenty-two feet long and tend to travel in large herds, or "pods." For as long as anyone has kept records they have stranded with some regularity, often in enormous numbers, on the beaches and tidal flats of Cape Cod Bay. The reasons for this are still not clear. To the early Cape Codders these strandings were considered a gift from Providence; in fact, "drift whales" constituted a portion of the salaries of local ministers. Blackfish supplied local residents with meat and high-grade whale oil from the rounded "melon" in the front of the whale's head. When a pilot whale herd was spotted coming inshore, they regularly set off in small boats to "help" the animals ashore.

William Martin's imaginative re-creation of an early stranding set upon by Vikings is distinguished by being the only opening of a novel I know of that is told from the perspective of a pilot whale. The early-nineteenth-century English traveler Edward Augustus Kendell may not have envied the Cape Codders' lot as a whole, but he certainly admired the pluck and resourcefulness of the young Truro boy who single-handedly subdued one of these stranded whales. Thoreau, who had learned not to pass quick judgment on local practices by the time he reached North Truro, gives a vivid but objective account of a mass beaching of blackfish near Great Hollow in 1855. The only criticism he expressed was academic: after returning home and hoping to learn more about blackfish, he was irritated to find that "neither the popular nor scientific name was to be found in a [state] report on our mammalia." Even for later writers, such as the socially liberal Berger, the exploitation of these stranded whales by Cape Codders produced, at most, ethical questions about the propriety of taking them on the Sabbath.

We are likely to forget how recently our views toward whales and whaling have changed. I have a photograph from the late 1930s showing several men in my town posing proudly with spearlike flensing knives, standing on the bodies of a couple of dozen stranded pilot whales. The stripped carcasses were buried in the dunes, and only a few years ago tides and currents exhumed the whitened skeletons, which tumbled out onto the tidal flats like a xylophone junkyard. Beachcombers picked up some of the vertebrae to use as drink coasters. By the 1960s, whales were no longer hunted or taken in Cape waters, yet Stanley Kunitz's magnificent poem on the stranding of a finback whale in Wellfleet reveals a deep ambivalence remaining in the reactions of the spectators.

In the past twenty years, with the explosion in cetacean research and the publicity generated by such environmental groups as Greenpeace, our understanding of the complexity of whale behavior and the threat that our own past and present behavior poses to the existence of several species has increased enormously. Whales have become, as much as any animal, a symbol of the modern environmental movement. Old Cape Codders would find it difficult to understand much of our current behavior toward them. Now instead of driving pilot whales ashore, we try to push stranded whales back into deep water. Whale watching has replaced whale hunting as a major source of income for modern Cape Codders and has given unprecedented numbers of us an opportunity to view these leviathans close up. The Center for Coastal Studies in Provincetown has emerged as a major research facility for the long-term studies of local whale populations, particularly humpbacks and the endangered right whale. They have identified and named hundreds of individuals, which supporters of their research have "adopted."

Few would deny that these changes have been for the good, both for the whales and for us. Yet as John Hay's compelling account of a recent stranding indicates, our actual knowledge of these creatures remains extremely sketchy and our responses to them more complex than we usually admit. When we view the whale as an entertaining god, or as correlative to our own human condition, are we seeing the animal more clearly or exploiting it any less than when we hunted it for lamp oil and corset stays? *What,* Leviathan still asks, *do you want of me?*

"Prologue—A.D. 1000—Strandings"

By William Martin

EACH YEAR THE whales went to the great bay. They followed the cold current south from seas where the ice never melted, south along coastlines of rock, past rivers and inlets, to the great bay that forever brimmed with life. Sometimes they stayed through a single tide, sometimes from one full moon to the next, and sometimes, for reasons that only the sea understood, the whales never left the great bay.

The season was changing on the day that the old bull led his herd round the sand hook that formed the eastern edge of the bay.

It had come time for them to fill their bellies and begin the journey to the breeding ground. The old bull did not need the weakening of the sunlight or the cooling of the waters to know this. He knew it because his ancestors had known it, because it was bred into him, in his backbone and his blood. And he knew that in the great bay, his herd had always fed well.

So he sent out sounds that spread through the water and came echoing back, allowing him to see without sight, to know the depth of the water and the slope of the beach, to sense the movement of a single fish at the bottom of the sea or the massing of a giant school a mile away.

And that was what the old bull sensed now.

He turned toward the school, and his herd turned with him. A hundred whales swam in his wake, linked by color and motion in a graceful seaborne dance, by the simple rule of survival to the fish before them, and by the deeper call of loyalty to the herd, their kin, and the old bull himself.

Then the sea was lit by a great flash. The fish felt the coming of the whales, and like a single frightened creature, they darted away. First east, then west, then south toward the shallows they went, and the sunlight flashed again and again on their silver sides.

The dance of the whales rose into a great black-backed wave and rolled, steady and certain, toward the shoal of fish. Soon the stronger fish were swimming over the weaker and splattering across the surface to escape. It did them no good. The wave struck, churned through them, and pounded on, leaving a bloody wake in which the gulls came to feast, while on the shore, other creatures watched and waited.

The old bull filled his belly, and as always in the great bay, the herd fed well. But their hunger was as endless as the sea, and their wave rolled on to the shallows where the last of the fish had fled. Black bodies lunged and whirled in the reddening water. Flashes of panic grew smaller and dimmer. Then came a flash that seemed no more than a moment of moonlight. The old bull turned to chase it, and the motion of his flukes brought the sand swirling from the bottom.

He had led the herd too close to shore and the tide was running out. In the rising turbulence, he could see almost nothing, so he made his sounds, listened for the echoes, and sought to lead the herd toward safety.

But something in the sea or the stars or his own head had betrayed the old bull. He followed his sounds, because that was what he had always done, and swam straight out of the water. The herd followed him, because that was what they had always done, and the black-backed wave broke on a beach between two creeks.

Still something told the old bull that he was going in the right direction. He pounded his flukes to drive himself into one of the creeks. But he did no more than send up great splashes and dig himself deeper into the eelgrass that rimmed the creek.

All around him, black bodies flopped uselessly in the shallows. The sun quickly began to dry their skin. And their own great weight began to crush them.

The old bull heard feeble warning cries, louder pain cries. He felt the feet of a gull prancing on his back. Then new cries, patterned and high-pitched, frightened the gull into the air.

From the line of trees above the beach came strange creatures, moving fast on long legs. They wore skins and furs. They grew hair on their faces. They carried axes that flashed like sunlight.

They were men. And they swarmed among the herd without fear, and drove their axes into the heads of the whales, and brought blood and death cries. And the biggest of them all raised his axe and came toward the old bull.

But before the axe struck, an arrow pierced the man's neck and came out of the other side. Blood and gurgling sounds flowed from his mouth. His eyes opened wide and the axe dropped from his hand.

Now men with painted faces came screaming from the woods. The old bull felt the clashing of the fight and heard sounds of fury unlike any he had known in the sea. Rage swirled around him, stone against iron, arrow against axe, bearded man against painted man. And with his last strength, he tried to escape.

He pounded his flukes but could do no more than roll onto his side, his great bulk burying the axe in the marsh mud beneath him.

Then a bearded man beheaded the painted chieftain and his painted followers fled. The victor lifted the head by the hair and flung it into the sea, but the other bearded men did not celebrate their victory. Instead, they ran off in fear.

For some time, the old bull lay dying on the beach between the creeks. Then the bearded men appeared once more, this time with a woman of their kind. Their axes flashed like the sides of panicked fish, and like the fish, they were fleeing. But the woman stopped and looked at the old bull. She made angry sounds. She picked up a boulder and raised it over his head. . . .

—from *Cape Cod* (1991)

—

Ministers and Whales

By Henry David Thoreau

THE ECCLESIASTICAL HISTORY of [Eastham] interested us somewhat. "In 1662, the town agreed that a part of every whale cast on shore be appropriated for the support of the ministry." No doubt there seemed to be some propriety in thus leaving the support of the ministers to Providence, whose servants they are, and who alone rules the storms; for, when few whales were cast up, they might suspect that their worship was not acceptable. The ministers must have sat upon the cliffs in every storm, and watched the shore with anxiety. And, for my part, if I were a minister, I would rather trust to the bowels of the billows, on the back-side of Cape Cod, to cast up a whale for me, then to the generosity of many a country parish that I know. You cannot say of a country minister's salary, commonly, that it is "very like a whale."

Nevertheless, the minister who depended on whales cast up must have had a trying time of it. I would rather have gone to the Falkland

Isles with a harpoon, and done with it. Think of a whale having the breath of life beaten out of him by a storm, and dragging in over the bars and guzzles, for the support of the ministry! What a consolation it must have been to him!

—from *Cape Cod* (1865)

———

The Provincetown Sea Monster

By Benjamin Franklin*

BOSTON, SEPT. 28, 1719. On the 17 Instant there appear'd in Cape-Cod harbour a strange creature, His head like a Lyons, with very large Teeth, Ears hanging down, a large Beard, a long Beard, with curling hair on his head, his Body about 16 foot long, a round buttock, with a short Tayle of a yellowish colour, the Whale boats gave him chase, he was very fierce and gnashed his teeth with great rage when they attackt him, he was shot at 3 times and Wounded, when he rose out of the Water he always faced the boats in that angry manner, the Harpaniers struck at him, but in vaine, for after 5 hours chase, he took him to see again. None of the people ever saw his like befor.

———

*This event, quoted in both Mary Heaten Vorse's *Of Time and the Town* and Josef Berger's *Cape Cod Pilot,* is attributed to Benjamin Franklin, uncle of the famous inventor and statesman.

"Stubb Kills a Whale"

By Herman Melville

THE NEXT DAY was exceedingly still and sultry, and with nothing special to engage them, the *Pequod*'s crew could hardly resist the spell of
sleep induced by such a vacant sea. For this part of the Indian Ocean
through which we then were voyaging is not what whalemen call a
lively ground; that is, it affords fewer glimpses of porpoises, dolphins,
flying-fish, and other vivacious denizens of more stirring waters, than
those off the Rio de la Plata, or the in-shore ground off Peru.

It was my turn to stand at the foremast-head; and with my shoulders
leaning against the slackened royal shrouds, to and fro I idly swayed in
what seemed an enchanted air. No resolution could withstand it; in that
dreamy mood losing all consciousness, at last my soul went out of my
body; though my body still continued to sway as a pendulum will, long
after the power which first moved it is withdrawn.

Ere forgetfulness altogether came over me, I had noticed that the
seamen at the main and mizen mast-heads were already drowsy. So that
at last all three of us lifelessly swung from the spars, and for every swing
that we made there was a nod from below from the slumbering helmsman. The waves, too, nodded their indolent crests; and across the wide
trance of the sea, east nodded to west, and the sun over all.

Suddenly bubbles seemed bursting beneath my closed eyes; like vices
my hands grasped the shrouds; some invisible, gracious agency preserved me; with a shock I came back to life. And lo! close under our
lee, not forty fathoms off, a gigantic Sperm Whale lay rolling in the
water like the capsized hull of a frigate, his broad, glossy back, of an
Ethiopian hue, glistening in the sun's rays like a mirror. But lazily
undulating in the trough of the sea, and ever and anon tranquilly spouting his vapory jet, the whale looked like a portly burgher smoking his
pipe of a warm afternoon. But that pipe, poor whale, was thy last. As
if struck by some enchanter's wand, the sleepy ship and every sleeper in
it all at once started into wakefulness; and more than a score of voices
from all parts of the vessel, simultaneously with the three notes from
aloft, shouted forth the accustomed cry, as the great fish slowly and
regularly spouted the sparkling brine into the air.

"Clear away the boats! Luff!" cried Ahab. And obeying his own order, he dashed the helm down before the helmsman could handle the spokes.

The sudden exclamations of the crew must have alarmed the whale; and ere the boats were down, majestically turning, he swam away to the leeward, but with such a steady tranquillity, and making so few ripples as he swam, that thinking after all he might not as yet be alarmed, Ahab gave orders that not an oar should be used, and no man must speak but in whispers. So seated like Ontario Indians on the gunwales of the boats, we swiftly but silently paddled along; the calm not admitting of the noiseless sails being set. Presently, as we thus glided in chase, the monster perpendicularly flitted his tail forty feet into the air, and then sank out of sight like a tower swallowed up.

"There go flukes!" was the cry, an announcement immediately followed by Stubb's producing his match and igniting his pipe, for now a respite was granted. After the full interval of his sounding had elapsed, the whale rose again, and being now in advance of the smoker's boat, and much nearer to it than to any of the others, Stubb counted upon the honor of the capture. It was obvious, now, that the whale had at length become aware of his pursuers. All silence of cautiousness was therefore no longer of use. Paddles were dropped, and oars came loudly into play. And still puffing his pipe, Stubb cheered on his crew to the assault.

Yes, a mighty change had come over the fish. All alive to his jeopardy, he was going "head out;" that part obliquely projecting from the mad yeast which he brewed.

"Start her, start her, my men! Don't hurry yourselves; take plenty of time—but start her; start her like thunderclaps, that's all," cried Stubb, spluttering out the smoke as he spoke. "Start her, now; give 'em the long and strong stroke, Tashtego. Start her, Tash, my boy—start her, all; but keep cool, keep cool—cucumbers is the word—easy, easy—only start her like grim death and grinning devils, and raise the buried dead perpendicular out of their graves, boys—that's all. Start her!"

"Woo-hoo! Wa-hee!" screamed the Gay-Header in reply, raising some old war-whoop to the skies; as every oarsman in the strained boat involuntarily bounced forward with the one tremendous leading stroke which the eager Indian gave.

But his wild screams were answered by others quite as wild. "Kee-hee! Kee-hee!" yelled Daggoo, straining forwards and backwards on his seat, like a pacing tiger in his cage.

"Ka-la! Koo-loo!" howled Queequeg, as if smacking his lips over a mouthful of Grenadier's steak. And thus with oars and yells the keels cut the sea. Meanwhile, Stubb retaining his place in the van, still encouraged his men to the onset, all the while puffing the smoke from his mouth. Like desperadoes they tugged and they strained, till the welcome cry was heard—"Stand up, Tashtego!—give it to him!" The harpoon was hurled. "Stern all!" The oarsmen backed water; the same moment something went hot and hissing along every one of their wrists. It was the magical line. An instant before, Stubb had swiftly caught two additional turns with it round the loggerhead, whence, by reason of its increased rapid circlings, a hempen blue smoke now jetted up and mingled with the steady fumes from his pipe. As the line passed round and round the loggerhead; so also, just before reaching that point, it blisteringly passed through and through both of Stubb's hands, from which the hand-cloths, or squares of quilted canvas sometimes worn at these times, had accidentally dropped. It was like holding an enemy's sharp two-edged sword by the blade, and that enemy all the time striving to wrest it out of your clutch.

"Wet the line! wet the line!" cried Stubb to the tub oarsman (him seated by the tub) who, snatching off his hat, dashed the seawater into it. More turns were taken, so that the line began holding its place. The boat now flew through the boiling water like a shark all fins. Stubb and Tashtego here changed places—stem for stern—a staggering business truly in that rocking commotion.

From the vibrating line extending the entire length of the upper part of the boat, and from its now being more tight than a harpstring, you would have thought the craft had two keels—one cleaving the water, the other the air—as the boat churned on through both opposing elements at once. A continual cascade played at the bows; a ceaseless whirling eddy in her wake; and, at the slightest motion from within, even but of a little finger, the vibrating, cracking craft canted over her spasmodic gunwale into the sea. Thus they rushed; each man with might and main clinging to his seat, to prevent being tossed to the foam; and the tall form of Tashtego at the steering oar crouching almost double, in order to bring down his centre of gravity. Whole Atlantics and Pacifics seemed passed as they shot on their way, till at length the whale somewhat slackened his flight.

"Haul in—haul in!" cried Stubb to the bowsman! and, facing round towards the whale, all hands began pulling the boat up to him, while yet the boat was being towed on. Soon ranging up by his flank, Stubb, firmly planting his knee in the clumsy cleat, darted dart after dart into the flying fish; at the word of command, the boat alternately sterning out of the way of the whale's horrible wallow, and then ranging up for another fling.

The red tide now poured from all sides of the monster like brooks down a hill. His tormented body rolled not in brine but in blood, which bubbled and seethed for furlongs behind in their wake. The slanting sun playing upon this crimson pond in the sea, sent back its reflection into every face, so that they all glowed to each other like red men. And all the while, jet after jet of white smoke was agonizingly shot from the spiracle of the whale, and vehement puff after puff from the mouth of the excited headsman; as at every dart, hauling in upon his crooked lance (by the line attached to it), Stubb straightened it again and again, by a few rapid blows against the gunwale, then again and again sent it into the whale.

"Pull up—pull up!" he now cried to the bowsman, as the waning whale relaxed in his wrath. "Pull up!—close to!" and the boat ranged along the fish's flank. When reaching far over the bow, Stubb slowly churned his long sharp lance into the fish, and kept it there, carefully churning and churning, as if cautiously seeking to feel after some gold watch that the whale might have swallowed, and which he was fearful of breaking ere he could hook it out. But that gold watch he sought was the innermost life of the fish. And now it is struck; for, starting from his trance into that unspeakable thing called his "flurry," the monster horribly wallowed in his blood, overwrapped himself in impenetrable, mad, boiling spray, so that the imperiled craft, instantly dropping astern, had much ado blindly to struggle out from that phrensied twilight into the clear air of the day.

And now abating in his flurry, the whale once more rolled out into view; surging from side to side; spasmodically dilating and contracting his spout-hole, with sharp, cracking, agonized respirations. At last, gush after gush of clotted red gore, as if it had been the purple lees of red wine, shot into the frightened air; and falling back again, ran dripping down his motionless flanks into the sea. His heart had burst!

"He's dead, Mr. Stubb," said Daggoo.

"Yes; both pipes smoked out!" and withdrawing his own from his mouth, Stubb scattered the dead ashes over the water; and, for a moment, stood thoughtfully eyeing the vast corpse he had made.

—from *Moby-Dick* (1851)

The Hardships of Whaling

By Henry C. Kittredge

IT IS EASY, dazzled by the glamour of far voyages to palm-fringed islands, to be deceived into false sentimentality toward this great dead industry. Many an up-state farmer's boy, lured by the will-o'-the-wisp of romance, left his plough in the furrow and went whaling—to end his days a beachcomber, disillusioned and beaten. It was a grim game, with the dollar always at the helm. But the financial side of it, with all its ruthlessness and with all that it led to—hazing men into deserting with money due them; overcharging for shoddy clothing from the slop chest and underfeeding until the hungry crew looked greedily on slices of broiled whale meat—all this was not more destructive to men's fiber than herding together in a forecastle, compared to which the forecastles of clippers were palatial, a miscellaneous crew composed of round-eyed lads from the Vermont hills and crime-hardened degenerates who ought to have been in jail. Men were not made to live by themselves; wherever circumstances force them to do so, they seek, like water, the level of the lowest and most vicious among them. The forecastles of whaling barks produced these circumstances as perfectly as they have ever been produced in the world, and our fresh-cheeked youngster, who embarked on a voyage as immaculate as a man can be, stood a fine chance of emerging from his four years' association with the dregs of the waterfront, as hardened a character as they.

> She'd a crew of blacks from the Cape Verde Isles
>   That spoke in Portagee,
> With men from Norway, Finland too,
>   And the shores of the Irish Sea.
>
> She'd whites from the rocky Yankee farms
>   Mixed up with Sandwich brown,
> With a skipper who hailed from New Bedford,
>   And a mate from Westport Town.

Beside learning vice, the young whalemen learned violence. A three months' voyage from New York to San Francisco in a clipper ship, with a ventilated deckhouse for the crew, was enough to beget frequent mutinies; what, then, can we expect from a forty months' cruise in a bobtailed blubber-boiler? Mutinies there were aplenty, and not without good reason did whaling captains sometimes sign on five mates to help them hold the lid on. Cook went through one Arctic winter with a mutinous crew—the only wonder is that crews in those latitudes ever refrained from mutiny. The sperm whalemen opened the petcock from time to time by calling at Honolulu, or Tahiti, or Guam, where men might desert instead of killing an officer, and where natives could easily be procured as replacements. But captains often neglected this safety valve, and stayed at sea as long as there was an unbroached barrel of salt horse in the hold, or a gallon of ropy water in the butts. Under such conditions, is it surprising that Captain Nathaniel Burgess, of Bourne, who made his last voyage with a crew that represented nine nationalities, called discipline the whaling captain's most serious problem?

Time has blurred the sharp and cruel outlines of life on a whaler. In our enthusiasm over those who returned victorious, we are likely to forget the many who were left behind, broken and polluted, to drag out the last years of their lives on the beach of a coral island. To-day there are those who lament the passing of this undoubtedly pictur-esque, though certainly ruinous industry. But the world is a better place without long-voyage whaling than it ever was with it. Keenly as we appreciate the skill and self-reliance and valor that it taught some of the men who practiced it, we cannot forget the merciless malignity with which it shattered the rest. The wreck of the *Wanderer,* New Bedford's last whaler, in the summer of 1925, was a happy event for the march of civilization.

—from *Cape Cod, Its People and Their History* (1930)

———

The Story of Viola Cook

By Josef Berger (Jeremiah Digges)

THE LAST WHALING skipper of Provincetown was Captain John Atkins Cook, who kept at it until 1916. Some of his voyages in the brigantine *Viola* actually paid better than those of the old days; a 25-month trip, ending in 1910, netted 2,200 barrels of sperm oil and 75 pounds of "first chop" ambergris—worth together $47,000. After he quit the sea, Captain Cook wrote a pretentious account of his voyages and had it published. But the story of Viola, his wife, will live long after the Captain and his book, his ambergris and his "ile," are all forgotten.

Viola went to sea with her husband. In 1893 he took her to the Arctic aboard his steam-bark *Navarch,* and returned to San Francisco in 1896. She spent the winter of 1900–01 aboard the *Bowhead* at Baillie Island, a hundred miles north of Herschel Island, where there was a 58-day spell of unbroken night, with the thermometer going to 57 degrees below zero. Boston and other New England newspapers were full of the story of the "courageous woman whose home was the frozen north." When she returned to Provincetown after her 1901 voyage, they quoted her as saying:

"Sewing helps to dispel the monotony that will manifest itself assertively at times."

On that voyage the Captain earned $115,000.

In the spring of 1903 he took her again. I have an old manuscript account of the trip, written by a relative and kept in a Provincetown home. It says:

"Two years were spent in the land of everlasting cold and desolation, only a few short weeks of summer whaling in partly open seas breaking the monotony of the ten-months lockup periods. The second summer in the ice was as fruitless as the first. . . . The weather of the second winter was unusually severe; the crew members were mutinous; scurvy and starvation were kept in abeyance only by Eskimo hunters."

Upon the Captain's failure to turn back, as had been expected of him, Viola, "inconsolable, hugged the privacy of her cabin for weeks on end, dwelling constantly upon her isolation. So great was the shock of her disappointment, her reason nearly fled, and for months following, Mrs. Cook remained mentally ill."

The townspeople say she was "mentally ill" not only for months, but until her death several years later.

In the meantime, two Irishmen came down the Cape. They were broke, and for several months they lived in the hulk of an old wreck half buried in the Truro beach. One of them, the elder, had once worked in a shoe factory, had had a row with his employer, and had made a solemn vow never to work again. His companion had dabbled in prospecting for gold, in newspaper work, and in a strange assortment of other professions.

Captain Cook had a housekeeper to take care of his home on Commercial Street, a French woman, who met these two wanderers, befriended them and told the younger man a strange story about a Provincetown sea captain, his wife, and a long and tragic imprisonment in the Arctic ice pack.

On November 30, 1917, the Provincetown Players gave a performance in their Macdougal Street theater in Greenwich Village, New York. It was a new play, by a young writer who had been chopping away at the stilted theater in which Broadway was encrusted at the time. The play was built around a grim search for oil in Arctic waters; a long imprisonment in the ice; the suffering of the ship's people; and finally, the lapse of the captain's wife into insanity, coming after his refusal to turn back when he had the chance.

"I know you're foolin' me, Annie," says "Captain Keeney" in one of the closing speeches. "You ain't out of your mind. (Anxiously) Be you? I'll git the ile now right enough—jest a little while longer, Annie—then we'll turn home'ard. I can't turn back now, you see that, don't you? I've got to git the ile. (In sudden terror) Answer me! You ain't mad, be you?"

The title of the play was *Ile;* the author, Eugene O'Neill.

—from *Cape Cod Pilot* (1937)

———

"Striped Whales"

By Thornton W. Burgess

I WAS BORN on old Cape Cod on January 14, 1874. . . . I am a Cape Codder by birth and by inheritance through a long unbroken line of ancestors back to Thomas Burgess, one of the founders of the oldest town on the Cape, Sandwich. Considerably more than half a century ago I left the Cape, yet in a sense I have never left it. It has been said that Cape Codders by birth rather than by adoption have salt in their hair, sand between their toes, and herring blood in their veins. Of these they never wholly rid themselves, nor do they want to. . . .

It is a land where the wind-whipped sand of the shore bites and stings, the beach grass cuts, and the facts of life are hard; but where the sky is blue, the air is soft, and the harshness of life is tempered by faith—it is where the real and the unreal meet, and the impossible becomes probable. One can believe anything on the Cape, a blessed relief from the doubts and uncertainties of the present-day turmoil of the outer world. If in truth there is a sea serpent, sooner or later it will be cast up on the shores of Cape Cod. If there are mermaids—when I am on the Cape I believe in them devotedly—it is there they will be found. I myself have seen there a red-and-white whale, striped like a barber's pole. And if a striped whale, why not a sea serpent and mermaids? Why not indeed?

In this atmosphere I was born and spent my boyhood. From it I have never wholly escaped. I can still close my eyes and see sea serpents and mermaids and striped whales. Though in my writing I strive not to deviate from the prosaic facts as Mother Nature presents them, I cannot avoid seeing them myself in the enchanted atmosphere in which I made my first field observation and whales became red-and-white for all time. Looking back through the years, I wonder if it was not then that the pattern of my life was set.

It was a Sunday morning in March, 1879. The church bells—Congregational, Methodist and Unitarian—were calling the faithful to worship. But this morning the faithful were few, for the sea also was calling and the voice of the sea was more persuasive than the sweetly solemn tones of the bells. A whale had come ashore on the beach directly opposite the village. Sunday worship was a weekly privilege, but a stranded whale the size of this one was an epochal event.

A day or two before, two whales had been harpooned off Province-town, which lies many miles straight across the bay from Sandwich. Both had broken away, but were thought to be fatally wounded. They had headed inside the bay. All the fishing hamlets on the inside of the Cape had been alerted to watch for the stricken monsters. One had been sighted off Sandwich. It had grounded on a bar off the beach and the whalers at Provincetown had been notified. I was five years old at the time. With a cousin a year or two older and his grandfather, I went to see the whale, along with most of the village folk.

The way led past the famous old Boston and Sandwich glass works, then across extensive salt marshes cut midway by a wide creek, and rimmed on the outer side by sand dunes. Because these marshes were flooded twice daily by high tides they were—and still are—crossed by a boardwalk raised some four or five feet above the marsh, with no guard rails except over the creek. A stiff wind gathered force as it swept unchecked over a long stretch of lowland and marshes. We small boys clung tightly to the old man's hands lest we be blown off the walk. The latter ended in loose sand behind the barrier dunes. With faces and hands stung by flying sand, breath whipped away in half-fearful gasps by the relentless winds, ears assailed by a meaningless babble of sound from shouting men and clamoring gulls on the other side of the dunes, we struggled up through the yielding sand and coarse razor-edged beach grass to the top of the nearest dune. With startling abruptness a never-to-be-forgotten scene burst upon us.

In the immediate foreground, in the shallows of low tide, was the ocean monster we had come to see. Some distance offshore, sharply etched against the flattened gray-green sea—for the wind was off-shore—rode the whaling ship. Boats were plying back and forth between shore and ship, those going out deeply laden while those returning were empty save for their crews.

But it was the huge, bulky mass of the monster in the foreground that challenged and held the wide-eyed gaze of the small boy clinging with one hand to his hat and with the other grasping tightly the elder's hand, catching his breath partly in awe at the strange scene and in part lest it be sucked away by the relentless wind. He was filled with awe and a bit frightened by the unexpected, unfamiliar, overwhelming sight of his first whale—a striped whale, a red-and-white whale. There it lay before his very eyes. I still can see it.

Since that long ago day of my first field observation I have seen many whales, but in their black or gray drabness none has ever looked as a whale should look. None has ever appeared in what I knew to be the true colors, red-and-white stripes like a barber's pole. Even when I read *Moby-Dick,* the whale was the wrong color.

The explanation? It is quite simple as are most explanations of the unfamiliar and the mysterious. The flensing knives of the whalemen already had been at work, exposing the white blubber. Much of this had been cut out in long strips down to the red flesh. It was all as simple as that. Yet, knowing this, whenever I am on the sea and hear the cry "Thar she blows!" I look with a feeling of half-expectation of seeing a living barber's pole. I almost still believe in striped whales. It would not shock my credulity in the least to see one. Not on Cape Cod anyway, for I am still a Cape Codder and vision beyond those not so blessed is my inheritance.

I am convinced that failure on the part of parents, teachers and others having to do with the guidance of the young to appreciate how extremely plastic is the child mind, how deep and lasting are the impressions for good or ill made therein by events and surroundings of daily life, is often at the root of many of the youth problems of today. There are countless striped whales among children everywhere. They are not to be ignored, denied or laughed away.

My first observation in the realm of Nature was completely in error. I found it out long, long ago. Nevertheless, whales never have looked right since. Always there is some gain in error if it leads to finding of truth in the end. It is sometimes pleasant, even helpful, to ignore the hard facts of science and exact knowledge and instead, gazing into the crystal globe of imagination, to see red-and-white whales. Who shall say that we are not the better for so doing?

The records show that that whale was no figment of the imagination. It was a seventy-four-foot Goliath, a sulphur-bottom or blue whale. It came ashore in March, 1879.

—from *Now I Remember* (1960)

———

A Truro Boy Kills a Blackfish

By Edward Augustus Kendell

IN THE MORNING I went from Truro to Provincetown.

For a short space, the road lay over hills, on which were crops of maize, now nearly ready for harvest. . . .

At the foot of these hills, I entered a tract of salt-marsh, inclosed at its head by a fence, and open, at the opposite extremity, to Province-town harbour. In all the lower part, the road lies along its edge, and is more or less commodious as the tide is higher or lower; the flood tide driving the traveller into the loose sand, and upon the sand-hills; while the ebb gives him the use of the lower part of the beach, itself but soft, and thrown into transverse ridges of sand, and interrupted by rills of fresh water, flowing from the springs in the hills. The length of this salt-meadow is about nine miles.

I had the company of an inhabitant of Provincetown. As we approached the mouth of the inlet, the vertebres of a small species of whale, here called *black-fish,* became frequent on the beach, together with other signs of fisheries, the sole objects of pursuit at Provincetown. Soon after, at the distance of half a mile, on the sandy flat from which the sea was now fast retiring, we discovered a boy, and, near him, what appeared to be a great fish. The solitary condition of the boy, and the smallness of his size, compared with that of the fish, formed a combination suffi-ciently remarkable to draw us to the spot; and, on our arrival, we found our fisherman, of about the age of ten years, astride a porpoise of about ten feet long, in the middle of a sea of blood, collected in the hollow of the sand. Alone, and with a table-knife for his instrument, he was cut-ting the blubber from the ribs of the monster, a task which he per-formed in a very workman-like manner.

Upon our inquiring of him who had killed the porpoise, he replied, that he had killed it himself; and gave us the following account of his adventure. His employment, in the morning, had been that of attend-ing his mother's cows; and from the hills on which he was, he had seen a shoal of porpoises enter the inlet. As the tide was ebbing, and the shore flat, many of them were soon embarrassed by the want of suffi-cient water to move in; and he flattered himself, that by leaving his cows, and coming down to the beach, he should be able to make a prize. Arrived at the water's edge, or rather going into it as far as he dared, he selected a porpoise, already embarrassed by the sand, and struggling to gain deep water. Him he boldly caught, from time to time, by the tail, thereby increasing his difficulties, till, in the end, the water, running fast away, left him upon the sand. The conquest so far effected, the boy had staid by his fish, to frustrate his efforts to escape, till escape had become quite impossible; and he had then gone home (a distance of a mile) to fetch a knife. Armed with the knife, he had proceeded to wound and kill the porpoise, a task of some labour and danger; and, according to the description, he had accomplished it only by watching for opportunities, and by alternately striking and retreating. The fish was now dead; and my companion supposed that it would yield ten gallons of oil, giving the little cowherd, at one dollar per gallon, ten dollars for his exploit.

—from *Travels Through Part of the United States* (1809)

———

A Blackfish Drive

By Henry David Thoreau

IN THE SUMMER and fall sometimes, hundreds of blackfish (the Social Whale, *Globicephalus melas* of De Kay; called also Black Whale-fish, Howling Whale, Bottle-head, etc.), fifteen feet or more in length, are driven ashore in a single school here. I witnessed such a scene in July, 1855. A carpenter who was working at the light-house arriving early in the morning remarked that he did not know but he had lost fifty dollars by coming to his work; for as he came along the Bay side he heard them driving a school of blackfish ashore, and he had debated with himself whether he should not go and join them and take his share, but had concluded to come to his work.

After breakfast I came over to this place, about two miles distant, and near the beach met some of the fishermen returning from their chase. Looking up and down the shore, I could see about a mile south some large black masses on the sand, which I knew must be blackfish, and a man or two about them. As I walked along towards them I soon came to a large carcass whose head was gone and whose blubber had been stripped off some weeks before; the tide was just beginning to move it, and the stench compelled me to go a long way round. When I came to Great Hollow I found a fisherman and some boys on the watch, and counted about thirty blackfish, just killed, with many lance wounds, and the water was more or less bloody around. They were partly on shore and partly in the water, held by a rope round their tails till the tide should leave them. A boat had been somewhat stove by the tail of one.

They were a smooth, shining black, like India-rubber, and had remarkably simple and lumpish forms for animated creatures, with a blunt round snout or head, whale-like, and simple stiff-looking flippers. The largest were about fifteen feet long, but one or two were only five feet long, and still without teeth. The fisherman slashed one with his jackknife, to show me how thick the blubber was,—about three inches; and as I passed my finger through the cut it was covered thick with oil. The blubber looked like pork, and this man said that when they were trying it the boys would sometimes come round with a piece of bread in one hand, and take a piece of blubber in the other to eat with it, preferring it to pork scraps. He also cut into the flesh beneath, which was firm and red like beef, and he said that for his part he preferred it when fresh to beef. It is stated that in 1812 blackfish were used as food by the poor of Bretagne.

They were waiting for the tide to leave these fishes high and dry, that they might strip off the blubber and carry it to their try-works in their boats, where they try it on the beach. They get commonly a barrel of oil, worth fifteen or twenty dollars, to a fish. There were many lances and harpoons in the boats,—much slenderer instruments than I had expected. An old man came along the beach with a horse and wagon distributing the dinners of the fishermen, which their wives had put up in little pails and jugs, and which he had collected in the Pond Village, and for this service, I suppose, he received a share of the oil. If one could not tell his own pail, he took the first he came to.

As I stood there they raised the cry of "another school," and we could see their black backs and their blowing about a mile northward, as they went leaping over the sea like horses. Some boats were already in pursuit there, driving them toward the beach. Other fishermen and boys running up began to jump into the boats and push them off from where I stood, and I might have gone too had I chosen. Soon there were twenty-five or thirty boats in pursuit, some large ones under sail, and others rowing with might and main, keeping outside of the school, those nearest to the fishes striking on the sides of their boats and blowing horns to drive them on to the beach. It was an exciting race. If they succeed in driving them ashore each boat takes one share, and then each man, but if they are compelled to strike them off shore each boat's company take what they strike.

I walked rapidly along the shore toward the north, while the fishermen were rowing still more swiftly to join their companions, and a little boy who walked by my side was congratulating himself that his father's boat was beating another one. An old blind fisherman whom we met, inquired, "Where are they, I can't see. Have they got them?"

In the mean while the fishes had turned and were escaping northward toward Provincetown, only occasionally the back of one being seen. So the nearest crews were compelled to strike them, and we saw several boats soon made fast, each to its fish, which, four or five rods ahead, was drawing it like a race-horse straight toward the beach, leaping half out of water blowing blood and water from its hole, and leaving a streak of foam behind. But they went ashore too far north for us, though we could see the fishermen leap out and lance them on the sand. It was just like pictures of whaling which I have seen, and a fisherman told me that it was nearly as dangerous. In his first trial he had been much excited, and in his haste had used a lance with its scabbard on, but nevertheless had thrust it quite through his fish.

I learned that a few days before this one hundred and eighty blackfish had been driven ashore in one school at Eastham, a little farther south, and that the keeper of Billingsgate Point light went out one morning about the same time and cut his initials on the backs of a large school which had run ashore in the night, and sold his right to them to Provincetown for one thousand dollars, and probably Provincetown made as much more. Another fisherman told me that nineteen years ago three hundred and eighty were driven ashore in one school at Great Hollow. In the Naturalists' Library, it is said that, in the winter of 1809–10, one thousand one hundred and ten "approached the shore of Hralfiord, Iceland, and were captured." De Kay says it is not known why they are stranded. But one fisherman declared to me that they ran ashore in pursuit of squid, and that they generally came on the coast about the last of July.

About a week afterward, when I came to this shore, it was strewn, as far as I could see with a glass, with the carcasses of blackfish stripped of their blubber and their heads cut off; the latter lying higher up. Walking on the beach was out of the question on account of the stench. Between Provincetown and Truro they lay in the very path of the stage. Yet no steps were taken to abate the nuisance, and men were catching lobsters as usual just off the shore. I was told that they did sometimes tow them out and sink them; yet I wondered where they got the stones to sink them with. Of course they might be made into guano, and Cape Cod is not so fertile that her inhabitants can afford to do without this manure,—to say nothing of the diseases they may produce.

—from *Cape Cod* (1865)

———

Joe Crocker and the Sabbath Whales

By Josef Berger (Jeremiah Digges)

THE LOWER-CAPE gibes at Wellfleet's "Bible-faces," like most schoolboy apocrypha, stemmed from truth. There were fishing captains of this town, a century ago, who ordered strict observance of the Sabbath, and who went wild-eyed in an agony of inner conflict as they read the Scripture to their crews while some godless Gloucester craft lay in plain sight off the starboard bow, hauling up a full fare of mackerel or cod. But there may have been some satisfaction for their regretful ghosts in the case of a man whom we will call Joe Crocker—because he is still a neighbor—and who once ran an establishment with a name something like "The Fisherman's Haven & Handy Outfitter."

One Sunday afternoon Joe was strolling down the beach when he came across a school of stranded blackfish—"puffin' pigs," as they were called. The sparm oil man, who "tried out" the heads of these creatures, would pay as high as four dollars for the "melon" under the skull. According to the law, the man who first cut his initials in a "beached pig" was the rightful claimant.

Joe got out his knife and worked like fury, "wishing his name was Ira so's he wouldn't have to bother cutting the jibboom on the J." He was finishing up the last few fish when Pastor Williams, the little old white-haired Methody minister, overtook him.

"Working on the Sabbath, eh, Mr. Crocker?"

"No such thing, Pastor," said Joe, taking his knife by the blade and letting fly to flick out a period in the last fish. "Just playing mumblety-peg."

127

The Pastor raked him crossways and departed with a last warning: "Laugh me off today, Joe Crocker, but you'll have the devil to pay tomorrow!"

Early next morning Joe was down at the try-works to sell his fish. But the sparm oil man handed Joe a copy of the newspaper. There, on the front page, was a long piece about new oil discoveries in Pennsylvania, and about how they were sure to scuttle the whale-oil market. The sparm man was buying no more!

Two days later a committee of townsmen called at the Fishermen's Haven. They came to tell Joe he'd have to clear his blackfish off the flats. He refused, pointing out that the fish were there of their own accord; he had not gone to sea and driven them ashore.

Next day Joe's fish turned "real severe." The wind had shifted to the s'uthard, bringing some relief to the town, but now delegations began coming in from towns further up-Cape. And they were furious. It looked like civil war. Then Pastor Williams stepped in. He declared Joe Crocker was responsible; the fish were his, they bore his mark.

Finally, Joe had to give in. He hired twenty men and half a dozen flounder-draggers to tow his fish out to sea. Joe Crocker, for one, had learned it paid to keep the Sabbath holy.

—from *Cape Cod Pilot* (1937)

"The Wellfleet Whale"

By Stanley Kunitz

A FEW SUMMERS ago, on Cape Cod, a whale foundered on the beach, a sixty-three-foot finback whale. When the tide went out, I approached him. He was lying there, in monstrous desolation, making the most terrifying noises— rumbling—groaning. I put my hands on his flanks and I could feel the life inside him. And while I was standing there, suddenly he opened his eye. It was a big, red, cold eye, and it was staring directly at me. A shudder of recognition passed between us. Then the eye closed forever. I've been thinking about whales ever since.

—Journal entry

I

You have your language too,
   an eerie medley of clicks
     and hoots and trills,
location-notes and love calls,
   whistles and grunts. Occasionally,
     it's like furniture being smashed,
or the creaking of a mossy door,
   sounds that all melt into a liquid
     song with endless variations,
as if to compensate
   for the vast loneliness of the sea.
     Sometimes a disembodied voice
breaks in, as if from distant reefs,
   and it's as much as one can bear
     to listen to its long mournful cry,
a sorrow without name, both more
   and less than human. It drags
     across the ear like a record
running down.

II

No wind. No waves. No clouds.
   Only the whisper of the tide,
     as it withdrew, stroking the shore,
a lazy drift of gulls overhead,
   and tiny points of light
     bubbling in the channel.
It was the tag-end of summer.
   From the harbor's mouth
     you coasted into sight,
flashing news of your advent,
   the crescent of your dorsal fin
     clipping the diamonded surface.
We cheered at the sign of your greatness
   when the black barrel of your head
     erupted, ramming the water,
and you flowered for us
   in the jet of your spouting.

III

All afternoon you swam
   tirelessly round the bay,
      with such an easy motion,
the slightest downbeat of your tail,
   an almost imperceptible
      undulation of your flippers,
you seemed like something poured,
   not driven; you seemed
      to marry grace with power.
And when you bounded into air,
   slapping your flukes,
      we thrilled to look upon
pure energy incarnate
   as nobility of form.
      You seemed to ask of us
not sympathy, or love,
   or understanding,
      but awe and wonder.

That night we watched you
   swimming in the moon.
      Your back was molten silver.
We guessed your silent passage
   by the phosphorescence in your wake.
      At dawn we found you stranded on the rocks.

IV

There came a boy and a man
   and yet other men running, and two
      schoolgirls in yellow halters
and a housewife bedecked
   with curlers, and whole families in beach
      buggies with assorted yelping dogs.
The tide was almost out.
   We could walk around you,
      as you heaved deeper into the shoal,
crushed by your own weight,
   collapsing into yourself,
      your flippers and your flukes

quivering, your blowhole
   spasmodically bubbling, roaring.
      In the pit of your gaping mouth
you bared your fringework of baleen,
   a thicket of horned bristles.
      When the Curator of Mammals
arrived from Boston
   to take samples of your blood
      you were already oozing from below.
Somebody had carved his initials
   in your flank. Hunters of souvenirs
      had peeled off strips of your skin,
a membrane thin as paper.
   You were blistered and cracked by the sun.
      The gulls had been pecking at you.
The sound you made was a hoarse and fitful bleating.

What drew us, like a magnet, to your dying?
   You made a bond between us,
      the keepers of the nightfall watch,
who gathered in a ring around you,
   boozing in the bonfire light.
      Toward dawn we shared with you
your hour of desolation,
   the huge lingering passion
      of your unearthly outcry,
as you swung your blind head
   toward us and laboriously opened
      a bloodshot, glistening eye,
in which we swam with terror and recognition.

V

Voyager, chief of the pelagic world,
   you brought with you the myth
      of another country, dimly remembered,
where flying reptiles
   lumbered over the steaming marshes
      and trumpeting thunder lizards
wallowed in the reeds.
   While empires rose and fell on land,
      your nation breasted the open main,

rocked in the consoling rhythm
  of the tides. Which ancestor first plunged
    head-down through zones of colored twilight
to scour the bottom of the dark?
  You ranged the North Atlantic track
    from Port-of-Spain to Baffin Bay,
edging between the ice-floes
  through the fat of summer,
    lob-tailing, breaching, sounding,
grazing in the pastures of the sea
  on krill-rich orange plankton
    crackling with life.
You prowled down the continental shelf,
  guided by the sun and stars
    and the taste of alluvial silt
on your way southward
  to the warm lagoons,
    the tropic of desire,
where the lovers lie belly to belly
  in the rub and nuzzle of their sporting;
    and you turned, like a god in exile,
out of your wide primeval element,
  delivered to the mercy of time.
    Master of the whale-roads,
let the white wings of the gulls
  spread out their cover.
    You have become like us,
disgraced and mortal.

———

"Stranded"

By John Hay

I HAD HEARD about the blackfish, also called pilot whales or potheads, from the time I moved to Cape Cod, but until recently I had never seen a live one. I did once come across some skeletons lined up along a local beach. The whales had apparently been part of a pod composed of family groups, because there were a number of young ones among them. According to local reports, the whales had died on this shore in the 1930s and been uncovered years later by storm waves.

Storms often bring revelations of hidden history in this sandy, malleable land. They periodically bury the evidence and then unearth it again. Not long ago, during a winter walk along the Great Beach, which faces the open Atlantic, I saw what looked like a giant sea turtle ahead of me, a dark brown, rounded back. It turned out to be the half-buried section of a hull from a wrecked sailing vessel, battered but well-crafted, with wooden pegs holding the planks together. Since the use of iron instead of wood for larger ships came in during the latter part of the nineteenth century, I supposed that this was a lighter, smaller craft, perhaps a hundred years old. The surviving portion of the boat was about fifteen feet long. Four days later, after a storm that kept the wind booming all night while heavy waves smashed onto the beach, displacing and relocating huge volumes of sand, the wreck had completely disappeared, tossed back into the nineteenth century.

A few miles from where I saw this remnant, archaeologists were excavating an Indian site at the head of the beach, working intensively against the possibility that another storm might wash away all their work. In the eroding banks of peat above the shore, they had uncovered large trees that might be several thousand years old. On the evidence of an Archaic spearpoint, they think that ten thousand years ago the bank was in a sheltered area five miles behind the present shoreline. So the world ocean beyond carves the land away and spreads its waters over whole continents, with supreme disregard of the way we measure time and history.

Under its shifting sands, the Great Beach hides the wrecks of a hundred ships or more, the debris of civilization. Where the beach slopes off into the Atlantic in fog, driving rain, sleet, sunlight, and showers, it becomes a broad highway of transformations, of tricks and illusions. Mysterious creations seem to rise before your eyes and disappear. The green primordial surf pounds down the shore, carrying intermittent sounds of dying ships, falling houses, and crashing rocks along with the clatter of its stones. Then it subsides, to repeat its histories. Nothing can claim it but creation.

The blackfish are relatively small—only twenty feet long—as compared to the big whales like finbacks and humpbacks, which are up to sixty or sixty-five feet in length. But they weigh some eighteen hundred pounds, two hundred pounds short of a ton. They once provided an extra source of income for generations of shore fishermen living in the towns along the inner circle of Cape Cod Bay. The whales were valued not for their meat but for their head oil, which was refined and used to lubricate light machinery, clocks, and watches. It fetched sixty-five dollars a gallon, good money in those days. The oil came from a lump the size of a watermelon in the whales' heads, which gave the animals the name of potheads. In the 1850s, according to Henry Kittredge's book *Cape Cod,* Captain Daniel Rich cut his mark on the sides of seventy-five blackfish stranded on the beach between Wellfleet and Truro and made one thousand dollars out of them.

When the spouts or rounded backs of the blackfish appeared offshore, townspeople would rush down to the shore and launch their dories or other small boats. They would surround the whales, yelling and beating on the water with their oars. The quarry panicked, headed in, and beached themselves. The "shore whalers," as they were called, then got to work with knives and lances, killing the poor beasts with great vigor. They usually shared the profits on an equal basis, possibly because there were not many lawyers and insurance people around in those days to complicate the business.

This method of whaling was convenient for those who did not want to hunt whales over deep water, and the whales aroused great excitement in the towns where they landed. "Drift whales" were thought to be a blessing sent through the grace of God, and in one instance grateful parishioners of the church in Eastham used part of the whaling proceeds to pay the minister's salary.

Those of us who rarely see blackfish and who certainly have never seen half a town engaged in cutting them up would not enjoy watching the process. Phil Schwind, a native of the Cape who died in the spring of 1992 at the age of eighty-five, has described a scene from the 1940s in his book *Cape Cod Fisherman:*

Then the murder started. I know of no other word that would fit. Those great beasts, their thin, external skin as black and shiny as patent leather, beat the sand with their tails; they sighed and cried like monstrous babies. Their gasping was pathetic to hear as the tide ran out and left them helplessly high and dry, but what fisherman stops to listen when there is money to be made? Armed with a razor-sharp lance on the end of a ten-foot hickory pole, Cal came up behind the flipper of the nearest blackfish and beat the creature three or four times over the head. When I protested, Cal explained, "You have to warn them you're here. I've lanced fish I didn't warn first and had them jump clear off the sand. Somebody could get hurt that way."

Cal drove the lance into the side of the creature, again and again, trying to make a bigger and bigger hole. Blood poured out in torrents, "gushed" is a more exact word. It splattered us and dyed the beach a bright red. One and then another he killed, working down the beach through the whole school.

It was dark before we finished lancing; my job was to hold a flashlight so Cal could see. Sometimes the fish were so close together we had to climb on one while it was still alive to lance another. Behind us blackfish in their death throes were heaving and moaning with blood-choked sighs. Their great tails lashed the sand, making a sound like a whole herd of horses galloping across hard ground.

Little more of the blackfish was used than the forty- to fifty-pound chunks in their heads, although their thick coats of blubber contained tons of oil, and their bodies contained tons of good meat. After the cutting was over, the remains were buried in the sand above the tideline before the stench became unbearable. Waste has been an almost built-in part of the economic thinking in this country. . . .

The blackfish, more often called pilot whales these days so as not to confuse them with fish, a race to which they do not belong, feed on squid in deep water along the edge of the continental shelf. During the summer and early autumn, the squid move closer inshore to feed, and the whales follow them. It was estimated that in the waters off Newfoundland during the late 1950s some forty-seven thousand pilot whales were taken. The original population is thought to have been no more than sixty thousand.

The tendency of these animals to herd closely together in family groups made it easier to drive them inshore. But what makes them strand voluntarily, if that is the right way to describe it? Theories have been advanced about parasitic infections of the inner ear, or inattention to what kind of bottom the whales might find themselves in, especially during frenzied feeding. It is possible that the whales become confused during migration when they swim out of deep water into Cape Cod Bay. The Cape is like a hook, starting from its stem on the mainland and curving around to its northern tip at Provincetown. The waters of the bay are relatively shallow, no more than eighty feet in depth. A sandy reef or bar near the mouth might confuse the whales if they swam inside it, and could not find their way out, or a storm might come up to further disturb their sense of direction. They might then swim in toward gradually shallowing waters and become even more disoriented as their geomagnetic sense was scrambled. It is also theorized that beaches with flat profiles disturb the whales' ability to echolocate. Whatever the explanation, after countless generations the pilots seem to have been unable to hand down the knowledge that a trap like Cape Cod must be avoided.

Each school has at least one leader, and if the leader panics, giving calls of distress, the rest follow. Phil Schwind, who is of the opinion that the leader is not necessarily a male, says these animals could be herded like sheep. People used to drive around them with their boats, which by the 1940s were equipped with motors. Their method was to wait until the moment when the tide started to turn back and then cut off one of the animals, which might be of either sex, and wait for the rest to follow. (After the forties, the once-precious head oil was replaced by refined petroleum and no longer had any value.)

The blackfish will not be separated, even under extreme conditions. They have a powerful sense of unity, and they are highly sensitive to each other's movements, needs, and inclinations. Such highly social animals communicate through a complex repertoire of underwater calls. Apparently each individual has a distinctive whistle. Pilot whales belong to the family of dolphins, so you might suppose them to have similar ways of communicating, although their social structure is much more tightly knit and familial than that of other species in the group. Dolphins trade information through a variety of clicks, whistles, and other strange sounds. A group of dolphins makes decisions as to when to move out to sea from near the coast, or when to go fishing at night. According to Kenneth Norris in his book *Dolphin Days,* about the spinner dolphins of the Pacific:

Each school member can detect the emotional level and alertness of the others, just as the wolf can tell by the itch and tension in another's call where it is in the chase. Under the greatest excitement, tension on its vocal chords may cause its voice to break just as our own voices break in heightened circumstances.

emotional glue that gives richness and nuance to a metaphoric communication system. Just as our spirits rise when we are listening to a symphony and its tempo increases, . . . so might something like emotion be transmitted throughout a school. . . . We routinely talk about future events when we say something simple like, "Let's go to the store." But the dolphin school, it seems, must match event and action while it acts out an emotionally based metaphor of what is going on.

What their refined use of signals means at any given moment remains to be understood and can only be found out, if at all, through patient, untiring research and a painstaking accumulation of data. Dr. Norris indicates that isolated signals may be symbolic, a given sound indicating a given circumstance. That, he says, is about halfway to being a word.

In a society so estranged from animals as ours, we often fail to credit them with any form of language. If we do, it comes under the heading of communication rather than speech. And yet the great silence we have imposed on the rest of life contains innumerable forms of expression. Where does our own language come from but this unfathomed store that characterizes innumerable species?

We are now more than halfway removed from what the unwritten word meant to our ancestors, who believed in the original, primal word behind all manifestations of the spirit. You sang because you were answered. The answers came from life around you. Prayers, chants, and songs were also responses to the elements, to the wind, the sun and stars, the Great Mystery behind them. Life on earth springs from a collateral magic that we rarely consult. We avoid the unknown as if we were afraid that contact would lower our sense of self-esteem.

Now I come to my first meeting with live pilot whales. It was on September 30, 1991. I had driven down to the parking lot at the head of the local beach in East Dennis where I often walk, especially at low tide, but I was stopped by a policeman. He told me that seventeen whales were stranded on the beach. So I left the car farther back in town and walked to the beach the long way around, through the thickets and dunes behind it. When I reached the beach, I saw a line of onlookers who were cordoned off on the sands just above the waterline. In their midst was a small, young whale lying dead on the sand. Others, still alive, had been removed and taken to the nearby channel of Sesuit Harbor to recuperate. In the shallow inshore waters were five knots of rescuers, or would-be rescuers, each holding on with quiet but obviously weary determination to a large, shiny black whale. The backs of the pilot whales were exposed, and the rescuers kept pouring water over them to keep them from drying out. In one case, a huge eighteen-hundred-pound animal was being carried onto the beach on a front-end loader by a number of people who had managed to get a stretcher under it. A line of people in deeper water farther out was trying to prevent another whale from moving in. The silent insistence in the animals was stunning to watch.

The rescuers were showing the strain. "I'm tired," one woman was heard to say. "It's more frustrating than discouraging. You try to help these animals but you don't know what to do. I wish we could learn the language of pilot whales."

In a later conversation, Phil Schwind, with memories of older and rougher realities, said to me that he felt sorry for those poor volunteers standing in cold water up to their waists for hours on end, desperately trying to hold back the whales, as if they could stop nature.

What nature is, we seldom seem to know. It is hard for us as "thinking animals" to understand behavior like that of the stranding whales, and we are too ready to confuse it with mass psychology. Yet in the great seas where these animals live, cohesion is a strategy for survival. When something happens to one animal, all the rest are in danger and respond.

The whales at East Dennis had been part of a larger group that had stranded four days before in Truro, farther down the shore of the Cape, where an effort had been made to save them from themselves. Later on, some of the survivors of the East Dennis stranding moved to Yarmouth. It was highly discouraging to the rescue teams, who had congratulated themselves on managing to persuade a whale to stay off the beach and swim away, to have it strand somewhere else. Other whales would simply wait offshore until the tide lowered and then strand themselves again.

During this period of stranding, five young whales, first three and then two more, were thought to be in good enough condition to be moved to the New England Aquarium. After a period of rest and careful feeding, they were successfully released at sea and their movements tracked in the months that followed. Science benefits from these efforts. The whales are an important source of information, a good, long-term investment in knowledge. Methods improve. Institutions are encouraged to tackle larger species of whales in the future, to add even more knowledge and hope. These very laudable efforts are also part of our need as a society to impose our will and to succeed in solving problems that face us. This need brings strong emotions with it—tears for hope, and tears for failure. But in the final analysis, we do not know why pilot whales strand, or what we could possibly do to prevent it.

There was something about that scene on the beach, with its ardent, tired people and the silent black whales bent on moving in to the terrible shore that affected me profoundly. As I was starting to leave, a buried memory welled up inside me, a waking dream. I remembered a feeling of being alone, of being detached, pulled away from all familiar surroundings and support. It had come to me a long time ago, when I was a boy, and I vaguely associated it with the dark weight of the city where we lived. Perhaps it was the immense drawing power of the ocean at my feet that helped bring this dreamlike memory out into the open. It was a very real feeling of removal and dislocation, but I do not equate it with fear, or dread anticipation of what was to come next. I had simply been pulled away from all familiarity and faced with some inexorable darkness of cavernous dimensions. But in some way, the memory brought me closer to those deep-sea animals than I could have imagined possible.

As I walked away down the beach, I passed a flock of sandpipers standing and scuttling along the wet sands at the edge of the beach. A blue light was cast around them from the water and the sky. Beyond them the ever present gulls watched the horizon, and a few crows scavenged for food over the tidelands. The sanderlings flew up spontaneously and sped off to land farther down the shore.

Ringing the coasts of the world, the birds are one measure of its tidal complexities. Each kind seems to stand out as an embodiment of light, commanded by the unknown depths of creation. They are on earth's inspired and urgent business, carrying its many worlds of being far into a future that requires of each of them a certain perfection.

Birds, fish, whales, and men live on the edge of oblivion, which often snatches them out of the air or the depths of the sea. During their varying spans of life they are all creation's people, each singularly endowed to follow out the life of the planet. Without this great company we would hang in a void. A chance meeting with a dying whale, a flock of sanderlings, or a passing bird testing the atmosphere, may be a revelation, however fleeting, of the underlying powers that lead us on and define our being. We come closest to nature, in its beginnings and endings, its Alphas and Omegas, in the darkest corners of our dreams.

*

On a recent visit to the city, I learned that pilot whales are known to dive down to at least eighteen hundred feet below the surface of the ocean. I was repeating this to my wife as we were traveling downtown in a bus. I heard a schoolboy sitting opposite us ask, "Do they really dive that deep?" When I answered, "I believe so," he turned his head and lapsed into a reverie, where we left him as we climbed down from the bus.

Men's Lives

~~~~~~

T HE THIRTY-MILE STRETCH of offshore water between the Monomoy Shoals south of Chatham and Provincetown's Race Point
is one of several parts of the East Coast known as "Graveyards of the
Atlantic." The first recorded shipwreck on Cape Cod was the *Sparrow-
hawk,* an English vessel that struck a sandbar off Orleans in 1627. Since
then an estimated three thousand vessels have been lost in the waters
off the Cape. I have never seen an estimate of the number of lives lost
in these shipwrecks, but in almost every one of the numerous small
graveyards scattered across the peninsula one can find epitaphs to those
"lost at sea."

Most of the Cape shipwrecks over the centuries have been connected
to the fishing industry. The most deadly areas were the shoals and rips
off Monomoy and the infamous Peaked Hill Bars off the Atlantic, or
back side, of Provincetown. Josef Berger's dramatization of an incident
among Provincetown's Portuguese fishermen is set in the community
of Helltown, a nineteenth-century fishing village near Race Point which,
as Berger points out, has been the locale of many colorful though fan-
ciful stories over the years. Provincetown historian George Bryant
maintains, in fact, that "Helltown" was never a contemporary term for
the village but an invention of later writers.

Not all losses occurred close to shore, however. Once fishing vessels
began making trips to Georges Bank and the Newfoundland Grand
Banks, entire fleets were sometimes caught in furious fall northeasters,
winter gales, and hurricanes. The largest loss of lives, however, usually
occurred on nonfishing vessels. One of Cape Cod's most famous wrecks
was the pirate ship *Whydah,* a three-hundred-ton galley commanded by
"Black Sam" Bellamy, which broke up on the bars off Eastham (now

South Wellfleet) on May 8, 1717, with a loss of 145 lives. Kittredge's account of the wreck and the subsequent frustrations of authorities who sought to locate the ship's booty is an early illustration of the ambivalent attitudes Cape Codders have always had toward the business of "wrecking."

Though fishing and whaling were, until recently, almost exclusively male professions, it was nonetheless women's lives as well as men's that were risked in the business of the sea. From the earliest days of the Cape's history, women went to sea in vulnerable vessels. *Mayflower* passenger Dorothea Bradford's drowning in Provincetown Harbor was the first recorded death of an Englishwoman in the New England. During the nineteenth century, waves of European immigrants sailed to America, often in overcrowded or unseaworthy vessels. Many of them came to grief in and around the waters off Cape Cod. In the first chapter of *Cape Cod,* for instance, Thoreau graphically describes the violent fate of 145 Irish immigrants—men, women, and children—in a wreck off Cohasset, an incident that seems to have obsessed him throughout his visit to the Cape. Many wives of local shipmasters and whaling captains accompanied their husbands on voyages that often lasted many months, or even years.

As several of the selections in this section reveal, even the lives of those women who stayed at home were intimately bound to and affected by the fate of the men who went to sea. A woman's economic fate was dependent upon her husband's success or failure at sea. Moreover, fishermen's wives were an integral part of their husbands' business, whether they were mending nets and rigging, or preparing bait, or cleaning and spreading cod on the fish flakes to dry. But often the consequences were personal and absolute. Thoreau's account of the grief and devastation wreaked upon the village of Truro following the great gale of 1841 is a masterpiece of understatement and condensation, speaking volumes in a few lines of conversation.

Frequently the most affecting testaments of the bonds and the losses between women and seagoing men are found in their own words, with no literary lens necessary. There exists, for instance, at the Sturgis Library genealogical collection in Barnstable, a remarkable correspondence, covering the years 1856–1870, between the parents of Joseph Lincoln, the popular early-twentieth-century Cape Cod novelist. His father, Joseph Sr., was a commercial ship captain from Brewster. His mother, Mary Crosby Lincoln, frequently went with her husband on his voyages. Their letters show a remarkably constant and strong affection over the years, and Mary's letters in particular give a lively picture of life in a small

Cape Cod town 125 years ago during an eventful period in American history. But during the winter of 1870 she remained at home, pregnant with their first child after twenty years of marriage and several miscarriages, while Joseph took the merchant bark *Aurelia* to ports in the South. Like Sullivan Ballou's famous letter to his wife just before the First Battle of Bull Run, the Lincolns' final correspondence is remarkable not only for its simple dignity and depth of emotion, but because it expresses a condition and fate at once so common and extraordinary that we today would not be able to imagine it properly without such testaments.

The lives that were risked at sea were not only those of men who went for fish, whales, or the profit of trade, but those of the men who tried to save them when their ships grounded on a bar, or froze their rigging in ice storms, or broke apart during offshore northeasters. The U.S. Life Saving Service, the predecessor to today's U.S. Coast Guard, was established in 1872. Nine stations were initially built along the coast of the Outer Beach from Provincetown to Monomoy, and eventually four others joined them, all manned almost entirely by local Cape Cod men. One of the original stations, the Old Harbor Lifesaving Station, was moved from its original site on Chatham's North Beach by the National Seashore to Provincetown's Race Point, where it is preserved as a museum. Another original station at Cahoon Hollow has performed a quite different function for many summers as the popular Beachcomber nightclub.

In the forty-three years of its existence, the Cape's Life Saving Service performed hundreds of sea rescues, some of truly heroic proportions. During the period August 1901–June 1902 alone, the Cape station crews saved 217 lives at sea. Despite their motto, "You have to go, but you don't have to come back," there was very little loss of life among the crews, a tribute to their skill and training. The most detailed account of these men and their exploits is given in *The Life Savers of Cape Cod* by J. W. Dalton (himself a crew member), originally published in 1902 and recently reprinted.

One of the most famous incidents in the Life Saving Service's annals was the Monomoy disaster of 1902. It was a tragic disaster in large part because, as Kittredge's account makes clear, it was a needless one. His footnote on the subsequent fate of Captain Elmer Mayo is a poignant reminder that life is not always as kind as art to its heroes.

With the opening of the Cape Cod Canal in 1914, ships were no longer required to make the dangerous outside passage around the Outer Cape. The number of shipwrecks declined dramatically, but did not cease. The wreck of the three-masted schooner *Montclair* on March 4, 1927, provides yet another example of how differently two authors can look at the same subject, or rather how the same subject can yield very different material. Henry Beston's moving description of the wreck has such a vivid immediacy that one may not realize on first reading that it is not an eyewitness report, but largely a secondhand narrative pieced together from the accounts of others. Kittredge's anecdote of the "cleaning out" of the *Montclair* provides a more local perspective on the wreck, and a fairly recent illustration of that peculiar blend of compassion and opportunism with which Cape Codders have always viewed such tragedies.

Not all sea disasters involved ships. One of the most harrowing, which has remained in local memory longer than most, involved the submarine *S-4,* which sank in Provincetown Harbor during the same year as the *Montclair* wreck. Like the Monomoy disaster, the loss of life was largely due to human error, compounded by an agonizing tragedy of errors. Berger, less forgiving of official bungling than Kittredge, tells the story with bitter irony.

Despite modern advances in ship safety, fishing equipment, and communications and navigation technology, Cape men and women continue to put their lives on the line when they go to sea, as recorded in Doug Carlson's and Alec Wilkinson's essays. The deep and earnest truths of Lincoln's lyrical tribute to "The Cod Fisher" are as true today as they were a hundred years ago.

"The Cod Fisher"

By Joseph Lincoln

Where leap the long Atlantic swells
In foam-streaked stretch of hill and dale,
Where shrill the north-wind demon yells,
And flings the spindrift down the gale;
Where, beaten 'gainst the bending mast,
The frozen raindrop clings and cleaves,
With steadfast front for calm or blast
His battered schooner rocks and heaves.

> *To some the gain, to some the loss,*
> *To each the chance, the risk, the fight:*
> *For men must die that men may live—*
> *Lord, may we steer our course aright.*

The dripping deck beneath him reels,
The flooded scuppers spout the brine;
He heeds them not, he only feels
The tugging of a tightened line.
The grim white sea-fog o'er him throws
Its clammy curtain, damp and cold;
He minds it not—his work he knows,
'T is but to fill an empty hold.

Oft, driven through the night's blind wrack,
He feels the dread berg's ghastly breath,
Or hears draw nigh through walls of black
A throbbing engine chanting death;
But with a calm, unwrinkled brow
He fronts them, grim and undismayed,
For storm and ice and liner's bow—
These are but chances of the trade.

Yet well he knows—where'er it be,
On low Cape Cod or bluff Cape Ann—

With straining eyes that search the sea
A watching woman waits her man:
He knows it, and his love is deep,
But work is work, and bread is bread,
And though men drown and women weep
The hungry thousands must be fed.

To some the gain, to some the loss,
To each his chance, the game with Fate:
For men must die that men may live—
Dear Lord, be kind to those who wait.

———

A Wall of Wrecks

By Henry C. Kittredge

IT HAS BEEN said that if all the wrecks which have piled up on the back side of the Cape were placed bow to stern, they would make a continuous wall from Chatham to Provincetown. This is a picturesque way of putting what is substantially the truth, for Peaked Hill Bars and the Monomoy Shoals are to sailors of to-day what Scylla and Charybdis were to Aeneas. Nauset Beach, which stretches along the whole coast line of Orleans and Eastham, holds in its fatal sands the shattered skeletons of vessels from half the seaports of the world; while farther north, the outer shores of Wellfleet and Truro have gathered in the hulls of a thousand ships, driven helplessly upon them by northeast gales. Even the comparatively sheltered waters of the Bay have had their share of shipwrecks, though there the hulls are not usually pounded to pieces as they are on the outer shore. It is not idle curiosity that makes the Cape-Codder a keen observer of the weather; it is habit inherited from ancestors who antedate lighthouses and life-saving stations, who have weathered typhoons and outguessed the fog.

—from *Cape Cod, Its People and Their History* (1930)

Mooncussers and the Wreck of the *Whydah*

By Henry C. Kittredge

A DILIGENT HISTORIAN has said that wrecks form no part of local history; and from one point of view he is right. Yet many wrecks that came ashore on the Cape presented the townspeople first with a problem in amateur life-saving, and second, with a more intricate problem in *meum and tuum*. On the whole, they had more success in solving the former than the latter, for the temptation of a rich cargo scattered along the beach is hard for a poor man to resist. So before passing on to the Cape-Codders' exploits as life-savers, it is necessary to glance at a few of their equally successful performances as mooncussers.

To be sure, the full significance of this picturesque term never applied to the Cape. Originally it meant the villainous practice of luring vessels to destruction by false lights in order to plunder them when the crews had perished. It went even further and included murdering survivors to give free play to the looting. A humorous Provincetown saying used to be, 'Don't get ashore on the back side of Truro; there's women waiting there on the beach with a brick in a stocking.' But nowhere on the Cape was there ever a case either of decoying a ship to its death, or of maltreating her crew. To-day mooncussing means no more than the pleasant and sometimes profitable practice of strolling along the beach looking for chance wreckage—a plank worth hauling home, an unbroken lobster pot, a vessel's quarterboard to nail over the barn door. But somewhere between the two extremes there exists a disagreeable truth, for unquestionably stranded vessels have been robbed of their cargo and gear by Cape-Codders; and who can say that mixed emotions did not sometimes exist in the breasts of men as they stood on the beach hills of Nauset and watched a ship pounding shoreward over the bars? . . .

The most sensational instance of pillaging a wreck in defiance of law occurred in the spring of 1717, when the pirate ship *Whidaw* was driven ashore on the back side of Wellfleet. It is a long story, but by no means a dull one; it involves, in fact, not one wreck but two. After a lurid cruise in southern waters, the notorious pirate, Samuel Bellamy, headed his ship *Whidaw* north to try his luck in Nantucket Sound. He was accompanied by a much smaller craft, a snow, which he had recently captured off the Virginia Coast. Between sunrise and sunset on April 26, Bellamy took two vessels near Nantucket Shoals. One of them was the *Mary Anne,* an Irish pink bound for New York with a cargo of Madeira; the other a Virginia sloop whose name is not recorded. Seven pirates from the *Whidaw* were put on board the *Mary Anne;* others took over the Virginia sloop, and the whole fleet of four vessels headed north into the night.

A gale came up from the northeast, and the pirates—none of them very sober—found themselves in trouble, driven off their course to the westward. The *Mary Anne* in particular made bad weather of it, no doubt because her crew had a larger supply of Madeira than the others, and toward midnight she got among breakers off Orleans and went aground. Not knowing what better to do, the pirates stayed on board. In the morning the *Whidaw* was nowhere in sight, but the snow and the Virginia sloop were riding it out at anchor in deep water. Those two vessels soon slipped their cables and made an offing—vanishing forever from the sight of the *Mary Anne* and from this narrative.

Before long a boat with two men, John Cole and William Smith, of Orleans, rowed off from the mainland and took the crew ashore. Not until they arrived at Cole's house did the rescuers know that they were entertaining pirates, but here the fact was announced in no uncertain language by one Mackonachy, cook of the Mary Anne, who demanded their instant arrest. Seven to three was too long odds for Cole and Smith; they did not hanker for a knife between the ribs. So by the time the startling news reached Joseph Doane, Esq., of Eastham, who as justice of the peace was the nearest official, the seven pirates had made off over the road, headed for Rhode Island. Doane and a posse of volunteers overtook them before they had gone far and sent them to the Barnstable jail for safekeeping. The pink went to pieces where she lay— but not, it is to be hoped, until her casks of Madeira had found their way into Eastham and Orleans cellars.

Meantime, the *Whidaw,* flagship of the pirate fleet, was having troubles of her own—divine retribution if ever there was a case of it. She had thrashed her way as far north as the ocean side of Wellfleet, but there Bellamy, realizing that he could keep off shore no longer, let go his anchors and tried to ride it out. The seas ran so high, however, that the *Whidaw* threatened to go under. As a last resort he set a little sail, cut the cables, and tried to claw off into deep water. He might have saved himself the trouble. Before morning his ship had capsized and was fast going to pieces in the breakers about two miles south of Cahoon's Hollow. Bellamy and one hundred and forty-four of his men were drowned. Only two survivors ever reached shore alive. They were Thomas Davis, a Welshman, who had been impressed from a captured ship, and John Julian, a Cape Cod Indian.

Davis found his way to the house of Samuel Harding in Wellfleet early in the morning of April 27, and told him of the wreck. Harding scented rich pickings; he hitched up his horse and, accompanied by Davis and the Indian, salvaged several wagonloads of the most valuable plunder before any one else knew that the *Whidaw* was ashore. But before long the beach was black with carts, half the able-bodied men of the village being on hand to haul what they could from the surf. The great prize would have been the chest of gold coins which was supposed to have been on board when the ship struck; but, like most pirate gold, it has never been found.

News of the wreck reached Justice Doane while he was still busy with the crew of the *Mary Anne,* but as soon as he had started them on their way to the Barnstable jail, he hurried to Cahoon's Hollow, only to find that the bones of the *Whidaw* had been picked clean. He arrested Davis and John Julian, who joined the seven men of the Anne at Barnstable, whence all were marched under an armed escort to Boston and tried for piracy—all but the Indian, that is, who vanished soon after reaching the city. Davis was acquitted; the others were hanged.

As soon as word came to the ears of Governor Shute that a pirate ship was ashore at Wellfleet, he did two things, both of them proper and both futile. First he issued a proclamation to all His Majesty's subjects whom it might concern, to seize all 'money, bullion, treasure, goods and merchandises,' from the wreck, that they might swell the royal exchequer. Second, he ordered Captain Cyprian Southack to sail to the Cape, collect the loot, and return with it to Boston. No man ever tried harder to achieve the impossible than Southack did. He anchored in Provincetown Harbor five days after the wreck, searched the town in vain for a horse, dispatched a detail of two men to Truro with orders to hire a pair there and proceed overland to the scene of the wreck, where they were to post themselves as a guard over the valuables on board her! Meanwhile, he himself set out for the spot in a whaleboat (with which the town was better supplied than it was with horses), skirted the Bay shore as far as Boat Meadow Creek in Orleans, and made his way across the Cape to the outer beach via this waterway, Jeremiah's Gutter, Town Cove, and Nauset Harbor, a feat which could have been accomplished even at that early date only on the very top of the spring tides.

All that was left of the least value on the *Whidaw* had been taken home by the citizens. The men whom Southack had sent to watch over the treasure had found nothing but fragments of the hull to guard. The cold rains of May, for which the Cape is famous, did nothing to improve the Captain's temper. It was a dour mariner who began knocking at the doors of the Wellfleet inhabitants, most of whom had a barn full of plunder from the wreck, and demanding that they hand it over. He was greeted variously. Some, with expressions of blank astonishment, asked him to what wreck he referred—they had heard of no wreck. Others laughed and bade him try to get it. Samuel Harding, at whose door the angry minion of His Majesty knocked loudest—for it was he who with Davis had skimmed the cream of the cargo—assured Southack that he was holding the goods for Davis until after the trial. It would be a breach of trust to give them up, even to so well authenticated an official as the Captain. In short, Southack returned to Boston with nothing but some second-hand rigging for his pains, convinced that all Cape-Codders were villains.

From the official point of view he was right, for the law expects men to do what it demands of them. But from the point of view of the observer of human nature, who realizes that temptations are sometimes too strong for mere man to resist, these same Cape-Codders appear as average samples of our race. Many an honest man has robbed the Crown who would not take so much as a stick of firewood from a neighbor. One may sympathize with Southack, without being prepared to denounce the men of Wellfleet.*

—from *Cape Cod, Its People and Their History* (1930)

———

*The legend of the *Whydah* (the original spelling of the ship's name), buried beneath the sands off the Outer Beach for over 250 years, came to life in 1984 when salvager Barry Clifford discovered the remains of the wreck on the ocean floor a half-mile off South Wellfleet.

Codfishing on the Banks

By Shebnah Rich

CODFISHING ON THE Banks was considered tough work. The boy who could graduate from that school with full honors, could take care of himself; fight his own battles. It was kill or cure; few, however, were killed; he was sure to come home hale and hearty. As an infallible remedy for most all complaints to which flesh is heir, a Bank voyage, as conducted thirty or forty years ago, challenges comparison. The radical change of life, the pure, bracing air, the regular labor, the sound sleep, the forced temperance and ravenous appetite are the medicine that will cure when all the mysteries of the *Materia medica* utterly fail. A trip on the Grand Bank, and "throw physic to the dogs!" I have known scores of men of various diseases, in various stages, who have made the trip, but rarely, if ever, heard of an instance that failed. It is understood that I am not speaking of helpless invalids, but more particularly of dyspeptics, liver, humorous or cutaneous diseases, and pulmonary complaints, in their early stages. I made the acquaintance of a gentleman of large fortune, on a Cunard packet, who said he had not made a square meal for thirty years. I believe a four months' trip to the Grand Bank, as a common hand, would enable this poor man to eat three square meals a day and look over his shoulder for a fourth. Charles Lamb says, "The foolisher the fowl or fish—woodcocks, dotterals, cod's heads, etc.—the finer the flesh thereof." Perhaps Lamb had eaten a codhead muddle at Old Margate Hoy. Who has not eaten a codhead muddle on the Banks, has something yet to do in the way of fine eating.

—from *Truro—Cape Cod* (1883)

———

The Hazards of Dory Fishing

By Henry C. Kittredge

HAZARDOUS AS THEIR calling was, even when all hands stayed on board and fished over the side, these progressive fishermen devised a yet more hazardous practice, justified in their own minds, if not in their families', because it caught more cod. They began in the late fifties to carry dories with them and to fish in pairs from these instead of from the schooner. It was believed that the quick motion of these little boats kept the bait dancing more conspicuously than the slower rise and fall of the schooner. Theoretically the dories did not venture too far away for safety, but fog and wind are unstable elements; a sudden blow, coming while the fish were biting, would often go too long unheeded by the dorymen. The schooner could no longer ride at anchor; the nicest handling could not keep her in sight of all her scattered dories. Some would get back to the safety of her deck; others would never be heard of again. Thus did the fearless Bankers add another hazard to their already hazardous calling.

Not content with running these risks, they employed another new device which took them still farther from the safety zone around their vessels. A Cape Cod fisherman conceived the idea of setting trawls— heavy lines anchored close to the bottom with short lines carrying baited hooks made fast to them at intervals. Sometimes there were a thousand hooks on a single trawl. The whole contrivance was buoyed and left, and the fisherman moved on to set the next one. Trawls had to be set and hauled from dories. If the men were reluctant to stop handlining when bad weather set in, what must have been their reluctance to abandon a half-hauled trawl with a codfish or halibut on every other hook? More fishermen were lost than ever, but there was no scarcity of volunteers to fill the gaps in their ranks.

What induced them to follow such a laborious, dangerous, and above all unprofitable business, it is hard to say. The Honorable Zeno Scudder, of Osterville, has calculated that a fisherman's earnings for four months for the decade between 1841 and 1851 were sixty-three dollars. The Government bonus brought the figure up to seventy-seven dollars but there is still nothing Croesan about it, even if a wide margin is allowed for statistical inaccuracy. The old jingle,

Sailor lads have gold and silver,
Fisher lads have nought but brass,

sums up the situation. The gambling element—which would account
for much—was reduced to a minimum with the Grand-Bankers. They
were almost certain to return with a full fare if they returned at all. The
best explanation is that the life itself appealed to a certain type of man.
Discipline on board a fisherman was as elastic as it could be made without actually removing the skipper from command. It could hardly have
been otherwise, indeed, for crews were composed for the most part,
not only of men who had been friends from boyhood, but of brothers
and fathers and sons. In 1789, a fishing vessel was lost on Nantucket
Shoals with a crew of eight Yarmouth men, six of whom were named
Hallett. The schooner Primrose of Yarmouth, which was lost in the
great gale of 1841, carried two Brays, two Matthewses, two Halls, and
two Wheldens. Of the twenty Dennis men lost in the same storm, twelve
were named Howes.

These crew lists, selected at random from the scores that sailed from
the Cape, suggest another answer to the question, 'Why did men spend
their lives fishing?' It was an hereditary calling. The sons of Cape Cod
fishermen were foreordained to the decks of schooners. It was taken for
granted that a boy would step on board his father's vessel as automati-
cally as the son of a business man nowadays steps into his father's office.
Brothers and fathers fished side by side. The *Dalmatia* of Truro carried
Gamaliel S. Paine and his fourteen-year-old son, Henry. The *Altair,* of
the same town, was commanded by Elisha Rich, aged twenty-six, and
sailing under him were his two brothers, Joseph and William. Boys
whose parents to-day would think them too young to be sent to boarding school went to sea as cooks on fishermen, and all hands fared
accordingly. Joseph Wheat shipped as cook on the *Cincinnatus,* of Truro,
at the age of thirteen. Thomas White was twelve when he sailed in the
Arrival, another Truro vessel, and he was not the youngest member of
the crew, either. Charles Nott was only eleven, and Dick Atwood was
fourteen. But these lads look like grown men when compared with
Ambrose Snow, Jr., who in 1842 at the age of eight sailed with his
father from Wellfleet for the Bay de Chaleur on the pink-sterned schooner
Mariner.

An important result of this family grouping on board fishermen, where
brother was often in command of brother, was to unfit men for the
navy or merchant service. Fine sailors they were, but savage commands,
such as issued from the brazen throat of the mate of a clipper ship, were

not their style. Discipline disagreed with them. If brother 'Lisha was shaving Monomoy too close or was slow in giving the order to shorten sail in a blow, Joe and William were there to tell him of it—captain or no captain. More informal, free-and-easy crews never sailed the sea. The ship's company of a Cape Cod fisherman was a floating democracy where freedom of speech was the order of every day, and democracy sorted ill with the routine of a deep-water merchantman. Coming up with the fishing fleet off Highland Light and tearing past with skysails set, the foremast hands of a lordly clipper looked with contempt at the tiny schooners and wondered how men could live on board them. The fishermen cocked an eye at the towering canvas of the clipper, spat over the side, and ejaculated, 'Monkeys on a stick.' So each went his way.

—from *Cape Cod, Its People and Their History* (1930)

———

Three Widows

By Henry David Thoreau

IT WAS SAID in 1794 that more vessels were cast away on the east shore of Truro than anywhere in Barnstable County. Notwithstanding that this light-house has since been erected, after almost every storm we read of one or more vessels wrecked here, and sometimes more than a dozen wrecks are visible from this point at one time. The inhabitants hear the crash of vessels going to pieces as they sit round their hearths, and they commonly date from some memorable shipwreck. If the history of this beach could be written from beginning to end, it would be a thrilling page in the history of commerce.

Truro was settled in the year 1700 as *Dangerfield*. This was a very appropriate name, for I afterward read on a monument in the grave-yard, near Pamet River, the following inscription:—

Sacred
to the memory of
57 citizens of Truro,

who were lost in seven
vessels, which
foundered at sea in
the memorable gale
of Oct. 3d, 1841.

Their names and ages by families were recorded on different sides of the stone. They are said to have been lost on George's Bank, and I was told that only one vessel drifted ashore on the back side of the Cape, with the boys locked into the cabin and drowned. It is said that the homes of all were "within a circuit of two miles." Twenty-eight inhabitants of Dennis were lost in the same gale; and I read that "in one day, immediately after this storm, nearly or quite one hundred bodies were taken up and buried on Cape Cod."

The Truro Insurance Company failed for want of skippers to take charge of its vessels. But the surviving inhabitants went a-fishing again the next year as usual. I found that it would not do to speak of shipwrecks there, for almost every family has lost some of its members at sea.

"Who lives in that house?" I inquired.

"Three widows," was the reply.

The stranger and the inhabitant view the shore with very different eyes. The former may have come to see and admire the ocean in a storm; but the latter looks on it as the scene where his nearest relatives were wrecked. When I remarked to an old wrecker partially blind, who was sitting on the edge of the bank smoking a pipe, which he had just lit with a match of dried beach-grass, that I supposed he liked to hear the sound of the surf, he answered:

"No, I do not like to hear the sound of the surf."

He had lost at least one son in "the memorable gale," and could tell many a tale of the shipwrecks which he had witnessed there.

—from *Cape Cod* (1865)

"Old Map of Barnstable County"

By Brendan Galvin

It doesn't show
how the cold edge of starlight
pierced woodpiles,

or the boy forking hay
who one afternoon cries out to no one
on the shore of Still Pond
and runs away to sea,

but crawls ashore years later,
to lie under this mapmaker's
pinpoint, which stands for "humane house,"
and gasp white-eyed on the straw floor,
his hands scrabbling his chest
for its breath.

Who would believe,
on this mapmaker's Atlantic
which looks safe as a strip of corduroy,
a schooner is floundering,

and soon heartbreak will walk
the sand roads up hollows
to Mrs. Small, Mrs. Snow, Mrs. Dyer,
sea widows whose lives will go on
in ways the cartographer's black squares
for houses can never explain?

A red dot for each vessel lost
would turn this map
to a rash like scarlet fever,
quick as a camera's shutter
that sea would close over islands,

and the griefs that went by the names
beside the black squares
would move on to other squares,

as on later maps
even the black squares
will have moved on.

———

from *The Captain Joseph Lincoln Papers*

Parimaribo Surinam Augst 10th 1860

MY DEAR WIFE. Your letter per Brig Cronstadt came to hand yesterday and happy was I Dear Em to hear that you was getting better. & I hope & trust by this time that you are entirely well again. as there is a vefsel to leave here tomorrow for Gloucester I thought I would write you a few lines, knowing that you would be happy to receive them. and nothing gives me more pleasure then writing to my Dear Emily when I cannot see her. or talk with her in any other way. then with my pen. but I thank god for that. & your letter dear Em I have read it over & over again. & if it gives you as much pleasure to rec'd mine, I am satisfied. although there is not much news in them. neither are they penned in quite so good a style as yours. but you must take them from whence they come. it has been but 34 days since I left you. but oh how long it seems to me—more then a year would spent in company with my dear wife. but never mind if nothing happens it will not be more then two months more before we meet again. then we will enjoy it I know. if my dear Em is only well again I shall be very thankful. & trust that I shall not have to go alone all of my days. but will have her with me part of the time if not all, then I should be willing to go any where. not but what I have other friends that I love & would like to see. but none like her. now Em I will tell you how I live out here. I take Breakfast & Dinner on Board of the vessel. take supper & lodgings on shore. for

157

the musquitoes are so thick on board could not sleep there unless I slept on deck. & that I would not like to do. so I have taken my bed on shore. & sleep in a large room alone. no paint on the floor nor plastering on the walls as I lay there can see out doors through the side of the building most any where. but the weather is very warm here all the year around. it rains here every afternoon. although they call it the dry season now. if it is so I dont know what the wet season can be. it must rain all the time. still it is very healthy here. do not hear of any sicknefs at all. & I think they would be pleasant voyages for a man to go. after he gets acquainted with the trade. think we shall get all of the cargo out tomorrow. & shall commence to load next week. think I shall get away in 3 or 4 weeks. tell Ella her letter was very goo. & I am much obliged to her for writing me all the news. & I will try & write her next time but I am so busy now discharging cargo that I can hardly get time to write you. as we have to watch the niggers in the lighters or they would steal the cargo. there is another vessel to leave here next week. then I shall write you again & tell mother I write her. in the mean time I am in hopes to get another letter from you. give my love to all of the folks & tell Martha she must excuse me for not writing her. & now Dear Em I must close as I have got to go on shore to see to the lighter.

> Yours truly
> Joseph.

Brewster Oct 1st [1861]

My Own Dear Husband,

I am writing you this letter with only a very faint hope of your getting it but there may be a chance to send it & I do not want you to be without letters again as you were before when you were there alone. You have only been from home a little more than two weeks and it seems to me to have been *at least* two months. I miss you and *long* for you evry day and about evry hour, I am *so lonely* Yes Joseph, if I am in a crowd yet I am *alone* when you are not with me is it not the same with you? but I know it is. How much I would like to be on board of the good bark called *the Wyman* this eve and see what you are all doing. I wonder where your thoughts are or if they have flew over the waters towards Cape Cod anwhere today. I dreamed of you last night but there was not much satisfaction in that for when I awoke I was just as much alone as when I went to sleep. I have been very well since you left home My Back troubles me sometimes but nothing *serious* & I have not grown *poor any* and hope I shall not at *present*. I am as busy as a Bee sewing making all the *little things* so as to have time to make you up a good lot of new shirts and have them ready for you when you get back. All the others are well. . . . I was down to Mother Thacher's and spent the day one day last week. they were all well Lucinda is real smart now, Uncle Benjamin had just finished the work down there and it looks firstrate he seemed to be very well was going to shingle Uncle Obed Snow's house this week he and Mr Watson Crocker, Mother says it was your Gin that cured him, and he wanted I should ask you if you could get him a gallon. I dont think you had better bring too much to people or you will get your name, but I am willing you should bring it to your own *folks*. Now I must try and think of some news to tell you, first comes the war. nothing very important has taken place since you went away. Washington is not in the hands of the rebels yet and they have not made any movement to try and get it as I can hear of. I saw by the papers a few days ago that the Sumpter left Surinam the first of Sept having been supplied with coal by Mr Hugh Wright an English planter. I suppose the same Mr Wright as used to come into Mr Mens. Well! if I was you American Captains I would have nothing to say to him I know. but should turn the cold shoulder to him whenever I met him, but he is a man of not much principles any way in my humble opinion, and if the old Sumpter is only out of your way I shall be very glad *that* is *all,* I can imagine Mrs Mens will give Mr Wright a few words *I should like to* but I suppose it would do no good, *so much for that*. . . . There was a man committed suicide here two weeks ago. Mr Freeman Dillingham you probably knew him. they do not know what caused it but he was probably insane. Old Mrs. Joseph Crocker is also dead I believe that is all since you left. there has been no weddings that I know of and but One birth, that is Capt Bela Berry's wife has a little girl, Capt Berry got home Saturday noon, & in the afternoon they rode down to her fathers and the next morning she got up and got their breakfast and before the folks went to meeting they went in to see her and her *babe*. What do you think of that I dont believe Capt Joseph Lincolns wife can beat that do you? . . . Brewster is quite lonely now no company and no going to the ponds or shore, but if there were ever so many parties going I should not want to go now as I have no one now to go with that I care about. I received that money that you sent by Henry Sears all right paid Mother hers, but have not paid Capt Foster the $25 dollars yet but shall in two or three weeks. Martha was going to Boston to buy her some Cambric[s] Cotton silks & c & c, and wanted conciderable money and Father could not spare her any then he has laid out so much on his shop this summer, so I let her have that money you sent for Capt Foster and shall have it again very soon when I shall immediately pay it over to him so that he need not suffer for the want of it. I do not need it I have enough without it and I shall be very glad to have *so much* of *that* debt paid off. . . . I believe I have written you all the news at any rate I have written you all I can think of and I do hope you will get it, and I hope I shall get some letters from you, some of your *lengthy* ones, but I will find no fault and I know you do not have so much to write about as I do. I hope you will not be gone over three months, and that will seem to me a very long time. I am so glad you do not go any longer voyages. I do know what I should do, but I suppose I should have to bear it as other women do. Be careful of yourself and dont get sick remember there is one at home watching for you and praying for your safe return. Now I think I must draw this letter to a close, but I hate to say good bye for writing to you seems a little like talking but I have about filled two sheets, and shall write again in a few days I think, So now Good bye my own dear Joseph, I hope it will not be very long before we meet again,

Ever yours with love
Your wife Em

New Orleans, Aug. 22cd 1870

My Dear Wife

   Your letter dated Brewster 14th received this day. and you can rest assured that I was much pleased to get it. for it was 14 days since I received your last. think you must have wrote me before, but it has not come to hand, but am much pleased to hear that you and baby are well also the other friends. should think by your writing that Susie and the young folks were having a good time, but think she might write me a few lines, if she is not too much taken up with work. Mr Lothrop got a line from John Baker this day saying that he was having a good time and hoped that the Bark did not run away with me, think that I am able to take care of my own vessel. How I wish you could have got Josie* picture should have been so elevated this day that no one could have touched me with a ten foot pole. I was disappointed for I was looking for it as much as I was a letter from you, but hope that you will both be spared, so that I will meet you again. think that I shall have double pleasure in meeting you dear Em. and my darling boy. take good care of him and dont hang him up on a nail unless he is very bad, for I long to see him and think I shall be a proud man if I can meet you both in good health. . . . When I shall leave here is more then I can tell as we are hung up now, but there is one thing certain she is got to

---

*Joseph C. Lincoln, the popular Cape Cod author, was born February 13, 1870.

leave here by Saturday night fill up with something. will write again before sailing with much love to Martha Susie & the Mothers
I close, Your loving Husband   J Lincoln

William Roach & Co.,
Charleston, S.C.   Dec 19th 1870

Mr J. Henry Sears
        I am busy tonight-laying out the body of Capt. Lincoln. Mr Roach has told me that he has written you today how we are getting along in loading, so I will confine myself to the particulars of Capt Lincolns sickness. He was taken with a violent headache yesterday morning, about day light, and at noon was taken with violent racking pains in the bowels. At three o'clock I went for a physician, and at six o'clock he seemed easier, At eight he was again attacked with spasms, called the physician who did all he could for his relief but did not help him much, He wished to consult with other physicians, I therefore called two more, of the best within my knowledge, They did everything that laid in there power, to procure an action, but did not succeed. This morning the[y] used there last redouce; Quicksilver, but were unsuccessful H[e] was suffering much less pain all day, and passed away at five and a half o'clock this eve. He had his senses to the last, but seemed hardly concious that he was so soon to go. He had a minister with him about an hour before he died, and wished his wife to be told that he died happy.

                              Your Obt Svt.
                              A. D. Lothrop Jr.
                              Mate Bark Aurelia.

———

" 'Tis Men's Lives"

By Josef Berger (Jeremiah Digges)

IN PROVINCETOWN, THREE miles across the sands of the "Province Land," the name of Helltown is still mentioned now and then; but local colorists have splashed it with nickel-magazine romance. Dirty doings, as hinted by the name, were the principal business of Helltown, one hears now. Beachcombing, a word which on Cape Cod can mean anything from scientific research to grand larceny, went the limit there; and men lived by wrecking, and mooncussing, and no one knows what else.

There is plenty of reason to suspect that on Cape Cod all these things have happened, in one spot and another alongshore; but Helltown itself had business of a wholly different sort. The twenty-odd little huts that squatted there, half a century ago, were simply winter quarters for Portuguese fishermen of Provincetown, men who had their homes and families in the village, who went to the banks on trawling schooners through the summer and fall, and who came out here to Helltown just after Christmas each year, to live in the shacks until the April following. By that time the schooners again were fitted out to go to the banks.

The men bunked eight or ten to a shack. They called it Helltown because it was just plain hell to live there; they lived there because from that beach they could sail their dories to the winter fishing grounds off Race Point early each morning and get back by night; and they fished in the winter because what was left of the $300 to $600 which they had earned on the schooners earlier in the year would not carry a big family through four idle months.

All New England fishing ports of that day had their Helltowns, or their men who had to work at the Helltowners' hazardous calling until the banks season began. Boats and gear came high, but life was cheap enough in Helltown; and gale, ice, and fog drove many a one-sided bargain. Maggie's eloquent retort to Monkbarns—"It's no fish ye're buying; it's men's lives"—held good on both sides of the Atlantic.

Yarns of the smugglers, the wreckers, the pirates of a place like Helltown are easy to listen to—and easy to spin. The tale of sacrifice, hardship, and death in the everyday fight for bread is elusive, and often left untold.

Minha maçã vermelhinha,
Picada do rouxinol . . .

Above the yaw and seethe of the surf outside, Senhor Miguel Bicho-Couve (Mike Cabbage-Bug) twangs at the six brass strings of his *guitarra* and lifts his baritone plaint:

My little apple of rosy hue,
The nightingale has sampled you . . .

The cigarette smoke rises, hovers above the "ram-cat" stove, and all at once vanishes into dark corners when a gust comes slapping through the east wall. Balancing on a keg-buoy near the stove, old 'Bastiao Dente-Ouro (Sebastian Gold-Tooth) is overhauling his gear. With skein of new gangin's draped on his shoulder and hook setter in hand, he goes over the coiled trawl round by round and, as he does so, sways on his keg to Mike Cabbage-Bug's lament over the state of his rosy little apple:

Quem te picou que te coma
Que te picou no melhor!

Let him who pecks devour you too,
For he has taken the best of you!

Captain Domingos Sou'west snores on a pallet of old sailcloth under the window, and draws his peacoat up closer under his chin. Captain Sou'west has turned in early, and has curtly ordered his sixteen-year-old son, Man'el, to do the same. With the market offering no better than $2 a hundredweight for day-old cod, a man has got to turn in early!

Figure it out for yourself. There is 50 cents a barrel haulage to be paid to the fellows who take your fish in their dumpcarts the three miles across the dunes to the depot. There's 25 cents for the sugar barrel in which they pack your fish, and which holds two hundred pounds. There's 10 cents for heading, 10 cents for ice; and the bait you need to catch a barrel of fish stands you an average of 70 cents. Well, there's $1.65 gone, before your fish is on the train! Add a dollar for freight, and you see what you've got for yourself at $2 the hundredweight—$4 less the $2.65 it costs you, or $1.35 for yourself. And if you can catch an average fare of three barrels a day, week in and week out, you're a damn big fisherman!

The lad Man'el turned in when his father told him to. All Sou'west's kids do as he commands. But now that the captain has settled down to

a log a good steady run—dreaming, most likely, of four-cent cod—
Man'el has taken up his perch by the stove again, to listen to the
singing.

Dark-eyed, round-faced, Man'el is spoken of by the men of Helltown
as "a fine boy when he wants to be." His father, gruff as a steam tug,
has been making a real fisherman out of Man'el, ever since he lost his
older boy at sea. But that Man'el, he still likes to play tricks, like painting black monkey-faces on a man's brand-new yellow sou'wester, or
slipping a live lobster under a man's blanket and leaving it there. Most
of the tricks he plays on the old man himself, though; and, so long as
he does that, the men of Helltown continue to speak of him as "a fine
boy when he wants to be."

Ah, but if you want to hear all about Man'el, go listen to his mother!
Then you'll hear something! You'll think he's a saint. And the old man—
well, the old man is really just as bad when Man'el isn't on deck to hear
him. At that, you have to admit it isn't every kid his age who's willing
to spend a winter at Helltown. Some you couldn't hold if you made
'em fast to a killick! But Man'el came out with his *Pai* the day after
Christmas, and a week's already gone by, and he isn't saying a word
about going back.

"Mike, sing the one about the light again," Man'el says, as he pours
himself a mug-up from the tall copper pot which is always kept on the
stove. "You know, the one you sang last night."

"Light? Ah!" Mike Cabbage-Bug grins and nods and winks at the
others. "You like thees song, eh? But you don't tell me for play thees
song while *Pai* is up—no?" And Mike laughs and sings:

> *Candeia que não da luz*
> *Não se espeta na parede . . .*

> Candle which gives no light
> Never is hung from the wall . . .

As he strums the intervening chords, Mike goes through a couple of
steps of the old *chamarita* and pauses to give Man'el a pat on the head.

> *O amor que não e firme*
> *Não se faz mais caso d'elle.*

> The love which is not passionate
> Never is noticed at all.

164

Through many stanzas, the song goes on. But not until Mike Cabbage-Bug has sung his last, and with a weary, "Ai, ai, ai!" has stowed his guitar safely behind a small forest of oars, masts, and gobsticks, does Man'el turn in for the night.

Tonight, out there in the sea, there is what fishermen call an "easterly rote"—uneven breaking and tumbling and backwashing, which trained old ears along the water front do not like to hear at night. But the ears of Man'el Sou'west are young, and in that broken whisper of the sea, that makes other men of Helltown fidget and roll even in their sleep, for Man'el there is only the laughing of Mike Cabbage-Bug, and the insistence of a stubborn little tune:

O amor que não e firme . . .

The night of the 2nd and the morning of the 3rd [of January, 1878] were terrible for those unlucky mariners who found themselves in a snow-storm, being driven on the treacherous sands of Cape Cod. Five vessels were lost. From the largest two not a soul was saved; every man, from the captains down to the deck boys, was buried beneath the cold waters. A few bodies were recovered, but the majority sleep in watery graves.
—*Fishermen's Own Book,* Gloucester, 1882.

"All right, boy?"
Steering with one hand, Captain Sou'west holds the mainsheet of his careening little craft with the other, ready to let go the instant she heels too far. Close-reefed mainsail and storm jib are all the dory can carry, the way it's come up to blow this afternoon. Off the Race, and with home a twelve-mile beat dead to windward, this little boat has a piece of work cut out for her! Spray hurls itself clear over the slender gaff, white water buries the "washboard" and comes in sheets across the weather rail. Ice gathers out of nowhere to drape rigging, sails, and the men themselves, ice that is like a death-sheet being spun for them by slow, invisible hands.

"All right, boy?"
Tack by tack, Sou'west thrashes her into it, makes her fight for her life. Sou'west knows the way home; but before a sign of home is given, before there is a hint of winning or losing, the snow ends all signs. Gale and the wicked tide of the Race—and now the snow.

"All right, boy?"
Man'el doesn't answer, but Man'el is all right. Under his oilskins, his clothes are drenched. Even with the work, he is chilled to the bone. But so is the Captain, and Man'el knows that. The old man thinks his

monotonous query is making Man'el feel that *he* is all right; but Man'el can see *Pai's* frozen hands.

So Man'el works on, and doesn't stop to answer now. With the bailer he works unceasingly, except when the boat goes in stays. Then he has to tend the jib sheets and jump back to the thwarts to shift the ballast bags to the other side. A man has to work fast, trimming ballast on one of these craft. The bags of sand are carried on the thwarts, not on the bottom where they ought to be, and they must be shifted at the exact moment of heading the gale; otherwise, over she goes—*zit!*—like that.

Through the dusk, Sou'west keeps her bowling along, and remembers every now and then that he must also keep offering some word of encouragement to the boy.

"I think we make it in a few more hours, boy, we keep up this way." And Man'el, his arms aching, fingers numb, looks at the old man and wonders if perhaps, after all, there is something more in the words than well-meaning show. For the old man does know these waters. He knows where he is with his eyes closed. And then Man'el looks at those hands again—and marvels at him.

With the hours, the wind rises, then abates a little and begins to look as if it might be blowing itself out, only to come back fiercer than ever. It is from one of these spells of easement, long after nightfall, while Man'el is chipping ice from the rigging, that the worst of it comes. Suddenly Sou'west calls Man'el to the tiller. Then, working frantically, using his wrists and his teeth when the blued, stiffened fingers fail him, he tries to get the mainsail in. But before he can manage it, a great sea bears down on the dory and "falls her off" in spite of all Man'el can do.

Into the trough go boat and crew, while the weight of unnumbered tons rolls over to snap a stick, sweep away a bit of rag, and swamp the pitiful little shell that was built for sea.

And yet, rocking sluggishly now down the long after-slope, it is not finished, this shell. Bottom-up, it is still something to cling to, still a hollowed hull that can be righted, bailed out, handled somehow, and yes, ridden at sea! Sou'west, his arms over the gunwale, hangs on and gasps and tries to get the water out of his eyes. Slowly, timing his movements with the rolling of the hull, he works himself back into the dory.

There is darkness, there is heaving water, there is the silent slant of snow—only these to hear the cry of Captain Sou'west:

"Man'el! Man'el!"

—from *In Great Waters* (1941)

"The Fish-Wife"

By Cynthia Huntington

I'll take a bath when it snows,
when I can look out the window up high
and see the sky all pale
and blank like a fish's eye.
And I know the boats won't go out tonight,
the fishermen drinking whiskey, locked
in a bar-dream, the music rocking them deeper.

It doesn't snow enough here,
though some would say otherwise,
fearing accidents. But the paper boy, skidding
uphill on his bike in light snow, knows better,
making S-tracks when his wheels slide sideways.

We really needed this snow, the old men will say,
putting to bed the surface roots of trees,
putting to bed the too-travelled streets.

When everything is covered
the earth has a light of its own;
the snow falls down from the moon
as everyone knows, and brings that light
back to us. I needed this light.

All day I kept by the window, watching the sky,
a prisoner in my clothes, the wind felt dry
and mean. Starlings stalked the yard with evil eyes
—I hated them, and hated, too, my neighbor's house
where sparks from the chimney fell back in a stinking
cloud—black ashes bringing no blessing.

When the roads are covered,
when the water is black and snow falls
into the waves, the birds' hunger swirls

the air, dark lovely shapes. All hungers
are equal now. I'll give them bread and seeds.

I have no money; the whiskey is gone,
and I must bathe in water. Fishermen, please
do not go out in your flimsy boats tonight
to chase after the cod and mackerel,
to hook the giant eels. Go safe,
go free. Let your feet leave trails
through streets and yards, wandering
home, your crooked voyages to bed.

The Wreck of the *Wadena*

By Henry C. Kittredge

IF LIFE-SAVERS COULD count on intelligent cooperation from the crews of stranded vessels, a large part of the danger of their calling would be eliminated. So expert are they in handling their surfboats in all weathers, and so perfect is their discipline, that hardly a man of them need be lost even in the worst storms, if those whom they are trying to rescue keep their heads and obey orders. But too often they do neither. The Monomoy disaster of 1902 is a terrible instance of this sort. Like so many other tragedies, it involved no more impressive a vessel than the stump-masted coal barge, *Wadena,* which struck on Shovelful Shoal, south of Monomoy Station, on March 11 in a heavy northeaster. Captain Eldredge and his men of the Monomoy Station brought the crew ashore and supposed that the incident was closed. The barge lay intact during the next few days, giving Boston wreckers a fine chance to salvage the coal.

At the same time that the *Wadena* struck, another barge, the *Fitzpatrick,* stranded not far from her, and two Chatham wreckers, Captain Elmer Mayo and Captain Mallows, were engaged by the owners to float her. They planned to begin work on the morning of the 17th, and accordingly spent the night before on board, after making the final arrangements with her captain. Toward evening it breezed up from the southeast, but Eldredge and his men at the station felt no anxiety, because they supposed that a tug which the wreckers were using had brought all hands ashore from the *Wadena*. What was their surprise, the next morning, to see a distress signal flying from the barge's rigging. Their surprise was mingled with concern, for the wind had increased during the night until it blew a gale which turned the water around the *Wadena* into a chaos of breakers.

Immediately Captain Eldredge, who had walked down to the end of Monomoy Point to look the situation over, telephoned back to the station for the lifeboat. When she arrived, he jumped aboard, and the crew, shipping a little water on the way, pulled off through the breakers to comparative shelter under the high leeward side of the *Wadena* and made fast. They found that five men had been left on board, all of whom had lost their nerve and were clamoring to be taken ashore. Worse still, they were in no sense of the word sailors, as appeared when their captain let go his hold of the rope by which he was lowering himself into the lifeboat and fell crashing aboard to the accompaniment of a smashed thwart.

Eldredge, ordering the five men to lie down in the bottom of the boat, braced himself for the return trip, and his crew shot the boat out from under the lee as he leaned against his long steering oar to head the craft into the seas. It was a beautiful piece of boatmanship; some water came aboard, but not enough to be dangerous. As soon as the trembling cargo in the bottom of the boat saw the top of the wave slop in over the side, however, they gave themselves up for lost, jumped to their feet, and seized the man at the oars around the neck—doubtless for the same reason that a drowning man winds himself around his rescuer.

In a second the boat was bottom up, with all hands in the water. Even now the Monomoy crew were calm. Twice they righted her, only to have waves capsize her before they could pull themselves on board. They had no strength for a third attempt, but clung to the bottom, determined to hang on till the last gasp. One by one, benumbed and battered, they let go and vanished, until the only man of that crew left was Seth Ellis, number one surfman of the station. Finding himself alone, he managed to wrap one arm around the centerboard which had floated up and protruded like a shark's fin from the bottom of the boat.

Up to this point the whole disaster had been shrouded in fog. Mayo and Mallows on board the *Fitzpatrick* had not even seen the crew put off to the other barge. But at this moment a hole was blown in the mist and revealed to the Chatham men on the *Fitzpatrick* the white bottom of a lifeboat with a single black figure sprawled across it. Deaf to the protests of Mallows and the Captain of the barge, Mayo in an instant had stripped to his underclothes, got a twelve-and-a-half foot dory over the side, seized a pair of clumsy oars which he cut down to somewhere near the right size, and was pulling toward Ellis and the lifeboat.

For any man who had not spent his life alongshore, as Mayo had, the attempt would have been suicide. But Mayo had been cradled in dories, spent his youth as fisherman, anchor-dragger and wrecker, and had substituted from time to time at various life-saving stations on the Cape. Now, at the age of forty, he knew all that a man can know about dories and the Monomoy Shoals. He knew that the boat which carried him was a poor specimen of her class; but even an indifferent dory is a remarkable sea-boat when handled by an expert, and that is how this one was handled. Yard by yard he pulled her to the side of the lifeboat, where the most ticklish part of the exploit awaited him. If Ellis had been another *Wadena* wrecker, both men would have perished. But numb and exhausted as he was, Ellis made not a single false move while Mayo helped him into the bottom of the dory. Then he headed for shore, came through the surf with the help of the shore detail of one, whom Captain Eldredge had left there, and assisted Ellis to the station. Six weeks later, Ellis who was soon as well as ever, became keeper of it. Mayo was given one medal by the Humane Society and another by the United States Government.

—from *Cape Cod, Its People and Their History* (1930)

———

The Fate of Elmer Mayo

By Henry C. Kittredge

MAYO EMERGED FROM the tragedy [described in the previous selection], furthermore, with a new schooner, the *Gleaner,* in which, as we have seen, he went wrecking and anchor-dragging, with the ups and downs of fortune attendant on the business. He took a flier in the Klondike during the gold rush, tried deep-sea codfishing out of Seattle, and afterward had charge of a string of fish traps in the South, whence he drifted back to Chatham to end his days, as helpless a hulk as any that he had ever helped to lighten of her cargo, his memory failing, his muscles useless, and an old tennis ball held feebly in his fingers in a vain attempt to keep them limber. Here he died in the summer of 1935. *Sic transit . . .*

—from *Mooncussers of Cape Cod*
(1937)

———

The Wreck of the *Montclair*

By Henry Beston

THERE HAS JUST been a great wreck, the fifth this winter and the worst. On Monday morning last, shortly after five o'clock, the big three-masted schooner *Montclair* stranded at Orleans and went to pieces in an hour, drowning five of her crew.

It had blown hard all Sunday night, building up enormous seas. Monday's dawn, however, was not stormy, only wintry and grey. The *Montclair,* on her way from Halifax to New York, had had a hard passage, and sunrise found her off Orleans with her rigging iced up and her crew dog-weary. Helpless and unmanageable, she swung inshore and presently struck far out and began to break up. Lifted, rocked, and pounded by the morning's mountainous seas, her masts were seen to quiver at each crash, and presently her foremast and her mainmast worked free, and, scissoring grotesquely back and forth across each other, split the forward two thirds of the vessel lengthwise—"levered the ship open," as Russell Taylor of Nauset said. The vessel burst, the two forward masses of the ship drifted inshore and apart, a cargo of new laths poured into the seas from the broken belly of the hold. Seven men clung to the rocking, drifting mass that was once the stern.

It was a singular fragment, for the vessel had broken as neatly crosswise as it had lengthwise, and the seas were washing in below deck as into an open barrel. Dragging over the shoal ground, the mass rocked on its keel, now rolling the men sickeningly high, now tumbling them down into the trampling rush of the seas. The fall of the two forward masts had snapped off the mizzen some twenty-five feet above the deck, and from the stump cracked-out slivers swung free with the rolling. Bruised, wet through, and chilled to the bone, the unfortunate men dared not lash themselves down, for they had to be free to climb the tilted deck when the ship careened.

Five clung to the skylight of the after deckhouse, two to the stern-rail balustrade. Laths filled the sea, poured over the men, and formed a jagged and fantastic wall along the beach.

One great sea drowned all the five. Men on the beach saw it coming and shouted, the men on the deckhouse shouted and were heard, and then the wave broke, hiding the tragic fragment in a sluice of foam and wreckage. When this had poured away, the men on the afterhouse were gone. A head was visible for a minute, and then another drifting southward, and then there was nothing but sea.

Two men still clung to the balustrade, one a seventeen-year-old boy, the other a stocky, husky-built sailor. The wave tore the boy from the balustrade, but the stocky man reached out, caught him, and held on. The tide rising, the stern began to approach the beach. A detail of men hurriedly sent over from Nauset Station now appeared on the beach and managed to reach and rescue the survivors. The *Montclair* had chanced to strand near a station classed as "inactive"—coast guard stations are discontinued if there is not enough work to justify their maintenance— and the two or three men who garrisoned the station could do little but summon instant aid. Men came from Nauset, circling the Eastham lagoon and Orleans cove in local automobiles, but the whole primitive tragedy was over in a moment of time.

As the vessel was breaking up, men came to the beach and helped themselves to the laths and what wreckage they fancied. Later on, there was a kind of an auction of the salvaged material. The other day I saw half-a-dozen bundles of the *Montclair*'s laths piled up near a barn.

A week after the wreck, a man walking the Orleans shore came to a lonely place, and there he saw ahead of him a hand thrust up out of the great sands. Beneath he found the buried body of one of the *Monclair*'s crew.

I can see the broken mast of the schooner from the deck of the Fo'castle. Sunday last, I walked over to the ship. The space under the after deckhouse from which the men were swept—officers' quarters, I imagine— is an indescribable flung mass of laths, torn wood, wrecked panelling, sopped blankets, and sailor's clothing. I remember the poor, stringy, cheap ties. In the midst of the débris a stain of soppy pink paper caught my eye: it was a booklet, "If You Were Born in February." I have often seen the set of twelve on newsstands. The scarlet cover of this copy had seeped into the musty pages. "Those who are born in this month," I read, "have a particular affection for home"; and again, "They will go through fire and water for their loved ones."

Who brought this thing aboard? one wonders. Whose curious hands first opened it in the lamplight of this tragic and disordered space? The seventeen-year-old boy is dead of the shock and exposure; the stocky, husky-built man, the only survivor, is going on with the sea. "He says it's all he knows," said a coast guardsman.

The wreck lies on the edge of the surf and trembles when the incoming seas strike its counter and burst there with a great upflinging of heavy spray.

—from *The Outermost House* (1928)

———

Stripping the *Montclair*

By Henry C. Kittredge

As soon as word reached town that a wreck was ashore, a migration started for the beach, Albert E. Snow among them. Knowing that there might be something to bring home, he took his Ford beach wagon and picked up a friend or two on the way, one of them an artist who has made Orleans his headquarters for a number of years. Having crossed the wooden bridge over Pochet Inlet, which brought them to the inside edge of the long, narrow barrier of beach hills which alone separated them from the sea, Snow turned right and, keeping this barrier beach still between them and the sea, followed the precarious route between the marsh on the one hand and the dunes on the other, trusting that the mud and the sand were both frozen hard enough to bear them. They left the car a little way beyond the lifesaving station and walked over to the beach. There lay the *Montclair* high enough to walk out to with hip rubber boots, the two halves of her hull a hundred yards or so apart, and, piled everywhere up and down the coast in chaotic confusion, millions of laths. Snow had his rubber boots, but the artist had come away without any; they therefore agreed that Snow should wade out to the wreck, collect what was to be had, and throw it ashore, where the artist should mount guard over it until they had a load for the beach wagon.

Snow climbed on board, where he found himself in the company of the best people in Orleans, twenty-five or thirty of them, young and old, who had come over to make a Roman holiday of it. The constable and his partner, who were house painters, were on hand, collecting enough running rigging for use in their business to last them the rest of their lives. Others were stripping her spars preparatory to towing them round to Orleans as underpinning for floats. One man was at work removing the wheel; two others got the compass and most of the signal flags; the bell was carried out of town somehow, and so was the binnacle. At the rate at which things were vanishing, Snow saw that unless he jumped in with considerable vigor he would have had his trip for nothing.

First he pried off one of the quarterboards with a sheath knife and, tossing it down to his friend on the beach, started for the other one, but someone had got it before him. As there was nothing else that particularly attracted him on deck, he made his way into the cabin, where a jovial group were making free with the stores, especially tea, ham, and condensed milk; almost everyone he saw had a five-ound ham under his arm. Snow soon had one too, as well as a set of four or five deep drawers and half a dozen cabin doors. These, too, along with the ham, went over the side to the waiting artist, and Snow returned to the cabin to emerge with a fine grating and, better still, the Captain's chart, showing the Montclair's course as straight as an arrow from Nova Scotia to the edge of the Handkerchief Shoal; the rest was silence.

Meantime lively doings had been going on outside the wreck. The artist found his duties as guardian of the goods a bit irksome, and, true to his trade, had drifted off somewhere to observe events from a new angle. He returned to his post to find that Snow's quarterboard—the prize item in the swag—had vanished. Well, that's the way it is; things are no safer on a beach, it seems, than they are when nailed to a wreck; yet mooncusser and hijacker are both honest men except on occasions like this. Being an enterprising young man, Snow rustled around and recaptured his quarterboard from the friend who had taken it, with no hard feelings on either side. You may take a quarterboard from a pile of goods which a man has just thrown from a wreck, but if you pry it off his barn you will go to jail.

No bad blood was caused, either, over another piece of sharp practice between citizen and citizen as they stood beside the wreck of the Montclair. One of them, pausing for a breather, was leaning against a big pile of laths, still neatly tied in bundles, that somebody had collected.

'That's a good-looking lot of laths you've got,' remarked a passerby to the man who was resting against them. 'What'll you take for them?'

The beach sharpens men's wits while it dulls their scruples.

'Five dollars,' he replied.

'You sold some laths,' said the other, and handed over a five-dollar bill.

The tired man put it in his pocket and sauntered off, leaving the purchaser of the laths to come to such terms with the man who collected them as their natures might dictate.

Snow and the artist loaded their trophies on the beach wagon, together with some goods that they were transporting for neighbors, and started back along the marshy route by which they had come. Halfway to the bridge they met another car, in which, as they soon discovered, was an angry man named Finnegan, a prohibition agent of some sort from Boston, who, as soon as he heard of the wreck, had started for Orleans to see how much truth there was in the rumor that she smelled of rum. Seeing the beach wagon loaded with stuff obviously from the wreck, he stopped his car and jumped out.

'Halt!' he cried. 'Stop! That's piracy! That's plain robbery! Take all that property back to the ship!'

Snow explained that they were not robbers, but that their names appeared well up in the Orleans social register; everybody knew them and liked them, he continued, and as for turning round and taking these few souvenirs back to the wreck, it was out of the question; no car had ever turned round on that marsh without getting bogged. Let Mr. Finnegan drop round to the house on his return from the beach, and if he thought that they had behaved improperly, he could then at his leisure particularize; with which urbane remarks Snow went his way, nor has he seen Mr. Finnegan since.

—from *Mooncussers of Cape Cod*
(1937)

———

The *S-4* Tragedy

By Josef Berger (Jeremiah Digges)

OFF WOOD END the submarine *S-4* was rammed and sunk on the afternoon of December 17, 1927, taking the lives of forty men.

Provincetown, long hardened to wrecks, now witnessed horror such as she had never known before. Slow suffocation within steel walls, 110 feet below the surface, went on for four days, while divers struggled to save the men with whom they could exchange messages by tapping in international code.

On the day of the accident, the Coast Guard destroyer *Paulding* had come across-Bay from Boston to comb the vicinity for rum runners. Through lack of coordination between the two branches of service, she was unaware that the submarine was at that time undergoing submerged trials in the deepwater course outside Provincetown Harbor. At the same time, storm warnings were flying, the wind was northwest—the worst possible weather for that particular stretch—and white water was already making over the submarine's projected course.

The *Paulding,* finding no rum-running craft in the outside waters, rounded Race Point and headed for the harbor, steaming straight into the submarine's testing-ground. Meanwhile the *S-4* had been put through several dives, and at the moment was proceeding with only a few feet of her periscopes showing. A heavy sea was running, but the periscopes would have been clearly visible to any alert observer aboard the destroyer. They had been seen and recognized from ashore by Lookout Frank Simonds of the Wood End Coast Guard Station. Boatswain Gracie, coming up to the observation room, asked Simonds what he had seen offshore. The lookout said, "Not much. But there was a submarine on the test run not long ago." Gracie anxiously took the telescope. Near the end of the measured mile he caught the little foaming wake of periscopes. "Good God, there's going to be a collision!" And he ran down to get his lifeboat ready for launching.

The *S-4* was just slanting to emerge, and her conning tower was half out of water when the speeding destroyer struck. She smashed her stem into the battery room of the submarine, just forward of the conning tower, on the starboard side. The hole was only about a foot across, but the impact and the leak it caused were enough to send the steel shell reeling to the bottom.

That the *Paulding* had been unaware of the *S-4*'s presence in those waters is clear from the radio message she sent out:

RAMMED AND SUNK UNKNOWN SUBMARINE OFF WOOD END PROVINCETOWN

From New London sailed the *Falcon,* the Navy's only salvage ship in the Atlantic, and from Newport came Divers Eadie, Carr and Michels. From Portsmouth came the mother-ship, *Bushnell*. From New York were sent pontoons—in tow of hopelessly slow tugs.

The collision occurred at 3:37 o'clock on a Saturday afternoon. The *Falcon* did not arrive on the scene until 7 the next morning. Meanwhile Boatswain Gracie of the Wood End Coast Guard Station, venturing out in his surfboat, spent twelve harrowing hours in a big sea, whipped by the icy nor'wester. He had found the submarine with his grapnel— and lost her again—before the *Falcon* arrived! Trying it once more, he struck at 10:45 o'clock Sunday morning, and about three hours later Diver Tom Eadie went down the grappling line.

Coming down with lead shoes on the steel hull, Eadie caught an answering signal from within. Forward, from the torpedo room, it came to him unmistakably—six taps—six men still alive! Aft, there came no answer.

The *S-4*'s conning tower was equipped with two emergency connections to the outside, one for an air line reaching crew compartments, the other for a line to the ballast tanks. It was now up to the rescue operators to decide which of these connections to make, for the divers could only take one line down at a time.

When Eadie came up, Diver Carr went down with an air line. He did as he had been instructed: instead of coupling it to the *S-4*'s crew compartment connection, which would have enabled the surviving men to breathe, he attached it to a connection designed to blow ballasts, with the object of raising the submarine herself. But two compartments were flooded and the ballast system was broken; and the result was that instead of lifting the *S-4,* the pumps at the surface were merely blowing air into the Atlantic Ocean through her punctured lungs.

Upon discovering that they had guessed wrong, the officers ordered Diver Michels down, to make the other connection. But now the sea was so great that diving itself looked like suicide. Michels went anyhow, became fouled in some wreckage, had to be rescued by Eadie, and was brought up three hours later in a serious condition. At this stage all vessels but the *Falcon* ran into Provincetown Harbor for shelter from the gale.

The prostrated diver was kept in the *Falcon*'s recompression tank. Monday morning the *Falcon* left the scene, going all the way to Boston to put Michels in a hospital. It was explained by those in charge that further diving would be impossible until the storm abated. When the salvage ship returned, diving was still out of the question.

Meanwhile communication with the imprisoned men had been continued by Morse signals sent on an oscillator. On Sunday evening the *Falcon* sent down the query:

"How many are there?"

"There are six." And the taps from below added, "Please hurry."

The next night the *Falcon* relayed a message to Lieutenant Fitch, in the submarine:

"Your wife and mother constantly praying for you."

No answer came, and through the night the message was repeated. Still there was no answer. Then, on Tuesday morning, from the sunken ship at last came a message:

"We understand."

After that, the six suffocating men sent no more messages.

On Wednesday morning, when the storm had abated and diving was possible again, the *Falcon* discovered that her single manila buoyline had parted. The submarine was lost again! Another grapnel was put down for her. While it was being dragged back and forth, the fishermen offered to help. They said they could line up their flounder draggers, moving abreast with their wide dredges dragging astern, and save time locating the wreck. The suggestion, though seemingly practical, was refused. And those last precious hours, when there might still have been some slight chance for the men below, were lost while the single grappling-iron went back and forth, back and forth, groping for the *S-4*.

That afternoon a line finally was made fast, divers went down, and the air line was attached to the crew compartment connection.

Then fresh air was pumped into the forward compartment—where lay six lifeless bodies.

When the Navy Department was informed that all on the *S-4* were dead, it decided to leave the submarine on the bottom until the spring. But "public opinion demanded a continuance of the salvage efforts," and so, work was resumed. The bodies were taken out, and three months later the ship was raised and towed to Charlestown Navy Yard.

The court of inquiry placed the blame on commanders of both the colliding craft, and also on Rear Admiral Frank H. Brumby, in charge of the "rescue" operations. Secretary of the Navy Wilbur overrode the decision of the court as it applied to Brumby and to Lieutenant Commander John S. Baylis, captain of the *Paulding*. Thus upon the dead commander of the *S-4* officially rests the full responsibility.

Since the tragedy, the Navy, according to newspaper accounts, has perfected "many escape devices to insure against a repetition of such losses." When the *S-51* went down off Block Island in 1925, snuffing out 33 lives, much the same sort of thing was said. Two years later the horror was repeated. From 1927, the record is clear.

—from *Cape Cod Pilot* (1937)

———

Raymond Duarte, Provincetown Fisherman

By Alec Wilkinson

RAYMOND DUARTE, A fisherman: "I was born in Portugal, in Viana do Castelo, in the northern part of the country, in 1946. . . .

"My father came to Provincetown in 1948. Arthur Duarte, my great-uncle on my father's side, was fishing here, and he sent for my father. My father fished with him a season, then brought the whole family. I learned English in school. They put me in a classroom and I had to figure it out. I wasn't allowed to speak anything but Portuguese at home, and that made it awkward with my friends. In Portugal, my father had been a fisherman, using hand lines and gill nets mainly. Gill nets for herring and hand lines for octopus in the rocks off the shore. My mother would help tar the nets and stretch them out in the sun to dry. . . .

"I quit school to go fishing. I learned to splice wire, I learned to cook for five men, I learned about the engine room and how to change oil. I learned about the nets. After a while, I knew enough that if a man was sick I could take his place for the day. If the engineer was sick, I would go out as engineer. If it was the cook, I would be cook. Those were in the days when boats had five-man crews. Nowadays, the cook and the engineer have been eliminated. Used to be there were so many fish that the boats couldn't handle them. All the fish now are getting caught outside, way offshore, by big trip boats out of New Bedford that are gone ten and twelve days at a time. You could put a Provincetown boat on the deck of a New Bedford boat. My father was a hard, hard man for a teacher. Anybody but me could make a mistake. He's all the time tinkering with his nets. He likes to add twine to get the shape he wants, and they regularly need repair. It's incredible to see him, he works so fast. It's like a sewing machine to see his hands moving. I would be holding the twine while he was mending, and if I wasn't going fast enough he would whack me with the mending needle across my knuckles and say, 'Pay attention!' I would go home with my knuckles bleeding. I once fished with him thirty-eight days. Several times, day and night, just coming home to unload—eat, sleep, get up, and go right back out. After a few weeks, I said, 'Captain, I need a rest. When are we going to take a break?' 'When the prices drop, we'll take it easy.' Come near the end of the thirty-eight days, I say, 'Captain, the prices have dropped,' and he says, 'I know—now we need to catch twice as many.' Another time, the back of the pilothouse caught fire, so I went to him and said, 'Captain you know the back of the pilothouse is on fire,' and he said, 'We're only going to make one more tow.' I've worked with him in a hundred-and-ten-mile-an-hour breeze. The wind was off the land, and we went in close to the beach to anchor. We put out two anchors and they didn't hold, so he decided to let out the nets—if we couldn't anchor up, then we'd fish. The sand was blowing off the beach and it felt like nails. We had a helicopter from the Coast Guard come over the top of us and they opened up their door and held out a big sign and it said 'Hurricane,' clear as a bell you could read it, and my father said, 'What do they want?' and I said, 'They say it's a hurricane,' and he said, 'Well, I know that.' . . .

"The problem with fishing is that your life is not your own. You get up at three or four in the morning. You're constantly away from home. My first son I didn't even see grow up. My wife figured it out—one week, I was home twenty-four hours. The rest of the time you're forever waiting by the phone—you never know when you are going to get a call. My father called one time at Thanksgiving. If he got the weather report in the evening and they gave him bad weather for the next two or three days and he thought he could get the night out of it, he would go out and fish the night. The only thing that stopped him was Good Fridays. We would fish until Thursday midnight, and then the net would come out of the water. He was a fanatic about that. Add to that, when you have the responsibility of a boat you are never comfortable at home.

You can't rest. It's on your mind constantly. The harbormaster will call in the middle of the night and say you parted lines, or you're taking on water, and you have to race to the pier to correct it.

"When I first went fishing, I got seasick for two years. It got so bad sometimes that I wanted to jump overboard. 'This business is not cut out for you,' my father said, and I said, 'Yes, it is.' I hung on, and then one day he came down to the wharf and let the lines go and said, 'I'm not going fishing. You are.' He must have called about fifty times that day on the radio, checking up. One time, he called and said, 'Where are you?' and I said, 'Off Nauset,' and he said, 'How deep?' and I said, 'Twenty-seven fathoms,' and he said, 'You're in a bad, bad place.' I said, 'What do you mean?' He said, 'You got a wreck at twenty-five fathoms, you got one at twenty-six, you got one at twenty-seven, and one at twenty-nine.' So I rang the bells and raised everyone up on deck and hauled the nets and steamed the hell out of there. I fished the rest of the day outside of the wrecks and came in with about eleven thousand pounds of yellowtails and blackbeats, and he was tickled.

"Why I put up with the seasickness I don't really know. I just liked fishing, ever since I was in grade school. My mother always knew where to find me—down at the wharf, or at the trap sheds, where the trap fishermen kept their boats and their nets. I see three or four kids hanging around the pier now that are hooked. They can't stay away. They are going to be fishermen."

—from *Riverkeeper* (1991)

———

"Eastham"

By Douglas Carlson

THE NIGHT OF October 28, 1976, seven fishermen drowned when the scalloper *Patricia Marie* went down off Nauset Light Beach in Eastham. More than seven years ago, and I still remember the day before, the night, the day after. Even I, an outsider living 500 miles away, remember.

Because my wife wanted to photograph the beach in autumn and I wanted a long weekend, we joined friends at an Eastham cottage over-looking Nauset Marsh and the entrance to Town Cove. On Sunday when the *Patricia Marie* was scalloping near Pollack Rip several miles off Chatham, we were deciding that high tide would be right for catching some flounder in the cove; the low tide following, just before dinner, would provide the fresh mussels we needed to complete our meal.

The first time I rowed a boat on salt water years earlier, I made a mess of it. I grew up on fresh water, which did nothing to prepare me for the oarlocks I faced that afternoon on Cape Cod Bay as I struggled from one lobster pot to another. Without a pintle and socket, these oarlocks held sleeveless oars that twisted and slid crazily. I had never felt helpless on the water before or since until we fished for flounder in the narrows between Nauset Marsh and Town Cove. We embarked from the point formed by the juncture of the Orleans arm of the cove and Skiff Hill Channel. In about fifteen feet of water, we started catching flounder and continued to catch them as the tide turned. Gradually, I realized that we were moving out to sea; the tide pouring out of the cove had easily overpowered our anchor's hold in the sand.

There was no danger; at worst we could have made shore on Porchy Marsh, wet and embarrassed, and faced the annoying task of crossing Skiff Hill Channel, beaching the boat and walking back to the cottage. But as I rowed against the tide, the points on the shore stayed immobile; I wasn't losing way, but I wasn't making way either. My back and arms ached, but I smiled and joked for my sons while my imagination pulled us with the tide, past Snow Point, past Inlet Marsh and out into the open sea. There was no danger; yet that power was so great, unforgiving and indifferent. Whether I kept rowing or not—even if I quit and allowed the boat and my family to drift—the tide would go out, turn, come in again. The flounder would still bury themselves in the sand below us.

The men of the *Patricia Marie* had loaded several thousand pounds of scallops on board, and they were heading home to Provincetown by the time the tide went out. We, by this time, had cleaned our flounder and gone back to the cove to gather mussels. On the mud flats, we were concentrating on filling our buckets when my son called out; he had sunk into soft mud that wouldn't release him. The harder we pulled, the deeper we sank into the darkness. I told myself that there was no danger, but we were being pulled down. The more we struggled, the more the mud and water filled our boots. Land turned to water; nothing could be trusted. There was no danger, but we had to leave Kevin's boots behind after pulling him out of them. The tide washed over them when it came in, and they rolled with the mussels in the current through the night.

The *Patricia Marie* sank before we went to bed that night. Some say the huge load of scallops suddenly shifted as the boat rolled, and she couldn't right herself. Some say she struck a whale. Boats returning to Provincetown heard a distress call, then voices on the water, then silence. During the night, I woke three times, hearing what I thought was our friends talking in the other room. The third time, I heard something on the cottage roof; I imagined a crow sitting there in the darkness; I felt us being pulled into the soft belly of the earth. In the morning, I thought about the dream. Had it been a night of birth or burial? Had we passed through darkness to light? But while I lay in bed, trying to make a poem about my nightmares, the Eastham Fire Department and a Wellfleet rescue squad were moving up and down the outer beach on the other side of the marsh, peering through the beach haze for traces of the *Patricia Marie*.

By noon the next day, we still hadn't learned what happened; we ignore radio and television when we are on vacation. We had seen the extra tire tracks on the beach but sensed nothing strange. The night's rain clung to the porch screens, obscuring the gray-green of the marsh and the gray-blue of the water. At Nauset Light, footprints in the sand at the stair's base fanned out to the surfline. The ORV's tracks led away to a point too far for us to reach. We turned on the radio in the car to see if the drizzle was expected to stop later and heard about the seven men and their families and the sea. There wasn't much to say. The drizzle didn't stop; we turned onto the highway and drove away from the ocean.

A friend of the *Patricia Marie*'s captain said this for the newspaper the next day: "I think I would rather be a farmer. If something breaks down, he can always get out and walk."

—from *At the Edge* (1989)

Natural Mystery

~~~~~

I F THERE IS one area in which the Cape has produced a nationally recognized literature, it has been what is loosely referred to as nature writing. At least two Cape-based books have achieved the status of classics of American nature writing, and the number of writers of note— essayists, poets, historians, novelists, and legitimate naturalists—who have chosen the Cape's natural landscape and its wild inhabitants as subjects is impressive by any standards.

In one sense this should not be surprising. From the very first writers have been impressed with this peninsula's unusual geography, striking natural beauty, and abundance of resources and wildlife. The first voyagers, as mentioned earlier, often had ulterior motives in praising, even exaggerating, the attractiveness and fertility of the Cape's natural scene. Still, they were probably not far off the mark.

After the first Pilgrim settlements, however, there is a period of over 150 years when very little seems to have been written about nature on Cape Cod. This is no doubt due in large part to the fact that the residents were too busy using up the natural resources, extirpating local flora and fauna, and transforming the landscape to record very much about them.

If we wish to get some idea of what the natural Cape was like during the years 1640–1800 it usually requires some reading between the lines. A seventeenth-century description of the Outer Cape's soil as "blackish and deep mold . . . excellent to a spit's depth" is typical of the time and suggests that the Cape's earth has not always been so sandy and barren. Some of the old public records and laws also give us glimpses of wildlife that was troublesome or valuable to the early Cape Codders. In 1717, for instance, the Town of Sandwich proposed building a wall along the

185

entire length of what is now the Cape Cod Canal in order to keep out wolves. At a meeting to consider the proposal, some wag remarked that such a barrier was more likely to have the effect of keeping the wolves in, and the idea was dropped. It was evidence, however, that larger predators—which also included bears, lynx, and bobcats—were still common on the peninsula at that time.

Records of fish landings, oyster harvests, blackfish strandings, barrels of whale oil, or even carloads of shorebirds sent to market attest—however jarring to modern environmental sensibilities—to the abundance of marine resources that were exploited during this period. There is even an eighteenth-century petition to the General Court on behalf of indentured Massachusetts apprentices that they "not be served lobster more than twice a week."

At the same time, contemporary records of the eighteenth and early nineteenth centuries provide hints that the fabric of the Cape's landscape, however tough and serviceable it may have seemed to the early inhabitants, was becoming unraveled. By 1700 several Cape towns had passed ordinances restricting the cutting and taking of wood. In 1725 much of the Provincelands, originally densely wooded, was described as "a Sahara"; laws against pasturing cows there were enacted by the Colonial General Court, but these proved largely unenforceable and ineffective. By 1800 the dunes behind Provincetown were advancing on the town at a rate of ninety feet a year. Salt marshes, originally valued as pastureland, were being dredged to expand existing harbors and create new ones, or filled to provide building sites. The towering white cedar swamps, once managed as the source of shingles and other rot-resistant wood products, began to be clear-cut in the early nineteenth century to provide bogs for the rapidly expanding cranberry industry.

When Thoreau, the first of the Cape's great landscape chroniclers, first visited in 1849, he found a landscape not only mostly desolate and barren in aspect, but largely shaped and altered by two centuries of intense human use and exploitation. Perhaps it was his recognition of the intimate relationship between human and natural processes here that prompted him to see its shape as a human arm, an image that has clung as tenaciously to this land as the name Gosnold bestowed on it. In *Cape Cod,* Thoreau gives us vivid descriptions of the interior Cape and some of its more colorful inhabitants; but the heart and true focus of his book is what he called "Cape Cod Beach"—that unsurpassed and uninterrupted stretch of shoreline backed by glacial cliffs that runs from Eastham's Coast Guard Beach to High Head in Truro.

The excerpts from *Cape Cod* in the following section were chosen to illustrate what seems to me to be the major achievement of the book: Thoreau's encounter with the sea ("to get a better view" of which was, after all, the reason he gives for his journey). Often in his travels beyond Concord, Thoreau's Transcendental view of nature, so neatly worked out in *Walden,* was shaken by encounters with genuine wilderness and the strong human drama he witnessed there. Cape Cod gave him a strong dose of both in the ocean and the human tragedy it had wreaked. His early, unbridled enthusiasm on first gaining the beach gradually gives way to more complex and troubled reactions, culminating in an extraordinary passage in which he comes to see the ocean as "naked nature, inhumanly sincere, wasting no thought on man, nibbling at the cliffy shore, where gulls wheel amid the spray."

In *Cape Cod,* Thoreau discovers a darker view of man's place in nature than he found beside the tamed shores of Walden Pond; yet it is also a strangely liberating one, in which the seashore becomes for him "a most advantageous point from which to contemplate this world." Along the way there is a wealth of perceptive and prescient observations, vivid images, gems of dry and morbid humor, and wonderful Thoreauvian sentences.

Many subsequent historians, nature writers, and poets have referred to Thoreau's classic account. John Bishop's "Nauset Sands," for instance, seems to be a footnote to Thoreau's famous statement about the Cape's ocean beaches, "A man may stand there and put all America behind him." Why, Bishop's poem seems to ask, would a man *want* to put America behind him?

The Great Beach of Cape Cod is also the focus of Henry Beston's 1928 classic *The Outermost House*. Unlike Thoreau, Beston spent his time on the beach in one place, letting nature come to him through the seasons of an entire year. His more stationary position allowed him to perceive nature as "a great ritual," one that gave poetry and meaning to human existence. He was one of the first to call for a "wiser and perhaps a more mystical concept of animals," granting them a status in this world equal to our own. In fact, Beston argued, "Nature is part of our humanity, and without some awareness and experience of that divine mystery man ceases to be man."

John Hay, the third of the Cape's great triumvirate of nature writers, also gave classic expression to its outer shores in his 1964 book *The Great Beach,* which in structure retraces Thoreau's beach walk in reverse, from north to south. For contrast, the selection here, "Dune Country," represents that other major focus of Cape nature writers, the mutable and mysterious dunes of the Provincelands. For Hay these changing and surprisingly rich shapes at the Cape Tip remind us that nature is in essence change, process, invention, and adaptation, lessons that more than ever we need to learn if we are to live in such a place without destroying it. In the same setting, poet Cynthia Huntington celebrates a summer sojourn in one of the quirky, indigenous dune shacks that dot the ridges and hollows of the Provincelands, and comes to find that exposure to natural processes in such a place shapes not only the dunes but our imaginations and sensibilities as well.

But, as the other selections here demonstrate, any number of facets of the natural world have fascinated Cape writers. The diary entries of Edmund Wilson are particularly interesting because, as a writer, he came to nature relatively late and willingly ignorant. The earlier entries reflect the eye of the artist, rich in image and response and—for such an informed intellect as Wilson's—refreshingly free of conceptual labels and the corrosive wit that often characterizes his human portraits. In his later years Wilson seemed to find increasing fascination, and even comfort, in the Cape's natural surroundings. The entry here on horseshoe crabs is notable, not so much for his comparison of that ancient arachnid's sex life with his own (in his diaries Wilson tended to compare most things with his sex life), but because the similarities he perceives have the effect not "of degrading human life . . . but of making me respect the animals."

In many of her poems, Mary Oliver, probably the Cape's most distinguished poet of nature, has claimed for herself an area overlooked by most previous writers: that borderland of shallow ponds, marshes, and low woods lying between the Provinceland dunes and the town itself. "The Truro Bear" is a reminder that Provincetown has not been the only source of unusual sightings. A few years ago, in fact, there was a rash of reports and even a fuzzy photograph or two of a cougar in the Truro region, which quickly became known as "the Pamet Puma." Whether she is contemplating the regular appearance of cold-stunned sea turtles on our beaches in autumn and early winter or the periodic winter incursion of snowy owls from their more northern range, Oliver's poetry, intensely lyrical, is also strongly rooted in natural history and accurate observation.

James D. "Skip" Lazell, Jr., is a genuine field biologist and something of an iconoclast in his penchant for asking seemingly simple but disturbing questions. His provocative article on Cape peepers (tree frogs, not voyeurs) reminds us that for all our vaunted scientific knowledge and field studies, the most ordinary local natural phenomena remain, at heart, an enduring mystery.

from *Cape Cod* (1865)

By Henry David Thoreau

CAPE COD IS the bared and bended arm of Massachusetts: the shoulder is at Buzzard's Bay; the elbow, or crazy-bone, at Cape Mallebarre; the wrist at Truro; and the sandy fist at Provincetown,—behind which the State stands on her guard, with her back to the Green Mountains, and her feet planted on the floor of the ocean, like an athlete protecting her Bay,—boxing with northeast storms, and, ever and anon, heaving up her Atlantic adversary from the lap of earth,—ready to thrust forward her other fist, which keeps guard the while upon her breast at Cape Ann.*

On studying the map, I saw that there must be an uninterrupted beach on the east or outside of the forearm of the Cape, more than thirty miles from the general line of the coast, which would afford a good sea view, but that, on account of an opening in the beach, forming the entrance to Nauset Harbor, in Orleans, I must strike it in Eastham, if I approached it by land, and probably I could walk thence straight to Race Point, about twenty-eight miles, and not meet with any obstruction.

*   *   *

At length we reached the seemingly retreating boundary of the plain, and entered what had appeared at a distance an upland marsh, but proved to be dry sand covered with beach-grass, the bearberry, bayberry, shrub-oaks, and beach-plum, slightly ascending as we approached the shore; then, crossing over a belt of sand on which nothing grew, though the roar of the sea sounded scarcely louder than before, and we were pre-

---

*Thoreau was not the first to compare the Cape to a "bare and bended arm," but in this extended metaphor he gave the image a definitive and enduring statement. Nearly every resident of the Cape, when asked where he or she lives, or the location of some local spot, instinctively flexes the map he or she was born with. Other writers have seen in its curved and elaborated shape other aspects of human anatomy. A contemporary of Thoreau's, N. P. Willis, referred to the Cape less flatteringly as "the raised leg of New England," and Monica Dickens, logically extending Thoreau's image, writes of Buzzard's Bay as "the armpit of the Cape."

pared to go half a mile farther, we suddenly stood on the edge of a bluff overlooking the Atlantic.

Far below us was the beach, from half a dozen to a dozen rods in width, with a long line of breakers rushing to the strand. The sea was exceedingly dark and stormy, the sky completely overcast, the clouds still dropping rain, and the wind seemed to blow not so much as the exciting cause, as from sympathy with the already agitated ocean. The waves broke on the bars at some distance from the shore, and curving green or yellow as if over so many unseen dams, ten or twelve feet high, like a thousand waterfalls, rolled in foam to the sand. There was nothing but that savage ocean between us and Europe.

Having got down the bank, and as close to the water as we could, where the sand was the hardest, leaving the Nauset Lights behind us, we began to walk leisurely up the beach, in a northwest direction, toward Provincetown, which was about twenty-five miles distant, still sailing under our umbrellas with a strong aft wind, admiring in silence, as we walked, the great force of the ocean stream,—

ποταμοῖο μέγα σθένος Ὠκεανοῖο.

The white breakers were rushing to the shore; the foam ran up the sand, and then ran back as far as we could see—and we imagined how much farther along the Atlantic coast, before and behind us—as regularly, to compare great things with small, as the master of a choir beats time with his white wand; and ever and anon a higher wave caused us hastily to deviate from our path, and we looked back on our tracks filled with water and foam. The breakers looked like droves of a thousand wild horses of Neptune, rushing to the shore, with their white manes streaming far behind; and when, at length, the sun shone for a moment, their manes were rainbowtinted. Also, the long kelpweed was tossed up from time to time, like the tails of sea-cows sporting in the brine.

* * *

I was comparatively satisfied. There I had got the Cape under me, as much as if I were riding it bare-backed. It was not as on the map, or seen from the stage-coach; but there I found it all out of doors, huge and real, Cape Cod! as it cannot be represented on a map, color it as you will; the thing itself, than which there is nothing more like it, no truer picture or account; which you cannot go farther and see. I cannot remember what I thought before that it was. They commonly celebrate those beaches only which have a hotel on them, not those which have a humane house alone. But I wished to see that seashore where man's works are wrecks; to put up at the true Atlantic House,* where the ocean is land-lord as well as sea-lord, and comes ashore without a wharf for the landing; where the crumbling land is the only invalid, or at best is but dry land, and that is all you can say of it.

*   *   *

There was but little weed cast up here, and that kelp chiefly, there being scarcely a rock for rock-weed to adhere to. Who has not had a vision from some vessel's deck, when he had still his land legs on, of this great brown apron, drifting half upright, and quite submerged through the green water, clasping a stone or a deep-sea mussel in its unearthly fingers? I have seen it carrying a stone half as large as my head. We sometimes watched a mass of this cable-like weed, as it was tossed up on the crest of a breaker, waiting with interest to see it come in, as if there was some treasure buoyed up by it; but we were always surprised and disappointed at the insignificance of the mass which had attracted us. As we looked out over the water, the smallest objects floating on it appeared indefinitely large, we were so impressed by the vastness of the ocean, and each one bore so large a proportion to the whole ocean, which we saw. We were so often disappointed in the size of such things as came ashore, the ridiculous bits of wood or weed, with which the ocean labored, that we began to doubt whether the Atlantic itself would bear a still closer inspection, and would not turn out to be but a small pond, if it should come ashore to us. . . .

The beach was also strewn with beautiful sea-jellies, which the wreckers called sun-squall, one of the lowest forms of animal life, some white, some wine-colored, and a foot in diameter. I at first thought that they were a tender part of some marine monster, which the storm or some other foe had mangled. What right has the sea to bear in its bosom such tender things as sea-jellies and mosses, when it has such a boisterous shore, that the stoutest fabrics are wrecked against it? Strange that it should undertake to dandle such delicate children in its arm. I did not at first recognize these for the same which I had formerly seen in myriads in Boston Harbor, rising, with a waving motion, to the surface, as if to meet the sun, and discoloring the waters far and wide, so that I seemed to be sailing through a mere sun-fish soup. They say that when you endeavor to take one up, it will spill out the other side of your hand like quicksilver.

---

*An old Provincetown inn still operating as a bar today. Eugene O'Neill and Tennessee Williams lodged there during their stays in Provincetown.

Before the land rose out of the ocean, and became *dry* land, chaos reigned; and between high and low water mark, where she is partially disrobed and rising, a sort of chaos reigns still, which only anomalous creatures can inhabit. Mackerel-gulls were all the while flying over our heads and amid the breakers sometimes two white ones pursuing a black one; quite at home in the storm, though they are as delicate organizations as sea-jellies and mosses; and we saw that they were adapted to their circumstances rather by their spirits than their bodies. Theirs must be an essentially wilder, that is less human, nature, than that of larks and robins. Their note was like the sound of some vibrating metal, and harmonized well with the scenery and the roar of the surf, as if one had rudely touched the strings of the lyre, which ever lies on the shore; a ragged shred of ocean music tossed aloft on the spray.

But if I were required to name a sound, the remembrance of which most perfectly revives the impression which the beach has made, it would be the dreary peep of the piping plover *(Charadrius melodus)* which haunts there. Their voices, too, are heard as a fugacious part in the dirge which is ever played along the shore for those mariners who have been lost in the deep since first it was created. But through all this dreariness we seemed to have a pure and unqualified strain of eternal melody, for always the same strain which is a dirge to one household is a morning song of rejoicing to another.

✳   ✳   ✳

Objects on the beach, whether men or inanimate things, look not only exceedingly grotesque, but much larger and more wonderful than they actually are. Lately, when approaching the seashore several degrees south of this, I saw before me, seemingly half a mile distant, what appeared like bold and rugged cliffs on the beach, fifteen feet high, and whitened by the sun and waves; but after a few steps it proved to be low heaps of rags,—part of the cargo of a wrecked vessel,—scarcely more than a foot in height.

Once also it was my business to go in search of the relics of a human body,* mangled by sharks, which had just been cast up, a week after a wreck, having got the direction from a light-house: I should find it a mile or two distant over the sand, a dozen rods from the water, covered with a cloth, by a stick stuck up. I expected that I must look very narrowly to find so small an object, but the sandy beach, half a mile wide,

---

*In July of 1850 Thoreau went to Long Island to search for the body and effects of Margaret Fuller, who, with her husband and child, had drowned in a wreck off Fire Island. Fuller was a well-known member of the Concord Transcendentalists and editor of *The Dial,* where Thoreau's first essays and poems appeared.

and stretching farther than the eye could reach, was so perfectly smooth and bare, and the mirage toward the sea so magnifying, that when I was half a mile distant the insignificant sliver which marked the spot looked like a bleached spar, and the relics were as conspicuous as if they lay in state on that sandy plain, or a generation had labored to pile up their cairn there.

Close at hand they were simply some bones with a little flesh adhering to them, in fact, only a slight inequality in the sweep of the shore. There was nothing at all remarkable about them, and they were singularly inoffensive both to the senses and the imagination. But as I stood there they grew more and more imposing. They were alone with the beach and the sea, whose hollow roar seemed addressed to them, and I was impressed as if there was an understanding between them and the ocean which necessarily left me out, with my snivelling sympathies. That dead body had taken possession of the shore, and reigned over it as no living one could, in the name of a certain majesty which belonged to it.

*   *   *

Though there were numerous vessels at this great distance in the horizon on every side, yet the vast spaces between them, like the spaces between the stars,—far as they were distant from us, so were they from one another—nay, some were twice as far from each other as from us,— impressed us with a sense of the immensity of the ocean, the "unfruitful ocean," as it has been called, and we could see what proportion man and his works bear to the globe. As we looked off, and saw the water growing darker and darker and deeper and deeper the farther we looked, till it was awful to consider, and it appeared to have no relation to the friendly land, either as shore or bottom,—of what use is a bottom if it is out of sight, if it is two or three miles from the surface, and you are to be drowned so long before you get to it, though it were made of the same stuff with your native soil?—over that ocean where, as the Veda says, "there is nothing to give support, nothing to rest upon, nothing to cling to," I felt that I was a land animal. The man in a balloon even may commonly alight on the earth in a few moments, but the sailor's only hope is that he may reach the distant shore. . . .

On Cape Cod the next most eastern land you hear of is St. George's Bank—the fishermen tell of "Georges," "Cashus," and other sunken lands which they frequent. Every Cape man has a theory about George's Bank having been an island once, and in their accounts they gradually reduce the shallowness from six, five, four, two fathoms, to somebody's confident assertion that he has seen a mackerel-gull sitting on a piece of dry land there. It reminded me, when I thought of the shipwrecks which had taken place there, of the Isle of Demons, laid down off this coast in old charts of the New World. There must be something monstrous, methinks, in a vision of the sea bottom from over some bank a thousand miles from the shore, more awful than its imagined bottomlessness; a drowned continent, all livid and frothing at the nostrils, like the body of a drowned man, which is better sunk deep than near the surface.

*   *   *

The ocean is but a larger lake. At midsummer you may sometimes see a strip of glassy smoothness on it, a few rods in width and many miles long, as if the surface there were covered with a thin pellicle of oil, just as on a country pond; a sort of stand-still, you would say, at the meeting or parting of two currents of air—if it does not rather mark the unrippled steadiness of a current of water beneath—for sailors tell of the ocean and land breeze meeting between the fore and aft sails of a vessel, while the latter are full, the former being suddenly taken aback. . . .

Yet this same placid Ocean, as civil now as a city's harbor, a place for ships and commerce, will erelong be lashed with tumult. It will ruthlessly heave these vessels to and fro, break them in pieces in its sandy or stony jaws, and deliver their crews to sea-monsters. It will play with them like seaweed, distend them like dead frogs, and carry them about, now high, now low, to show to the fishes, giving them a nibble. This gentle Ocean will toss and tear the rag of a man's body like the father of mad bulls, and his relatives may be seen seeking the remnants for weeks along the strand. From some quiet inland hamlet they have rushed weeping to the unheard-of shore, and now stand uncertain where a sailor has recently been buried amid the sand-hills.

*   *   *

Perhaps what the Ocean takes from one part of the Cape it gives to another,—robs Peter to pay Paul. On the eastern side the sea appears to be everywhere encroaching on the land. Not only the land is undermined, and its ruins carried off by currents, but the sand is blown from the beach directly up the steep bank, where it is one hundred and fifty feet high, and covers the original surface there many feet deep. If you sit on the edge you will have ocular demonstration of this by soon getting your eyes full. Thus the bank preserves its height as fast as it is worn away. This sand is steadily traveling westward at a rapid rate, "more than a hundred yards," says one writer, within the memory of inhabitants now living; so that in some places peat-meadows are buried deep under the sand, and the peat is cut through it; and in one place a large peat-meadow has made its appearance on the shore in the bank covered many feet deep, and peat has been cut there. This accounts for that great pebble of peat which we saw in the surf.

The old oysterman had told us that many years ago he lost a "crittur" by her being mired in a swamp near the Atlantic side east of his house, and twenty years ago he lost the swamp itself entirely, but has since seen signs of it appearing on the beach. He also said that he had seen cedar stumps "as big as cartwheels" (!) on the bottom of the Bay, three miles off Billingsgate Point, when leaning over the side of his boat in pleasant weather, and that that was dry land not long ago. Another told us that a log canoe known to have been buried many years before on the Bay side at East Harbor in Truro, where the Cape is extremely narrow, appeared at length on the Atlantic side, the Cape having rolled over it, and an old woman said,—"Now, you see, it is true what I told you, that the Cape is moving."

*   *   *

Sometimes, when I was approaching the carcass of a horse or ox which lay on the beach there, where there was no living creature in sight, a dog would unexpectedly emerge from it and slink away with a mouthful of offal.

The seashore is a sort of neutral ground, a most advantageous point from which to contemplate this world. It is even a trivial place. The waves forever rolling to the land are too far-traveled and untamable to be familiar. Creeping along the endless beach amid the sun-squawl and the foam, it occurs to us that we, too, are the product of sea-slime.

It is a wild, rank place, and there is no flattery in it. Strewn with crabs, horse-shoes, and razor-clams, and whatever the sea casts up,—a vast *morgue*, where famished dogs may range in packs, and crows come daily to glean the pittance which the tide leaves them. The carcasses of men and beasts together lie stately up upon its shelf, rotting and bleaching in the sun and waves, and each tide turns them in their beds, and tucks fresh sand under them. There is naked Nature,—inhumanly sincere, wasting no thought on man, nibbling at the cliffy shore where gulls wheel amid the spray.

*   *   *

When we reached Boston that October, I had a gill of Provincetown sand in my shoes, and at Concord there was still enough left to sand my pages for many a day; and I seemed to hear the sea roar, as if I lived in a shell, for a week afterward. . . .

We went to see the Ocean, and that is probably the best place of all our coast to go to. If you go by water, you may experience what it is to leave and to approach these shores; you may see the Stormy Petrel by the way, θαλασσοδρόμα, running over the sea, and if the weather is but a little thick, may lose sight of the land in mid-passage. I do not know where there is another beach in the Atlantic States, attached to the mainland, so long, and at the same time so straight, and completely uninterrupted by creeks or coves or fresh-water rivers or marshes; for though there may be clear places on the map, they would probably be found by the foot traveler to be intersected by creeks and marshes; certainly there is none where there is a double way, such as I have described, a beach and a bank, which at the same time shows you the land and the sea, and part of the time two seas. . . .

The beach which I have described, however, is not hard enough for carriages, but must be explored on foot. When one carriage has passed along, a following one sinks deeper still in its rut. It has at present no name any more than fame. That portion south of Nauset Harbor is commonly called Chatham Beach. The part in Eastham is called Nauset Beach, and off Wellfleet and Truro the Backside, or sometimes, perhaps, Cape Cod Beach. I think that part which extends without interruption from Nauset Harbor to Race Point should be called Cape Cod Beach, and do so speak of it. . . .

The time must come when this coast will be a place of resort for those New-Englanders who really wish to visit the seaside. At present it is wholly unknown to the fashionable world, and probably it will never be agreeable to them. If it is merely a ten-pin alley, or a circular railway, or an ocean of mint-julep, that the visitor is in search of,—if he thinks more of the wine than the brine, as I suspect some do at Newport,—I trust that for a long time he will be disappointed here.

But this shore will never be more attractive than it is now. Such beaches as are fashionable are here made and unmade in a day, I may almost say, by the sea shifting its sands. Lynn and Nantasket! this bare and bended arm it is that makes the bay in which they lie so snugly. What are springs and waterfalls? Here is the spring of springs, the waterfall of waterfalls. A storm in the fall or winter is the time to visit it; a lighthouse or a fisherman's hut the true hotel. A man may stand there and put all America behind him.

———

"Nauset Sands"

By John Peale Bishop

I

Elude the dunes! By sunken pace
Through struggling sands,
Patched by the panting beach grass, come
To the long coast arrayed by sea-piled storms.

The north stands
Dissolute sands,
Sea-borne bulwarks against the sea.

South is an unlimited strand,
A waste of noon
Paced by no shadow.

And here the lonely man may stride
Unmeasured by the beach,
Strip, run and plunge
Through inborn sunburnt spray,
Then glistening stretch
Where in the destroying radiance
Of the aroused day
No shell survives. An imagined east
The sea! And all America is west!
And here at last a naked man may rest
Undaunted by the ancestral quest
As though it had not been,
In azure assumption of pure space
Untortured by the undaunted dream,
An hour stay, unshadowed of the sun,
And this the first as now the ultimate coast.

II

Domain that has no confines but in light,
Destroying space! Brute blue of noon now glared
Its death upon me. I saw them on their coast,
Their hearts as big with winds as though they had been sails,
And all their purpose prows turned into the sun.
Undream their doing. Lie down! Lie down!
The sea returns upon an instant and all their voyages
End at last in a bare body on the sand.
Into the world naked I came
And now once more lie naked to the sky.

———

"Prof. George Washington Ready—Seeing the Serpent"

By Herman A. Jennings

IN 1886, PROFESSOR Ready* alleges that he saw this monster and furnished a reporter with the facts, which were written out and published in the *Cape Cod Item,* at Yarmouthport, from which paper it was largely copied into other papers throughout the country. I believe that there has been no *reliable* account of the appearance of the serpent since. At considerable expense, I have been able to secure the original document, together with the professor's likeness and affidavit.

Sea Serpent in Provincetown

The recent earthquakes have so disturbed the bottom of the ocean, that many of the huge creatures which it is believed exist there have come to surface. Sea serpents and other nondescript monsters, it is alleged,

* "Professor" George Washington Ready (1832–1920) was, according to Josef Berger in *Cape Cod Pilot,* one of the last of Provincetown's original town criers and "the grandest of the lot."

have been seen in various places besides Marblehead, the sea serpent's home. The latest and most colossal in dimensions has visited Province-town. Mr. George W. Ready, a well-known citizen here, was going from the town to the backside of the Cape, and in crossing one of the sand-dunes, or hills, saw a commotion in the water, about a half a mile from the shore in the Herring Cove. It looked like a whirlpool and from his standpoint appeared to be about twenty feet in diameter, from the center of which jets of spray, looking like steam, were ejected to the height of fifty feet. Intently watching this strange phenomenon, he presently saw a huge head appear above the surface, and point for the shore. The head was as large as a two hundred gallon cask, concave on the under side and convex on the upper. Mr. Ready saw the creature coming towards the shore and secreted himself in a clump of beach plum bushes, where he got a good view of the monster. The creature swam to the shore with a slow and undulating motion and passed within about thirty feet of where Mr. Ready was secreted. It was about three hundred feet long, and in the thickest part, which was about the middle, he judged as it passed him to be about twelve feet in diameter. The body was covered with scales as large as the head of a fish barrel, and were colored alternately green, red and blue. They did not overlap each other, but seemed as if they were joined together by a ligature some four inches broad. The most curious feature was the head. The open mouth disclosed four rows of teeth, which glistened like polished ivory, and were at least two feet long, while on the extreme end of the head or nose, extended a tusk or horn at least eight feet in length. The crea-ture had six eyes as large as good-sized dinner plates, and they were placed at the end of moveable projections, so they were, at least, three feet from the head. In the creatures moving along these projections were continually on the move so that the reptile could see before, behind, and sideways, at the same time. Three of the eyes were of a fiery red hue, while the others were of a pale green. A strong sulphurous odor accompanied him, and intense heat was emitted, so much, that the bushes and grass over which he moved have the appearance of being scorched with fire. When the tail came out of the water it was seen to be of a V shape, the broadest part towards the body, to which it was joined by a small bony cartilage about twenty feet long, and only ten inches in diameter. This tail on the broad part was studded with very hard, bony scales, shaped like the teeth of a mowing machine, or reaper, about one foot long, and eight inches at the base, and cut everything smooth to the ground as it was dragged over the surface; pine and oak trees, nearly one foot in diameter, were cut off as smoothly as if done by a saw, and have the appearance of being seared over with a hot iron. The creature made for one of the large fresh water ponds called Pasture Pond. When in the center the head, which had all the time been raised some thirty feet in the air, began slowly to descend and was soon under water, the body slowly following it. As the tail disappeared, the water commenced to recede from the shore till the pond was left completely dry with a large hole in the center some twenty feet in diameter, perfectly circular, down which sounding leads have been lowered two hundred and fifty fathoms and no bottom found. By standing on the brink of the hole, what appears to be water, can be seen at a long distance down. Preparations are being made to investigate the matter, and thousands are going to see and examine the track of the huge sea monster. For fear that this statement should be doubted, and any one try to contradict it, I here append a copy of Mr. Ready's affidavit and signature:

"I, George Washington Ready, do testify that the foregoing statement is correct. It is a true description of the serpent as he appeared to me on that morning, and I was not unduly excited by liquor or otherwise."

GEORGE W. READY.

—from *Provincetown or Odds and Ends from the Tip End* (1890)

NOTE. Mr. Ready resides at the head of Pearl Street in this place, and can be interviewed on the subject at any time. [Jennings' note]

———

from *The Outermost House* (1928)

By Henry Beston

EAST AND AHEAD of the coast of North America, some thirty miles and more from the inner shores of Massachusetts, there stands in the open Atlantic the last fragment of an ancient and vanished land. For twenty miles this last and outer earth faces the ever hostile ocean in the form of a great eroded cliff of earth and clay, the undulations and levels of whose rim now stand a hundred, now a hundred and fifty feet above the tides. Worn by the breakers and the rains, disintegrated by the wind, it still stands bold. Many earths compose it, and many gravels and sands stratified and intermingled. It has many colours: old ivory here, peat here, and here old ivory darkened and enriched with rust. At twilight, its rim lifted to the splendour in the west, the face of the wall becomes a substance of shadow and dark descending to the eternal unquiet of the sea; at dawn the sun rising out of ocean gilds it with a level silence of light which thins and rises and vanishes into day.

At the foot of this cliff a great ocean beach runs north and south unbroken, mile lengthening into mile. Solitary and elemental, unsullied and remote, visited and possessed by the outer sea, these sands might be the end or the beginning of a world. Age by age, the sea here gives battle to the land; age by age, the earth struggles for her own, calling to her defence her energies and her creations, bidding her plants steal down upon the beach, and holding the frontier sands in a net of grass and roots which the storms wash free. The great rhythms of nature, today so dully disregarded, wounded even, have here their spacious and primeval liberty; cloud and shadow of cloud, wind and tide, tremor of night and day. Journeying birds alight here and fly away again all unseen, schools of great fish move beneath the waves, the surf flings its spray against the sun. . . .

. . . The peninsula stands farther out to sea than any other portion of the Atlantic coast of the United States; it is the outermost of outer shores. Thundering in against the cliff, the ocean here encounters the last defiant bulwark of two worlds.

The cliff I write of and the bordering beach face the Atlantic on the forearm of the Cape. This outer earth is now scarce more than a great dyke or wall some twenty-five miles long and only three and four miles wide. At Provincetown it rises from the sea, beginning there in a desert of dunes and sand plains of the ocean's making. These sands curve inland toward the continent, bending toward Plymouth even as a hand may be bent down at the wrist, and Provincetown harbour lies in the curve of palm and fingers. At Truro, the wrist of the Cape—the forearm simile being both exact and inescapable—the land curve falls from the east and west down through an arc to the north and south, and the earth cliff begins and rises rather suddenly to its greatest elevation. South by east from the Highland Light to Eastham and Nauset Coast Guard Station, the rampart fronts the sea, its sky line being now a progress of long undulations, now a level as military as a battlement, hollows and mounded hills here and there revealing the barren moorland character of the country just above. At Nauset, the cliff ends, the sea invades the narrowing land, and one enters the kingdom of the dunes.

The cliff ends, and a wall of ocean dunes carries on the beach. Five miles long, this wall ends at a channel over whose entrance shoals the ocean sweeps daily into a great inlet or lagoon back of the dunes, an inlet spaced with the floors of tidal islands and traced with winding creeks—the inlet of Eastham and Orleans. Very high tides, covering the islands, sometimes turn this space into bay. Westward over the channels and the marshland one looks to the uplands of the Cape, here scarce a good two miles wide. At Eastham, the land is an open, rolling moor. West over this lies Cape Cod Bay. A powerful tribe of Indians, the Nausets, once inhabited this earth between the seas.

Outermost cliff and solitary dune, the plain of ocean and the far, bright rims of the world, meadow land and marsh and ancient moor: this is Eastham; this the outer Cape. Sun and moon rise here from the sea, the arched sky has an ocean vastness, the clouds are now of ocean, now of earth. Having known and loved this land for many years, it came about that I found myself free to visit there, and so I built myself a house upon the beach.

*   *   *

My house completed, and tried and not found wanting by a first Cape Cod year, I went there to spend a fortnight in September. The fortnight ending, I lingered on, and as the year lengthened into autumn, the beauty and mystery of this earth and outer sea so possessed and held me that I could not go. The world to-day is sick to its thin blood for lack of elemental things, for fire before the hands, for water welling from the earth, for air, for the dear earth itself underfoot. In my world of beach and dune these elemental presences lived and had their being, and under their arch there moved an incomparable pageant of nature and the year. The flux and reflux of ocean, the incomings of waves, the gatherings of birds, the pilgrimages of the peoples of the sea, winter and storm, the splendour of autumn and the holiness of spring—all these were part of the great beach. The longer I stayed, the more eager was I to know this coast and to share its mysterious and elemental life; I found myself free to do so, I had no fear of being alone, I had something of a field naturalist's inclination; presently I made up my mind to remain and try living for a year on Eastham Beach. . . . So, choosing to remain upon the beach, I look forward to October and winter and the great migrations. Earliest autumn and September now enclose the earth.

My western windows are most beautiful in early evening. On these lovely, cool September nights the level and quiescent dust of light which fills the sky is as autumnal in its colouring as the earth below. There is autumn on the earth and autumn overhead. The great isles of tawny orange smouldering into darkness, the paths of the channels stilled to twilight bronze, the scarlet meadows deepening to levels of purple and advancing night—all these mount, in exhalation of colour, to the heavens. The beam of Nauset, entering my northern casement, brushes a recurrent pallor of light across a part of my bedroom wall. A first flash, a second flash, a third flash, and then a little interval as the dark sector of the lens travels between the Fo'castle and the flame. On bright moonlit nights, I can see both the whitewashed tower and the light; on dark nights, I can see only the light itself suspended and secure above the earth.

It is dark to-night, and over the plains of ocean the autumnal sky rolls up the winter stars.

*   *   *

There is a new sound on the beach, and a greater sound. Slowly, and day by day, the surf grows heavier, and down the long miles of the beach, at the lonely stations, men hear the coming winter in the roar. Mornings and evenings grow cold, the northwest wind grows cold; the last crescent of the month's moon, discovered by chance in a pale morning sky, stands north of the sun. Autumn ripens faster on the beach than on the marshes and the dunes. Westward and landward there is colour; seaward, bright space and austerity. Lifted to the sky, the dying grasses on the dune tops' rim tremble and lean seaward in the wind, wraiths of sand course flat along the beach, the hiss of sand mingles its thin stridency with the new thunder of the sea.

I have been spending my afternoons gathering driftwood and observing birds. The skies being clear, noonday suns take something of the bite out of the wind, and now and then a warmish west-sou'westerly finds its way back into the world. Into the bright, vast days I go, shouldering home my sticks and broken boards and driving shore birds on ahead of me, putting up sanderlings and sandpipers, ringnecks and knots, plovers and killdeer, coveys of a dozen, little flocks, great flocks, compact assemblies with a regimented air. For a fortnight past, October 9th to October 23d, an enormous population of the migrants has been "stopping over" on my Eastham sands, gathering, resting, feeding, and commingling. They come, they go, they melt away, they gather again; for actual miles the intricate and inter-crisscross pattern of their feet runs unbroken along the tide rim of Cape Cod.

Yet it is no confused and careless horde through which I go, but an army. Some spirit of discipline and unity has passed over these countless little brains, waking in each flock a conscious sense of its collective self and giving each bird a sense of himself as a member of some migrant company. Lone fliers are rare, and when seen have an air of being in pursuit of some flock which has overlooked them and gone on. Swift as the wind they fly, speeding along the breakers with the directness of a runner down a course, and I read fear in their speed. Sometimes I see them find their own and settle down beside them half a mile ahead, sometimes they melt away into a vista of surf and sky, still speeding on, still seeking. . . .

The tide being high these days late in the afternoon, the birds begin to muster on the beach about ten o'clock in the morning. Some fly over from the salt meadows, some arrive flying along the beach, some drop from the sky. I startle up a first group on turning from the upper beach to the lower. I walk directly at the birds—a general apprehension, a rally, a scutter ahead, and the birds are gone. Standing on the beach, fresh claw marks at my feet, I watch the lovely sight of the group instantly turned into a constellation of birds, into a fugitive pleiades whose living stars keep their chance positions; I watch the spiralling flight, the momentary tilts of the white bellies, the alternate shows of the clustered, grayish backs. The group next ahead, though wary from the first, continues feeding. I draw nearer; a few run ahead as if to escape me afoot, others stop and prepare to fly; nearer still, the birds can stand no more; another rally, another scutter, and they are following their kin along the surges.

No aspect of nature on this beach is more mysterious to me than the flights of these shore-bird constellations. The constellation forms, as I have hinted, in an instant of time, and in that same instant develops its own will. Birds which have been feeding yards away from each other, each one individually busy for his individual body's sake, suddenly fuse into this new volition and, flying, rise as one, coast as one, tilt their dozen bodies as one, and as one wheel off on the course which the new group will has determined. There is no such thing, I may add, as a lead bird or guide. Had I more space I should like nothing better than to discuss this new will and its instant of origin, but I do not want to crowd this part of my chapter, and must therefore leave the problem to all who study the psychic relations between the individual and a surrounding many. My special interest is rather the instant and synchronous obedience of each speeding body to the new volition. By what means, by what methods of communication does this will so suffuse the living constellation that its dozen or more tiny brains know it and obey it in such an instancy of time? Are we to believe that these birds, all of them, are *machina,* as Descartes long ago insisted, mere mechanisms of flesh and bone so exquisitely alike that each cogwheel brain, encountering the same environmental forces, synchronously lets slip the same mechanic ratchet? or is there some psychic relation between these creatures? Does some current flow through them and between them as they fly? Schools of fish, I am told, make similar mass changes of direction. I saw such a thing once, but of that more anon.

We need another and a wiser and perhaps a more mystical concept of animals. Remote from universal nature, and living by complicated artifice, man in civilization surveys the creature through the glass of his knowledge and sees thereby a feather magnified and the whole image in distortion. We patronize them for their incompleteness, for their tragic fate of having taken form so far below ourselves. And therein we err, and greatly err. For the animal shall not be measured by man. In a world older and more complete than ours they move finished and complete, gifted with extensions of the senses we have lost or never attained, living by voices we shall never hear. They are not brethren, they are not underlings; they are other nations, caught with ourselves in the net of life and time, fellow prisoners of the splendour and travail of the earth.

The afternoon sun sinks red as fire; the tide climbs the beach, its foam a strange crimson; miles out, a freighter goes north, emerging from the shoals.

*   *   *

The three great elemental sounds in nature are the sound of rain, the sound of wind in a primeval wood, and the sound of outer ocean on a beach. I have heard them all, and of the three elemental voices, that of ocean is the most awesome, beautiful, and varied. For it is a mistake to talk of the monotone of ocean or of the monotonous nature of its sound. The sea has many voices. Listen to the surf, really lend it your ears, and you will hear in it a world of sounds: hollow boomings and heavy roarings, great watery tumblings and tramplings, long hissing seethes, sharp, rifle-shot reports, splashes, whispers, the grinding undertone of stones, and sometimes vocal sounds that might be the half-heard talk of people in the sea. And not only is the great sound varied in the manner of its making, it is also constantly changing its tempo, its pitch, its accent, and its rhythm, being now loud and thundering, now almost placid, now furious, now grave and solemn-slow, now a simple measure, now a rhythm monstrous with a sense of purpose and elemental will. . . .

The surf is high, and on the far side of it, a wave greater than its fellows is shouldering out of the blue, glinting immensity of sea. . . . Two thirds of a mile out, the wave is still a sea vibration, a billow. Slice it across, and its outline will be that of a slightly flattened semicircle; the pulse is shaped in a long, advancing mound. I watch it approach the beach. Closer and closer in, it is rising with the rise of the beach and the shoaling of the water; closer still, it is changing from a mount to a pyramid, a pyramid which swiftly distorts, the seaward side lengthening, the landward side incurving—the wave is now a breaker. Along the ridge of blue forms a rippling crest of clear, bright water; a little spray flies off. Under the racing foam churned up by the dissolution of other breakers the beach now catches at the last shape of sea inhabited by the pulse—the wave is *tripped* by the shoaling sand—the giant stumbles, crashes, and is pushed over and ahead by the sloping line of force behind. The fall of a breaker is never the work of gravity alone.

It is the last line of the wave that has captured the decorative imagination of the world—the long seaward slope, the curling crest, the incurved volute ahead.

Toppling over and hurled ahead, the wave crashes, its mass of glinting blue falling down in a confusion of seething, splendid white, the tumbling water rebounding from the sand to a height almost always a little above that of the original crest. Out of the wild, crumbling confusion born of the dissolution of the force and the last great shape, foamy fountains spurt, and ringlets of spray. The mass of water, still all furiously a-churn and seething white, now rushes for the rim of the beach as it might for an inconceivable cataract. Within thirty-five feet the water shoals from two feet to dry land. The edge of the rush thins, and the last impulse disappears in inch-deep slides of foam which reflect the sky in one last moment of energy and beauty and then vanish all at once into the sands.

*   *   *

I have now to tell of the great northeast storm of February 19th and 20th. They say here that it was the worst gale known on the outer Cape since the *Portland* went down with all hands on that terrible November night in '98.

It began after midnight on a Friday night, and the barometer gave but little warning of its coming. . . .

I woke in the morning to the dry rattle of sleet on my eastern windows and the howling of wind. A northeaster laden with sleet was bearing down on the Cape from off a furious ocean, an ebbing sea fought with a gale blowing directly on the coast; the lonely desolation of the beach was a thousand times more desolate in that white storm pouring down from a dark sky. The sleet fell as a heavy rain falls when it is blown about by the wind. I built up my fire, dressed, and went out, shielding my face from the sleet by pulling my head down into the collar of my coat. I brought in basket after basket of firewood, till the corner of the room resembled a woodshed. Then I folded up the bedclothes, threw my New Mexican blanket over the couch, lighted the oil stove, and prepared breakfast. An apple, oatmeal porridge, toast made at the fireplace, a boiled egg, and coffee.

Sleet and more of it, rushes of it, attacks of it, screaming descents of it; I heard it on the roof, on the sides of the house, on the window-panes. Within, my fire fought against the cold, tormented light. I wondered about a small fishing boat, a thirty-foot "flounder dragger" that had anchored two miles or so off the Fo'castle the evening before. I looked for her with my glass, but could not see into the storm.

Streaming over the dunes, the storm howled on west over the moors. The islands of the marsh were brownish black, the channels leaden and whipped up by the wind; and along the shores of the desolate islands, channel waves broke angrily, chidingly, tossing up heavy ringlets of lifeless white. A scene of incredible desolation and cold. All day long I kept to my house, building up the fire and keeping watch from the windows; now and then I went out to see that all was well with the Fo'castle and its foundations, and to glimpse what I could, through the sleet, of the storm on the sea. For a mile or so offshore the North Atlantic was a convulsion of elemental fury whipped by the sleety wind, the great parallels of the breakers tumbling all together and mingling in one seething and immense confusion, the sound of this mile of surf being an endless booming roar, a seethe, and a dread grinding, all inter-twined with the high scream of the wind. The rush of the inmost break-ers up the beach was a thing of violence and blind will. Darkness coming early, I closed my shutters on the uproar of the outer world, all save one shutter on the landward side.

With the coming of night the storm increased; the wind reaching a velocity of seventy to eighty miles an hour. It was at this time, I am told, that friends on the mainland began to be worried about me, many of them looking for my light. My lamp, a simple kerosene affair with a white china shade, stood on a table before the unshuttered window facing the land. An old friend said he would see it or think that he saw it for a half minute or so, and then it would vanish for hours into the darkness of the gale. It was singularly peaceful in the little house. Pres-ently, the tide, which had ebbed a little during the afternoon, turned and began to come in. All afternoon long the surf had thundered high upon the beach, the ebb tide backed up against the wind. With the turn of the tide came fury unbelievable. The great rhythm of its waters now at one with the rhythm of the wind, the ocean rose out of the night to attack the ancient rivalry of earth, hurling breaker after thundering breaker against the long bulwark of the sands. The Fo'castle, being low and strongly built, stood solid as a rock, but its walls thrummed in the gale. I could feel the vibration in the bricks of the chimney, and the dune beneath the house trembled incessantly with the onslaught of the surf. . . .

I did not go to bed, for I wanted to be ready for any eventuality. As the hour of flood tide neared, I dressed as warmly as I could, turned down my lamp, and went out upon the dunes.

An invisible moon, two days past the full, had risen behind the rushing floor of cloud, and some of its wan light fell on the tortured earth and the torment of the sea. The air was full of sleet, hissing with a strange, terrible, insistent sound on the dead grass, and sand was being whirled up into the air. Being struck on the face by this sand and sleet was like being lashed by a tiny, pin-point whip. I have never looked on such a tide. It had crossed the beach, climbed the five-foot wall of the dune levels that run between the great mounds, and was hurling wreckage fifty and sixty feet into the starved white beach grass; the marsh was an immense flooded bay, and the "cuts" between the dunes and the marsh rivers of breakers. A hundred yards to the north of me was such a river; to the south, the surf was attempting to flank the dune, an attempt which did not succeed. Between these two onslaughts, no longer looking *down* upon the sea, but directly into it and just over it, the Fo'castle stood like a house built out into the surf on a mound of sand. A third of a mile or so to the north I chanced to see rather a strange thing. The dune bank there was washing away and caving in under the onslaught of the seas, and presently there crumbled out the blackened skeleton of an ancient wreck which the dunes had buried long ago. As the tide rose this ghost floated and lifted itself free, and then washed south close along the dunes. There was something inconceivably spectral in the sight of this dead hulk thus stirring from its grave and yielding its bones again to the fury of the gale.

*   *   *

Night is very beautiful on this great beach. It is the true other half of the day's tremendous wheel; no lights without meaning stab or trouble it; it is beauty, it is fulfilment, it is rest. Thin clouds float in these heavens, islands of obscurity in a splendour of space and stars: the Milky Way bridges earth and ocean; the beach resolves itself into a unity of form, its summer lagoons, its slopes and uplands merging; against the western sky and the falling bow of sun rise the silent and superb undulations of the dunes.

My nights are at their darkest when a dense fog streams in from the sea under a black, unbroken floor of cloud. Such nights are rare, but are most to be expected when fog gathers off the coast in early summer; this last Wednesday night was the darkest I have known. Between ten o'clock and two in the morning three vessels stranded on the outer beach—a fisherman, a four-masted schooner, and a beam trawler. The fisherman and the schooner have been towed off, but the trawler, they say, is still ashore.

I went down to the beach that night just after ten o'clock. So utterly black, pitch dark it was, and so thick with moisture and trailing showers, that there was no sign whatever of the beam of Nauset; the sea was only a sound, and when I reached the edge of the surf the dunes themselves had disappeared behind. I stood as isolate in that immensity of rain and night as I might have stood in interplanetary space. The sea was troubled and noisy, and when I opened the darkness with an outlined cone of light from my electric torch I saw that the waves were washing up green coils of sea grass, all coldly wet and bright in the motionless and unnatural radiance. Far off a single ship was groaning its way along the shoals. The fog was compact of the finest moisture; passing by, it spun itself into my lens of light like a kind of strange, aërial, and liquid silk. Effin Chalke, the new coast guard, passed me going north, and told me that he had had news at the halfway house of the schooner at Cahoon's.

It was dark, pitch dark to my eye, yet complete darkness, I imagine, is exceedingly rare, perhaps unknown in outer nature. The nearest natural approximation to it is probably the gloom of forest country buried in night and cloud. Dark as the night was here, there was still light on the surface of the planet. Standing on the shelving beach, with the surf breaking at my feet, I could see the endless wild uprush, slide, and withdrawal of the sea's white rim of foam. The men at Nauset tell me that on such nights they follow along this vague crawl of whiteness, trusting to habit and a sixth sense to warn them of their approach to the halfway house.

Animals descend by starlight to the beach, North, beyond the dunes, muskrats forsake the cliff and nose about in the driftwood and weed, leaving intricate trails and figure eights to be obliterated by the day; the lesser folk—the mice, the occasional small sand-coloured toads, the burrowing moles—keep to the upper beach and leave their tiny footprints under the overhanging wall. In autumn skunks, beset by a shrinking larder, go beach combing early in the night. The animal is by preference a clean feeder and turns up his nose at rankness. I almost stepped on a big fellow one night as I was walking north to meet the first man south from Nauset. There was a scamper, and the creature ran up the beach from under my feet; alarmed he certainly was, yet was he contained and continent. Deer are frequently seen, especially north of the light. I find their tracks upon the summer dunes.

Years ago, while camping on this beach north of Nauset, I went for a stroll along the top of the cliff at break of dawn. Though the path followed close enough along the edge, the beach below was often hidden, and I looked directly from the height to the flush of sunrise at sea. Presently the path, turning, approached the brink of the earth precipice, and on the beach below, in the cool, wet rosiness of dawn, I saw three deer playing. They frolicked, rose on their hind legs, scampered off, and returned again, and were merry. Just before sunrise they trotted off north together down the beach toward a hollow in the cliff and the path that climbs it.

Occasionally a sea creature visits the shore at night. Lone coast guardsmen, trudging the sand at some deserted hour, have been startled by seals. One man fell flat on a creature's back, and it drew away from under him, flippering toward the sea, with a sound "halfway between a squeal and a bark." I myself once had rather a start. It was long after sundown, the light dying and uncertain, and I was walking home on the top level of the beach and close along the slope descending to the ebbing tide. A little more than halfway to the Fo'castle a huge unexpected something suddenly writhed horribly in the darkness under my bare foot. I had stepped on a skate left stranded by some recent crest of surf, and my weight had momentarily annoyed it back to life.

Facing north, the beam of Nauset becomes part of the dune night. As I walk toward it, I see the lantern, now as a star of light which waxes and wanes three mathematic times, now as a lovely pale flare of light behind the rounded summits of the dunes. The changes in the atmosphere change the colour of the beam; it is now whitish, now flame golden, now golden red; it changes its form as well, from a star to a blare of light, from a blare of light to a cone of radiance sweeping a circumference of fog. To the west of Nauset I often see the apocalyptic flash of the great light at the Highland reflected on the clouds or even on the moisture in the starlit air, and, seeing it, I often think of the pleasant hours I have spent there when George and Mary Smith were at the light and I had the good fortune to visit as their guest. Instead of going to sleep in the room under the eaves, I would lie awake, looking out of a window to the great spokes of light revolving as solemnly as a part of the universe.

All night long the lights of coastwise vessels pass at sea, green lights going south, red lights moving north. Fishing schooners and flounder draggers anchor two or three miles out, and keep a bright riding light burning on the mast. I see them come to anchor at sundown, but I rarely see them go, for they are off at dawn. When busy at night, these fishermen illumine their decks with a scatter of oil flares. From shore, the ships might be thought afire. I have watched the scene through a night glass. I could see no smoke, only the waving flares, the reddish radiance on sail and rigging, an edge of reflection overside, and the enormous night and sea beyond.

One July night, as I returned at three o'clock from an expedition north, the whole night, in one strange, burning instant, turned into a phantom day. I stopped and, questioning, stared about. An enormous meteor, the largest I have ever seen, was consuming itself in an effulgence of light west of the zenith. Beach and dune and ocean appeared out of nothing, shadowless and motionless, a landscape whose every tremor and vibration were stilled, a landscape in a dream.

The beach at night has a voice all its own, a sound in fullest harmony with its spirit and mood—with its little, dry noise of sand forever moving, with its solemn, overspilling, rhythmic seas, with its eternity of stars that sometimes seem to hang down like lamps from the high heavens—and that sound the piping of a bird. As I walk the beach in early summer my solitary coming disturbs it on its nest, and it flies away, troubled, invisible, piping its sweet, plaintive cry. The bird I write of is the piping plover, *Charadrius melodus,* sometimes called the beach plover or the mourning bird. Its note is a whistled syllable, the loveliest musical note, I think, sounded by any North Atlantic bird.

Now that summer is here I often cook myself a camp supper on the beach. Beyond the crackling, salt-yellow driftwood flame, over the pyramid of barrel staves, broken boards, and old sticks all atwist with climbing fire, the unseen ocean thunders and booms, the breaker sounding hollow as it falls. The wall of the sand cliff behind, with its rim of grass and withering roots, its sandy crumblings and erosions, stands gilded with flame; wind cries over it; a covey of sandpipers pass between the ocean and the fire. There are stars, and to the south Scorpio hangs curving down the sky with ringed Saturn shining in his claw.

Learn to reverence night and to put away the vulgar fear of it, for, with the banishment of night from the experience of man, there vanishes as well a religious emotion, a poetic mood, which gives depth to the adventure of humanity. By day, space is one with the earth and with man—it is his sun that is shining, his clouds that are floating past; at night, space is his no more. When the great earth, abandoning day, rolls up the deeps of the heavens and the universe, a new door opens for the human spirit, and there are few so clownish that some awareness of the mystery of being does not touch them as they gaze. For a moment of night we have a glimpse of ourselves and of our world islanded in its stream of stars—pilgrims of mortality, voyaging between horizons across eternal seas of space and time. Fugitive though the instant be, the spirit of man is, during it, ennobled by a genuine moment of emotional dignity, and poetry makes its own both the human spirit and experience.

*   *   *

So came August to its close, ending its last day with a night so luminous and still that a mood came over me to sleep out on the open beach under the stars. There are nights in summer when darkness and ebbing tide quiet the universal wind, and this August night was full of that quiet of absence, and the sky was clear. South of my house, between the bold fan of a dune and the wall of a plateau, a sheltered hollow opens seaward, and to this nook I went, shouldering my blankets sailorwise. In the star-shine the hollow was darker than the immense and solitary beach, and its floor was still pleasantly warm with the overflow of day.

I fell asleep uneasily, and woke again as one wakes out-of-doors. The vague walls about me breathed a pleasant smell of sand, there was no sound, and the broken circle of grass above was as motionless as something in a house. Waking again, hours afterward, I felt the air grown colder and heard a little advancing noise of waves. It was still night. Sleep gone and past recapture, I drew on my clothes and went to the beach. In the luminous east, two great stars aslant were rising clear of the exhalations of darkness gathered at the rim of night and ocean—Betelgeuse and Bellatrix, the shoulders of Orion. Autumn had come, and the Giant stood again at the horizon of day and the ebbing year, his belt still hidden in the bank of cloud, his feet in the deeps of space and the far surges of the sea.

My year upon the beach had come full circle; it was time to close my door. Seeing the great suns, I thought of the last time I marked them in the spring, in the April west above the moors, dying into the light and sinking. I saw them of old above the iron waves of black December, sparkling afar. Now, once again, the Hunter rose to drive summer south before him, once again autumn followed on his steps. I had seen the ritual of the sun; I had shared the elemental world. Wraiths of memories began to take shape. I saw the sleet of the great storm slanting down again into the grass under the thin seepage of moon, the blue-white spill of an immense billow on the outer bar, the swans in the high October sky, the sunset madness and splendour of the year's terns over the dunes, the clouds of beach birds arriving, the eagle solitary in the blue. And because I had known this outer and secret world, and been able to live as I had lived, reverence and gratitude greater and deeper than ever possessed me, sweeping every emotion else aside, and space and silence an instant closed together over life. Then time gathered again like a cloud, and presently the stars began to pale over an ocean still dark with remembered night.

During the months that have passed since that September morning some have asked me what understanding of Nature one shapes from so strange a year? I would answer that one's first appreciation is a sense that the creation is still going on, that the creative forces are as great and as active to-day as they have ever been, and that to-morrow's morning will be as heroic as any of the world. *Creation is here and now.* So near is man to the creative pageant, so much a part is he of the endless and incredible experiment, that any glimpse he may have will be but the revelation of a moment, a solitary note heard in a symphony thundering through debatable existences of time. Poetry is as necessary to comprehension as science. It is as impossible to live without reverence as it is without joy.

And what of Nature itself, you say—that callous and cruel engine, red in tooth and fang? Well, it is not so much of an engine as you think. As for "red in tooth and fang," whenever I hear the phrase or its intellectual echoes I know that some passer-by has been getting life from books. It is true that there are grim arrangements. Beware of judging them by whatever human values are in style. As well expect Nature to answer to your human values as to come into your house and sit in a chair. The economy of nature, its checks and balances, its measurements of competing life—all this is its great marvel and has an ethic of its own. Live in Nature, and you will soon see that for all its non-human rhythm, it is no cave of pain. As I write I think of my beloved birds of the great beach, and of their beauty and their zest of living. And if there are fears, know also that Nature has its unexpected and unappreciated mercies.

Whatever attitude to human existence you fashion for yourself, know that it is valid only if it be the shadow of an attitude to Nature. A human life, so often likened to a spectacle upon a stage, is more justly a ritual. The ancient values of dignity, beauty, and poetry which sustain it are of Nature's inspiration; they are born of the mystery and beauty of the world. Do no dishonour to the earth lest you dishonour the spirit of man. Hold your hands out over the earth as over a flame. To all who love her, who open to her the doors of their veins, she gives of her strength, sustaining them with her own measureless tremor of dark life. Touch the earth, love the earth, honour the earth, her plains, her valleys, her hills, and her seas; rest your spirit in her solitary places. For the gifts of life are the earth's and they are given to all, and they are the songs of birds at daybreak, Orion and the Bear, and dawn seen over ocean from the beach.

"Going Out to the Traps"

By Edmund Wilson

AUGUST 12, 1930. Beautiful night, with light marine blue of sky above sand dunes, with white cloud to the east shaped low and undulated like a sand dune, with the stars sprinkled close around its edges—almost (the stars) as informal and unnightlike as if they were some phenomenon of day—perfect calm night with full moon up.—Moonlit sand dunes: pure and bluish pale soft outlines.—In the town, all the houses, packed full with their large green-blinded windows in their compact white boxes, looked clear and fine in the bluish moonlight, with that New England dignity, one of the only things we have comparable in that line to Europe—a conversation, something in the nature of an argument, coming out of one of the only houses that were lighted.—We had taken along shredded-wheat biscuit and condensed milk and coffee, with orange-peel alky [local argot for alcohol] in it.

Everything was dark on the gray long pier, with its wooden apparatus overhead and its stink of fish—we sat on the end and had a drink—the moon was so thin, a bright disc placed lightly on the light night blue of the west, and toward Truro, the low gray-pink above the opaque blue of low clouds was reflected in the blue porcelain (a softer zinc) of the water, where the darker dories and rowboats lay parallel to the darker clouds—dark-faced shapeless figures on the wharf—they got down into a dory, five of them, from the other tine of the pier and rowed out toward the traps with regular heavy and funereal rhythm of oars, not saying a word.

We visited a series of four traps—the laborious pulling up of the nets: the butterfish, great flapping silver flakes, making a smacking crepitation of fireworks when they were thrown onto the floor of the boat—the squid would usually be the first to appear, streaming through the water in rusted streaks—they seemed so futile, so unpleasantly uncannily incomplete flimsy forms of life, with their round expressionless eyes, like eyes painted—a white iris with a black spot—on some naïve toy, their plumes like the ostrich feathers of some Renaissance woman of the court in an engraving by [Jacques] Callot, and their squirting method of propulsion, they couldn't even swim like fish—when pulled up, they would squirt their last squirt, trying to propel themselves away,

214

then expire indistinguishably in a mixed bluish and amberish carpet of slime, when they would be sold by the basket as bait for trawlers.— Combined squeaking of squids and slapping of other fish, as baskets are emptied.—The first things we saw, however, were little sea crabs, clinging to the meshes of the net, which seemed, with their blue and pink, to match the dawn.—The mackerel, with their little clean-clipped tails like neat little efficient propellers: everything the squids were not— iridescent mother-of-pearl along the bellies and striped distinctly black and green along their blacks—a big goosefish: the old Portuguese fisherman held him up for us to see his great gullet with the limp slimy squids drooling out of it, brutally grasping him with his thumb and finger in the fish's dull eyes, then flung him overboard—dogfish with their mean smug sharks' mouths on the white underside and their ugly absurd sharks' eyes with a gray cat-pupil on a whitish lozenge of iris— when you held them up by the tail, they snapped up like springs and tried to bite you.—A few whiting and cod-headed hake—rather prettily mottled sand dabs.

It was cold perched on the roof of the little cabin, but as the full summer sun rose, we could feel its heat growing steady.—A gray warship of some kind farther out in the harbor.—The blue shirts and the dirty yellow oilcloth of the five fishermen matched the sky and the sea and the unseen presence of the sand.

When we returned, the tide was out, and the wharf spindled on the bent stems of its piles, green-slimed almost to the top—we walked into shore on the hard smelly slime of the harbor bottom.

—from *The Thirties* (1980)

"Horseshoe Crabs"

By Edmund Wilson

AT THE BAY, in July, I found many of them lying on their backs and bent at an angle, with their sharp tails sticking up in the air, still alive but unable to get back to the water, because, except in the water, they could not turn themselves over. I would pick them up by the tail and throw them back. Their heavy bronze carapaces, six spider legs with small claws, thick laminations (?) and their [illegible]. One could see how they had been able to survive from before the days of the mammals—practically indestructible. The dead ones were making a stink.

Then I saw what I thought was a small crab pushing a large one, which had been stranded, out to sea. I picked him up by the tail, and he hung on to the one in front with his two front claws, so that this one was dangling, too. Then I saw others of these pairs. In one case, the big one (always in front) was buried in the sand, and I assumed that the small one was digging it out—I tried to help. Later, when I looked them up, I discovered that the big ones were the females and smaller ones the males. This was the mating season, when the females would drag the males in and lay their eggs at the line of the surf, burrowing into the sand. Then they would pull the male along, and he would fertilize them. At other times of year they lived in the deeper water (eating sea worms). Those who were left on their backs by the surf in the sun had no chance of getting back. It was extraordinary to think of the creatures perpetuating themselves in their present form through all those thousands of years. It inspired one with a certain respect for them. I remembered that John Bishop had also been struck by them: *Colloquy of a King Crab*. He seems to have found in them a symbol for his own later life: crawling but never destroyed. I thought rather of the superficial differences, but underlying identity, between their sexual life and ours—driven to carry on the species, resisting any attempts to interfere with it (as when I picked one up by the tail). Amount of thought one gives to sex, even at my age, when one no longer needs to. This doesn't have the effect, for me, of degrading human life (though it makes me realize that we waste time and energy on these primitive impulses), but of making me respect the animals.

—from *The Forties* (1983)

———

"Spectacle Ponds"

By Edmund Wilson

EARLY JULY '48: I went there for the first time with Reuel; then with Elena, not long afterward. I had expected to find them interesting, from what I had heard, and they enchanted me when I found them, after several futile expeditions, and had on me an emotional effect.

One sees the big one first, coming down the sandy road: its dark blue hill-and-tree-locked water. At the bottom of the road, on the left, are the gray boards of some old shack, of unrecognizable shape and purpose, and in the little clearing that leads to it, the white shriveled-up splinters of turtle eggs that lay about the holes for the nests—Reuel took them for the bones of crabs. (When I first came, however, I made my way down through the bushes.)

There is a flat stretch of ground between the two ponds, a sort of wild cranberry bog covered with little cranberry blossoms and with marvelous pogonia and adder's mouth, larger than at Higgins Pond, and intensified to vivider tinges. The colors vary in proportion to whether they have sprung up in places where they got more or little sun—the adder's mouth from a fainter to a flamelike mauve (?), startling as it rises against the green of cranberry shoots and bog grass—with the fine little wings of its flowers and its bearded crazy flap that, in this exceptional orchid, rises at the top like a crest instead of hanging down like a tongue. There is something snakelike about these pogonia blossoms while the adder's mouth, with its colubrine name, is shyer and less defiant.

On the left is the smaller and muddy pond, with both the white bowl-like and the yellow ball-like water lilies. If you wade in, you sink through a layer of goo but find firm ground underneath. The clay is absolutely red, as if the soil had a lot of iron.

On the other side, the larger pond lies, half enclosed by a hilly bank, solitary, deep, wild, and mysterious. A zone of some water plant with tiny white flowers runs all the way around a little out from the shore. Between the shore and this is white sand, where great pollywogs lie; but the stems of the waterweeds make a forest where it is black below. On the hither side, the bottom drops steeply, and the middle is deep and dark. But inshore it is limpid and still, a contrast, full of dignity and distinction, to its muddy probably shallow neighbor. Jack Phillips once saw under the water what he thought was a fabulous monster but turned out to be an enormous snapping turtle wrestling with an enormous eel. We found a painted turtle's shell, with the red markings very bright, completely cleaned out. The bullfrogs had the finest voices that I ever remember to have heard: they were really musical, tuneful. I felt about the place a wildness unlike anything one finds at the ponds we frequent. It was as if it existed for itself, as if the frogs and the orchids flourished and perfected themselves, had their lives, for their own satisfaction. Nobody came to see them. They did not have to be on their guard against being picked or caught (the frogs were not troubled by our presence but, after a moment, went on with their singing). There it was, walled in, complete in itself, absorbing its summer days, lying open from sun to sun, with the ponds bending water lilies and water grass, frogs and turtles, pickerel and perch, in their unplumbed unfished-in depths.

The emotional effect of this spot was due, I suppose, to some affinity that I felt between it and my life at this time—and a darkness into which I sink and a clear round single lens, well guarded and hidden away. Many things nourished and lurking at the bottom that have not yet been brought to light.

Elena, when she swam across it, said that it was a little stagnant.

—from *The Forties* (1983)

———

"The Herring-Run"

By John Hay

By day and night, out of the law of leaden tides,
Migration and death through the inland gauntlet, where the gulls,
Like vultures hunting high air of dying, circle and scream.

The pale blind fish, in millions, move from the ocean walls—
Salt gulfs and dark devouring—to fight the sun,
In the shallow waters crystal to a hunter's eye.

On the stream bed flowing, their sinuous shadows on the sand,
They waver backward with the weeds; processional
In tide and stars, pulsed forward by the drums of time.

Soft in the currents, spineless as the water's flow;
And then they leap! Taut daring at the wires, the high
And highest trial; their wounds; their white resplendent scales!

The male and female, power and spawn, rocket through rage
Of rocks, black storms and flailing torrents on their flesh,
To meet the silent lakes, perfection's morning womb.

They die shining. The splash of moons and golden lust
Of rivers loads the nets, as they protest and praise,
In the last quick leaps and running of their great desire.

———

"Dune Country"

By John Hay

SAND DUNES, AS distinct from sandspits, or the banks at the head of
the beach, are found in a few restricted areas on the Cape, but their two
primary locations are the Provincetown hook and at Sandy Neck in
Barnstable, on the Bay side. Inland of the beach, far enough not to be
exposed to the constant wash of the tides or to flooding seas during
storms, the dunes have forms and motions of their own. They were
originally produced by the wind, and it is the wind that reshapes them,
blows over their shoulders and down their slopes, making mounds and
ripples on their surfaces, and also undoes them and makes new ones
again.

The Provincetown dunes, which I had passed by on my June hike
down the beach, represent an exposed region of several miles in extent,
uninhabited for the most part except for a few gray beach houses perched
on the dunes overlooking the sea. They are continually being added to

by sand which the dry northwest wind picks up along the shore and blows inland. Because of its dryness, this wind also has the greatest effect in moving the dunes. Damper winds causing moisture on grains of sand, make them more resistant to being moved.

Much of the region is held down by low vegetation. Its sandy reaches are patched everywhere by Hudsonia, or beach heather, pitch pines kept down almost flat on the ground by wind and salt spray, and its slopes and hummocks kept intact by beach grass; but in other areas, and they are extensive, the dunes have broken loose and roam like the waves of the open ocean, with great crests and long, deep troughs. They look as if they should have a slow, massive momentum of their own, but they are moved by the wind, migrating in a west to east direction at the rate of some ten to fifteen feet a year, creating a considerable problem at the point where they skirt the highway across from the town of Provincetown. On the far end of Pilgrim Lake high dunes loom over the highway and are continually drifting down on to it, hardly deterred by snow fences and the planting of beach grass, so that the sand has to be cleared off frequently.

It is a young country, even compared with the rest of the Cape, which, in geologic terms at least, is by no means an ancient land. It is postglacial and is made of material brought along the shore and added to a reef of glacial debris. It begins where the glacial material of the lower Cape ends, easily seen where the cliff at "High Head" breaks off above Pilgrim Lake, and then it stretches and curves out very close to sea level. Samples of material taken in the area showed a carbon dating of 5000 years, comparatively recent times. Also there seems to be good reason for believing that much of the dune country was broken free and set to wandering by the hand of man. . . .

There is a small hill called Mt. Gilboa on one side of the highway at Provincetown, facing another Biblical peak called Mt. Ararat on the other, and if you climb it you can overlook the harbor and the roofs of the town, as well as the dunes and sea in the other direction. (Provincetown, incidentally, consists of a belt of houses narrowly strung along the inner shore with its streets directly oriented toward the harbor, appropriate to a people whose trade and thoughts were toward the sea. This is also true of the houses, which were built longitudinally, parallel to the streets.) In the fall, clam diggers bend down over dark flats at low tide between stretching fingers of water. Dories are stranded in the mud, or move gently on low water. Beyond them are the curving, stockadelike enclosures of the fish weirs, and draggers move in to the mouth of the harbor out of the bay. The sunlight fires the sandy faces of the long, low cliffs that extend down the inner shore of the Cape.

The town, which is so thick and crowded with cars during the summer months, a host to the cities, teeming with talk and color, a variety of human shapes, sizes, and exclamations, so reclaimed that you can hardly conceive of its austere past, becomes diminished again to a mere cluster of houses, a tenuous edge on water and sand. On the far-going Atlantic side, the dunes billow and toss. The Ararats are everywhere, peaks, crowns, domes held down by yellow beach grass on the mounds and hillocks from which the slopes dive down.

As the world's dunes go, these may not be of major size and extent. On the other hand they have been measured at heights between sixty and eighty feet, and at times dune ridges may have reached elevations up to 100 feet. Also, their scale is such, leading from one open face to another, that human figures climbing a steep side across an intervening slope of no great distance seem tiny. The walls keep looming up and the valleys dip between, so that the whole landscape is full of a wide motion.

In all this bare largesse of sand, the texture is clean and clear. Shadows move over it like loving hands. The wind's touch in turn has made grooves, grains, and ribs on the surface. In some areas the black mineral magnetite joins with garnet to make blackish-purple ripples in the sand, or irregular masses, or little brushstroke feathers and clouds. Everything shows clearly, from human footprints and the long ruts made by beach buggies, to mice or rabbit tracks. And I suppose that in the summer—if you pounce in time—you can see insects leaving their traces, like dune grasshoppers, colored and grained like sand, or a spider that buries down in the sand, thus avoiding extreme temperatures; or even a toad. I once found a Fowler's toad quite far out on the beach where it must have wandered away from the dunes.

A stick that drops down from one of those shrubs so besieged by wind and sand waggles down a dune making a fine tracery, or what looks like a stamping of birds when it is lodged in one place and blown back and forth. An oak leaf merely blown for a slight distance down the sand makes a track, with all its lobe ends imprinted like a long tassel or thin strands of separate strings. Except for the beach-buggy tracks, that follow one route fairly consistently, and may be visible for months at a time, and the beach grasses, continually renewing their precise circles on the sand, most of these tracks soon disappear. There is a constant moving of sand particles, a sweeping over by the wind. The open dunes are trackless areas where tracks take on great significance.

During winter days when the northwest wind blows with fury along the exposed shores of the Cape, it may be too uncomfortable to stay in the dunes for any length of time. You gasp in the polar air and hide your face from the stinging sand. Each sand grain is lifted and sent with the speed of a projectile along the surface of the dunes. Given a little shelter from which to watch you could see the dunes change shape in an afternoon, or an hour. It is on days like this that they migrate like waves, with long slopes on their upwind sides, steep ones on their lee.

On their bright and stable days, the long dune shoulders at the top of each rise tilt you up, body and vision, into the dizzy heights of a sky graded from cobalt to indigo, the way the scale of things in the landscape goes from sand grains to rocking seas without distraction. The dunes almost seem to ask for a long-distance running from both men and clouds. They are a place of flying, falling, and tumbling, shaping the motion of what comes to them, asking for an approach that soars. . . .

I sat on the top of a high dune one afternoon and watched a beach buggy swaying and swinging up in my direction along a track that led from the shore. It droned up and careened by me, plowing and slipping through the sands, and away down a long slope it went on the dunes' free forms, cutting across the shadows that were spearheading toward the sea. Then I heard children's voices in the distance coming over quite clear and shrill, falling off at intervals before the wind. The slopes and valleys stretched with pure travel in between. It was the kind of place where all views and associations keep on, across a shifting range. It lacked fixed ways, decided roads. Only packed in by the open ocean and the long reaches of time, the roving dunes made a continually majestic statement which no amount of cans, broken glass, or human footprints could erase.

Off on the end, the edge, past the cities and the suburbs, the fixed house lots, the fields, and plains that make a patchwork of an entire nation, here is a country let go, barren, down to an essential minimum, but tossing and flowing with its own momentum in an envious proximity to the sea. It is the first and last land in America.

—from *The Great Beach* (1963)

———

"The Gulls"

By Howard Nemerov

I know them at their worst, when by the shore
They raise the screaming practice of their peace,
Disputing fish and floating garbage or
Scraps of stale bread thrown by a child. In this,
Even, they flash with senseless beauty more
Than I believed—sweet are their bitter cries,
As their fierce eyes are sweet; in their mere greed
Is grace, as they fall splendidly to feed.

And sometimes I have seen them as they glide
Mysterious upon a morning sea
Ghostly with mist, or when they ride
White water or the shattered wind, while we
Work at a wooden oar and huddle inside
Our shallow hull against the sea-torn spray;
And there they brutally are emblems of
Soul's courage, summoners to a broken love.

Courage is always brutal, for it is
The bitter tooth fastens the soul to God
Unknowing and unwilling, but as a vise
Not to be torn away. In the great crowd,
Because it gathers from such empty skies,
Each eye is arrogant and each voice loud
With angry lust; while alone each bird must be
Dispassionate above a hollow sea.

White wanderers, sky-bearers from the wide
Rage of the waters! so may your moving wings
Defend you from the kingdom of the tide
Whose sullen sway beneath your journeyings

Wrinkles like death, so may your flying pride
Keep you in danger—bless the song that sings

Of mortal courage; bless it with your form
Compassed in calm amid the cloud-white storm.

———

"Note: The Sea Grinds Things Up"

By Alan Dugan

It's going on now
as these words appear
to you or are heard by you.
A wave slaps down, flat.
Water runs up the beach,
then wheels and slides
back down, leaving a ridge
of sea-foam, weed, and shells.
One thinks: I must
break out of this
horrible cycle, but
the ocean doesn't: it
continues through the thought.
A wave breaks, some
of its water runs up
the beach and down
again, leaving a ridge
of scum and skeletal debris.
One thinks: I must
break out of this
cycle of life and death,
but the ocean doesn't: it
goes past the thought.
A wave breaks on the sand,
water planes up the beach
and wheels back down,
hissing and leaving a ridge
of anything it can leave.

One thinks: I must
run out the life
part of this cycle,
then the death part
of this cycle, and then
go on as the sea
goes on in this cycle
after the last word,
but this is not the last
word unless you think
of this cycle as some
perpetual inventory
of the sea. Remember:
this is just one sea
on one beach on one
planet in one
solar system in one
galaxy. After that
the scale increases, so
this is not the last word,
and nothing else is talking back.
It's a lonely situation.

———

"How grey, how wet, how cold"

By Marge Piercy

They are bits of fog caught in armor.
The outside pretends to the solidity of rocks
and requires force and skill bearing in
to cut the muscle, shatter the illusion.

If you stare at them, your stomach
curls, the grey eyes of Athene

pried out, the texture of heavy phlegm,
chill clots of mortality and come.

They lie on the tongue, distillations
of the sea. Fresh as the morning
wind that tatters the mist.
Sweet as cream but with that bottom

of granite, the taste of deep well
water drawn up on the hottest day,
the vein of slate in true Chablis,
the kiss of acid sharpening the tongue.

They slip down quick as minnows
darting to cover, and the mouth
remembers sex. Both provide
a meeting of the primitive

and worldly, in that we do
little more for oysters than the gull
smashing the shells on the rocks
or the crab wrestling them open,

yet in subtle flavor and the choice
to taste them raw comes a delicacy
not of the brain but of the senses
and the wit to leave perfection bare.

———

"Pitch Pines"

By Brendan Galvin

Some trees loft their heads
like symmetrical green bells,
but these, blown one-sided
by winds salted out of the northeast,
seem twisted from the germ.
Not one will lean the same way as another.

Knotted but soft, they mingle
ragged branches and rot to punkwood,
limbs flaking and dying
to ribs, to antlers and spidery twigs,
scaly plates slipping off the trunks.

Hanging on, oaks rattle maroon clusters
against winter. But these, resinous in flues,
blamed for a history of cellar holes,
snap in the cold and fall
to shapes like dragons asleep,

or thin out by dropping sour needles
on acid soil. For one week in May
they pollinate windows, a shower
that curdles water to golden scum.

From Bartholomew Gosnold's deck,
Brereton saw this cape timbered to its shores
with the hardwoods that fell to keels
and ribbing, to single meetinghouse beams
as long as eight men.

Stands of swamp cedar, cleared for cranberries,
were split to shakes or cut lengthwise
for foundations, while sheep cropped

elm and cherry sprouts
and plows broke the cleancut fields.

Fifty cords at a time, birch and maple
melted bog iron in pits; elm and beech
boiled the Atlantic to its salts; red oak
fired the glassworks at Sandwich—

till the desert floundered
out of the backlands and knocked
on the rear doors of towns
and this peninsula drifted
in brushfire haze,

and, clenching their cones
under crown fires, the grandfathers
of these pines held on until
heat popped their seeds
to the charred ground.

———

"Mussels"

By Mary Oliver

In the riprap,
   in the cool caves,
      in the dim and salt-refreshed
       recesses, they cling
in dark clusters,
   in barnacled fistfuls,
      in the dampness that never
       leaves, in the deeps
of high tide, in the slow
   washing away of the water

in which they feed,
  in which the blue shells
open a little, and the orange bodies
 make a sound,
   not loud,
    not unmusical, as they take
nourishment, as the ocean
 enters their bodies. At low tide
   I am on the riprap, clattering
    with boots and a pail,
rock over rock; I choose
 the crevice, I reach
   forward into the dampness,
    my hands feeling everywhere
for the best, the biggest. Even before
 I decide which to take,
   which to twist from the wet rocks,
   which to devour,
they, who have no eyes to see with,
 see me, like a shadow,
   bending forward. Together
    they make a sound,
not loud,
 not unmusical, as they lean
   into the rocks, away
    from my grasping fingers.

"The Truro Bear"

By Mary Oliver

There's a bear in the Truro woods.
People have seen it—three or four,
or two, or one. I think
of the thickness of the serious woods

around the dark bowls of the Truro ponds;
I think of the blueberry fields, the blackberry tangles,
the cranberry bogs. And the sky
with its new moon, its familiar star-trails,
burns down like a brand-new heaven,
while everywhere I look on the scratchy hillsides
shadows seem to grow shoulders. Surely
a beast might be clever, be lucky, move quietly
through the woods for years, learning to stay away
from roads and houses. Common sense mutters:
it can't be true, it must be somebody's
runaway dog. But the seed
has been planted, and when has happiness ever
required much evidence to begin
its leaf-green breathing?

—

"In Blackwater Woods"

By Mary Oliver

Look, the trees
are turning
their own bodies
into pillars

of light,
are giving off the rich
fragrance of cinnamon
and fulfillment,

the long tapers
of cattails
are bursting and floating away over
the blue shoulders

of the ponds,
and every pond,
no matter what its
name is, is

nameless now.
Every year
everything
I have ever learned

in my lifetime
leads back to this: the fires
and the black river of loss
whose other side

is salvation,
whose meaning
none of us will ever know.
To live in this world

you must be able
to do three things:
to love what is mortal;
to hold it

against your bones knowing
your own life depends on it;
and, when the time comes to let it go,
to let it go.

———

"How Turtles Come to Spend the Winter in the Aquarium, Then Are Flown South and Released Back into the Sea"

By Mary Oliver

Somewhere down beach, in the morning, at water's edge, I found a sea turtle,
its huge head a smoldering apricot, its shell streaming with seaweed,
its eyes closed, its flippers motionless.
When I bent down, it moved a little.
When I picked it up, it sighed.
Was it forty pounds, or fifty pounds, or a hundred?
Was it two miles back to the car?
We walked a little while, and then we rested, and then we walked on.
I walked with my mouth open, my heart roared.
The eyes opened, I don't know what they thought.
Sometimes the flippers swam at the air.
Sometimes the eyes closed.
I couldn't walk anymore, and then I walked some more
while it turned into granite, or cement, but with that apricot-colored head,
that stillness, that Buddha-like patience, that cold-shocked but slowly beating heart.
Finally, we reached the car.

The afternoon is the other part of this story.
Have you ever found something beautiful, and maybe just in time?
How such a challenge can fill you!
Jesus could walk over the water.
I had to walk ankle-deep in the sand, and I did it.
My bones didn't quite snap.

Come on in, and see me smile.
I probably won't stop for hours.
Already, in the warmth, the turtle has raised its head, is looking around.
Today, who could deny it, I am an important person.

———

"White Owl Flies into and out of the Field"

By Mary Oliver

Coming down
out of the freezing sky
with its depths of light,
like an angel,
or a buddha with wings,
it was beautiful
and accurate,
striking the snow and whatever was there
with a force that left the imprint
of the tips of its wings—
five feet apart—and the grabbing
thrust of its feet,
and the indentation of what had been running
through the white valleys
of the snow—

and then it rose, gracefully,
and flew back to the frozen marshes,
to lurk there,
like a little lighthouse,
in the blue shadows—
so I thought:
maybe death

isn't darkness, after all,
but so much light
wrapping itself around us—

as soft as feathers—
that we are instantly weary
of looking, and looking, and shut our eyes,
not without amazement,
and let ourselves be carried,
as through the translucence of mica,
to the river
that is without the least dapple or shadow—
that is nothing but light—scalding, aortal light—
in which we are washed and washed
out of our bones.

———

"The Spiral"

By Cynthia Huntington

I

I live on the inside curve of a spiral, where the peninsula turns around on itself and curls backward. The tip of this spiral is still building, extending and growing thin as waves wash sand along the outer shore, nudging it north and west. The movement of this curve is inward, counterclockwise, winding back to set this place apart in its own self-willed dreaming.

Out here beyond the last bedrock, past the crust of the glacial deposit, I live on a foothold of sand that is constantly moving. Everything eroded and nudged along shore ends up here, broken. Whole coastlines, boulders, good earth perhaps: they arrive at last as sand. Sand keeps its forms barely longer than water; only the most recent wave or the last footprint stays on its surface.

Sleeping, I wake to sounds of water. Day and night the ocean mutters like a restless dreamer. I never catch a word. The water is full of life; it is nothing but life, yet it is not itself a living thing. I live beside it and sleep falling into its voice. Repeating, obsessive, the liquid syllables might almost become words, but do not, just as the sand pushed back and forth at the tide line will not quite take a form, though the ocean shapes it again and again.

At night the oil lamps shine on the boards and windows hold the flames in their black pools, yellow and welcoming if you were returning here after some journey. The only other lights are down past the beach where boats sail into the night sky; the furthest ones blink like low stars on the horizon. Then one star may take flight, glowing yellow or red or green, and turn out to be a small plane patrolling this outpost, scanning the black water with its radar. The shack rocks gently in wind. Set up on wood pilings against the second dune, it lets the wind under it, gently lifting. In the high bunk, when the lamps are put out, we feel the whole place sway like a boat at anchor, and there is nothing fixed or steady, only these currents carrying us along in the dark. Bert turns in his sleep, smacking the bottom bunk with an outflung arm, and the bed shakes and resettles. I lie still above him in the upper berth with its view of four windows. They are effacing themselves now, as the inner and outer darkness fade toward equilibrium. I can still see a little bit of sky there when I turn, or, lying flat on my back, I can put out my hand and touch the boards of the ceiling. During storms rain hits the shingles and thrums against the roof's thin skull. Wobbling on its axis, the earth twirls off in space, spun in thrall to a star. Only the pull of that great fire, and our opposite thrust away from it holds us on course.

Where are we going? By night and day traveling, we follow a circular motion, imperfect, an elliptical orbit that wheels us back around, but never to quite the same place. Through tug and counter-pull of orbits, gravity and centrifugal force, sphere within sphere we go, taking the long way round each time, just missing the point where we began. We move in time, in our circling, and so can never return to where we were. The spiral opens out, and vanishes.

We live on the outermost, outward-reaching shore of Cape Cod, at no fixed address. In seven years there have been a series of rooms, houses, cabins, borrowed nests. Of all the borrowed places, this one is best, a little board shack stuck up on posts in the sand, two hundred yards from the ocean, surrounded by beach roses, shorebirds, grass and rolling dunes, anchored in sand that flows straight down into the sea. We return here every summer, coming as early and staying as late as the season allows. It is my "pied-à-terre"—a true foot on the earth—just one foot because I am moving, not standing still.

The shack has a name, Euphoria, which at first I thought sounded a little silly and high-flown, but not anymore. It means elation, and has to do with the wind. The name came with it along with other bits of history that belong to it more than we do. In its present incarnation it is the property of Hazel Hawthorne Werner, who holds a lifetime lease with the Cape Cod National Seashore, where it stands. Hazel bought Euphoria in the 1940s from a woman from Boston who had come out to join her lover, who had another shack three hundred yards down the beach. He camped in that shack and she camped in Euphoria, until the war came and he went off to fight. The woman from Boston bought it, years before that, from a Coast Guardsman who built it to house his wife in summers; she saw the place and promptly fled to town. Back then these were the Provincelands, unclaimed by man nor beast, though people from Provincetown would often tramp across to cook picnic suppers over a bonfire of wreckage. It was called "the back side," the town facing otherwise toward the harbor, and the Coast Guard patrolled the beach on foot at night.

Every spring we pack up our books and winter clothes to store in a friend's basement and get together our boxes of provisions, load them on Bill Fitts' four-wheel-drive truck and move out to the dunes. The pump handle is screwed together, the outhouse retrieved from bushes and set up at a discreet distance from the shack, its peaked roof rising jauntily toward the sky. I unpack what we've brought: rice and oil, and beans, and canned things, flashlight, radio, sweatshirts, and things for the beach. Everything fits, in a corner or on a shelf, stowed neat and tight as on a small boat, which is what Euphoria most nearly resembles. I fill the paraffin lamps while Bert fixes the propane tank to the stove and we're in business. It's an hour's walk to town, uphill and down in soft sand, so the summer crowds won't reach us. We carry our supplies overland in knapsacks—and carry our garbage out—along the old Coast Guard supply route, Snail Road, a ghost highway in the sand. Beach buggies and vans roll up and down the beach, a regular parade on weekends, and there are scattered lights at night where fishing boats hang offshore. From where we sit they look small, their sound lost in the constant turning of the waves.

This is my favorite place in all the world. The shack measures twelve by sixteen, perched on stilts in front of a sand dune on the wild side of the cape, where the dunes slope down to the water only to rise up a little further out as sand bars, creating treacherous, spectacular currents. Those are the Peaked Hill Bars, once called the graveyard of the Atlantic. Here over three thousand shipwrecks were counted: four hundred in one terrible winter. The ocean beats hard on the unsheltered coast and the shoreline is wild and bare, dotted with roses and bayberry, set between long austere vistas of dunes and stonelike waves. Behind the shoreline lie eight miles of dunes.

Set high on the second dune, Euphoria has a view of dune or sea from every window. It is a room of windows, the two big ones in front looking north, that we raise by tugging on a rope slung over a pulley, and the one behind that pulls inward from a top hinge and hooks up to the roof beam by a hook and eye. Day blows straight through: newspapers, books, and notebook pages ruffle under their rock weights. The wind carries dust of sand, a fine powder that coats every surface and sifts down to lie in the floorboards. Outside, the sand scours the sides until the grain of the boards stands out in relief, glowing silver gray.

Euphoria is unpainted except for the sky-blue trim on the screen door, and a little worn yellow on the shelf we use for dishes. The rest is the color of old wood—or I should say colors, sometimes gray or silver, sometimes brown, depending how much damp is in it and how the light falls. Today it has a glint of silver rising behind the dark grain, as if it were glowing from within. The sand is pale brown and the ocean is dark blue.

We haul our water uphill from a well pipe sunk in the valley. There is fresh water under the sand and above sea level: the sweet water floats like a lens on top of the denser salty water. The water from the pump has a great deal of iron, giving it a brownish tinge that stains our teeth, but it is delicious and cold as water out of the earth is always cold and fresh and bright with minerals.

The shack has a tiny porch, and a weather vane that twirls like crazy in the constant winds. There are gaps between the boards and around the door and windows. Sunlight and rain leak in equally, making this a not-quite substantial shelter, the idea of a house, but with none of a real house's constriction. Inside are three tables built under the windows, bunk beds, a gas stove for cooking, and a wood stove for heat. A camp chair tucks under the small rear table. The east wall has an open closet and some shelves for blankets. We are provided with oil lamps, an enormous kettle bestriding both burners of the range, a dry sink, and a propane refrigerator which invariably breaks down in the heat of August. I sweep under the table, pull out the backless bench made of many pieces of scrap wood where we sit side by side to eat and look out over the ocean.

*

Days pass; we live by the sun. Some days are lazy and long; we wander in and out, bang the screen door shut, curiously not at home, uneasy in all this great stretch of space. A bird cries in the bayberry, far away in its life. The sun climbs up and slides down again, and eventually we relent to its timekeeping, sit staring at the water for hours, and dissolve into the measure of tides, and honorably do nothing. I have perhaps two ideas a day: one usually concerns food. The appetite this air inspires is legendary.

We returned three days ago and are full of wonder. Mornings the beach roses open their small petals to the cold salt air, and we shiver in the chill that is May on the North Atlantic, feeding newspaper and driftwood to the stove. Now in late afternoon I sit on the steps with a piece of driftwood in my hand, turning it over and over, touching the curves and spirals of the grain. A good weariness slows me to enter the touch of the wood, tracing its softness and resistances. My legs are heavy, my lungs light with oxygen. I feel my bones and the good boards under me, and the cold in the seawind rising. Behind me, the shack trembles slightly, holding its shape against all that blows.

I spent this morning pacing the shoreline and tramping back among dunes, rediscovering valleys and reclaiming hilltops. I climbed the high dune to stare down at the shack, at the pale, still line of beach molded to the changing water. The shack is the center from which I venture and to which return, in love with its shade and plain dimensions, its slanted roof and scarred pilings. A safe retreat under the wide sky, it offers an interior life to put against the expanse of gold and blue that surrounds us here. The sand is slowly breaking up underfoot as the sun dries it; each day my feet scuff a finer dust rising like pollen as the swollen grains loosen and begin to lift, going from brown to ivory. The first bloom of spring is on the sand itself, changing its color and texture, growing lighter, tracked by birds. I added my tracks to theirs, and to the scratches left by wind-blown driftwood, as I walked along kicking at bones the wind uncovered, poking my nose into white bits of shell, and green upstarting in clumps. I walked along intently, feeling as if I was looking for something, though I couldn't figure quite what it was. Returning this afternoon, I set to reinhabiting the shack, which sat empty all winter and has gone wild. Funny winds teased its balance against the hill, and birds, dune mice, and red squirrels skittered across the porch and down the roof. Those sounds of scratching, scuffling, and blowing are in the boards, caught in the hollow spaces they frame. Now the clink of cups swung gently, lip to bottom, swayed on their hooks by a window breeze, enters and passes through, adding an over-sound to the wild ones, and the smell of food cooking over a gas flame domesticates the atmosphere. I sit in proprietary fashion gazing out from the doorstep, the house at my back and the world before me, while dinner simmers on the stove.

Bert is walking down to the beach; his back-lit shape recedes slowly as he crosses down the path and up the first dune. The sun is still high at five o'clock, but a chill is crawling up from the beach. Soon the wind will rise. Bert is going down for the hundredth time to examine waves and poke through beach wrack. Like me, he doesn't know exactly what he is looking for, but it is important, even compelling, this search among the tides' leavings. I see his strong back, his loose stride as he walks up the path toward the horizon of dune and sky, and disappears over the edge. Clouds fly over and an agreeable loneness surrounds Euphoria, weighting it here, in its own piece of world that is quiet and out of the way of the world's traffic.

II

These sand dunes were made by the ocean. They are ground the sea gave back, returned from every shore its storms have ripped or currents tugged or tides unraveled, and it is an odd, sometimes unearthly-seeming place. The dunes rise up like monuments; the ocean took thousands of years to build them but they may be seen, in slow-time, to breathe and move, rising and falling and lapping forward. Now in spring the skittish birds touch down briefly and lift off again, leaving scratches in the sand. Waves keep pushing up against the shoreline, and beneath the waves, with every beat, a new line of dunes is forming as a sand bar slowly rises offshore.

When the ocean makes land it creates something different from land's land. No bedrock, or heavy humus and clay, no hard-packed soil to clasp the roots of big trees and fold records of time in its layers. It builds with what its currents can carry, floating piece by piece, and grain by grain, by slow accumulation. The ocean, in its disquiet, can only imagine—that is, bring forth an image of—flux, and so it creates a shoreline that moves in waves, and hills that rise and fall and toss one over another, and take the print of the wind on their surfaces.

From where I'm sitting, high up, the landscape takes on a peculiar unity. My gaze takes in dunes and ocean, miles of water and sand in either direction. They look like images of the other, though the dunes lie still and the waves keep churning toward shore. This is an illusion, of course; in fact it is the dunes which are moving, some fifteen feet a year, walking inland toward the highway on a course bent to cover the town in sand one fine day. The water's not going anywhere; a pulse moves through it and lifts and lets it go. In a time-lapse photo, over a season, or a year perhaps, the impression would I think be reversed: the waves must freeze to an average stillness, a little blurred at the edges, and the slow moving dunes would be seen to crawl forward, cresting and tumbling over themselves, grain by wind-borne grain. This new world risen from the sea. Quietly, magically, in smallest increments over millennia the frozen wave turns to stone, and the stone dances.

The ocean is waves and the dunes are also waves; I can see that clearly. Are they a form of a motion? Cadences of water and mineral, the gulls' wings rippling V-shapes over the beach, a shape I can see clearly in my mind, a shape that exists nowhere, only momentarily glimpsed in the instant of opening, closing. That pulse that thrums through bare matter, arranging visible molecules in its reflection, is not a life pulse but something older than life, and more absolute. The grass lies down under the wind and the vines tangle and tumble down into the valleys. Life is still very small here—it is like the beginning of the world every day, among bare elements. Water, stone and salt, wind and currents and endless waves of light, rays from the sun . . . and life arranges, it organizes itself among these forces, absorbs energy and makes itself places to be. Grass starts out of bare sand; lichen covers the rock; ants crawl forward out of cool crevices.

A marsh hawk circles the valley and up the side of the hill, tipping her wings, listening closely in the grass. Her flight winds up and back, looping one trail on the next to comprehend the ground below her. She weaves a trap from the air and pounces, dropping out of the sky.

The beach grass at my foot bends and draws spirals in the sand. I scuff out the marks, and it starts over. Pale grains pile up against the stem as the least, invisible motion of air impels the blade to wave, and the weight of the grasshead pulls it down toward the root. It is blank and particular, this little pile of sand pushed up at the base of the grass stem, apparently without impulse, pure undistinguished matter. Sweep it away and more falls in. This mass appears indivisible; though no two grains are alike there is no real difference in them either.

If this world moves in waves, sand is the matter that is displaced, lifted by minutest particles, singly and in droves, to change the structure of appearances. Sand follows motion, riding inside waves or currents. Its weight is nothing; it can blow away or float or be carried along by any agency. The shapes it makes have nothing to do with the structure of its pieces, old eroded crystals, particles of quartz and feldspar, flakes of silica. Gathered up, they make plains and pleats, cliffs and dunes, and long sloping beaches where terns and plovers scratch out nests.

Sand grains are very old, worn down from rock and mineral, finally nearly irreducible. They are the particular, the acted-upon, *"material."* Each grain is so much empty space: a succession of hard ridges arrayed around holes. They are imaginary arrangements, as all matter is: ninety-nine and ninety-nine hundredths percent empty space. Lifted and carried, held in the motions of water and air, without force or strength of their own, they offer a physical record of the evanescent: "This is the direction the wind came; here is the meeting of wave and cliff."

"I will multiply thy seed as the stars of the heaven, and as the sand which is upon the seashore. . . ."

"And yet the number of the children of Israel shall be like the sand of the sea, which cannot be measured nor numbered."

The breath of the Lord moved over the dust and the dust stirred and rose up. The breath of the Lord was a gale force, immense, irresistible. How was the dust gathered; why wasn't it set fleeing before that storm wave of God's own breath? The Hebrew word for creature also translates as soul—what brings the two together, dust and spirit, to make a creature that walks about, builds walls and cities, that utters the outgoing breath shaped in words of praise? What force holds us, to compel the disparate particles to return, and makes them utter the stillness of a single form? The spider's spiral web, the moon snail's curling shell, and the marsh hawk's coiled orbit—all these speak of return. Something makes the movement turn back as it builds, some desire for unity or coherence. The breath of waves across sand, the sun's radiant energy spilled forward endlessly, breath of spirit entering the dust, these move the dead matter forward, but still something holds back, slowing the movement, adding a curve to every line.

A flight of small, indistinct birds skittering past the weathervane tugs my gaze after them, up into the sky. They flitter into bushes, a score of impulses whirled up as one, and scatter into the dusty miller where they pull and dig, making quick, decisive motions with their heads, tearing the seedheads apart, holding on with their feet.

Down on the beach some seabirds are diving. Their wings tuck in against their sides as they plummet, head down, hurtling toward the water; then a quick opening to sheer off at the surface. The fall forward is entire, giving in to gravity's quick tug, and then the virtuoso flourish at the end, unfurling wings. For every fall forward is a compensating holding back that keeps a balance, a hesitancy that makes it circle back to complete itself. Straight lines are the will's fantasy; the world is round and we move in orbits, sphere within sphere, pivoting from an unseen center and, ". . . the way from any point to any other point," as Lawrence wrote, "is around the bend of the inevitable."

But sand advances like a ghost across the surface of sculpted sand. It gleams like skin, wide and white, heaped uprising, its surfaces bright polished as if a dune were a single thing. Elements cohere, like this *body* of land, this cape whose form curls backward, a shrimp's tail, a cocked fist. Thrust out to sea, the peninsula clings to itself at the end, reversing direction. Countering the force that moves things forward is a force of resistance. It drags the act behind the intention, it thinks again, looks over its shoulder, repeats. The sandbar that trips the wave and sends it sprawling, in curls and spirals in the air, to where it breaks in the sun in a million filaments, is the visible form of "wave."

A moon snail as big as my thumb, bleached white by the sun, lies on the step beside me. I picked it up on the beach this morning, God knows why. I collect things for no reason, liking the feel of a thing in my hand, wanting to return with a token, something tangible and perfectly useless. This shell is worn, fragile as old crockery. It has been empty a long time, buried and tossed about, cracked along the edges. Why I chose this and not another I can't say; shells are scattered everywhere and this one had nothing special to recommend it, whether in size, perfection of shape or state of preservation. But if I must collect, why not, after all, choose the ordinary specimen? The extraordinary speaks of exception, insisting on itself, while the ordinary speaks for its type. This one will do for all the shells I have found and kicked aside, picked up and carried and dropped again, the way people always do at the beach in summer, in the long afternoons. I hold it and move my finger along its furls and feel it turn, still spiraling in my hand, small coracle in which the animal floated to sea. It is dark inside, where the soft-bodied mollusk pressed against the wall, curled up, dreaming its one life. That life was ravenous, and blind, a sucker of life juices from clams and mussels and other moon snails when necessary. Now empty, it keeps that impress, that turn and return; the animal has long since died. I study it awhile, turning it over, then pitch it into the sand where it will become sand.

III

These three then: spiral, sand and wave—the shape, the matter, and the meter of this place. The wind seems like another body of the sea, extending its tides and currents inland, rippling the tops of the dunes, everything in motion, the ocean urging its grains of sand forward, licking and lapping at the land's edge like an animal mother, slowly building the spiral that makes and unmakes the world.

These three—I would like to say that is all. But there is a fourth thing always before me that I can't forget. It is there in the engines that comes across the dunes at sunset, and in the little red and green lights of airplanes that skim the beach all night, in the questioning blips on radar screens that track them, and the oil tankers looming at dawn on the horizon. It is the presence of history, as close to us here as ever, and I can read it here as plainly as I read the other forces. It is history that beats its straight path across every wave and curve and piles up stones into monuments, with its old story of force and shortcuts, will and nightmare, and never treading the same ground twice. Engine, dynamo, drumbeat, whirlwind—history is said to march, and it marches in loud boots, clomping forward with a great willful noise best played by drum and tuba. I would turn away from it here if I could and just listen to the water, which is full of longing but never articulates a demand. I would turn away and only listen, but it is not possible. The radar domes in Truro glow in the sky at night above the dune called Ararat and planes practice maneuvers overhead. Fishing boats trail oil and purple spumes of spilled gasoline and garbage of their trade. Tankers carrying oil from feudal kingdoms sit like gray slugs on the horizon and Highland Light sends its white beam around and around, cutting through clouds with its peremptory light.

All summer Air Force pilots train against attack of this seacoast; their loops and turnings overhead remind us who owns this shore. The jets leave curling vapors behind them, looping the air as if they wanted to return. But cannot. Impossible, can't turn back. Even in sleep, as we fall, the hemisphere is turning back to light, to the new day loud with news, its noises and demands.

On a very still night, when the wind picks up suddenly from the south we may hear the traffic from Route 6. We aren't so far from anything here at all—the big blue water tower sits on one horizon with the lights of the town ranged beyond it, and the Park Service rangers come down the beach in their green pickups at regular intervals. We are settled, here in this trammeled wilderness, smack in the middle of the world, with both feet in time—and yet. And yet time does let go a little here and there, for intervals when the other world takes over. Then we are closer to something we do not know well, and we feel another life, the life of the continent and the unformed sphere of water touching it, still touching and forming. And even though the air is full of death and terrible radio signals, and full color pictures of war zones from satellites sent overhead, it is peaceful beneath all that. It is the peaceful-ness within creation, which will not save us, but which is nevertheless full, essential, and needing to be known. A fat gull rows across the sky, ponderously, deliberately, flying. When we have come back from our winter rooms, when we have returned at the end of a day's wandering, we settle ourselves for another look around, fill the small blue cups with brandy, and watch and listen as evening comes on. Then day and night pour into one another like water, each day is a slice of eternity—each day is the whole thing. Then it is time to light the lamps, and not so much later, to put them out.

We live on the outside arm of a spiral, about halfway from the center of a galaxy which, from a particular angle no one can see anyway, has been said to resemble a fried egg. We live on a rare green jewel of a planet, wound up in clouds and vapor, under a membrane so tough that objects strike it and burst into flames.

From where we stand it looks as if the universe is coming apart. The galaxies whirl like sandstorms, stars and planets flung outward, scatter-ing fragments of fire and dust. The outward thrust of this universal explosion pushes everything away, and gravity, the force of attraction, pulls back and draws the receding stars and planets into new orbits, to skitter and wobble and make trails across the sky.

The universe expanding outward from every point makes every point the possible center of an infinite expansion. Ptolemy was right: we are, every one of us, at the center, and against the swirl of matter and light out there, we may sense ourselves occupying a relative stillness.

This is all we know. The wind luffs the boards of the shack and night comes again. The house stands, straining in what the poet Tomas Tran-stromer calls "its constellation of nails." The moon pulls at the earth's waters and the earth draws them back down. In a high wind I hear the nails tug in the flesh of the wood, and feel the shack leaning, lifting, *straining*. Hold on. We're going to soar right over that far dune one day and wake up on Plymouth Rock; I dream it often, that ungainly triumphant flight of the shack Euphoria, unwinding itself board by board. Everything we touch is flying, years in its breath. Expanding, pushed beyond bounds, we rush straight ahead into chaos, rebounding and falling forward, like water bouncing down rocks.

Where are we going? despite our best instruments, calculations, and predictions, we don't know. We can measure speed and direction, but there's no destination in sight. We are unwheeling the bound energies, fleeing the center, as a plant leaves the seed in shoots, that in time-lapse photography might seem to break forward with the abrupt violence of sunflares. This dissolution makes another shape, a new form, entirely called-for and necessary. And in this grand amazement I sit, still, for all practical purposes, and breathe in the momentary world.

The geese go north in April, flying over night and day. Sun slaps the broken surfaces of water and reflects off the sand, but the Atlantic stays hard and cold. In May a cock pheasant displays, parading around the shack, stamping his feet and tossing back his head as he calls in strangled tones for a lady-love. Any love will do, only come soon! He is gorgeous, all bright gold and flame colors, calling and calling; his voice is raucously bad.

Our first night back we stumbled over boxes we were too tired to unpack before dark. The room filled with moonlight reflected up from the sand. The clock ticked too loud and I got up to put it outside. What possessed me to bring a clock at all? It ends up in the outhouse, loudly singing to itself, time's cricket in a cage, keeping count just in case we need to know the time, any time at all this summer.

Waking, I wash at the basin; water swirls into the drain, tugged sideways by the earth's rotation. The water spirals down, swallowing itself, breaking up whatever images it held. The morning pulls forward in time; pulled through space we turn from the sun and back, our return set against the straight downward fall of a day that never returns. I feel a lingering motion in descent, some reluctance, as if this life could hold us.

Waking, I turn back to the day. A new day, in its one-time-only appearance. A drowned moth floats in widening circles in the water bucket, and suddenly, for no reason at all, a red-winged blackbird drops out of the sky onto our weather vane and begins his willful, joyful noise.

The day spins out real dream forms, conjuring a world scratched on sand, all ridges and shadow, almost a trick of light, moving faster than my mind can track it. A jet trail swirls across the blue sky, loops, and blows away again, curling, lost.

———

"Difference"

By Mark Doty

The jellyfish
float in the bay shallows
like schools of clouds,

A dozen identical—is it right
to call them creatures,
these elaborate sacks

of nothing? All they seem
is shape, and shifting,
and though a whole troop

of undulant cousins
go about their business
within a single wave's span,

every one does something unlike:
this one a balloon
open on both ends
but swollen to its full expanse,
this one a breathing heart,
this a pulsing flower.

This one a rolled condom,
or a plastic purse swallowing itself,
that one a Tiffany shade,

this a troubled parasol.
This submarine opera's
all subterfuge and disguise,

its plot a fabulous tangle
of hiding and recognition:
nothing but trope,

nothing but something
forming itself into figures
then refiguring,

sheer ectoplasm
recognizable only as the stuff
of metaphor. What can words do

but link what we know
to what we don't,
and so form a shape?

Which shrinks or swells,
configures or collapses, blooms
even as it is described

into some unlikely
marine chiffon:
a gown for Isadora?

Nothing but style.
What binds
one shape to another

also sets them apart
—but what's lovelier
than the shapeshifting

transparence of *like* and *as:*
clear, undulant words?
we look at alien grace,

unfettered
by any determined form,
and we say: balloon, flower,

heart, condom, opera,
lampshade, parasol, ballet.
Hear how the mouth,

so full
of longing for the world,
changes its shape?

"Where Do All the Peepers Go?"

By James Lazell

THE NAME PINKLETINK is the delightful favorite of the inhabitants of Martha's Vineyard for *Hyla crucifer crucifer,* the little cinnamon treefrog and famed harbinger of spring. Peepers are among the most abundant of all vertebrate animals from the valley of the St. Lawrence to the Gulf of Mexico. There is a different subspecies in southern Georgia and northern Florida.

Peepers begin their breeding activities in early March, as a rule, but can be heard at least giving their "rain call" during any month of the year. The sheer volume of a peeper chorus on a warm spring evening is amazing.

Where do all the peepers go? Along with "how can owls live without drinking water?" and "how do green turtles find Aves Island?" this is, for me, one of the great unsolved biological puzzles. I have carefully estimated numbers of *calling* peepers all over the Cape and Islands. My figures indicate there are often more than a thousand per marshland acre. Of course, the calling ones are just the males. Females are bigger— up to an inch-and-a-half, versus less than an inch on the average. Perhaps they are more succulent to snakes, raccoons, fish, other frogs, birds, and all the other things that eat them. Let's say there are only half as many females as males. That makes a total population of at least 1500 concentrated at one acre of breeding marsh. From aerial photos, automobile reconnaissance, and topographic maps, I estimate about thirty percent of Cape Cod's approximately 350 square miles is breeding ponds and marshes. That mounts to more than 100 square miles. Now, there are 640 acres in every square mile, as near as matters. That's 100 × 640 × 1500 = 96,000,000. That is the same thing as ninety-six million, for those of you, like me, who don't think well in terms of large numbers. It is awfully close to a hundred million. Now where do all those peeper go?

Numi and I were examining frogs in the Provincelands one rainy August night. Right off, about the second frog we came to (and there were hundreds) was a peeper. "See," Numi said, "there's no problem. Peepers are right out here with all the rest of the frogs, just as you should expect." We never saw another one.

Sometimes I have found peepers away from their breeding grounds. I once found a half dozen in tangles of Nantucket greenbriar. I once found one in tall grass. One popped in the window of my truck near the Hidden Forest as I drove along one afternoon (I stopped and searched for more—none). I have recorded a dozen or more hopping around in wet woods, like the State Forest on Martha's Vineyard, over the past eight years. None of that gets close to an explanation. There is no way to extrapolate a hundred million little frogs from that scanty data.

I have heard a lot of facile, specious explanations for where they go (and how owls live, and how turtles find Aves), but none that would ever stand up to a little cogent criticism. I challenge *anyone* to go out in the field with me at any time other than breeding season and show me those peepers.

Let's do a little more arithmetic. Let's presume that all 96 million spread out evenly all over Cape Cod's 350 square miles. That means 274,286 (to the nearest whole frog) per square mile. I'll settle for 275 thousand. Now, there are still 640 acres in each square mile, so there must be about 430 of the little beggars out there on every average acre.

Of course, they aren't evenly distributed. There must be optional areas where they live, and quite a few acres (like all the paved part of Route 6 and the bottom of Wequaquet Lake) where they do not live. All right, if you think you know where peepers go, pick your absolute favorite, best-of-all-possible acres, and let's go. If you can show me four peepers on it—less than one hundredth—less than one lousy percent of all the ones that must be somewhere—I will be snowed.

Come on all you canny, old New England naturalists, all you sharp young students, all you nature lovers, hikers, and campers: put your minds to it. They are little, brown to pinkish, disk-toed froggies. They look like they ought to climb, but I never heard of anyone who found one very far up in a tree (maybe fifteen feet?). Get out there. Observe. Maybe my figures are off by a factor of a hundred or so. Refute me if you can. Even so, *where do all the peepers go?*

—from *This Broken Archipelago* (1967)

Land's End

~~~~~~

F ROM ITS BEGINNINGS to the present day, the tip of Cape Cod
(encompassing Provincetown and parts of North Truro) has been
a world apart from the rest of the peninsula. To begin with, its geological origins are different. The glacial Cape ends at High Head in North
Truro, where the topography slopes dramatically downward toward
the dunes, swamps, shallow ponds, low forests, and elongated barrier
beaches of the Provincelands. All of the Provincelands are postglacial,
formed from material eroded from the Outer Beach and carried north
by ocean currents, where, over the past six thousand years, it has gradually formed the broad "hook" which encloses Provincetown's magnificent harbor.

The Provincelands (which, like the Australian desert, were called "the
outback" by the old Provincetowners) have been under public ownership—first colonial, then state, and now federal—since before the town
itself was founded. Ironically, their public ownership—or public confis-
cation, depending on your point of view—has long been and continues
to be a bone of contention. From the beginning, local inhabitants have
used the Provincelands for their own purposes—cutting wood, pasturing cows, drying fish—and have always ignored or bristled at what they
consider unfair and unnecessary restrictions. It is a question of suitable
use that has been going on now for almost three hundred years, and it
is not likely it will be resolved soon.

Because of the protection and anchorage its harbor afforded early
European fishermen, it is quite likely, as Kittredge suggests, that Provincetown was informally settled, at least seasonally, long before any of
the other Cape towns. It is also likely that from its earliest days it had a
more cosmopolitan makeup than the Pilgrim settlements, one that soon

gave it a reputation for license, smuggling, resistance to authority, and a character that has changed over the centuries in nature, but not in distinctiveness.

The Yankees eventually recognized the value of its harbor and settled there in numbers in the early eighteenth century, bringing with them a measure of law and order to the town. (Its somewhat belated incorporation in 1727 was, according to Kittredge, regarded by the populace as "an amusing detail.") Provincetown's rise during the nineteenth century to preeminence among the Cape's fishing ports (surpassed only by Gloucester and New Bedford in New England) seems to have increased and emphasized its distinctive character. Even a next-door Truro native like Shebnah Rich describes it almost as some foreign land. For Thoreau, it was the only Cape Cod village worth his attention, because both the town and its inhabitants so uniquely reflected their relationship to the sea and the dunes that bracketed them.

Thoreau's description of Provincetown takes unabashed delight in its physical and sociological oddities, yet it leaves an indelible impression on him as "the most completely maritime town that we were ever in." He was less impressed, however, with its tourist accommodations. His account of a night spent at the venerable Pilgrim House is, like his bout with the clam at the Wellfleet oysterman's house, an unusually candid view of Thoreau, and of his ability to turn personal discomfort into something approaching farce. (One can only speculate on how he—not to mention the Pilgrims—might have responded to the spectacle of transvestite costume balls that were held at the same hotel during its latter days.)

During the late 1800s, Provincetown's position as the Cape's leading fishing port was bolstered by the arrival of large numbers of Portuguese immigrants, mostly from the Azores. Provincetown, with its cosmopolitan heritage, seems to have absorbed this new ethnic element with remarkable ease, in large part because of the skill and courage demonstrated by the new arrivals. Portuguese fishermen quickly rose to captain many of the boats, and their descendants and more recent immigrants dominate the local fleet to this day. Sympathetic writers like Mary Heaton Vorse, Josef Berger, and Wilbur Daniel Steele embraced the rich addition of the Portuguese culture in essays, fiction, and plays.

Vorse and Steele were early figures in Provincetown's phenomenal growth as an art colony in the early 1900s, an era that officially began in 1899 when Charles Hawthorne opened Provincetown's first art school. 1916 saw the formation of the Provincetown Players, one of the most important small theaters in the history of American drama, which launched the career of Eugene O'Neill on a Provincetown fish wharf.

By the 1920s, Provincetown's summer community had taken on a distinctly bohemian flavor. Many of its local fishermen had abandoned long-lining and dragging and were casting their nets in the more profitable waters of rum-running. These "Days of the Locust," as Vorse termed them, resulted in some serious disruptions of the traditional life of the town, an effect recorded in her portraits of "Mrs. Mooncusser" and other local residents at the time.

One writer who was drawn to this new artistic community was Edmund Wilson, who spent most of his summers at the Cape tip in the late 1920s and 1930s. Wilson was part of a younger generation of writers and artists, many of whom eventually bought houses and became part of their communities on the Outer Cape. With his critic's temperament, he was fascinated by his colleagues' personalities and chronicled their feats and foibles copiously in his extensive diaries. Few writers have paid more moving tribute to their fellow artists, or expressed more strongly the sense of community that sustained them, than did Wilson in his reflections on "the life all finished" at the funeral of Katy Dos Passos.

Provincetown, like the rest of the Cape, has changed dramatically since the end of World War II. In some ways it has been transformed more than most towns, but in other ways it has changed the least; or rather, it has continued to change in ways it has always done. Because of its urban connections, particularly with New York, Provincetown has always reflected sociological changes more rapidly than most towns its size. During the 1950s it emerged as one of the major gay and lesbian communities on the East Coast. During the late 1960s and 1970s the town was inundated with the nation's youth counterculture. Roger Skillings's *Provincetown Stories,* a series of dramatic monologues that form a kind of modern *Spoon River Anthology,* reflects some of the darker and darkly humorous aspects of that era, when the strung-out drug culture and the culture clash between P-Town's disparate groups reached a peak. Susan Mitchell's memoir, on the other hand, attests to the enduring and complex aesthetic appeal that its environs continue to have for each new generation of artists.

During the 1980s the homosexual community has become not only more open but also more integrated into all aspects of Provincetown life. It has also had to come to grips more than most small communities with what novelist Jacquelyn Holt Park calls "the Age of the Sword"—the advent of AIDS. At the same time, local gay and lesbian literature has come of age. Its sensibility has achieved a history and a self-acceptance that allows it to be less defensive and more celebratory of itself, as in the eloquent lyrics of poet Mark Doty.

Provincetown today is generally considered the most commercialized Cape Cod town. It even seems to advertise that fact in the name of its main street. But the gaudy human carnival that swamps Commercial Street each summer is essentially a veneer that at most dominates a small stretch of the town. In fact, more than any other Cape town, Provincetown has managed to remain a community, in the traditional sense of that word—an identity unto itself. It is still primarily a collection of distinct neighborhoods, full, even in summer, of their local residents tending gardens, painting chairs, walking dogs, riding bicycles. It strikes me, in fact, as a kind of poem, not in any sentimental sense, but rather as fitting Robert Frost's hard-nosed description of himself as "a unity of bursting opposites." It contains a greater—and more notorious—ethnic and social diversity than any town over the Canal, yet its diverse parts not only manage somehow to coexist, but to form a recognizable and vital identity, one, as Mary Heaton Vorse put it, that is "quick with creation."

Tales of Early Provincetown

By Henry C. Kittredge

PROVINCETOWN, THE FIRST place on the Cape to be visited by white men, was one of the last to be dignified with the title of town. Its geographic situation is responsible for both facts: an explorer, groping his way in New England waters, could hardly fail to stumble over the tip of the Cape, and Provincetown Harbor was pretty sure to tempt him to anchor. The settlers, on the other hand, making their way overland from various parts of the Bay Colony, found plenty of good sites long before they reached the sand spit that is Provincetown. If they had been seafarers from the outset, instead of farmers and herdsmen, there would have been a different story to tell. But they were looking for hay grounds and arable fields, and took small interest in harbors.

Other Europeans had been interested in Provincetown Harbor, however, long before the *Mayflower* found shelter there—long before the *Concord* skirted its outer shore, carrying Gosnold and Archer. Landlords of sixteenth-century fishermen's taverns anywhere along the coast of Brittany or the Bay of Biscay had heard all about Provincetown from the picturesque villains who dropped in to drink brandy and sour wine of an evening between one fishing season and the next. They told tales of lurid sojourns ashore where a sickle-shaped arm of sand made a harbor in which their vessels could ride out storms from any quarter, and where natives gave them venison and strange corn for rum; tall trees stood close to the water's edge; all day great flocks of wild fowl flew about the marshes; they could fill their holds with fish without going a mile from shore. This was better than facing the rigors of the Grand Banks to the north; here they lived in houses, and the savages were their friends. 'An island, perhaps?' the landlord suggested. An island, perhaps; perhaps a cape; of that they knew nothing. So the conversation drifted along, and by and by the fishermen went to bed.

—from *Cape Cod, Its People and Their History* (1930)

Provincetown, Circa 1840

By Shebnah Rich

FORTY YEARS AGO the shores of Provincetown were lined with wind-mills, called in the vernacular, "salt-mills," used for pumping ocean water into the hundreds of acres of "salt works" that completely flanked the town and came up almost into their houses and bed-chambers. What with the salt ocean rolling on the back side, the salt bay washing the front, the thousands of hogsheads of pure salt crystallizing in shallow vats or high piled in storehouses, waiting market, and miles of salt cod-fish curing the autumnal sun, Provincetown could lay good claim to being a well-preserved community. A view of the town is better worth seeing from any approach than hundreds of places of wider fame, but fifty years ago an approach at highwater from Truro, the only land communication, was a rare view.

The quaint village hugging the crescent shore for three miles, hundreds of mills from the shore, wharves and hill-tops all in lively motion and commotion, the tall spars of the vessels in port, the steep hills rising like huge earth-works of defence, and the low sandy point half-coiled around the harbor, anchored at the tip by the lighthouse of old Darby fame, was a sight that could be seen nowhere else in this land, and was more like the old Dutch and Flemish pictures of Hobbema and Van Ostade than anything I have seen. About this time a profane visitor wrote in a weekly newspaper, "Houses, salt-works, and curiously-built hovels, for uses unknown, are mixed up together. It would seem that the God of the infidels, which they call chance, had a hand in this mys-terious jumble." The citizens properly resented this fling at their prac-tical architecture, and intimated they knew their own business.

In 1829, the Provincetown minister, Mr. Stone, said to Dr. Cornell, then a Wellfleet schoolmaster, "Would you believe that there is a town in the United States with 1800 inhabitants and only one horse with one eye? Well, that town is Provincetown and I am the only man in town that owns a horse and he is an old white one with one eye." . . .

There was then no road through the town. With no carts, wagons, carriages, horses or oxen, why a road? A road was well enough where there was use for it. The first sleigh ever used in the town was a dory; a good substitute and suggestion for the North Pole explorers. A Prov-

incetown boy seeing a carriage driving through the town wondered
how she could steer so straight without a rudder. . . . Here every man
had a path from his house to his boat or vessel, and once launched, he
was on the broad highway of nations, without tax or toll. There were
paths to the neighbors, paths to school, and paths to church; tortuous,
perhaps, but they were good pilots by night or day, on land or water.
Besides, at lowwater there was a road such as none else could boast,
washed completely twice a day from year to year, wide enough and free
enough and long enough, if followed, for the armies of the Netherlands.

> For you, they said, no barriers be,
> For you no sluggard rest;
> Each street leads downward to the sea
> Or landward to the West.

The cob wharves were then not as frequent or long as now, and travel
passed under and around them. Washing fish is one of the cherished
institutions of Provincetown. It might not inappropriately be adopted
as her coat of arms. The division of the United States surplus revenue
was the beginning of a new era in Provincetown. When the question of
appropriating the money for laying out a road and building a sidewalk
through the town was being discussed, a citizen in town meeting said:
"As this money has proved a bone of contention in most places, I think
the best place for bones is under our feet; I am therefore in favor of
appropriating this fund to a sidewalk throughout the town." Like all
great improvements, it met with bitter opposition. The old were wed
to old ways and content. They had known no inconveniences. Houses,
stores, saltworks, fish flakes and mills were to be removed, wells to be
filled, and rough places made smooth, before the road could be laid out
and sidewalks built. All of which was done, and the five-plank walk on
one side of the street, the whole length of the town, substantially as
now, was opened for travel in February, 1838, at a cost of two thousand dollars. Tradition says that some of the old people, particularly the
ladies, who had strenuously opposed the project, declared they would
never walk on it, and were as good as their word, walking slip-shod
through the sand as long as they lived. In some of the old pictures the
people are represented without feet, it being understood so much was
covered by the sand.

—from *Truro—Cape Cod* (1883)

Provincetown

By Henry David Thoreau

AFTER THREADING A swamp full of boxberry, and climbing several hills covered with shrub-oaks, without a path, where shipwrecked men would be in danger of perishing in the night, we came down upon the eastern extremity of the four planks which run the whole length of Provincetown street. This, which is the last town on the Cape, lies mainly in one street along the curving beach fronting the southeast. The sand-hills, covered with shrubbery and interposed with swamps and ponds, rose immediately behind it in the form of a crescent, which is from half a mile to a mile or more wide in the middle, and beyond these is the desert, which is the greater part of its territory, stretching to the sea on the east and west and north.

The town is compactly built in the narrow space, from ten to fifty rods deep, between the harbor and the sand-hills, and contained at that time about twenty-six hundred inhabitants. The houses, in which a more modern and pretending style has at length prevailed over the fisherman's hut, stand on the inner or plank side of the street, and the fish and store houses, with the picturesque-looking windmills of the Saltworks, on the water side. The narrow portion of the beach between forming the street, about eighteen feet wide, the only one where one carriage could pass another, if there was more than one carriage in the town, looked much "heavier" than any portion of the beach or the desert which we had walked on, it being above the reach of the highest tide, and the sand being kept loose by the occasional passage of a traveler. . . .

This was the most completely maritime town that we were ever in. It was merely a good harbor, surrounded by land, dry if not firm,—an inhabited beach, whereon fishermen cured and stored their fish, without any back country. When ashore the inhabitants still walk on planks. A few small patches have been reclaimed from the swamps, containing commonly half a dozen square rods only each. We saw one which was fenced with four lengths of rail; also a fence made wholly of hogshead staves stuck in the ground. These, and such as these, were all the cultivated and cultivable land in Provincetown. We were told that there were thirty or forty acres in all, but we did not discover a quarter part so much, and that was well dusted with sand, and looked as if the desert was claiming it. They are now turning some of their swamps into Cranberry Meadows on quite an extensive scale.

Yet far from being out of the way, Provincetown is directly in the way of the navigator, and he is lucky who does not run afoul of it in the dark. It is situated on one of the highways of commerce, and men from all parts of the globe touch there in the course of a year. . . .

Early the next morning I walked into a fish-house near our hotel, where three or four men were engaged in trundling out the pickled fish on barrows, and spreading them to dry. They told me that a vessel had lately come in from the Banks with forty-four thousand cod-fish. Timothy Dwight says that, just before he arrived at Provincetown, "a schooner came in from the Great Bank with fifty-six thousand fish, almost one thousand five hundred quintals, taken in a single voyage; the main deck being, on her return, eight inches under water in calm weather."

The cod in this fish-house, just out of the pickle, lay packed several feet deep, and three or four men stood on them in cowhide boots, pitching them on to the barrows with an instrument which had a single iron point. One young man, who chewed tobacco, spat on the fish repeatedly. Well, sir, thought I, when that older man sees you he will speak to you. But presently I saw the older man do the same thing. It reminded me of the figs of Smyrna.

"How long does it take to cure these fish?" I asked.

"Two good drying days, sir," was the answer.

I walked across the street again into the hotel to breakfast, and mine host inquired if I would take "hashed fish or beans." I took beans, though they never were a favorite dish of mine. I found next summer that this was still the only alternative proposed here, and the landlord was still ringing the changes on these two words. In the former dish there was a remarkable proportion of fish. As you travel inland the potato predominates. It chanced that I did not taste fresh fish of any kind on the Cape, and I was assured that they were not so much used there as in the country. That is where they are cured, and where, sometimes, travelers are cured of eating them. No fresh meat was slaughtered in Provincetown, but the little that was used at the public houses was brought from Boston by the steamer.

A great many of the houses here were surrounded by fish-flakes close up to the sills on all sides, with only a narrow passage two or three feet wide, to the front door; so that instead of looking out into a flower or grass plot, you looked on to so many square rods of cod turned wrong side outwards. These parterres were said to be least like a flower-garden in a good drying day in midsummer. There were flakes of every age and pattern, and some so rusty and overgrown with lichens that they looked as if they might have served the founders of the fishery here. Some had broken down under the weight of successive harvests. The principal employment of the inhabitants at this time seemed to be to trundle out their fish and spread them in the morning, and bring them in at night. I saw how many a loafer who chanced to be out early enough, got a job at wheeling out the fish of his neighbor who was anxious to improve the whole of a fair day.

Now then I knew where salt fish were caught. They were everywhere lying on their backs, their collar-bones standing out like the lapels of a man-o'-war-man's jacket, and inviting all things to come and rest in their bosoms; and all things, with a few exceptions, accepted the invitation. I think, by the way, that if you should wrap a large salt fish round a small boy, he would have a coat of such a fashion as I have seen many a one wear to muster. Salt fish were stacked up on the wharves, looking like corded wood, maple and yellow birch with the bark left on. I mistook them for this at first, and such in one sense they were,— fuel to maintain our vital fires,—an eastern wood which grew on the Grand Banks. Some were stacked in the form of huge flower-pots, being laid in small circles with the tails outwards, each circle successively larger than the preceding until the pile was three or four feet high, when the circles rapidly diminished, so as to form a conical roof. On the shores of New Brunswick this is covered with birch-bark, and stones are placed upon it, and, being thus rendered impervious to the rain, it is left to season before being packed for exportation.

It is rumored that in the fall the cows here are sometimes fed on cod's heads! The godlike part of the cod; which, like the human head, is curiously and wonderfully made, forsooth has but little less brain in it,—coming to such an end! to be craunched by cows! I felt my own skull crack from sympathy. What if the heads of men were to be cut off to feed the cows of a superior order of beings who inhabit the island in the ether? Away goes your fine brain, the house of thought and instinct, to swell the cud of a ruminant animal!—However, an inhabitant assured me that they did not make a practice of feeding cows on cod's heads; the cows merely *would* eat them sometimes, but I might live there all my days and never see it done. A cow wanting salt would also sometimes lick out all the soft part of a cod on the flakes. This he would have me believe was the foundation of this fish-story.

—from *Cape Cod* (1865)

A Night at the Pilgrim House

By Henry David Thoreau

JUNE 21, 1857. At the Pilgrim House,* though it was not crowded, they put me into a small attic chamber which had two double beds in it, and only one window, high in a corner, twenty and a half inches by twenty-five and a half, in the alcove when it was swung open, and it required a chair to look out conveniently. Fortunately it was not a cold night and the window could be kept open, though at the risk of being visited by the cats, which appear to swarm on the roofs of Province-town like the mosquitoes on the summits of its hills. I have spent four memorable nights there in as many different years, and have added con-siderable thereby to my knowledge of the natural history of the cat and the bedbug. Sleep was out of the question. A night in one of the attics of Provincetown! to say nothing of what is to be learned in entomol-ogy. It would be worth the while to send a professor there, one who was also skilled in entomology. Such is your *Pilgerruhe* or Pilgrims'-Rest.

Every now and then one of these animals on its travels leaped from a neighboring roof on to mine, with such a noise as if a six-pounder had fallen within two feet of my head,—the discharge of a catapult,—a twelve-pounder discharged by a catapult,—and then followed such a scram-bling as banished sleep for a long season, while I watched lest they came in at the open window. A kind of foretaste, methought, of the infernal regions. I didn't wonder they gave quitclaim deeds of their land here. My experience is that you fare best at private houses. The barroom may be defined a place to spit.

> Soon as the evening shades prevail,
> The *cats take* up the wondrous tale.

At still midnight, when, half awake, half asleep, you seem to be wel-tering in your own blood on a battlefield, you hear the stealthy tread of

---

*The Pilgrim House burned down in the fall of 1990.

padded feet belonging to some animal of the cat tribe, perambulating the roof within a few inches of your head.

—from *The Journal of Henry David Thoreau* (1906)

———

from *Time and the Town* (1942)

By Mary Heaton Vorse

CAPE COD IS thrust out from the coast of Massachusetts sixty miles into the Atlantic like an arm with a fist on the end. Within the fist's shelter sits Provincetown.

When we saw it first from the deck of a boat making the trip from Boston to the Cape, it seemed to rise out of the sea. It stretched out as we approached it, low-lying and gray, its skyline punctuated with a standpipe and the steeples of churches. Gray wharves ran out into the bay. It was a seafaring place that lived from the sea and by the sea and whose one crop was fish.

When I drove around the town in a horse-drawn accommodation, I knew that here was home, that I wanted to live here always. Nor have I changed my mind in these thirty-five years, nor for one moment wished to live anywhere else, though I have been over half the globe.

The town is three miles long and two streets wide. The front street follows the bay's curve. The two main streets are woven together with a tangle of narrow lanes so numerous no one person knows them all.

Portuguese fishermen made an informal meeting place midtown. Down the narrow streets ran beautiful dark-skinned children. Old women stood in doors of Cape Cod houses, looking as though they had come yesterday from the Western Islands.

The vast harbor can hold the entire Atlantic fleet. The combination of wild and austere country bordered by the Atlantic Ocean, flanked by glittering dunes, holds one forever. You are in a populous, exciting town, yet a five minutes' walk takes you to untamed, back country. You live in a land place and yet all the ships of the sea touch here.

What I experienced when I first drove through Provincetown's long street, when I walked through the low, scrubby woods "in back" through the dunes to the outside shore, was as definite, as acute, as falling in love at first sight. The knowledge that this was to be my home forever did not come as a shock, or with any sense of surprise; it was rather as though I were invaded by the town and surrounded by it, as though the town had literally got into my blood. I had also the sense of completion that a hitherto homeless person has on discovering home.

I am not the only person who came here to spend two weeks and remained a lifetime; I am not the only one who if exiled would feel as though my taproot were cut. I have read letters written back from the Azores by homesick boys. I have seen letters from the Pacific Coast from other children—"Oh, if I could only see Provincetown again!" On holidays by boat, by train, in car, hitchhiking, the young people come streaming back. There are boys and girls who exist only for the times when they can return home.

It is almost as if this devotion to Provincetown were secret or a special sense. People either like it extravagantly or see nothing but a town of small houses built too close together, existing on a barren sandspit, surrounded by scrubby woods and inhospitable dunes, rimmed by a beach covered, more often than not, with broken bottles and dead fish. Many loathe the town on sight and see only that it is crowded, noisy, dirty; they hate the very landscape and long for lush pastures and green trees.

There seems to be no middle ground, unless one excepts those tourists who call Provincetown "quaint." And it is not quaint. It is a serious town; the way it is built has to do with the difficult and dangerous manner in which its living has always been earned. Provincetown lives by skill and daring, by luck and chance, for fishing is an immense gamble—riches on the one hand and death on the other. So tragedy, the imminence of death, and adventure prevent that stagnation which is the usual fate of small towns.

When I try to account for the passion which Provincetown rouses in the hearts of the people who have lived here, it is these elements which determine its quickened, high sense of life. People here have been nourished by beauty and change and danger.

Children who listen to tales of adventure, improbable escapes, heroism, and sudden death, as events which have happened in their front yards, find other places tame. A boy can see living heroes walk the streets, men who have been through hairbreadth rescues or who have made miraculous catches of fish, men who gamble with death to make a quick market.

If Provincetown were wiped out—my house and my town gone—I

would be as vulnerable as a hermit crab without its shell. Wherever I go I carry Provincetown around with me invisibly. And as I am, so are most of those who live here.

*   *   *

I still call my house Kibbe Cook's house, as though it were only lent me. Last summer on the New Beach I got to talking with an old lady, who turned to her husband to say,

"Isaiah, here are the folks who live in Kibbe Cook's house!"

The name of the old owner sticks partly because no one but the Cooks ever lived in this house before us, partly in the unconscious recognition that this house and the Cook family spanned an important part of Provincetown history.

Within this Provincetown, which differs from every other town in the world and which has its own individual shape, aspect, essence, is Kibbe Cook's house, which again is different from all other houses in the world.

The first week we were in Provincetown we saw Kibbe Cook's house sitting under its big willow. The shingles were gray. The big square chimney was tumbling down. A board was nailed across the sagging front door. An unkempt path led to this closed door and grass grew high around it. Bricks had fallen from the underpinnings.

It had that untenanted and miserable air of a house whose people had died and left it abandoned. For this old house was not merely closed. It was a home going begging. The front windows with crooked shutters aswing seemed to peer out into the world, seeking for a family to make it live again. It had been lived in from father to son and had been planned and built by them, and how good were its proportions, how comfortable was its outline.

All the weeks of that first summer, there the house sat; and we in our first excitement about Provincetown, when we were not out on the bay or exploring the back country, did not give it the half-hour which would have made it ours.

When we looked at it next year, it had been painted and repaired by David Stull, "the ambergris king," and was for sale. The first time I went through it I knew that this low-lying yellow house was my own house, the place for me to live, forever, as the year before I had known that Provincetown was to be forever my home.

Seen from the street it looks small; in reality it is ample, rambling on room after room. Its wide fireplaces can hold big logs. Its best rooms are wainscoted, and the woodwork has been fitted in with nice workmanship. The rooms have a comfortable dignity for all their low ceilings and their modest size. There are plenty of cupboards and closets. It is so old that the doors are not planed but gouged, with door latches on many of the doors instead of knobs and old H L (Holy Lord) hinges to keep away the witches.

And best of all it is a house comfortable for a woman to work in. I like to live in an old house. I like the careful, leisurely workmanship of a former day, the patina which comes only with time, the golden dimness that the years lay across a well-constructed dwelling. Above all, give me a house whose work I can do myself if need be. In a house of a shape and size where I can do my own work I am insured against fate. No home means home to me that must have paid service, a house where you must necessarily be overworked and uncomfortable if you cannot find someone to do your work for you. . . .

It was on this piece of land and in the house with its windows on the sea that we struck deep roots. I have had as valid and important relation with this house as a woman can possibly have with another human being. I have had it lie obedient under my hand, humming along like a fine, well-running machine. I have had it impersonal, when it was run by some person other than myself. It has got away from me like a runaway horse. I have had it jerk and jump, be cross-grained, as though it resented the lack of my proper care, and tried to thwart me and to come between me and my work.

It has had times of such stillness and quiet enclosure that it seemed an extension of myself. There have been strange and phantasmal times, when all the doors have swung wide open and people have come hurtling through until it had not the privacy of a railway station. It has been sanctuary to me and it has supported me.

I have gone far away from this house, and have seen war and famine and watched history being made, and always in the back of my mind there it was, waiting for me. Away, I can reconstruct every knothole and I remember the malignity of the former back kitchen which was always a glory hole. Through the many side and back doors of my house has poured a stream of youth, a stream of friends, from the first days until now.

*   *   *

Provincetown from its earliest days has been freer, richer in life than its neighbors. Back in 1727 Truro asked to be severed from Provincetown because of the goings-on there. Provincetown gloried in this separation and laughed to itself. Truro sitting discreetly in the folds of her moors looked down her nose at Provincetown and still does. The Cape early wrote, in legend, its opinion of the folk on Land's End.

Captain Jeremiah Snaggs lived up the Cape and he did not die in the odor of sanctity. The story is he tried to escape the devil by various devices. He dodged the devil in Barnstable, he eluded him in a hollow tree in Orleans, he escaped from him in Wellfleet by putting a jack-o'-lantern which looked like him in a tree, but in Provincetown the devil caught up with him.

"Well," said Captain Jeremiah, "you caught me fair and squar'. Whar do we go from here?"

"Go?" said the devil. "Nowhar. Ain't we to Provincetown?"

*   *   *

At one end of the incredible gamut of character in Provincetown one might place Captain Cook of Peaked Hill Bars, a great lusty, life-loving man with the quality of command that any captain must have. He was a rock of a man, a landmark of the old days, salty, humorous, just, impatient, a man of stature.

Mrs. Cook was one of the many older women I got to know who had suffered too much from the sea. She had lost at sea father, brothers, cousins. It had taken toll of one generation in her family after another, so she never looked at the sea if she could help it.

Every sunup she drove in from Peaked Hill Bars. Every sunset she drove back again, through the dunes' splendid desolation, but she turned her eyes away from the blue line of ocean. She had never seen the breeches-buoy drill or the boat drill. She had watched that horizon too often from the time she was a girl for the return of menfolk who were not to come. She was a lovely woman and a notable one, but permanently saddened by tragedy.

The story of Mrs. Mary Mooncusser was also an emanation of Provincetown, but she seems to me to stand for the revenge of all the frustrations of New England and of small towns. I can tell her story because she is dead and if she had any relatives in this town I never knew it. This all happened a quarter of a century ago or more.

One summer I needed a cook, and a gray-haired, neat, elderly woman applied for the place. She dressed in gray percale with spotless white aprons, and the respectability of her appearance and speech could not be exaggerated. There was never such a tidy body, the lamp chimneys shone, the kitchen was scrubbed, she was a good cook. One day one of my neighbors came to me in embarrassment and said,

"I think you ought to know about Mrs. Mooncusser, with a young girl taking care of Mary Ellen and all. Poor thing, it's not her fault, her husband got her into drinking ways, but once in a while, not often, well, she drinks, and then she doesn't know what she does and she lets in anybody—fishermen, old men, little boys, she don't know." It was like finding a sewer where you thought there was a brook.

So one day when Mrs. Mooncusser didn't come, I went to her house with a lame excuse that I couldn't afford two girls any more. I knocked on the front door and no one answered, and I went to the back door and it gave under my knock. I went through a spotless kitchen into a spotless living room. There was an antimacassar on the padded back of a rocker. A tortoise-shell cat sat purring in the sun. Geraniums bloomed at the windows. You could have "et from the floor," as the saying goes. Everything was order and peace in the bright morning, and I called,

"Oo-hoo, Mrs. Mooncusser!" And out from the bedroom off the sitting room came Mrs. Mooncusser.

Her neat hair was drawn back from her face and done in the accustomed gray knot. She was so old that already she had the gray look of age. There was nothing whatever the matter with Mrs. Mooncusser except that she was stark naked. and she said,

"Good morning, Mrs. Vorse, sit down," and she herself sat down and rocked gently, with the morning sun streaming in on her bareness.

And I said, "Good morning, Mrs. Mooncusser," and then told her what I had come to say.

"I was expecting this but I'm sorry to leave you, Mrs. Vorse, because you've been very nice to me," said she, rocking gently, her bare feet padding the floor.

And I said, "I am sorry to have you go, Mrs. Mooncusser, as you have been very nice to me too." Then she got up and I got up.

And she said, "Let me let you out the front door, Mrs. Vorse."

So standing there, naked, and apparently unconscious of it, she opened the front door, and I went down the neat path bordered with zinnias. She watched me go. The personification of the dark things hidden in all small towns.

*　　*　　*

The very houses are subject to change and move about as though not anchored to the land. In most places when a man builds a house he builds it and there it stands, practically unchanged, keeping the same form in which it began, and almost invariably in the same place. This is not true in Provincetown. Houses there do not remain upon their foundations. Formerly, every summer one saw houses cumbrously moving down the front street.

People in Provincetown do not regard houses as stationary objects.

A man will buy a piece of dune land above the town and a cottage on the front shore, and presently up the hill toils the little house. Or he buys a piece of shore front and a cottage on the back street, and presently the house is wambling along to take its place on the water.

It has always been so since the old days. Provincetown people got a habit of moving their houses long ago when there was a settlement of forty-eight houses over by Long Point. This sickle of sand which encloses one of the finest harbors on the North Atlantic was so narrow that encroaching storms played havoc with it and threatened at one time to sweep the narrow point away. It was too valuable a harbor to be destroyed and the government took it over. But the thrifty Provincetowners asked the government:

"What are you going to do with these houses?"

"Nothing," responded the government.

"Well, can we take them?"

"If you take them away," answered the government. The Provincetown fathers consulted together. And next, houses supported on wrecking barrels bobbed solemnly across the bay. They "figgered" it this way.

If wrecking barrels can support and bring up from the sea's bottom a vessel of many tons' burden, why can't a raft of wrecking barrels support a house on the surface of the water? It could and did. Arnold's Radio Shop, formerly Matheson's Department Store, then our principal store in town, was once the schoolhouse, and though a large building it went to sea and became an amphibious animal. They say that so gently were these houses eased off that the moving didn't interfere with the housewife cooking her dinner.*

*   *   *

No group of people ever had less sense of having a mission than did the Provincetown Players. This theater which began so modestly with no aim except the amusement of its own members altered the course of the history of the theater in America. Why it should have had such a success and had such far-reaching results was more than the happy chance which brought plays, actors, and theater together with a leader like George Cram Cook.

The success of the Provincetown Players was, in a small degree, one of those explosions of talent which from time to time transform art and

---

*Several dozen of these former Long Point houses, most of which were relocated on the east end of Commercial Street, can be identified today by small blue plaques depicting a house on a barge.

science. Such explosions come only in times when a creative breath is blowing through all of society. The Provincetown Players were part of the wave of creation to which the war put an end. . . .

Living in Provincetown the summer of 1915 among others were Susan Glaspell and George Cram Cook, Hutchins Hapgood and Neith Boyce, the Steeles, the Zorachs, the Henry Marion Halls, Edward and Stella Ballantine, Robert Edmond Jones, and Joe O'Brien and myself.

From the first the leadership was with Jig Cook, without whom there could never have been any Provincetown Players. The plays touched off a fire in him since for years he had been thinking of the theater as a community expression—the old dream of people working together and creating together.

The first plays were given at the Hapgoods' house, with settings improvised by Robert Edmond Jones. One of the plays was given on the porch with the sea for a background. The audience then went on the porch to look into the house for the second play.

Neith Hapgood had written a play called *Constancy,* which was a witty take-off on the stormy loves of Jack Reed and Mabel Dodge. Joe O'Brien and Neith were the actors.

Jig and Susan's play, *Suppressed Desires,* had been written in a moment of gaiety the year before. This famous play was a satire on the Freudian fad of the moment. No one would buy it; theatrical producers called it too special. This "special" play has had thousands of performances. It has been played all over the country by every kind of theatrical group. Through twenty-five years and more, *Suppressed Desires* has sold and still sells.

These two plays were so amusing, there was such a breath of life in the performance, that we wanted to do more. Our wharf, with the fishhouse on the end, was conveniently at hand to serve as a theater. The fishhouse was a hundred feet long and fifty feet wide. It had a dark, weathered look, and around the piles the waves always lapped except at extreme low tide. There was a huge door on rollers at the side and another at the end which made it possible to use the bay as a backdrop. The planks were wide and one could look through the cracks at the water. The color of the big beams and planks was rich with age.

We dragged out the boats and nets which still stood there. We all made contributions to buy lumber for seats and fittings. We made the seats of planks put on sawhorses and kegs. We ransacked our houses for costumes and painted our own scenery. Our first curtain was a green rep curtain my mother had made for me for "theatricals" in our attic in Amherst. Out of these odds and ends we made a theater, which was to have such unsuspected and far-reaching effects beyond the borders of Provincetown.

The night for the first performance came. Four people stood in the wings with lamps in their hands to light the stage. Lanterns with tin reflectors were placed before the stage like old footlights. Four people stood beside the lamp bearers with shovels and sand in case of fire, and with these lights the fishhouse took on depth and mystery. . . .

I sat in the audience on the hard bench, watching the performance, hardly believing what we had done. The theater was full of enthusiastic people—a creative audience. In spite of its raining in torrents, everyone had come down the dark wharf lighted here and there by a lantern. People had leaned their umbrellas against one of the big timbers which supported the roof. I noticed an umbrella stirred, then slowly slid down an enormous knothole to the sand thirty feet below. With the stealth of eels, other umbrellas went down the knothole to join their fellows under the wharf. The dark interior, the laughing audience, the little stage with its spirited performance, and the absconding umbrellas are all part of the memory of the first night of the Provincetown Players.

All the next winter Jig Cook was thinking in terms of a community theater. The play and the response of the group were stimulating to his imagination. Susan Glaspell wrote of this time in *The Road to the Temple:*

It might have ended there—people giving plays in the summer, if it hadn't been—Do you remember Jig's dream city, how there was to be a theater, and "why not write our own plays and put them on ourselves, giving writer, actor, designer, a chance to work together without the commercial thing imposed from without? A whole community working together, developing unsuspected talents. The city ought to furnish the kind of audience that will cause new plays to be written."

The summer people had gone. Jig would go out on the old wharf and "step" the fish-house. Wasn't there two feet more than he had thought? He would open the sliding-door that was the back wall, through which fish, nets, oars, anchors, boats, used to be dragged, and stand looking across the harbor to the Truro hills, hearing the waves lap the piles below him. He would walk back slowly, head a little bent, twisting his forelock.

"One man cannot produce drama. True drama is born only of one feeling animating all the members of a clan—a spirit shared by all and expressed by the few for the all. If there is nothing to take the place of the common religious purpose and passion of the primitive group, out of which the Dionysian dance was born, no new vital drama can arise in any people." He and Neith Boyce said it together. He came home and wrote it down as an affirmation of faith.

The original group had new members the next summer—Frederick Burt, the B. J. O. Nordfeldts, Jack Reed and Louise Bryant, Harry Kemp and Mary Pyne and Hutch Collins. Terry Carlin, an old anarchist whom all of us knew, took a shack on the water with a young fellow named Eugene O'Neill. Terry was a tall, beautiful old man, with gay blue eyes and a shock of iron-gray hair. He had fine, muscular workman's hands. I remember meeting him, looming out of the fog, in the back country, with him beautiful Mary Pyne, Harry Kemp's wife. Mary had on a gray cape and her red hair shone through the fog. Together they looked like a symbolic picture of Ireland.

Terry's young friend, Gene O'Neill, was dark and good-looking. He told us shyly that he had written some plays.

When Frederick Burt read *Bound East for Cardiff* at the Cooks', Gene went into the next room while the reading was going on, for his tough, hard-boiled pose covered extreme sensitiveness. There was no one there during that reading who did not recognize the quality of this play. Here was something new, the true feeling of the sea. O'Neill had spent a couple of years as a seaman in his young, turbulent days and he had brought back from the experience the Glencairn cycle. Nothing that O'Neill did later had more truth than his early plays. From that moment he took his place as an important writer.

No one of us who heard that play reading will ever forget it, nor the reading of *Trifles* by Susan Glaspell, which took place at my house. Listening to the plays and giving them the instant recognition they deserved was a company of young people whom destiny had touched. Strange fates awaited them. Gene was to be America's greatest playwright and to withdraw completely from the world. Jack Reed was to be buried under the Kremlin in Moscow, and Jig Cook was to die in Greece and be laid in his grave by the women of the village, a stone from the Parthenon for his head given by the Greek government. . . .

These different personalities all touched with greatness formed the center of the group who so quickly recognized the talent of Eugene O'Neill and who gave *Bound East for Cardiff.*

It has never been more authentically played than it was by our group of amateurs, on the old wharf, with the sound of the sea beneath it. Susan Glaspell describes it this way:

The sea has been good to Eugene O'Neill. It was there for his opening. There was a fog, just as the script demanded, fog bell in the harbor. The tide was in, and it washed under us and around, spraying through the holes in the floor, giving us the rhythm and the flavor of the sea while the big dying sailor talked to his friend Dris of the life he had always wanted deep in the land, where you'd never see a ship or smell the sea.

*   *   *

When the big whaling fleet went out from Provincetown on voyages to the South Seas after whales and sea elephants, and our coasters plied from Boston to the West Indies, our skippers stopped at the Western Islands to recruit their crews, and the Portuguese sailors who were landed in Provincetown from our vessels liked this country and sent for their wives and children or for their sweethearts.

The Portuguese immigration which began in the great whaling days continued until legislation put an end to immigration. The greatest number came in the decade between 1911 and 1920. This immigration is divided almost evenly between the Atlantic seaboard and the Pacific coast. In the west more Portuguese work in the mills, while six thousand fishermen are divided between Provincetown and the other fishing towns.

Those who came to Provincetown were almost all from the Western Islands, the Azores, and in the early days there was a considerable immigration of Bravas from the Cape Verde Islands. These are people of pride and character, a mixture of Sudanese Negro, who were a proud and superior warrior race, of Arab and Portuguese.

Many Portuguese families have American names. A cabin boy would be brought over by some old sea captain and raised as a son of the family. First he would be known, perhaps, as "Snow's Manell," and then he would become known as "Manny Snow," his old name forgotten but his religion kept. Other names became Anglicized. Perriaras or Perez became Perrys, Diaz became Deers.

A little Provincetown boy once landed at Ponta Delgada in São Miguel. He looked around at the children and the sailors loafing at the water front, and the signs on the shops, and his comment was:

"Why, this is just like home!"

And no wonder. Fayal, Flores, Pico, São Miguel, began over seventy years ago sending their handsome, clean-blooded people to us and have been doing so ever since. "The Lisbons," people from Portugal, came much later.

By the first of the century, ninety per cent of the fishing was being done by the Portuguese. The great fresh fishermen were mainly captained by Portuguese and manned by Portuguese. The fleet of "gasoliners" was almost entirely in the hands of the Portuguese.

The Western Islanders bought their homes and their vessels, went into business, or became coast guards. The tax list of Provincetown shows more Portuguese names than it does those of Americans.

The Portuguese weren't tucked away in one little quarter of the town as were the early Irish settlements through the New England towns. On three-mile-long Commercial Street, that spreads along the water front, are perpetual little crowds of brilliantly colored Portuguese children; by Railroad Wharf are always knots of fishermen—handsome, strong-looking fellows—and as you go farther along toward the West End, " 'way up along," you seem to be in a foreign community altogether. The names on the shops are Coreas, Silvas, Cabrals, Mantas; the very language of the street is foreign.

At six-o'clock Mass, the priest still preaches first in Portuguese for the benefit of the old folk who had never learned English and then in English for the children who know English better than the tongue of their fathers. Saint Peter's Church was built by the Portuguese fishermen who each gave the money from a "fare" until the church was completed.

Formerly posters advertised the Thanksgiving Dance in the Town Hall: Dances—American, São Miguel, Flores, Pico, Fayal. Thus, this merrymaking, commemorating a day so essentially American, became half Portuguese. The American dances were danced upstairs; those of old Portugal, the Charmelita and others, were danced downstairs by young people and old. . . .

Formerly there were always men knotting new nets in their "stores," as they called the little sheds on the water front where the gear is kept. Making and mending nets were as unceasing a work as that of housekeeping. Fish nets are fragile things, and the fury of the storms and the struggles of the fish are constantly rending their meshes. From the fishhouse would come the sound of a *guitarre,* the seven-string Portuguese instrument. Carts laden with nets to spread out to dry their accumulation of seaweed and sea creatures went down the street. When they were finally dried, the nets were tarred and piled, black and dripping, from the great tar kettles, to be laid again over the blueberry bushes to dry, like a mourning veil.

If you stopped inside the fishhouse you would hear stories of miraculous catches, of strange creatures seen—stories like that of Louis Tindrawers and his dory mate, Lopez, who were separated from their vessel by fog, and when the fog lifted the vessel was gone. They rowed for two days and two nights and finally came upon the back side, thinking themselves in hard luck, only to find they were the only ones left alive of their crew and that their vessel had been cut down by a steamer in the fog.

Or you might hear a legend like that of how the gray moss that covers the dunes and blooms with a yellow flower happens to be called "Mary's flower" by the Portuguese. A fisherman took his wife and baby to live in one of the deserted shacks up at Helltown. He was so poor he didn't have a power dory and still used sail. As he didn't return, food grew low and there was only enough flour left for one loaf of bread for his wife and baby.

One night there was a terrible storm and the woman heard a knocking on the door and hastened to open it. It was a woman with a baby wrapped in a shawl. The fisherman's wife warmed her visitors before the fire and gave them the last of the bread and used the last bit of coffee.

The next morning was beautiful. The woman said good-by and started off across the gray moss of the dunes, the baby in her arms. Then a wonderful thing happened. The gray moss bloomed under her feet in golden flowers, and as she went away in the mist, the fisherman's wife could see a shining halo around her head, so she knew she had been visited by the Blessed Virgin, who had come to comfort her in her husband's absence, and that her husband would soon return. So Portuguese story and song and legend and nickname have been woven into our lives.

———

The Portuguese of Provincetown

By Josef Berger (Jeremiah Digges)

LAST TIME I took a pair of boots in to Joe Halfdollar, the old Portuguese fisherman who has gone into cobbling, I stopped to admire a new window display he had set out.

At the left side he had a big old shark-bitten seaboot, which he must have picked up off the beach, frayed and stringy around the top and showing a great gaping hole in the forepeak. Under this he had placed the legend, "BEFORE." At the right side, over a card printed "AFTER," a silver high-heeled dancing pump glittered in immaculate daintiness.

When I went in to congratulate old Joe on this achievement, he seemed shy. Then he gave me a wrinkly smile and explained—as he had heard so many others in Provincetown explain—it was just "his art."

Provincetown, whatever the summer may bring it, is a fishing town, and its people are fisherpeople. In July and August, when the population suddenly triples, there is some tendency to forget this. I have read wonderful descriptions of the town, from which one would gather that it is principally an art colony, festooned with nets and "picturesque" Portuguese fishermen who presumably have been planted for the convenience of the artists who paint them.

In the Cape-end eddies of summer traffic, which work into a dizzy whirlpool here, it is true that for two months of each year the town practically loses itself. One might add that it is beside itself. The tourists are now the most numerous, the artists and writers by long odds the most articulate. Hence it may come as a surprise to the visitor, when he is told that of the more than four thousand residents of the town—"year-round people"—three-fourths are Portuguese, seeking their livelihood in the fishery or indirectly from its earnings.

They are an engaging people. I do not see how Provincetown can be very life-like to writers who treat the Portuguese as incidental. Cape Cod, of course, has a rich historical interest without them, because the Cape's history goes back beyond their time; but the Cape today is very much with them, and has been so since the last quarter of the Nineteenth Century, when large numbers came to New England, attracted

275

by success stories of pretty much the same stamp that all fish stories bear. . . .

In introducing them, one must use their nicknames. For they have an odd custom of bestowing nicknames on one another—not in a spirit of levity, but in dead earnest. They practically forget their real names. Sometimes the sobriquets are not very delicate, but always they are highly descriptive; and once a man comes by his nickname, there is no escape. As it is always the surname that is replaced, whole families must abide by the practice. There is the "Rat family," for instance; there are the "Codfishes"—Manuel Codfish, Maria Codfish, and all the little Codfishes; there is the fisherman who lost both his legs—"Tom Low;" and there are Mike Molasses and Mrs. Jazzgarters. With good grace, the Rats, the Codfishes and all the rest accept what they cannot reject; cheerfully they answer to the names. Some have been in use so long that in the course of generations the real family names have become obscured, and legal problems have arisen.

—from *Cape Cod Pilot* (1937)

———

from *The Twenties*

By Edmund Wilson

COMING INTO PROVINCETOWN, exquisite delicacy of mother-of-pearl sea thinning to a fragile shelly blade along the shallow shore—a sort of iridescence of violet, blue and green—a few gulls.

Provincetown, June 20 [1927]. "Full of fairies that keep antique shops"—"The Anchorite," with its pseudo-stained glass (ecclesiastical) in the door—that soft and plumy gray-white sky, the wide westward gold such as one sees aboard ship—the lavender-ashy harbor, so fresh and lovely, full of little craft, less lavender and more ashy as the evening fell—a large clear star in the dark above the eaves of a clear white house. Excellent mackerel fried in butter and some kind of sweet oyster soup—old captain in hotel—talk of swordfish at so much a pound—clean sea-washed olive but not ruddy-tanned or swarthy slight Portuguese, black-eyed, not often handsome, nor the women beautiful, but a scrubby growth like the dune weed of the northern sand—a pretty black-eyed baby who smiled, in the arms of a weather-seasoned woman talking to another weather-seasoned woman. —I recognized the spire of the church, among roofs, that Charles Demuth had painted—the green-looking, high, dark, ominous house about which there had been some strange story that delighted O'Neill had been put into excellent shape and changed into a historical museum. —Harry Kemp on forgotten English poets, drunk and inconsequent, discouragement with study of literature— "dozens of dumb artists—literary people gone"—John Francis's gentle, appealing voice and gentlemanliness (an eccentric real estate agent)— painted wooden figurehead of woman with head thrown up and one hand clasping wreath across breast over doorstep shelter of yellow house, sunk like an old water-logged ship in a dooryard of long uncut grass, with an old woman sitting at the window—"a drink distilled from the sand on the sand dunes." —Episcopal Church of St. Mary's of the Harbor, singing *Holy, Holy, Though the darkness hide thee,* in the clean evening in the little cabin-church with the minister in his white surplice.

The sun of late afternoon glowing silver in a sky lightly iron-shadowed above a white house whose dark-blue blinds respond to the shadows of the sky—a Chinese-white house with bright lettuce-green shutters. —A fine white house with a low white fence, braided in, of long flattened rectangles latticed with diagonals, behind which the clear evening light showing the leaves of the trees on the lawn like precise silhouetted green lace, all delicate and in the flat; light-green shutters on high slender white houses, vaulted gold canary cages in windows—Pete Carr (the Carrs were two brothers who had a cart that we depended on for transferring baggage) knew better how to talk to O'Neill's guests than Dick—neither ever seemed to get married—"kept bachelor's hall" in house with radio and round sanded receptacle for tobacco juice; man who was frightened of black snake, woman who took adder by the tail and snapped its head right off. Bright blues of bachelor's-buttons, oranges, vermilions of nasturtiums, reds of poppies, deep yellows with brown-orange centers of those small sunflower-looking flowers, such bright primary colors against the meager greenery and the pale sandy soil, and the white houses.

———

from *The Thirties*

By Edmund Wilson

THIS SUMMER AT PROVINCETOWN ('32) like fifty years ago—men on wagon and getting restive, falling in love with young girls, going to New York and looking for jobs. —Picnic at Gull Pond—blue little very slightly wind-roughed inland fresh-water lake—Sambo and Toto, cocktails in thermos bottle, little chickens, Sunday papers, Dudley Poore—water creamy and warm—a sort of sentimental swim—I used to crawl all over lakes like this.

—Harbor back of the Dos Passos house—diving raft—tanned groups with legs standing up on it—sometimes people (big children) just lying on it like logs in the sun—the Russian with the narrow-striped jersey who had brought a water bicycle from the banks of the Seine—people apparently taking a big police dog for a ride in a boat—a whole pack of police and other dogs single-footing around on the sands when the tide was out—a boy in a boat dragging another boy on what looked like a cellar door—a row of sailboats like white butterflies—the small waves from the *Dorothy Bradford* which caused Stella to think that the tide had gone out as far as it was going and was now turning back—a boy in bathing trunks in a kayak, rotating the double oar like a propeller—the salad and hors d'oeuvre of the garbage—other days absolutely clear—stumps of the piles of the old pier just sticking up in a rectangular patch like the worn-down bases of old teeth. —On rainy days and in dreary winter weather you felt cooped up on the narrow land, however, like all places where life is so much the water. —A sailboat slipping by at night refreshing the night by a tracing of silent life across it—the dark church of Truro set high on its hill on one side of the harbor and white Long Point light at the end of its sandspit on the other. . . .

*   *   *

Provincetown, August 1, 1936. Old life all finished: people working now, not drinking so much, not giving so many dissolute parties, but with much less relation to one another, no longer a real community—two boatloads of Boston trippers a day—the *Romance* and the *Steel Pier*—we arrived in town with the Stutz [an old car which I had bought for this trip with Betty Huling] just at the moment of the irruption—a herd of dumb clucks with sordid faces wandering in the middle of the streets, hooked into the tourist traps. —Poor Carl Van Vechten had been up there looking for the Provincetown of twenty years ago, wanted to photograph O'Neill's house, the Wharf Theatre. —Anti-Red feeling— Ernest Meyer of the *Post* had been arrested on the lawn of the Vernon Inn as he was coming out of a meeting of the League Against War and Fascism—the cops had previously frisked it for minors—they put him in jail for a night. —Dos thought that it had practically reverted to the status of an ordinary small town, the town boys were all in the night clubs.

"Katy Dos Passos"*

By Edmund Wilson

—AFTER THE DAYS of horrible weather—the day before had been at once hot and sticky and drenched with dismal heavy rain—it brightened up in the afternoon, and the view from the cemetery was lovely. The Given plot is just on the edge of the hill, across from the church on the neighboring hill, and just below it is a big grove of unusually tall pine— beyond is Pamet River and the bay, all silver in the four o'clock light— the waterway winding in between the sands and the marshes. The little cemetery looked light, clean, and dry—with its millstone and its old-fashioned tombstones, up there, along with the bold town-square characters, above what had once been the seafaring community. I had tried more or less to dissociate myself from them, as Dos had done at first, but we had been living there, dining together, struggling with the native

---

*Katharine Smith Dos Passos had been instantly killed when riding with her husband, John, at Wareham, Massachusetts, en route to Connecticut on September 12, 1947. Dos Passos, who was driving, was blinded by the sun and crashed into a parked truck. The top of the car was sheared off. The novelist lost the sight of his right eye and suffered minor injuries. He was under the shock of the accident and loss when [Edmund Wilson] visited him a few hours later. He remained hospitalized and could not attend his wife's funeral, which took place on the Cape. [Leon Edel's note]

tradesmen and workmen, bringing . . . I thought how they had lived on that water—and how much, in spite of all that was frivolous and "escapist," childish and futile in our lives, we had derived something from it and belonged to it—and Katy's death for the moment had given the whole thing dignity. I felt, as I had not done before, that we (Givens, Shays, Chavchavadzes, Walkers, Dos Passoses, Susan, Matsons, Vorses, ourselves) had all become a group, a community, more closely bound up together than we had realized or perhaps wanted to be. It was already a whole life that we had lived there—since Dos—who had always scoffed at Provincetown as a middle-class artist colony—had come up there to court Katy and had first moved in to "Smooley Hall." All the parties, the days at the beach, the picnics, the flirtations, the drinking spells, the interims of work between trips, the moldy days of winter by stoves, the days of keeping going on a thin drip or trickle of income, stories and articles, bursts of prosperity, local property and cars, bibelots from Mexico or elsewhere, pictures and figures by local artists accumulated in P'town front rooms, walled in against the street—that was what our life had been when we had dedicated ourselves to the Cape, to the life of the silver harbor—and all the love and work that had gone with it, that we had come there to keep alive.

—from *The Forties* (1983)

—

from *P-Town Stories* (or *The Meatrack*) (1980)

By Roger Skillings

Home

Provincetown aspires to the condition of Venice. It'll never make it, except maybe in smells. Coming down Ciro's white-shelled alley on a hot murky night you get the luxuriant gardens, roses and honeysuckle, then a tinge of rotting garbage, then a whiff of skunk and finally—back of that, subtler, pervasive, for a stiffening instant unrecognizably nostalgic—the cesspools. Then your breath blows it away and you go on to your pleasures, oblivious to the pitted finger of land lapped by the treacherous sea.

Sweet Necessity

Paula had been on the meatrack since morning, strungout, hungry and hungover. Her shoes and bathing suit were rolled up in her jacket under the bench and her anxious eyes searched the passing mob.

In three days she'd never got to the beach once, though that was why she'd come. She could see a little bit of the bay glittering between the shops across the street, like a piece of a picture puzzle, white sand and blue sea with bathers, fifty yards away, but she couldn't leave the meatrack.

The speed freak limped by again and she looked away. "How you doin?" he'd shouted once when she'd met his eyes. Face burned red, bare feet blistered, he'd been walking the street all day, up and down, like an angry scarecrow, going past in opposite directions every 20 minutes, and finally he'd become aware of her always there watching him, while the other inhabitants of the benches changed with the hours. He hated the sight of her and she knew it.

Billy Birdman came strolling. "Where'd you disappear to?" he said.

"You seen Alma? She's supposed to meet me here."

"I haven't seen anybody, I just got up," said Billy "What did you leave for?"

"I've got to get back to New York," she said. "Alma's got my bus fare, I gave it to her so I wouldn't drink it."

"She probably drank it," Billy said.

"She can't," Paula said, "she took some pills that'll make her sick. She took so many she probably got off on them."

"The last bus goes at six," said Billy.

"Then I'll have to hitch," she said.

"It's going to rain," Billy said, cocking his eye at the black sky. A wind was coming up.

Paula bared her dry teeth in a bitter smile. What had she ever learned, except she was doomed to repeat? Three days she'd lived in the bars, crashing on floors or in cars, and eating crap. She'd meant to walk the beach alone, swim and embrace her soul, but the minute they arrived they met some guys with mescaline and then it was a continuous trance of parties and pills and confused migrations from place to place. She couldn't remember where she'd met Billy, only that he'd sat by the bed for hours, rubbing her belly.

"Come," he said, "I'll buy you a slice of pizza."

"Will you bring me one?"

"I'm not coming back this way. How come you left, you don't like balling me?"

"Sure," she said. "Why not?"

"Then come on," he said, jerking his head. "I know somebody who's got dynamite dope."

"I've got to get back to New York."

"No you don't," he said, his black eyes darting everywhere in the summer crowd, "you don't have to do anything, you can stay here, you can go to New York, you can do whatever."

"I'm on methadone," she explained in exasperation, "if I don't get back soon I'm going to be very sick."

Billy did a deft little soft-shoe two-step with his head on one side. "Then I guess you'll go," he said and walked off.

"Give me a cigarette at least," she called but he didn't stop.

From the other direction four cops moving so fast and smooth they might've been on wheels hustled down the block each carrying a limb of the speed freak who kept shouting, "You're liars, you killed him, not me."

The clot of struggle swirled along the walk and disappeared down the basement steps under the Town Hall. The pennants on the roof of the outdoor cafe where tourists were drinking ices snapped in the rising wind and the first drops fell.

In terror Paula grabbed her bundle and ran for the bus, praying Alma would be there. Where was she, her oldest friend? Between the shops laughing streams of people were coming off the beach. Paula had a momentary vision of Alma drowning, eyes wide and blind, seaweed in her hair, and knew when the bus left she would start for the highway without a search.

Demography

Two straight college guys
sitting on the meatrack
amazed at the gays going by
began counting them
on a matchbook cover
They got to a dozen, no end
in sight. There's another!
Look at that one! Look at him!

I wanted to say And them darling
and them and them and all of them.
They were only getting the queens
of course.

The Meatrack

I used to sit on the benches every day before the Selectmen took them away, they had to, there're so many hippies. The benches are for the townspeople not pigs like them, they leave their filth underneath, they commit sex crimes at night, they burn incense inside our law-abiding town hall, they smell, don't ever sit downwind, they look awful, they have no pride, some of them come from good families too. I don't mind long hair on girls.

Well look at Sally Souza! Who does she think she is? She can hardly fit inside those pants. Wait till her mother finds out, I'm not going to be the one to tell her. I wish there was some place to sit down, coffee costs a quarter everywhere now, I won't pay that. It's a sad day for this town when they have to take the benches away.

Either/Or

Sometimes I see the advantages. One night I was in Piggy's, George and Philip were both there, both giving me a hard time. I kept trying to keep away from them, it was like being in a vice, I kept moving around and one or the other would keep popping up, demanding I go home with him. I just wanted to be left alone.

Royal could see my troubles, he came over and stood beside me. He puts his cheek right close to mine, he says When that happens to me darling I just wait till closing time and then leave with a man.

The Ultimate Question

I'm leaving.
I know I say it
all the time but
I'm going away
one of these days, make
the big break, move
to New York, L.A.,
Shanghai. I'm getting my shit
together, I'm really going
to do it, you'll see, you'll be
amazed, you'll get a card
from Tulsa or Toledo
or some other slum
and you'll remember
what I said tonight
when you thought I was drunk.
By then I'll be long gone,
free and clear. Of course
I've only been here 17 years.
You can't stay forever
can you?

"Dreaming in Public: A Provincetown Memoir"

By Susan Mitchell

THE WINTER OF 1979, I lived in a condominium down by the tennis courts at the east end of Provincetown. The apartment was large enough to span the land world and the sea world, each with its own flora and fauna, sounds and smells. When I stood under the skylight on the land side and looked out on Commercial Street, men slim as their ten-speed bicycles shadowed past, and pink-jeaned girls with enormous eyes whizzed by on roller skates faster than my IBM Selectric could type "anorexia" or "cocaine." Under the skylight was a waterbed, and drifting out on it, I stared up into sky. "I have done a good deal of skying," Constable wrote in 1822, the year he painted most of his cloud studies. I did a good deal of skying, too—into the green and black foliage of cumulonimbus, into that gaseous, chloroformed light that precedes sudden and violent storms. Sometimes a strong wind tossed and lowered a tree branch against the skylight. In fine weather, that tree pulsed with small golden birds, finches that must have eaten food touched by Midas— even their excrement was liquid gold. I loved skying into weather just developing: clouds rapidly changing to mist, swirling apart until suddenly the skylight framed shades of blue; blurs and blots of clouds, a vast calligraphy that kept erasing, then rewriting itself in an excess, an exuberance of alphabets, or into a patois of bruises, a jargon of violet streakings, thick squid ink that seemed the very opacity of language and desire.

The bedroom, with its white chest of drawers, white chair, blue rug, and white curtains was on the bay side. The low bed seemed a part of that bay: propped on one elbow, I could look out at 4 A.M.—the fishing boats returning to Provincetown harbor, all thirteen of them, their lights a rope pulling toward shore. Their return was a clock chiming, a parent's key turning in the lock of childhood. At high tide, waves would break against the foundation of the building, so that even in the dark, even with eyes closed, I knew, as if something had shifted in my own blood and marrow, the bay was at flood. During hurricanes and gales, the Atlantic was shaken into me, a vibration so deep—that boom, boom of fist against body bag when Marvin Hagler worked out at the Provincetown Inn the following fall—its percussions became part of my sleep, a disturbance of the flesh. Even after I left that apartment and Provincetown, even in Charlottesville and in those breathtaking absences of the Midwest, I could have sworn I felt it—the tide changing, the Atlantic heaving itself on Truro, Wellfleet, Race Point, the waist-high grass of Indiana prairie bending westward.

I grew up in N.Y.C., where I learned to drift with crowds, to be one shining particle in those streaming currents of phosphorescense that merge and intersect around Fifth and Fifty-seventh, especially on late winter afternoons. As one sparkling corpuscle, I delighted in the speed, the thrust, even the bumps and jolts of all those other glittering corpuscles. Black, white, Hispanic, Asian, Native American, we made up one Amazonian bloodstream. In those crowds, I savored my anonymity, that deliciously sensuous private space where I could dream in public, sensing the outermost edges of other people's dreams: that woman striding past me in a green suede coat, lighting up a Mary J—the burned eggplant smell drifted back to me, spreading, smudging the purely olfactory calligraphy of her dream. Long after she disappeared into the crowded distance, her dream flowed from her nostrils, enigmatic, persistent.

In Provincetown, everyone seems to dream in public. The summer I lived in a studio at the west end, Georgie would stand in front of me as I sunbathed in the garden and dream out loud. We had moved into the cottage on the same day, Georgie in the studio below mine. "Hi," he said, "I'm Georgie the Whore," the only name I ever knew him by. Midmorning, as I stirred silty coffee with a twig and watched black islands break loose from the sun, Georgie would read to me from the dream diaries clients had left with him, clients he usually met at Tuesday afternoon tea dances at one of the restaurants on Commercial Street. Georgie was a perfectionist who found ways to concretize down to the last detail his clients' amorphous yearnings for mingled pain and pleasure. But what Georgie loved to dream most was the male body. If he could have found a way, he would have entered through the anus and exited from the mouth, having traveled every tortuous channel of mazy entrails, as if lovemaking, to be any good, had to re-enact our births, the cry of orgasm recalling the glistening moment when we scream out our arrival on earth. How many times that summer I heard his clients arrive, four maybe five arrivals each night, the cars racing up, then falling back down the gravel driveway, as the men replaced one another, their cries always sounding somehow the same. As Georgie talked, the male body turned inside out or rolled into a gleaming ball, arms grasping ankles, or became a wheel, legs reaching back toward the head—all those intricate combinations of cat's cradle I played as a child, Georgie never tiring of the game, the knots never slipping through his fingers, but only through his heart: they were all "teddy bears" whose small bodies nestled against his chest. Georgie's lovers were contortionists, sexual acrobats, so that finally, for me, the image that represented them all was Picasso's *Femme Couche,* with its simultaneous, all-embracing view of breasts, buttocks, and vaginal face. What Georgie dreamed out loud each morning was sex as collage: every possible way of taking a man, fantasy superimposed on fantasy, maps and ground plans for fantastic cities of desire, the cities lapping and overlapping one another, each city with its own lymphatic network pumping, pulsating, spilling from fountain to baroque fountain.

Sometimes when a morning listening to Georgie made me feel too lethargic to write, I'd devote the afternoon to a small shop on Commercial Street that sold magic tricks and costumes. The magic tricks—hats that promised disappearance, rubber spiders quivering on black legs, glasses with false bottoms—were not what interested me: it was the masks, those rubber faces that fit over my own like a second, or a first, skin. There were animal masks—cat, gorilla, bear, and an odd one-of-a-kind fanged face that reminded me of Cocteau's dream animal for *Beauty and the Beast.* The fanged face even came with a costume that swathed and engulfed the body in velvet. Masks are not to be put on frivolously. All through the filming of *Beauty and the Beast* Cocteau was so disfigured by eczema that he wore "a veil made of black paper, fastened to the brim of his hat with clothespins, with holes for his eyes and mouth." What I never tired of were masks that opened to reveal still another mask: a dream inside a dream—or a dream with its own false bottom, the shock of mistaken identity. There was, for example, the Beautiful Lady mask from Italy, with her straight nose, thick mascaraed lashes, porcelain skin blushing at the cheeks—and a black chiffon scarf draped across the mouth. Unfasten the scarf: the mouth bloomed up a crimson gash, a gaping blood-smeared wound. The Beautiful Lady was so versatile, an alluring woman who, at the drop of a veil, could transform herself into something hideous—or, depending on the viewer's taste, perhaps something more alluring. Beautiful Lady reminded me of the mask worn by the Echo Dancer in Kwakiutl winter ceremonies. When the Echo Dancer appears, he wears a mask bearing human-like features. Moving around the fire, he covers his face with the corner of his blanket, then suddenly lets the covering drop to reveal a different mouthpiece on the mask. As the dance progresses, the performer displays a series of mouthpieces—animal, bird, sea creature. But the Beautiful Lady also brought to mind those Ovidian myths where the hunter is transformed into the victim—Actaeon changed into a stag, then torn to pieces by his own dogs, which mistake him for the animal he was pursuing. But unlike Actaeon, the Beautiful Lady had the ability to heal herself: only cover her mouth, and what was bloody and torn is made whole; cover her mouth, and whatever story she inspires can start over from its innocent beginning.

I approached the Beautiful Lady mask gingerly, with respect, but never tried it on. It was the King Kong hands that I loved to slip over my own like burglar's gloves, that leathery black skin exchanging cells with mine: the gorilla hands were somewhat humanized by my gestures while some animal trace revived my body, electrifying each hair on my head. I have seen every one of the King Kong films, each refilming a reflection of some subtle change in our idea of the erotic. In the version that stars Jessica Lange, the essence of the heroine's sexuality is amnesia, her ability to forget each narrow escape as soon as it's over. As a result, she starts each adventure anew, fearless. When the geological team arrives on Kong's island, Jessica rushes ahead on the stony beach, despite the foreboding chill created by the ominously swirling mists. It's not a beach I would care to walk alone. But Jessica, ignorant of the cues that immediately alert the aficionado of the fantasy genre, senses no danger. Like the Beautiful Lady, she is self-healing, a perpetual virgin in the garden of fantasy sex.

During the winter of 1979, as I read in front of a window overlooking Provincetown Bay, I often thought of Keats the reader: "I should like the window to open onto the Lake of Geneva," he wrote Fanny, "and there I'd sit and read all day, like the picture of somebody reading." Perhaps like those women looking out of windows in paintings by Caspar David Friedrich and M. V. Schwind that had such a vogue in the early and mid 1800s. Backs turned on the dark interiors that make up most of the pictorial space, these women seem to drift out of the paintings—not toward, but away from us, out over the horizon where our own thoughts are traveling. Painters of this period frequently portrayed themselves before windows, and there is even a painting, attributed to M. Drolling the elder, of a Paris interior (Wadsworth Atheneum, Hartford) where the view through the open window is depicted on a canvas on the easel. Like these artists, like Keats looking out on Lake Geneva, I was simultaneously inside and outside, snug and far away, contained and dispersed as I sat by my window. The natural world with its gulls, sandpipers, boats, and winding windrows of kelp and seagrape intermingled with the poems and novels I read, such as in Spenser's Bower of Bliss living vines and tendrils entwine themselves around artificial plants. That strange long-drawn cry that Emma Bovary hears after making love with Rudolphe, the cry that hangs on the air of Steegmuller's superb translation before it mingles with Emma's own jangled nerves seemed to come from out over the bay, the cry of a gull suddenly rising from the silence. The natural world flowed into, washed over, and nurtured whatever I read, dreamed, and wrote. I was a creature in a tidal pool, sometimes drinking the incoming waves at flood, other times breathing air and that extraordinary Provincetown light that always comes from several directions at once—bouncing off the bay, raining down through the skylight, crackling out of the wood stove. I was a straddler, inhabiting a world of art prolonged by dream and a natural world guided by some deeper dream. On sunny, surprisingly warm December afternoons, I sipped margaritas at the Red Inn, and as the sun set, licked salt from the rim of the ocean. This was my third year in Provincetown. No longer a fellow at the Fine Arts Work Center, I stayed on with a grant from the Artists Foundation, sometimes sharing the sunset with two other former fellows, a sculptor and a painter. What I remember now were our long, impassioned talks about Nancy Holt, whose *Sun Tunnels,* constructed during the seventies in Utah's Great Basin Desert, invited us to meditate on inside and outside, sensations from within the body and perceptions sucked in through openings in the tunnels and pipes. Late at night, when the moon loomed, an enormous floating city that illuminated whatever I was reading, I thought of the moon penetrating Holt's tunnels, the different shapes that light takes as it encroaches on darkness. Even when I read in the bath, glass of scotch beside the soap, I could sense the lunar tug, the pull the moon exerted on the bay, on the syrupy undulations of the waterbed, on the water I bathed in. On the stereo, John Anderson slurred "Going Down Hill," the moon dragging at his vocal cords, thickening the sound.

Late at night, I drifted through all the apartments I had ever lived in: the little apartment on the rue du Cherche Midi that looked down on a cobblestone courtyard that gleamed on chill, wet October nights; the hotel room in Paris, its windows opening onto a garden of blossoming pear trees—my home for a year, it also looked into another room where each night a man and woman made love without bothering to draw the curtains; the pink stucco apartment that looked out on Porto Cervo where a harbor vendor sold bright orange roe of sea urchins, the sticky tickertape of history I gulped down with lemon and the rough burn of Sardinian Vernaccia, future urchin beds swallowed whole; the balcony in N.Y.C. that looked down on swaying barges of light, hanging bridges, neon gardens floating miraculously thirty stories above the street; the dark blue tiles of the apartment overlooking Positano, cool under bare feet, the *persiani* half closed on hot afternoons, the ocean boiling at the cliff bottom, sizzling, breeze of garlic and onion. Through the window at Provincetown I looked out through all those other windows, the window in Paris opening to reveal the window in Porto Cervo, which opened wide to reveal the balcony in N.Y.C.—as if I were pulling a spy glass to its furthest extension. Or as if the windows opened onto each other like those stories in the *Arabian Nights* that do not really end but, instead, spill into one another, story overflowing into story, until I am standing in the garden at Positano where Danish's cat has just given birth to the rhythm of "Sergeant Pepper's Lonely Hearts Club Band." The rooster crows and dawn arrives with the smell of lemon and mimosa. The rooster knows the exact moment. All roosters everywhere know the moment. In Provincetown, it's conch pink, slippery, the thin line that separates night from day, the exact moment when morning appears like a sail on the horizon. Such thresholds have always seemed magical to me, those fine threads of the world that have the power to renew us if we can only grab hold of them: the flicker of light that appears between bands of color in Rothko's paintings, that marginal world, the dividing line, the moment of change when everything still seems possible. Once, walking near Pilgrim Heights, I tried to follow the shrill of peepers to its source, that spring where the sound wells up and spills into rivulets of water. Louder and louder the shrilling grew—and then, just when I had almost found its source, the shrilling stopped, all the peepers holding their breath at once. So the source is secret, magical, withholding itself, retreating into what Mallarmé called the "last spiritual casket."

It was at Pilgrim Heights that William Bradford and an exploring party from the *Mayflower* had their first drink of American water. Before going on to Plymouth and founding our nation on rock, the Pilgrims first tried to found it on water in Provincetown Harbor. It was in Provincetown Bay that the women of the *Mayflower* washed their clothes after the long crossing. And it was in Provincetown Bay that Bradford's wife, Anne, in a state of despair, drowned herself. You will not find her mentioned in the *Encyclopaedia Britannica,* though William's career is summarized there. You will not find her suicide mentioned in Bradford's chronicle, *The History of Plimoth Plantation:* not a ripple of her passing disturbs his account of the Pilgrim venture. Within the fullness of the first Thanksgiving there is this absence, Anne's: within the desire to build, to construct, to found, to create something new, this tug in the opposite direction, this desire not to begin, not to, not to—the secret absence out of which all great things start up.

I have visited the spring where supposedly Bradford and his exploring expedition had their first taste of "sweet water." The first time alone, the second time with Otukwei Okai, a poet from Ghana in residence at the Fine Arts Work Center. This was my second year as a fellow, the spring of 1979. The car I had bought the previous year still smelled new, and its shiny black exterior had not yet lost its sex appeal. Every afternoon, Otukwei passed the car, patted the hood, and said something complimentary, until finally it dawned on me: he wanted us to go for a drive and fulfill his version of the American dream—fast car, loud rock, hamburgers, shakes and fries, and all the windows open. It seemed so clichéd to me, this dream, but well, why not do it?—especially since my own myth of Africa was probably just as hackneyed: tawny lions, as marvelously unreal as Rousseau's, creeping up on villagers. My pleas for lion stories invariably reduced Otukwei to frowning silence. The day I satisfied his dream down to the last greasy fried potato, Otukwei, his wife Beatrice, and their infant daughter, swaddled in pink, drove with me to Pilgrim Heights for our own taste of the famous spring. Along the way Otukwei and I spilled out ideas for poems, our creative juices keeping pace with the rock music, the membranes of our fetal poems so thin that images swam back and forth between us. It was one enormous poem we were writing as we got out of the car and walked the spongy forest trail covered with amber needles to a high place that looks down on the water, which barely seems to move between banks of yellow-brown reeds. An egret shuddered up, its flight hardly faster than the river's. The air was redolent of pine. It was here, supposedly, that the Pilgrims saw footprints made by local Native Americans. I spared Otukwei my skepticism about the role of this particular spring in American history and simply knelt with him: it tasted as before— warm, sandy. On the drive back to Provincetown, suddenly out of the flow of conversation, it erupted—Otukwei's lion story. A very large lion. The men carrying it on a pole back to the village, its tail so long it dragged in the dust.

Recently, on a flight to West Palm Beach, as a south wind carried wave after wave of rain against the windows, I felt it again, the deep boom of Provincetown Bay slapping at foundations, sucking its breath in, holding it, holding it, then heaving it out. We were threading our way between storm systems in an eerie yellow-green light, the wake of a passing tornado. Bouldery clouds, stacked precariously on one another, trembled, stretching, towering higher and higher above the plane, then suddenly toppled, the plane falling with them as if through a trap door. I had entered the realm of process, where skying was all that mattered.

To the left, racing us, was a thick black cloud, flat as a mattress, a flying carpet with three dark threads tentacling down. As we banked, cloud after cloud tumbled toward us, breakers, whitecapped, foaming, spewing spray—and then it was the ocean, all its teeth bared.

Sometimes the ocean returns to me in surprising ways—as this past Christmas in the powder room of a N.Y.C. department store. It was my favorite hour. Outside, the lights had just come on, snow was beginning to fall, each flake a momentary jewel in the hair of passersby. As I yawned into the mirror, a stall door opened behind me: the woman enthroned on the toilet puckered her glossy red lips, sweeping her hands up her shiny black hair caught in a chignon. Still sitting, she wiggled out of black lace pantyhose and into crotchless panties. The woman who had just left her stall resembled the woman I had chatted with the night before at a dinner party: same blond bangs, same thick hair squared at the jaw, same sad eyes and drained face. Now I watched them both in the mirror. The prostitute was radiant, glowing, as she removed the crotchless panties, lowering them slowly to the floor, a gesture that suddenly seemed the essence of her appeal. Nothing can dirty me, that gesture said. Not the dirt on the floor. Not the water oozing out of the toilets. Not the urine spotting the toilet seats. Not the faded blonde whose sadness leaves a sour taste only in her own mouth. The prostitute waved a leg in my direction and smiled: "Boy, oh boy, oh boy," she said, her voice entirely different from what I had expected; it seemed to come from another body, from a delivery boy's or a cab driver's. Still looking in the mirror, I smiled back, thinking of the ocean licking itself clean all those nights in Provincetown as I listened in the dark. The ocean that heals instantly around whatever penetrates it. The ocean lubed to a shine. In a mirror, the ocean looks at itself and sees that it is wearing a rose. And sees that it has no hats. This ocean that goes on talking in my sleep, that keeps kneading itself like dough, like prayer.

———

The Age of the Sword

By Jacquelyn Holt Park

IT WOULD COME later—the Age of the Sword. In the 1980s the Plague would bring the young men back to Provincetown to die.

On beaches where waves rode in like horses to bend their necks at the shore, the waves would ride out carrying the mourners. Up from Florida they would come—parents, friends, lovers. Up from Georgia and North Carolina—sisters, brothers, cousins. Back from Minnesota and Los Angeles they would ride the wooden barges, boats of death, pausing on the swirling plate of the Atlantic to pay tribute, scattering the remains. Farewell glad son, proud friend, apple of my eye—farewell. All but ashes now, death's feed. In the 1980s skeletons would walk the streets in Provincetown, stiffgaited, pale, their eyes like dried leaves in standing water, fingerwidth limbs, stick-armed, leaning on canes, half blind, torturously summoning breath for one more step. Their time had come, and they knew it. Soon they too would float seaward into the bleeding horizon, into the sun's last squirt beyond the rim. Float to oblivion, young men turned old, men who in the summers of their youth, in the bright mornings of their passion, in the red marrow of their sexuality, had come to Provincetown to find out who they were, young men now to rest permanently where once they had relaxed. That would be the 1980s.

But when Emily arrived two decades before, the town was full of life. And always beautiful. Long before, the pilgrims had developed it by the sea. They spun paths on its natural elevations. They erected houses on those paths as quaint and picturesque as boats carved inside bottles. Their ships fed on the harbor like pups nursing at an earthen teat, bringing in a harvest of seaweed and ocean, smells of fish. They traveled to a light that artists would call the purest in the land. They became fishermen who took the sea as their mistress, who felt that mistress up in their imaginations, who entered that mistress with their dreams of plunder, who lay with her at night under God's jewelry, a million stars. Then, as now, the fishermen are everywhere. So is the fog. In Provincetown, fog drools over the pavement, backs up in alleys, squats on rooftops from which it leaps like a ghostly feline, builds like smoke in cramped quarters winding bayward from Hyannis through Orleans, Eastham, Wellfleet, Truro, flowing between the sandtears of dunes that weep across highway 6. In winter, Provincetown sleeps. In summer, it rings with dance. Artists come. Families come. So do the queers. Provincetown is yet another bead on the string that connects the empires of Queer—Ogunquit, Fire Island, Greenwich Village, Key West. In the 1960s queer was in the thighsoft sands, inside the singing of the surf, the wet and lonely ringing of the wind where egrets ran, where men were eager and women were independent. In the shothot summers of the 1960s, Provincetown was one long party. Everyone was invited, including Emily—or so she wanted to believe.

—from *A Stone Gone Mad* (1991)

———

"Rope"

By Mark Doty

Our street unspools toward the harbor,
    swerving past guesthouses,
the ancient jumble of roses,
    fencepickets in a formal tumble
crowded as a Persian miniature:
    a crazy quilt,

every corner filled. Where there might
    be a vacant spot there's a boat
in drydock—*Chlorox,* unfortunate moniker—
    and an intricate strip of garden
where someone's knotted a tapestry
    of kale and sweetpeas

beside a roped pyramid of lobster traps.
    It's the first place
I've ever really wanted to live.
    Art, Milton Avery wrote,

"Rope"

is turning a corner; you don't know
   what's around the bend

till you go there. Our curve
   surprises with harbor glitter:
a bobbing dinghy, a sunstruck triangle
   of boats, two trawlers
idly going about whatever
   their business is . . .

Here, just where the street bends
   is my favorite house: shingled, narrow,
an elaborate Edwardian toaster
   of a house, covered with moss
and drifting, almost perceptibly,
   towards collapse.

Antony lives there, and Charley.
   They walk early or late
to escape the heat; Charley,
   the antique spaniel, on his rope leash,
so much time elapsed between steps
   you might take him

for porcelain, an incredibly decrepit
   Staffordshire figurine,
or a particularly far gone carpetbag
   of buffalo hide, something allowed
to molder in a heap in the barn until mice
   made of it

their own version of the granaries
   of Babylon. He is that old.
I don't know if Antony would move faster
   on his own—I've never seen him
without Charley—but his pace
   precisely matches

his dog's, as if together they were
   one thing (something submarine,
adapted to the pressure of great depths).
   I've seen them down on the shore

in the evening, leaning against the shoulder
   of an upturned dory;

"We're soaking up some moonshine,"
   Antony calls. The truth is
I avoid them, since Antony delivers monologues
   which do not have endings—lucid,
interesting even, though often concerning
   the role of amino acids,

the quality of donuts—and to listen
   is a commitment of uncertain,
considerable length. I don't see them
   for days, and then I worry,
since you can almost smell
   the fragility

of their age, and when Charley
   cries a little, from the difficulty
of picking himself up on those no longer
   reliable legs, Antony cannot hear him.
I am a little surprised, every time
   they reappear,

and glad. They stand for hope,
   and seem as tentative and constant
as the steeple of the Unitarian church,
   which leans a little to the right,
but stands. Lately Charley
   is not walking well;

a few steps and those legs buckle
   beneath him, so Antony has constructed
a sort of rope harness,
   which the good soldier
of ongoingness wears, and when he falls
   and looks up

from those droozed, ancient eyes,
   which have seen the rise
of empires, from which the face
   has sagged away, relinquishing its form

to the steady pull of earth,
   Antony can lift him

up again, even hold him
   suspended a while
so that Charley can move his failing legs
   and feel that he has been for a walk.
The neighbors say,
   When that dog goes . . .

But who'd suggest Charley's lived
   long enough? Think of Solomon, who commanded
the child be divided between mothers;
   who could cut apart one living thing,
or sever the rope that holds them both
   in the world?

It's frayed as it is.
   Art is this strong,
exactly: love's gravity,
   the weight of Charley's body,
in his rope harness, suspended
   from his master's hand.

———

"A Letter from the Coast"

By Mark Doty

All afternoon the town readied for storm,
   men in the harbor shallows hauling in small boats
      that rise and fall on the tide. Pleasure,

one by our house is called. I didn't think
   the single man who tugged her in could manage
      alone, though he pushed her up high enough,

he must have hoped, to miss the evening's
   predicted weather: a huge freight of rain
      tumbling up the coast. There's another storm

in town, too, a veritable cyclone
   of gowns and wigs: men in dresses here for a week
      of living the dream of crossing over.

All afternoon they braved the avenue
   fronting the harbor, hats set against the wind,
      veils seedpearled with the first rain,

accessoried to the nines. The wardrobes
   in their rented rooms must glitter,
      opened at twilight

when they dress for the evening,
   sequin shimmer leaping out of the darkness . . .
      Their secret's made visible here, public,

as so many are, and in that raw weather
   I loved the flash of red excess, the cocktail dress
      and fur hat, the sheer pleasure

of stockings and gloves.
   I'm writing to tell you this:
      what was left of the hurricane arrived by ten.

All night I heard, under the steep-pitched shallows
   of our sleep, the shoulders of the sea flashing:
      loaded, silvering with so much broken cargo:

shell and rusted metal, crabclaw and spine,
   kelp and feathers and the horseshoe carapace,
      and threading through it all the foghorns'

double harmony of warning, one note layered
   just over and just after the other. *Safety,*
      they said, or *shelter,* two inexact syllables

repeated precisely all night, glinting
   through my dream the way the estuaries
      shone before sunup, endless

invitation and promise, till dawn
   beat the whole harbor to pewter.
      Pleasure was unmoved and burnished a cobalt

the exact shade of a mussel's hinge,
   and every metal shone in the sea: platinum,
      gunmetal, tarnished chrome.

The law of the tide is accumulation, *More,*
   and our days here are layered detail,
      the shore's grand mosaic of detritus:

tumbled beach glass, endless bits
   of broken china, as if whole Nineteenth Century kitchens
      went down in the harbor and lie scattered

at our feet, the tesserae of Byzantium.
   Those syllables sounded all night,
      their meaning neither completed nor exhausted.

What was it I meant to tell you?
   All I meant to do this storm-rinsed morning,
      which has gone brilliant and uncomplicated

as silk, that same watery sheen?
   How the shore's a huge armoire
      full of gowns, all its drawers packed

and gleaming? Something about pleasure
   and excess: thousands of foamy veils,
      a tidal wrack of emerald, glamor

of froth-decked, dashed pearl bits.
   A million earrings rinsed in the dawn.
      I wish you were here.

Summer Rituals

~~~~~~

To MILLIONS OF visitors and seasonal residents today, Cape Cod still *means* summer—though its permanent population continues to burgeon and the tourist season now essentially lasts the year round. A century and a half ago, however, off-Cape visitors were so rare that Thoreau and his traveling companion, William Ellery Channing, were initially mistaken by the locals for bank robbers. One of the few groups that regularly migrated to the Cape in the summer at that time were Methodists who held their religious retreats in such outdoor settings as Eastham's Millennium Grove. Thoreau gives a skeptical view of these "camp-meetings," with more than a hint that sexual frustration was the source of the women's "hysteric fits."

At the time of his visit Thoreau observed, "At present [Cape Cod] is wholly unknown to the fashionable world." Yet he was perceptive enough to realize that "[t]he time must come when this coast will be a place of resort for those New Englanders who really wish to visit the seaside"— though even he could not have imagined how complete that transformation would be.

Before the "fashionable world" could discover the Cape, however, it had to have means to get there. In fact, as reflected in the literature, "getting away to the Cape" has been as much of a ritual as actually being here. Prior to the Civil War, overland travel to the Cape was difficult and comfortable public lodgings scarce. Most of the relatively few tourists restricted their visits to day or weekend trips on the steamer service that ran between Boston and Provincetown. Thoreau took the Old Colony Railroad as far as Sandwich in 1849; the line was gradually extended down-Cape, reaching Provincetown in 1873. Its completion linked Cape towns to the rest of New England, and for the first time Cape Cod became accessible to the region's urban population.

After World War I the first paved roads were constructed down-Cape. With the arrival of the automobile the second phase of the Cape's transformation into a summer resort began. The weekender appeared. Cottage colonies began to spring up in the towns and on the beaches. Having lived with change throughout their history, Cape Codders adjusted to these outside influences with philosophy and pragmatism. Cape historian Henry Kittredge observed in 1930: "If whales no longer visit their shores, rich city folk do, and with easy adaptability Cape men and women take the goods the gods provide them." Some local residents began to rent out rooms in their old Cape houses, while others added on a front porch for a restaurant, set up a gas station or a beach plum jelly stand in the front yard or an antique store in the barn.

Celebrities and literary figures have long been a part of the Cape's summer scene. Two presidents have had summer homes here. Grover Cleveland spent many summers at Gray Gables in the 1890s; this large rambling structure on Buzzard's Bay burned down several years ago. John F. Kennedy had vacationed since boyhood at the family compound in Hyannis Port. Berger's humorous anecdote about Cleveland is also a significant measure of change: less than a century ago, a U.S. president could wander off alone into the local woods and become lost. Kennedy's election, on the other hand, not only transformed Hyannis Port into a tourist mecca, but was probably the catalyst that assured the establishment of the Cape Cod National Seashore in 1961. It also, as Alfred Kazin's satiric portrait documents, brought a wave of famous and not-so-famous political summer immigrants to another Cape community.

Older Cape Codders remember that the Depression did not make as much of an impact here as most places, since they had been poor for so long they didn't know it. Yet as the nation slowly emerged from that economic debacle, the Cape attracted more and more writers as summer residents. Some, like poet Conrad Aiken, decided to remain year-round. Aiken's letters are among the best written this century, and the one reproduced here vividly describes another Cape ritual, that of "moving in." Still another time-honored summer ritual among Cape writers, wittily caught by E. J. Kahn, Jr., is that of pretending *not* to write.

Other selections reflect a generally unrecognized, yet pervasive aspect of the Cape: its connection to war. Everett Allen's "Cape Cod Idyll," for instance, illustrates how the very peace and refuge he finds on a Cape Cod beach can, by contrast, call up darker memories of a very different beach. The S.S. *Longstreet* target ship in Cape Cod Bay, on the other hand, provides an unintentional perspective on the Cape's view of itself as a "summer playground."

One of the most enduring summer chronicles in Cape literature is an unassuming book written in the late 1940s by a Quincy doctor, Wyman Richardson. The Richardson family have summered for generations in Eastham, and the two-hundred-year-old farmhouse that is memorialized in *The House on Nauset Marsh* is still used today. It is only a stone's throw from the National Seashore's Visitors Center. One can look out from the Visitors Center at the same vista of Salt Pond, Nauset Marsh, and the Outer Beach that Richardson describes in his book. Through the grace of his writing and the geniality of his personality, Richardson may have created the perfect Cape Cod summer idyll. In fact, he did it so well that his wife once told me that after the book came out people from as far away as California would show up on their doorstep announcing that they had come to have a "Do-Nothing Day." The sense of peace and contentment that pervades this book is even more remarkable when one realizes that most of it was composed late at night when Richardson could not sleep because of pain from the cancer that killed him in 1948.

During the past forty years the summer scene has increasingly been viewed, often with a jaundiced eye, by the "washashore," or non-native year-rounder. Some, like poet Marge Piercy, have expressed with lyric appreciation the many subtle pleasures of "Cod Summer"; others, like Monica Dickens, have observed with satiric relish the misadventures of the summer tourist.

Still, the outsider's perspective remains a strong strain in contemporary Cape writing. Ira Wood's city-smart character in *Kitchen Man* is not a little bemused by the culture clash of the white-wine-and-brie summer crowd and Wellfleet locals. On the other hand, Cape Cod has long been a favorite subject for *New Yorker* writers, and Adam Gopnik's piece on Nauset Beach is a perfect specimen of that magazine's sophisticated journalism: urbane, articulate, entertaining, self-deprecatingly superior, perceptive in matters literary and cultural, and, in matters more mundane, such as geography, often quaintly ignorant.

Finally, Mary Lou-Weisman's "Letter"—which has probably been tacked up on more local refrigerators than any other recent piece of Cape writing—is a hilarious testament to the longevity and perils of perhaps the oldest seasonal ritual of all: the summer house guest.

Millennium Grove

By Henry David Thoreau

THIS WAS THE Eastham famous of late years for its camp-meetings, held in a grove near by, to which thousands flock from all parts of the Bay. We conjectured that the reason for the perhaps unusual, if not unhealthful development of the religious sentiment here, was the fact that a large portion of the population are women whose husbands and sons are either abroad on the sea, or else drowned, and there is nobody but they and the ministers left behind. The old account says that "hysteric fits are very common in Orleans, Eastham, and the towns below, particularly on Sunday, in the times of divine service. When one woman is affected, five or six others generally sympathize with her; and the congregation is thrown into the utmost confusion. Several old men suppose, unphilosophically and uncharitably, perhaps, that the will is partly concerned, and that ridicule and threats would have a tendency to prevent the evil."

How this is now we did not learn. We saw one singularly masculine woman, however, in a house on this very plain, who did not look as if she was ever troubled with hysterics, or sympathized with those that were; or, perchance, life itself was to her a hysteric fit,—a Nauset woman, of a hardness and coarseness such as no man ever possesses or suggests. It was enough to see the vertebrae and sinews of her neck, and her set jaws of iron, which would have bitten a board-nail in two in their ordinary action,—braced against the world, talking like a man-of-war's-man in petticoats, or as if shouting to you through a breaker; who looked as if it made her head ache to live; hard enough for any enormity. I looked upon her as one who had committed infanticide; who never had a brother, unless it were some wee thing that died in infancy,—for what need of him?—and whose father must have died before she was born.

This woman told us that the camp-meetings were not held the previous summer for fear of introducing the cholera, and that they would have been held earlier this summer, but the rye was so backward that straw would not have been ready for them; for they lie in straw. There are sometimes one hundred and fifty ministers, (!) and five thousand hearers, assembled. The ground, which is called Millennium

Grove,* is owned by a company in Boston, and is the most suitable, or rather unsuitable, for this purpose of any that I saw on the Cape. It is fenced, and the frames of the tents are, at all times, to be seen interspersed among the oaks. They have an oven and a pump, and keep all their kitchen utensils and tent coverings and furniture in a permanent building on the spot.

They select a time for their meetings, when the moon is full. A man is appointed to clear out the pump a week beforehand, while the ministers are clearing their throats; but, probably, the latter do not always deliver as pure a stream as the former. I saw the heaps of clam-shells left under the tables, where they had feasted in previous summers, and supposed, of course, that that was the work of the unconverted, or the backsliders and scoffers. It looked as if a camp-meeting must be a singular combination of a prayer-meeting and a picnic.

—from *Cape Cod* (1865)

———

from *The Bostonians* (1886)

By Henry James

THE TRAIN FOR Marmion left Boston at four o'clock in the afternoon, and rambled fitfully toward the southern cape, while the shadows grew long in the stony pastures and the slanting light gilded the straggling, shabby woods, and painted the ponds and marshes with yellow gleams. The ripeness of summer lay upon the land, and yet there was nothing in the country Basil Ransom traversed that seemed susceptible of maturity; nothing but the apples in the little tough, dense orchards, which gave a suggestion of sour fruition here and there, and the tall, bright

---

*The Millenium Grove campground, located at the junction of Campground and Herring Brook Roads in North Eastham, is long gone, but the oaks remain. Even though most of the Lower Cape has become reforested over the past century, the area is conspicuous for the density and relatively large size of the trees. The ministers and their "hearers," have been replaced by a thriving population of gray squirrels, though they will preach at you if you are too curious about their activities.

golden-rod at the bottom of the bare stone dykes. There were no fields of yellow grain; only here and there a crop of brown hay. But there was a kind of soft scrubbiness in the landscape, and a sweetness begotten of low horizons, of mild air, with a possibility of summer haze, of unregarded inlets where on August mornings the water must be brightly blue. Ransom had heard that the Cape was the Italy, so to speak, of Massachusetts; it had been described to him as the drowsy Cape, the languid Cape, the Cape not of storms, but of eternal peace. He knew that the Bostonians had been drawn thither, for the hot weeks, by its sedative influence, by the conviction that its toneless air would minister to perfect rest. In a career in which there was so much nervous excitement as in theirs they had no wish to be wound up when they went out of town; they were sufficiently wound up at all times by the sense of all their sex had been through. They wanted to live idly, to unbend and lie in hammocks, and also to keep out of the crowd, the rush of the watering-place. Ransom could see there was no crowd at Marmion, as soon as he got there, though indeed there was a rush, which directed itself to the only vehicle in waiting outside of the small, lonely, hut-like station, so distant from the village that, as far as one looked along the sandy, sketchy road which was supposed to lead to it, one saw only an empty land on either side. Six or eight men, in 'dusters', carrying parcels and handbags, projected themselves upon the solitary, rickety, carry-all, so that Ransom could read his own fate, while the ruminating conductor of the vehicle, a lean shambling citizen, with a long neck and a tuft on his chin, guessed that if he wanted to get to the hotel before dusk he would have to strike out. His valise was attached in a precarious manner to the rear of the carry-all. 'Well, I'll chance it,' the driver remarked, sadly, when Ransom protested against its insecure position . . . He liked the very smell of the soil as he wandered along; cool, soft whiffs of evening met him at bends of the road which disclosed very little more—unless it might be a band of straight-stemmed woodland, keeping, a little, the red glow from the west, or (as he went further) an old house, shingled all over, grey and slightly collapsing, which looked down at him from a steep bank, at the top of wooden steps. He was already refreshed; he had tasted the breath of nature, measured his long grind in New York, without a vacation, with the repetition of the daily movement up and down the long, straight, maddening city, like a bucket in a well or a shuttle in a loom.

———

By Train to Provincetown

By Thomas Merton

MOTHER'S DEATH HAD made one thing evident: Father now did not have to do anything but paint. He was not tied down to any one place. He could go wherever he needed to go, to find subjects and get ideas, and I was old enough to go with him.

And so, after I had been a few months in the local school at Douglaston, and had already been moved up to the second grade, in the evil-smelling grey annex on top of the hill, Father came back to New York and announced that he and I were going somewhere new.

It was with a kind of feeling of triumph that I watched the East River widen into Long Island Sound, and waited for the moment when the Fall River boat, in all her pride, would go sweeping past the mouth of Bayside Bay and I would view Douglaston, as I thought, from the superiority of the open water and pass it by, heading for a new horizon called Fall River and Cape Cod and Provincetown.

We could not afford a cabin, but slept down below decks in the crowded steerage, if you could call it that, among the loud Italian families and the colored boys who spent the night shooting craps under the dim light, while the waters spoke loudly to us, above our heads, proclaiming that we were well below the waterline.

And in the morning we got off the boat at Fall River, and walked up the street beside the textile mills, and found a lunch wagon crowded with men getting something to eat on the way to work; and we sat at the counter and ate ham and eggs.

All day long after that we were in a train. Just before we crossed the great black drawbridge over the Cape Cod Canal, Father got off at a station and went to a store across the street and bought me a bar of Baker's chocolate, with a blue wrapper and a picture of a lady in an old-fashioned cap and apron, serving cups of chocolate. I was almost completely overwhelmed with surprise and awe at the fact of such tremendous largesse. Candy had always been strictly rationed.

Then came the long, long journey through the sand dunes, stopping at every station, while I sat, weary and entranced, with the taste of chocolate thick and stale in my mouth, turning over and over in my mind the names of places where we were going: Sandwich, Falmouth,

Truro, Provincetown. The name Truro especially fascinated me. I could not get it out of my mind: Truro. Truro. It was a name as lonely as the edge of the sea.

That summer was full of low sand dunes, and coarse grasses as sharp as wires, growing from the white sand. And the wind blew across the sand. And I saw the breakers of the grey sea come marching in towards the land, and I looked out at the ocean. Geography had begun to become a reality.

The whole town of Provincetown smelled of dead fish, and there were countless fishing boats, of all sizes, tied up along the wharves; and you could run all day on the decks of the schooners, and no one would prevent you, or chase you away. I began to know the smell of ropes and of pitch and of the salt, white wood of decks, and the curious smell of seaweed, under the docks.

—from *The Seven Story Mountain*
(1948)

———

"Route Six"

By Stanley Kunitz

The city squats on my back.
I am heart-sore, stiff-necked,
exasperated. That's why
I slammed the door,
that's why I tell you now,
in every house of marriage
there's room for an interpreter.
Let's jump into the car, honey,
and head straight for the Cape,
where the cock on our housetop crows
that the weather's fair,
and my garden waits for me
to coax it into bloom.

As for those passions left
that flare past understanding,
like bundles of dead letters
out of our previous lives
that amaze us with their fevers,
we can stow them in the rear
along with ziggurats of luggage
and Celia, our transcendental cat,
past-mistress of all languages,
including Hottentot and silence.
We'll drive non-stop till dawn,
and if I grow sleepy at the wheel,
you'll keep me awake by singing
in your bravura Chicago style
Ruth Etting's smoky song,
"Love Me or Leave Me,"
belting out the choices.

Light glazes the eastern sky
over Buzzards Bay.
Celia gyrates upward
like a performing seal,
her glistening nostrils aquiver
to sniff the brine-spiked air.
The last stretch toward home!
Twenty summers roll by.

—

President Cleveland Gets Lost

By Josef Berger (Jeremiah Digges)

THE SANDWICH WHICH is your first taste of Cape Cod is not slapped on a plate and pushed under your nose; to get to it, you must go around the counter. And so, when you have returned from the Freeman graves to the intersection, instead of turning onto the highway again, continue straight across, passing the information booth on the detour leading to the beautiful old village.

On your way you pass Bay View Cemetery, where Joseph Jefferson is buried. Jefferson, greatest comedian of his time, won renown as Rip Van Winkle, as Bob Acres, and in a score of other leading roles. On that corner of the Cape where the Canal now opens into Buzzards Bay, he and Grover Cleveland were neighbor summer residents, both attracted by the hunting and fishing in Sandwich woods. Jefferson wanted to buy a house in Sandwich, but Sandwich didn't want Jefferson. To the townsfolk, "the stage" was a remote, godless world, whence no good neighbor could have come. Jefferson went south, but before he left, he bought a lot in Bay View Cemetery, and told his friends, "They won't let me live in Sandwich, but I'll stay there yet!" And he is staying—yet.

Of Cleveland, too, there is a story worth retelling. The then President was lost in the Sandwich woods. Drenched by a heavy rain and tired from his day's fishing, he knocked at a lonely house in a clearing. A voice from aloft asked what he wanted. "This is the President," Cleveland said. "I'm lost, and I'd like to stay here tonight." "Well," came the answer, "stay there." And down went the window.

—from *Cape Cod Pilot* (1937)

—

A Summer in Brewster

By Helen Keller

JUST BEFORE THE Perkins Institution closed for the summer, it was arranged that my teacher and I should spend our vacation at Brewster, on Cape Cod, with our dear friend, Mrs. Hopkins. I was delighted, for my mind was full of the prospective joys and of the wonderful stories I had heard about the sea.

My most vivid recollection of that summer is the ocean. I had always lived far inland and had never had so much as a whiff of salt air; but I had read in a big book called "Our World" a description of the ocean which filled me with wonder and an intense longing to touch the mighty sea and feel it roar. So my little heart leaped high with eager excitement when I knew that my wish was at last to be realized.

No sooner had I been helped into my bathing-suit than I sprang out upon the warm sand and without thought of fear plunged into the cool water. I felt the great billows rock and sink. The buoyant motion of the water filled me with an exquisite, quivering joy. Suddenly my ecstasy gave place to terror; for my foot struck against a rock and the next instant there was a rush of water over my head. I thrust out my hands to grasp some support, I clutched at the water and at the seaweed which the waves tossed in my face. But all my frantic efforts were in vain. The waves seemed to be playing a game with me, and tossed me from one to another in their wild frolic. It was fearful! The good, firm earth had slipped from my feet, and everything seemed shut out from this strange, all-enveloping element—life, air, warmth and love. At last, however, the sea, as if weary of its new toy, threw me back on the shore, and in another instant I was clasped in my teacher's arms. Oh, the comfort of the long, tender embrace! As soon as I had recovered from my panic sufficiently to say anything, I demanded: "Who put salt in the water?"
—from *The Story of My Life* (1928)

—

Edna St. Vincent Millay

By Edmund Wilson

OF THE HOUSEHOLD in which Edna grew up I had a glimpse, in the summer of 1920, when I went at her invitation—she had John Bishop and me on different weekends—to visit her at Truro, near the tip of Cape Cod. It was already dark when I got there—there was in those days a train that went all the way to Provincetown, shuffling along so slowly that it might have been plodding through the sand—and though I was met by a man with a cart, he did not, for some curmudgeonly Cape Cod reason, drive me all the way to the house, but dropped me some distance away from it, so that I somehow got lost in a field and dragged my suitcase through scrub-oak and sweetfern in the breathless hot August night. At last I saw a gleam—a small house—which I approached from the fields behind it, and there I found the Millays: Edna, with her mother and her two sisters, none of whom I had met. The little house had been lent them for the summer by George Cram Cook (always known as "Jig"), the organizer of the Provincetown Players, who with Susan Glaspell lived across the road. It was bare, with no decoration and only a few pieces of furniture; a windmill that pumped water and no plumbing. Norma has told me since that, when it rained the first night they got there, before they knew they had neighbors who could see them, they had all taken a shower under the spout from the roof. They gave me a dinner on a plain board table by the light of an oil-lamp. I had never seen anything like this household, nor have I ever seen anything like it since. Edna tried to reassure me by telling me that I mustn't be overpowered by all those girls, and one of the others added, "And *what* girls!" Norma, the second sister, was a blonde, who looked a little like Edna; Kathleen, the youngest, was different, a dark Irish type. Edna was now very freckled. All were extremely pretty. But it was the mother who was most extraordinary. She was a little old woman with spectacles, who, although she had evidently been through a good deal, had managed to remain very brisk and bright. She sat up straight and smoked cigarettes and quizzically followed the conversation. She looked not unlike a New England schoolteacher, yet there was something almost raffish about her. She had anticipated the Bohemianism of her daughters; and she sometimes made remarks that were startling from the lips of a little old lady. But there was nothing sordid about her: you felt even more than with Edna that she had passed beyond good and evil, beyond the power of hardship to worry her, and that she had attained there a certain gaiety. The daughters entertained me with humorous songs—they sang parts very well together—which they had concocted in their girlhood in Maine. . . .

Since there were only two rooms on the first floor, with no partition between them, the only way for Edna and me to get away by ourselves was to sit in a swing on the porch; but the mosquitoes were so tormenting—there being then no mosquito control—that we soon had to go in again. I did, however, ask her formally to marry me, and she did not reject my proposal but said that she would think about it. I am not sure that she actually said, "That might be the solution," but it haunts me that she conveyed that idea. In any case, it was plain to me that proposals of marriage were not a source of great excitement.

The next morning she sat on the floor and recited a lot of new poems—

she rarely read her poetry, she knew it by heart. The Millays were rather vague about meals and only really concentrated on dinner, but they never apologized for anything. We played the Fifth Symphony on a primitive old phonograph that had been left with them by Allan Ross Macdougall. She was committing the whole thing to memory, as she liked to do with music and poems; and, raspy and blurred though it sounded, the power of its bold or mysterious motifs came through to me—surcharged with her power—as it never had done before. Jig Cook and Hutchins Hapgood dropped by and sat on the edge of the porch. The conversation was light but learned, and I was rather astonished when Jig quoted a poem in Sanskrit: I did not know at that time that he was a liberated Greek professor. But the things that remain with me most vividly—because she called my attention to them—are the vision of Jig Cook's daughter, Nilla, a handsome and sturdy little girl in a bright red bathing-suit walking along the beach, as we looked down from the cliff above; and a gull's egg we found on the sand—gulls do not build nests—which made Edna stop and stare. It came back to me seven years later when, going up to Cape Cod in the early summer, I found myself alone in Provincetown:

Provincetown

We never from the barren down,
    Beneath the silver-lucid breast
Of drifting plume, gazed out to drown
    Where daylight whitens to the west.

Here never in this place I knew
    Such beauty by your side, such peace—
These skies that, brightening, imbue
    With dawn's delight the day's release.

Only, upon the barren beach,
    Beside the gray egg of a gull,
With that fixed look and fervent speech,
    You stopped and called it beautiful.

Lone as the voice that sped the word!—
    Gray-green as eyes that ate its round!—
The desert dropping of a bird,
    Bare-bedded in the sandy ground.

Tonight, where clouds like foam are blown,
   I ride alone the surf of light,
As—even by my side—alone
   That stony beauty burned your sight.

For I was not "the solution," nor was anyone else she knew.
                      —from *The Shores of Light*

———

"Memory of Cape Cod"

By Edna St. Vincent Millay

The wind in the ash-tree sounds like surf on the shore at Truro.
I will shut my eyes . . . hush, be still with your silly bleating, sheep on
   Shillingstone Hill . . .

*They said: Come along! They said: Leave your pebbles on the sand and come
   along, it's long after sunset!*
*The mosquitoes will be thick in the pine-woods along by Long Nook, the wind's
   died down!*
*They said: Leave your pebbles on the sand, and your shells, too, and come
   along, we'll find you another beach like the beach at Truro.*

Let me listen to wind in the ash . . . it sounds like surf on the shore.

———

Moving In

By Conrad Aiken

To Edward Burra

w brewster mass
sept 7 40

Dear Ed: . . . We moved in a month ago, viz. Aug. 4 . . . after a
simultaneous struggle to get that cottage clean for incoming tenants
and this one habitable, where the carpenters and plumbers etc. were
still working. It was chaos and no mistake. . . . And so it went, with
Mary trying to get meals and make beds and lighten a little the darker
corners of unswept rooms, and myself weeding the vegetable garden,
mowing lawns, cutting down trees, shooting at woodchucks and squirrels, attacking poison ivy with a squirt-gun; and both of us wrestling
with the problems of building and paying for the building. The workmen became so devoted they wouldn't leave, and actually worked two
and a half weeks without pay, or in the hopes of deferred pay: we then
had to shoo them off, lest our whole future be mortgaged. Result of
everything, a three-quarters finished house, with wrecked purlieus and
bad gaps, but pretty damned nice. It is really a lovely place. The country
is as simpatico as any I've seen—rolling, wooded, with cleared patches,
and far views to the sea, marshy as it approaches sea level, then fine
broad sand beaches. Fishing weirs far out, far glimpses of Provincetown. Pines, oaks, deer, and wild life of every sort—quite alarming.
You meet giant wasps in the garden, dragging giant caterpillars by the
throat—six foot blacksnakes—woodchucks eating the lettuce—swarms
of maggots an inch long trying like salmon to swim up out of the garbage pit—there are times when it seems better to stay indoors! But the
whole thing is good. And we both thrive on hard physical work, and
feel extremely well. Mary is at the moment scrubbing the kitchen—I
spent the morning scything tall grass and weeds and poison ivy, taking
an occasional shot at a red squirrel who is trying to nest in the outhouse. Summer folk have largely gone—our road is very quiet—life is
simple. (If it weren't for the daily paper and the wireless, dammit.) (The
wireless this minute reports that Princess Martha of Norge is arriving
this p.m. at Hyannis for a month on the Cape.) On Saturday we had a
house-warming for the builders and masons, with a sprinkling of others—everyone got tight as ticks, and we ended by having dinner at a

quarter to eleven, quite spanish dearie, and much fun was had. If ever
there was a time when drinking served a useful purpose by gosh it's
now. . . . meanwhile our loves—
Conrad

—from *Selected Letters of Conrad
Aiken* (1978)

———

"The Rituals of Summer"

By Clare Leighton

EACH JUNE, WHEN school got out, my neighbor friends arrived. Then
we began our summer rituals together. Life was filled with the many
little things that must be done if the pattern of the year were rightly to
be fulfilled.

And because the family included three young boys, there was a constant sense of the wonder of life—that wonder which dims as we reach
adulthood but which can illuminate the world.

I lived, with them, the inevitable "firsts" of the season: the first visit
to the bay, the first swim, the first sight of the ocean. The Cape, then,
in early summer, held an especial clarity of light, imparting a first-day-
of-Creation feeling, like the opening movement of Beethoven's Ninth
Symphony. The leaves of the honey locusts shone yellow-green in the
sun against the clean blue of the sky. Everything so brimmed with youth
that it held the power to peel back the years and restore the excitements
of childhood to us older persons. The heat of summer had not yet tired
the countryside; meadows were white with daisies, yellow with coreop-
sis, purple with vetch. The dunes glowed golden with poverty grass in
bloom. Little white boats tossed on the bay, shining in their new coats
of paint. This moment of clear joy was preciously transient. It would
never more exist until the following June.

The first general ritual of the year, controlled by impersonal timing,
was the annual Blessing of the Fleet, in Provincetown. This was followed by the bonfire and fireworks on the Fourth of July. We watched
this always from the little cove at the bottom of our road, with fire-

works and stars doubled in the water. Robbie, the youngest boy, stayed up late for the event, enchanting us with his diminutive, Promethean magic as he caught the stars and fireworks in his tiny hands and presented them to us, delicately and guardedly, secure in the belief that he held within those little hands stars of silver and gold from the midnight sky.

After that came the annual blueberry gathering, with its elaborate rituals. This merged into the picking of water lilies from our secret lily pond.

We drive along the narrow sand roads through the woods, the sweet pepper bushes and bay swishing against the car. Down below, through breaks in these bushes, we can see the chain of bright blue ponds. But our particular lily pond is none of these. It is a hidden one, and—we like to believe—known to nobody but us.

Our pond is never blue like the others. It is covered with algae and scum. If you look down into its depths, it is like a three-dimensional world of pond life, in horizontal layers of vegetation.

What hazards abound in picking water lilies. Some years it is simpler than others, for then the pond is shrunken in size and we can walk along the edge, upon dry land. But at other times, even in a season of extreme heat and drought, the pond is bigger than usual, swollen from early spring rains. And then we have to wade around it, in all the slime and muck.

We go to this pond always in the morning, while still the water lilies are opened wide. The sun glistens on the surface scum in a quiver of light. It is like a painting by a French Impressionist. I find myself thinking of Monet as I sweep aside the heavy bushes that protect the pond from vulgar view and see the sparkle of water on the flat green plates of lily pads. There, all along the edge of the pond, squat the little frogs. Their gold eyes catch this morning sunlight, till, as I glance towards them, it is almost like the signaling of countless heliographs. Rich, deep gold is held within the eyes of these bright green frogs.

And then, as I look around me, I see a thick patterning of the pretty, tiny, pink water orchids, and the green spearing arrowheads which are the young leaves of the water hyacinths, pointing upright out of this scummy pond. We follow the fringe of the pond, treading upon the thick wet softness of cranberry vines. Before us when we tread, frogs hop across our path, from the cool little green caves in the depth of this foliage. As they plop into the pond they make spreading, overlapping circles upon the surface of the water.

"Better not take off our shoes," Ellen and I say each year, knowing how much we want to feel this cool thick growth beneath the soles of our bare feet. "Remember there are supposed to be blood suckers in this pond. And they are frightening things."

For we never forget that one of these ponds, not far from ours, carries the name of Horse Leech Pond.

And so, while ashamed of our cowardice, we keep on our sneakers when we go water-lily picking.

The flowers seem always to grow just beyond our reach.

"One of these days we'll have to get hold of a tiny collapsible boat," I suggest. "Then we can go far out and find the best and biggest of the water lilies." But in the meantime we must invade this horrible slime, scared of what we may come up against as we wade further into the pond, away from the edge.

Low in the air around me, like a fugue of flight, I see the dragonflies: sapphire-blue darning needles everywhere, thin and clear, delicate as gauze; large, gray-blue dragonflies, resting on lily pads and on the white flowers themselves; and the huge russet-orange ones, of the color of a wood thrush. The dragonflies hover and dart, smooth yet abrupt in their manner of flight, so swift of movement that their wings are invisible. As I look down into the pond, between the clumps of algae where the water is clear, I see tiny fish, with their shadows beneath them, darting in the same rhythm of movement as that of the flight of the dragonflies. The stagnant, static world of the lily pond is threaded with life.

We have to wade far out, till the water is halfway up our thighs. Like little girls paddling at the ocean's edge, we have tucked our skirts high, into our belts.

"I've got the first one," calls Ellen, as she holds a lily high in the air, the long red-brown stem hanging limply down like a water snake. "And there are heaps of them further along—if only I dare go there."

The bottom of the pond is squelchy and slimy. I do not know upon what I tread. I feel insecure, as though I might at any moment step into a quicksand and vanish beneath the surface.

The sun is high in the sky, and the lilies are still wide open. Drops of water glisten on their petals, which have an artificial quality of cold perfection as though they were made of flawless china, or modeled in wax. Even the yellow of their stamens seems false. I need to get close to one of them, that its subtle perfume may assure me it is a plant and not an exotic, man-made work of art.

Soon, as the afternoon passes, these flowers of visionary whiteness will close for the night and become, until the sunlight of tomorrow opens them once more, tight, creamy-green buds.

We wade back to dry land, our legs covered with filthy slime and scum. But my hands are filled with lilies and I am satisfied. . . .

—from *Where Land Meets Sea*
(1954)

———

Two Beaches

By Everett S. Allen

I DO NOT know yet what wind and weather will do this morning, so we shall sit here at the mooring for a while and bask in the snugness of being afloat without having to be alert. . . .

There is much merit in sitting aboard a boat at a mooring. It allows you to look back at the land you have left, and if you would find a new country within an old one, you need only look at it from the opposite direction. Now it is very early morning and what is so breathtaking, apart from the crystal quality of hour and season, is that, being land-based creatures, our view of environment usually is from shore to sea— but on this day, we swing at anchor and look to the land as if it were another world.

Two differences afforded by the change in perspective are astounding. Even at this short distance, helped by the dawn's stillness, what yesterday was familiar and even dull now well might be a foreign country. Although only a half water-mile away, its edges are smoothed and there are beauty and mystery hidden within them. It is easy to imagine that the inhabitants ashore bear no resemblance to those of yesterday, and for all I know they may speak a foreign tongue, wear doublets, and traffic in Eastern spices.

It is pleasantly incredible that, tucked into the shoreline's blur, there actually are such unimaginative things as gasoline pumps and laundromats. . . .

It is good to live close to the weather; in watching the poetic machinery of the bowl overhead there is both peace and adventure. I once knew a man who deliberately had no windows in his office, and I felt that he had sacrificed a great deal in choosing not to be distracted by sun or rain, or the wet and silver splendor of late fall fog.

Now over all is morning quietness, except for the sad and raucous two-toned laughter of a gull; or perhaps he is not laughing, I do not know. How bright is the coming sunlight on white boats; on smooth wood it sparkles, and on the sea's face it is dappled and interspersed with the darkening wind ripples. . . .

The quality of atmosphere is changing from day to day at this time of year and the new kind of world is particularly noticeable in the early hours. There is a clarity, as if everything were freshly washed; it is a powerful beauty and it etches, as with a diamond-bladed cutter, the sharp ridgepoles, the spires, and even the tree clumps against the sky's line.

Like the mute, moving targets of a shooting gallery, lines of clumsy, impatient vehicles push along the distant highways and it is happily strange to see them so far away as to be noiseless and fumeless, their insistent horns too weak to reach me.

Coffee, rich in a white china mug and light dancing on its dark surface, titillates every sense and is an experience of the spirit as well. Steam from the cup rises to embrace the nostril; married to the wind of daybreak across the cheek, to the warming sun that prompts an emotional uncoiling, it infuses an attitude of well-being—not ambition, just well-being.

The quiet houses ashore are tucked in and out of stately elms so ancient that they must remember all the long-lost idioms, the leisurely provincialism of some earlier life. That is the key to the spell; this morning, time is pushed back at arm's length for a moment and the values—lapping of water, the equation of sun, sea and sky—are much the same as they have been for hundreds of years. That is why, when someone ashore slams a screen door, I wonder how he could bear to do it, but I remind myself that he has not made this journey I have made; has not lost time as I have lost it, and his sleeve of care is still raveled.

The mind—my mind anyway—is occasionally too insistent to be denied. Over the years, I have never sat here at the mooring, looking ashore at this beach, without recalling in exhaustive detail much that I would rather not remember. This is because, in a war largely forgotten because there have been other wars since, I spent weeks memorizing the configurations of the Normandy beach called Omaha which this one unfortunately resembles more than any other I have ever seen. It is an irony, for this is a place of peace; it has never known war; yet it pulls the trigger of recollection for me and I shall tell you what I remember, because I must.

The raw taste and smell of fear began with the time of dawn or earlier, when the crumpling explosions, dull blast of mine in mud, singing shell, and roar of flame commenced to transform the summer land into wounds, and man into shapeless, black-wet mounds, lapped by the tide.

It was chilling in the fresh northwesterly. Four-foot breakers curled along the beach, and the steel gunwales of bobbing landing craft scraped off the sides of the transports those shivering soldiers who forgot how to come down a scramble net properly. Smoke and dust from naval fire and a slight mist made the land purple and the enemy therein more terrible by virtue of invisibility. Landmarks we sought were obscured, undoing our assignments catastrophically. The fuzziness of shoreline contributed to the unreality of the blistering shattered air, the headless infantryman bobbing by, the boat disintegrating in a fountain of white water.

Offshore were the great gray hulls of the fighting ships, *Texas, Arkansas, Ancon* and *Augusta*. Inshore, a dozen rolling destroyers slammed five-inch shells into the strongpoints, for we could not land artillery and all but two of the thirty-two "swimming tanks" foundered short of the beach. A French cruiser, muzzles blazing orange, broke out an ensign of incredible size, a tricolored assurance to those natives ashore who had refused to evacuate, that they were being shot at by friends.

Most of the landing craft grounded on sandbars. Under fire as they came within a quarter mile of the shore, the infantry suffered its heaviest casualties just after touchdown. Rapid gunfire beat on the landing crafts' bows, and when the ramps were lowered you could see the spatter of bullets whipping the surf just beyond them. Some soldiers dove underwater or went over the sides of the ramps to try to duck the machine gun's pattern.

Chilled from cold spray, stiff from cramped positions, green-faced from seasickness, and often loaded so heavily that they sank when they waded into a deep hole, the debarking troops could not move fast in water knee-deep or higher, and they stumbled on the runnels, crossing the tidal flat. Many were exhausted before they reached the shore, where they faced two hundred yards of open sand before gaining the seawall or shingle beach. Those who made it did so by walking into or crawling under heavy fire; most of those who stopped to organize, rest or take shelter, joined the dead.

Behind the survivors of the beach crossing, the rising tide was drowning the wounded who had been cut down on the sand. At Sector Dog

White, LCIs 85 and 91, which had sailed with us, were mined and shelled; clothes burning, the living jumped or fell into the sea and tried to swim in under the artillery fire. The ships burned for hours under palls of black smoke. As the tide rose, underwater obstacles—posts, angle-iron "hedgehogs," gatelike "Element Cs" and log ramps—all carrying teller mines, blew up more boats.

Up ahead were wire and minefields to get through, the exposed beach flat and, beyond, bare and steep bluffs with enemy strongpoints. In addition to mines, there were fougasses, TNT charges set off by trip wire that ran along much of the beach. Enemy pillboxes, casemates, rocket pits and antitank guns poured plunging and grazing fire along the tidal flat and beach shelf.

At 0830, approximately two hours after the landing, destroyers were no longer able to bring fire to bear on the German strongpoints for fear of hitting our infantry clinging to the foot of the smoke-obscured cliff. The tidal current and poor visibility had caused innumerable units to land in the wrong places; heavy casualties among commissioned and noncommissioned officers produced further confusion.

Sometime during those hours of fear and interminable explosion, of outrageous introduction to an outrageous world—and do not ask me what time, for time was gone—something offshore in that gray, milling armada caught my eye. What a remarkable thing it is that a split-second glance at some familiar line or shape prods the subconscious. What was it I had seen that called to me to look again?

Then I saw her, bright bone in her teeth, threading her way through the fleet and bound inshore, the two-hundred-and-fifty-foot steamer *Naushon,* once queen of the New Bedford, Martha's Vineyard and Nantucket Steamship Line, and requisitioned in 1942 by the War Shipping Administration for use as a hospital ship. She had come to Omaha Beach to take back the first wounded to England.

Oh, she too had changed; gray paint for white; no insignia on her black stack, and reinforced steel plating where none was before. But her lines were unmistakable as she stood in, and it just happened she was starboard side to and turning, exactly as I used to see her, day after day, as she rounded the breakwater at Vineyard Haven, with a long and two shorts of the whooming whistle to let everybody know she was coming.

Squatting among the broken poppies and the junk of war, I wept until I vomited. It was sacrilege for this symbol of tanned women in summer hats, of children playing in sand to be in such a place and on such a bitter errand. It was unbearable to be reminded of a time when my principal concern was whether the mackerel were biting at the steamboat dock—and to try to relate that time, or myself, to the new corpse upon the sand six feet away, a thing of open mouth and vacant eyes. . . .

—from *This Quiet Place, A Cape Cod Chronicle* (1971)

———

"First Landfall: Ararat"

By Charles H. Philbrick

Lofted together alone on the sky-bared mound
Of Mount Ararat, just east of Provincetown—
East of nearly everywhere—and west of Spain,
In Spanish air we knelt, panting, hot, held
Together by being alive, we two, one, applauded
With beautiful buttocks the large round of sand.

Then, with still-swallowing, tucked-under prides,
Back we came down the sashayed slopes, one-two.
Pair from an ark and parties in covenant, we
Stood zipped and buttoned beside the black river
Of tar. We crossed it at last in a lope between
The shiny currents of steeled, seeking people.

Cushioned, powered, glassed against sand in the wind,
Visored from sun and sped under time, they kept on,
Past us and passing each other: dry, desperate people.

Welcome, we mouthed, being over, *Welcome to more
Of what you think you've left behind.*
                                    Finally we found
Our cottaged friends in the dusk, where the bottle
        went around.

And that was the first time we fell on this land,
　　　in our youth,
But far from the first or last time we have rubbed
　　　bare a truth.

———

"Do-Nothing Day"

By Wyman Richardson

JUST HOW ONE tells when a "do-nothing" day arrives, I have never been able to make out. There is some combination involving both weather elements and human physiology which, when it occurs, makes it clear to all that such a day is at hand. Although it may come at any time of year, it may, of course, be masked by some urgent necessity such as duck shooting or bass fishing. Even then, an extremely severe do-nothing day may show up, causing everyone, often somewhat to his surprise, to give up plans for the usual strenuous activities.

It is September. A before-breakfast weather observation has revealed a sparklingly clear day. A deep blue sky already is beginning to be spotted with fluffy white cumulus clouds, carried before a fresh northwest breeze. Just the day for energy and activity, you say? No! It soon becomes apparent that this is a do-nothing day.

Breakfast is prepared in a leisurely fashion, starting with a large glass of freshly prepared orange juice, squeezed in the old-fashioned blue china contraption with a hump in the middle, not in the modern metal gadget. This is followed by fried eggs, bacon, and toast, and topped off with a large cup of coffee—made as coffee should be made, in a regulation coffeepot. We sit around the table for a long time, sipping coffee and enjoying a smoke while talk drifts to this subject and that. Through the south windows we look out across the hill where waves of yellow-brown grass, borne by a fresh breeze, seem to climb up and over. After a long time, first one person and then another stirs, and eventually the dishes get washed.

"What'll we do today?" someone asks.

There is a long silence.

"Nothing," comes the reply, most likely from me.
And nothing it is.

Then comes a period of sitting on the edge of the low platform on the south side of the house, with bird glasses near at hand. A gray marsh hawk, looking almost blue in the bright light, follows his customary beat between the hills and down across the little meadow by the Salt Pond Creek. He sails along close to the grass with very little effort, and sometimes hangs almost motionless on an updraft as he scans the grass for sign of mouse or other succulent morsel. Suddenly, over toward the Cedar Bank, the crows begin a great racket. From all directions more crows can be seen, flying fast and true to the scene of the disturbance. Shortly, the cause of all this commotion becomes thoroughly annoyed. A very large red fox, pursued by fifty chattering crows, comes out of the cedars, lopes down through the hollow and up back of the barn, and disappears through Mrs. Doane's orchard. Undoubtedly, he will cross the road and make for the thicket the other side of Robbins' Pond.

Now butterflies claim our attention. The stunning black swallowtail comes floating gracefully by and obligingly lights on the short grass not far away. She seems not a bit skittish and will allow a quiet approach to within a few feet, as she spreads her lovely iridescent wings to catch the warmth of the sun and to show off the brilliant coral spot in her lower wing. Her mate is never very far away. He is perhaps not so beautiful as his colorful spouse, but he carries a fine yellow band near the margin of his wings that contrasts sharply with his otherwise dark coloring. He is a great fighter, too, as any black swallowtail who makes the mistake of wandering too close will soon find out. We see occasionally the tiger swallowtail, and the powerful monarch is not uncommon, but the black swallowtail belongs particularly to the Farm House.

The American copper should perhaps be considered the Farm House butterfly. He has coppery-red wings, speckled with black, and is very tame, though he makes a fast getaway when disturbed. He has been attracted in great abundance by the presence of large areas of sorrel. The grayling, with eye-like spots on his wings, annoys us by his habit of closing his wings when resting, but he is, withal, a charming butterfly. Occasionally we see a painted beauty or his close relative, the cosmopolite, a streak of beautiful pink contrasting sharply with the dull gray of the under surface of his wings.

It is fun to study the butterflies in the field and to try to identify them without collecting them. In many instances this can be done, especially with the help of bird glasses; in others, only the family, such as the skippers, can be identified.

*

It is time, now, for the day's major activity. This consists of a long walk down the hill to the boathouse, a matter of two hundred and fifty yards or so. For a while we sit on the boathouse platform. The tide has started to flood up the Salt Pond Creek and the lower flats are rapidly being covered. Terns, finding the water of the bay too rough for successful fishing, circle around and around in the lee of the hill, and then make their way up the creek to see what is doing in the Salt Pond.

We spend a long time inspecting them closely in the attempt to identify the species. The arctic tern, with his bright red bill, has a somewhat more graceful flight, looks a trifle larger, and has some characteristic arrangement of the black edging to the outer wing feathers, all of which make him relatively easy to differentiate. The roseate tern, so named because of the beautiful pink wash on his spring-plumaged breast, can be told by his black bill and somewhat smaller size. He also seems a little whiter. The common tern's bill is usually tipped with black and he is not so regal a bird as his cousin, the Arctic, nor quite so graceful. The young of the year, with white forehead and rather stubby wings, are so much alike we do not try to tell them apart. A possible exception might be the Forster's tern, whose offspring have a black line through the eye, but one must be sure that it does not run all the way around the back of his head, as it does in some of the commoner species.

As the tide rises further, a steady stream of shore birds begins to pass by. They are of all sizes. Flocks of tiny least and semipalmated sandpipers turn and twist with incredible rapidity as they make their way to windward. Fast-flying black-bellied plover, often in more or less of a line, are interspersed with straggling flocks of big winter yellowlegs whose long yellow legs trail out beyond their tail tips.

In about half an hour the flight is over. We take to watching the antics of a very large orange and black wasp with a long, narrow waist— one of the sphecid wasps. We have previously noted a slanting, half-inch hole in front of which the sand is piled up in a little mound. This wasp has succeeded in killing (or drugging?) one of those big flying grasshoppers which are so common down here, and is obviously trying to drag the monster, which is twice her length and three times her weight, to the hole. The distance is six feet, and what to the wasp must seem like a jungle of grass and weeds separates her from the hole. Her method is to grasp the grasshopper near his head with her front legs, and back up towards her destination. Unfortunately, this largely deprives her of the use of her best eyes, her delicate antennae, and she frequently goes astray. Then she lets go her prey and makes a reconnaissance, after which she hurries back. In fact, the most striking thing about her is her panic of haste.

Nothing else can be done until we have seen the feat accomplished. After a long time, the hole is reached and the wasp backs down, dragging the grasshopper after her. For a while nothing happens. Then the wasp comes out minus the grasshopper. How she managed to by-pass him in the tunnel remains a mystery. Feverishly, she starts plugging up the hole, using the mound in front, until it is completely plugged. Then she circles around a few times, comes back once and again to tamp down the plug, and finally flies away—where, we do not know. I suppose she has laid her eggs in the tunnel, and, having supplied her future offspring with food, has gone off with the feeling that she has accomplished her mission.

There follow a few desultory remarks about the desirability of cleaning up the boathouse, restringing and painting the decoys, mending the gear, and so forth, but no one makes any such move. There is also some talk of a swim, but the air is too cool and comfortable, and the flood tide, with its flotsam and jetsam, does not look inviting. Besides, the sun is in the south, and the inner man begins to grumble a bit. So we wander back up the hill.

When we reach the house, the surrounding cedars are found to be alive with birds. They turn out to be pine warblers—olive-brown little birds with conspicuous white patches on their outer tail feathers. The driveway is filled with chipping sparrows; there are three robins in the thick, unpruned apple tree by the barn; and five bluebirds are sitting on the barn roof. This curious combination of species—the thrushes (robins and bluebirds), the sparrows, and the warblers—is a very common one here at this time of year, and I have come to realize that it represents a very definite migratory unit.

For instance, you may find such a group of birds busily feeding among the pitch pines near the road north of the "Quawkery." Suddenly the robins and bluebirds fly up to the telephone wires, or to the top of a large cedar, and begin to call. The sweet warbling note of the bluebirds is especially reassuring. For several minutes they continue their calls, while little "chips" and other very faint calls grow in volume from all about. After three or four minutes, the robins and bluebirds take off in a leisurely way toward the southwest. The little call notes increase in intensity, as one after another the pine warblers follow their leaders. Soon the chipping sparrows join the flight, intermingling with the last of the warblers but definitely forming a rear guard. It takes about ten minutes for the whole flock to get under way. At the end of that time, the last sparrow has disappeared and the pine trees are deserted.

It is perfectly obvious that the bigger birds, the robins and the bluebirds, are leading the way and shepherding their flock toward warmer climes. I do not think they cover much distance at one time, at least during the day, but, day or night, they keep in touch with each other by constant calling. Some still night, during the height of the migration, sit outdoors and listen. You may suddenly become conscious of a constant chorus of chirps and calls coming out of the darkness from overhead. And should you hear the soft warble of a bluebird, you may imagine him encouraging his trusting group of smaller brethren and guiding them to their destination. The thought of this relationship has somehow given me great comfort. Through the dark passages that must sometimes be negotiated, what better guide could one have than the cheerful, sagacious robin or the unpretentious, caretaking, sensible bluebird?

The time has come to prepare the big meal, a process that will take one and one half to two hours. We have very definite ideas about food and how it should be prepared. We like it simple but properly cooked. We do not go in for rare spices, unusual combinations, difficult sauces and such things. We like good fresh fish of all kinds, or shellfish, or ducks. Bass head chowder is our specialty, but we can make a good, simple quahog or clam chowder that you will not soon forget. And by chowder, I mean chowder and not a kind of glorified tomato bouillon.

Today's dinner is to be broiled striped bass and creamed potatoes—nothing more. Some of us may feel the need of topping this off with one or two of those cookies that the Orleans bakery specializes in, and, of course, coffee, a fortified edition of the morning's brew, is essential.

The trick about broiling bass is to have the fire in the stove at just the right point. This requires a certain judgment when the wind is due west, for under such circumstances there is for some reason a draft which sweeps down over the peak of the roof and sends puffs of smoke swirling out around the edges of the stove covers.

Fortunately, on this day, the wind has a definite northerly slant and the stove will draw. The fire is started, and while it is getting under way, the fish cleaning ceremony takes place. The cleaning board was built onto the south side of the barn and its specifications called for dimensions that would accommodate a seventy-five-pound bass—so far, it has not been tested to its full capacity. A bass is a delightful fish to clean. If he has been wrapped in newspaper and put directly onto the ice in the fish box, he will remain moist. Consequently, the scales are easily stripped off. Then the dorsal and anal fins are ripped out, the ventrals sliced, and the pectorals dissected off. When the fish is gutted, the head and tail cut off, and the remainder split, the backbone can be removed, leaving two fillets of firm flesh containing absolutely no bones except for a few large ribs in the flank. Head and tail are carefully preserved for a future chowder. Today's fish is a nice little five-pounder and his head will hardly, of itself, do for a chowder, but we ate his twin yesterday and the two heads will be just enough.

While all this has been going on, the womenfolk have been setting the table, preparing potatoes, making cream sauce, and such things. The kettles are singing softly, indicating a good fire, and by the time the fish has been cleaned, observations made as to sex and latest feeding habits, the fish board swashed off, and so forth, it is almost time to start broiling.

To broil a fish properly, the fire should be burning down. Too hot a fire will burn the flesh before it is cooked. On the other hand, if it is too low, the flesh will get dry. This is quite a delicate point. The other delicate point comes in cooking the fish just the right length of time. There is a very narrow range between not enough cooking, so that the shoulder meat has a slippery, raw look, and too much cooking, so that the flesh is mealy, dry, and tasteless. Frequent turning is, of course, necessary, and I like to do most of the cooking with the skin side down, not worrying if it gets burned.

On do-nothing day, the fish usually comes out pretty well. When he appears on the table, lightly browned, and gently bathed in melted butter with just a touch of lemon juice added, there is no further delay. All hands set to and silence reigns.

With the ending of dinner and the inevitable cleanup afterwards, do-nothing day is about over. A long nap is in order, from which we wake up relaxed and contented. We may take the car to Round Pond to see if it holds any teal, or to catch a glimpse of a deer coming down for a sip of water, or we may drive over to the West Shore to watch the sunset. A light supper of soup, toast, and jam satisfies everybody. Afterwards, a small fire in the fireplace feels pleasant. The northwest wind has died out, the air has a distinct Fall tinge and the stars are very bright and clear.

When we take our last outdoor observation before going to bed, we find a bright show of northern lights. For a while we stand and watch the shimmering streamers suddenly shoot up toward the zenith and as suddenly disappear. At one end of the arc an orange-yellow color appears, and at the other, over near the house, the color becomes almost blood red.

"Some folks say," Tom, our iceman, once remarked after asking us if we had, the night before, seen the northern lights, "some folks say it means the END."

Well, we begin to shiver, and it means the end of the day for us. One by one, we disappear into our respective bedrooms. The last to go blows out the lamps and stands for a moment before the fireplace, while the flickering light of the dying fire casts an enormous shadow against the ceiling.

Yes, we have all kinds of days here at the Farm House. They are all good, but one of the best is do-nothing day.

—from *The House on Nauset Marsh*
(1947)

———

"Wellfleet: The House"

By Richard Wilbur

Roof overwoven by a soft tussle of leaves,
The walls awave with sumac shadow, lilac
Lofts and falls in the yard, and the house believes
It's guarded, garlanded in a former while.

Here one cannot intrude, the stillness being
Lichenlike grown, a coating of quietudes;
The portraits dream themselves, they are done with seeing;
Rocker and teacart balance in iron moods.

Yet for the transient here is no offense,
Because at certain hours a wallowed light
Floods at the seaside windows, vague, intense,
And lays on all within a mending blight,

Making the kitchen silver blindly gleam,
The yellow floorboards swim, the dazzled clock
Boom with a buoy sound, the chambers seem
Alluvial as that champed and glittering rock

The sea strokes up to fashion dune and beach
In strew by strew, and year by hundred years.
One is at home here. Nowhere in ocean's reach
Can time have any foreignness or fears.

———

"The Hyannis Port Story"

By Kurt Vonnegut, Jr.

THE FARTHEST WAY from home I ever sold a storm window was in Hyannis Port, Massachusetts, practically in the front yard of President Kennedy's summer home. My field of operation is usually within about twenty-five miles of my home, which is in North Crawford, New Hampshire.

The Hyannis Port thing happened because somebody misunderstood something I said, and thought I was an ardent Goldwater Republican. Actually, I hadn't made up my mind one way or the other about Goldwater.

What happened was this: The program chairman of the North Crawford Lions Club was a Goldwater man, and he had this college boy named Robert Taft Rumfoord come talk to a meeting one day about the Democratic mess in Washington and Hyannis Port. The boy was national president of some kind of student organization that was trying to get the country back to what he called First Principles. One of the First Principles, I remember, was getting rid of the income tax. You should have heard the applause.

I got a funny feeling that the boy didn't care much more about politics than I did. He had circles under his eyes, and he looked as though he'd just as soon be somewhere else. He would say strong things, but they came out sounding like music on a kazoo. The only time he got really interesting was when he told about being in sailboat races and golf and tennis matches with different Kennedys and their friends. He said that there was a lot of propaganda around about what a fine golfer Bobby Kennedy was, whereas Bobby actually couldn't golf for sour apples. He said Pierre Salinger was one of the worst golfers in the world, and didn't care for sailing or tennis at all.

Robert Taft Rumfoord's parents were there to hear him. They had come all the way from Hyannis Port. They were both very proud of him—or at least the father was. The father had on white flannel trousers and white shoes, even though there was snow on the ground, and a double-breasted blue coat with brass buttons. The boy introduced him as *Commodore* William Rumfoord. The Commodore was a short man with very shaggy eyebrows and pale blue eyes. He looked like a gruff, friendly teddybear, and so did his son. I found out later, from a Secret Service man, that the Kennedys sometimes called the Rumfoords *"the Pooh people,"* on account of they were so much like the bear in the children's book *Winnie the Pooh*.

The Commodore's wife wasn't a Pooh person, though. She was thin and quick, and maybe two inches taller than the Commodore. Bears have a way of looking as though they're pretty much satisfied with everything. The Commodore's lady didn't have that look. I could tell she was jumpy about a lot of things.

After the boy was through pouring fire and brimstone on the Kennedys, with his father applauding everything he said, Hay Boyden, the building mover stood up. He was a Kennedy Democrat, and he said some terrible things to the boy. The only one I remember is the first thing he said: "Son, if you keep blowing off steam like this during your Boy Scout days, you aren't going to have an ounce of pressure left when you're old enough to vote." It got worse from there on.

The boy didn't get mad. He just got embarrassed, and answered back with some more kazoo music. It was the Commodore who really cared. He turned the color of tomato juice. He stood up and he argued back, did it pretty well, even though his wife was pulling at the bottom of his brass-buttoned coat the whole time. She was trying to get him to stop raising such an uproar, but the Commodore loved the uproar.

The meeting broke up with practically everybody embarrassed, and I went over to Hay Boyden to talk to him about something that didn't have anything to do with Kennedy *or* Goldwater. It was about a bathtub enclosure I had sold him. He had insisted on installing it himself, saving himself about seven dollars and a half. Only it leaked, and his dining-room ceiling fell down, and Hay claimed that was the fault of the merchandise and not the installation. Hay had some poison left in his system from his argument with the boy, so he used it up on me. I answered him back with the truth, and walked away from him, and Commodore Rumfoord grabbed my hand and shook it. He thought I'd been defending his boy and Barry Goldwater.

"What business you in?" he asked me.

I told him, and, the next thing I knew, I had an order for storm windows all around on a four-story house in Hyannis Port.

The Commodore called that big old house a cottage.

"You're a Commodore in the Navy?" I asked him.

"No," he said. "My father, however, was Secretary of the Navy under William Howard Taft. That's my full name: Commodore William Howard Taft Rumfoord."

"You're in the Coast Guard?" I said.

"You mean the *Kennedy Private Fleet?*" he said.

"Pardon me?" I said.

"That's what they ought to call the Coast Guard these days," he said. "Its sole mission seems to be to protect Kennedys while they water-ski behind high-powered stinkpots."

"You're *not* in the Coast Guard?" I said. I couldn't imagine what was left.

"I was Commodore of the Hyannis Port Yacht Club in 1946," he said.

He didn't smile, and neither did I, and neither did his wife, whose name was Clarice. But Clarice *did* give a little sigh that sounded like the whistle on a freight train far, far away on a wet morning.

I didn't know what the trouble was at the time, but Clarice was sighing because the Commodore hadn't held any job of any description since 1946. Since then, he'd made a full-time career of raging about whoever was President of the United States, including Eisenhower.

Especially Eisenhower.

So I went down to Hyannis Port in my truck to measure the Commodore's windows late in June. His driveway was on Irving Avenue. So was the Kennedys' driveway. And President Kennedy and I hit Cape Cod on the very same day.

Traffic to Hyannis Port was backed up through three villages. There were license plates from every state in the Republic. The line was moving about four miles an hour. I was passed by several groups of fifty-mile hikers. My radiator came to a boil four times.

I was feeling pretty sorry for myself, because I was just an ordinary citizen, and had to get stuck in lines like that. But then I recognized the man in the limousine up ahead of me. It was Adlai Stevenson. He wasn't moving any faster than I was, and his radiator was boiling, too.

One place there, we got stuck so long that Mr. Stevenson and I got out and walked around a little. I took the opportunity to ask him how the United Nations were getting along. He told me they were getting along about as well as could be expected. That wasn't anything I didn't already know.

When I finally got to Hyannis Port, I found out Irving Avenue was blocked off by police and Secret Service men. Adlai Stevenson got to go down it, but I didn't. The police made me get back into line with the tourists, who were being shunted down a street one block over from Irving Avenue.

The next thing I knew, I was in Hyannis, going past the *Presidential Motor Inn,* the *First Family Waffle Shop,* the *PT-109 Cocktail Lounge,* and a miniature golf course called the *New Frontier.*

I went into the waffle shop, and I called up the Rumfoords to find out how an ordinary storm-window salesman was supposed to get down Irving Avenue without dying in a hail of lead. It was the butler I talked to. He took down my license number, and found out how tall I was and what color my eyes were and all. He said he would tell the Secret Service, and they would let me by next time.

It was late in the afternoon, and I'd missed lunch, so I decided to have a waffle. All the different kinds of waffles were named after Kennedys and their friends and relatives. A waffle with strawberries and cream was a *Jackie.* A waffle with a scoop of ice cream was a *Caroline.* They even had a waffle named *Arthur Schlesinger, Jr.*

I had a thing called a *Teddy*—and a cup of *Joe.*

I got through next time, went right down Irving Avenue behind the Defense Minister of Pakistan. Except for us, that street was as quiet as a stretch of the Sahara Desert.

There wasn't anything to see at all on the President's side, except for a new, peeled-cedar fence about eight feet high and two hundred feet long, with a gate in it. The Rumfoord cottage faced the gate from across the street. It was the biggest house, and one of the oldest, in the village. It was stucco. It had towers and balconies, and a veranda that ran around all four sides.

On a second-floor balcony was a huge portrait of Barry Goldwater. It had bicycle reflectors in the pupils of its eyes. Those eyes stared right through the Kennedy gate. There were floodlights all around it, so I could tell it was lit up at night. And the floodlights were rigged with blinkers.

A man who sells storm windows can never be really sure about what class he belongs to, especially if he installs the windows, too. So I was prepared to keep out from under foot, and go about my business, measuring the windows. But the Commodore welcomed me like a guest of great importance. He invited me to cocktails and dinner, and to spend the night. He said I could start measuring the next day.

So we had martinis out on the veranda. Only we didn't sit on the most pleasant side, which looked out on the Yacht Club dock and the harbor. We sat on the side that looked out on all the poor tourists being shunted off toward Hyannis. The Commodore liked to talk about all those fools out there.

"Look at them!" he said. "They wanted glamour, and now they realize they're not going to get it. They actually expected to be invited to play touch football with Eunice and Frank Sinatra and the Secretary of Health and Welfare. Glamour is what they voted for, and look at 'em now. They don't even get to look at a Kennedy chimney up above the trees. All the glamour they'll get out of this administration is an over-priced waffle named *Caroline*."

A helicopter went over, very low, and it landed somewhere inside the Kennedy fence. Clarice said she wondered who it was.

"Pope John the Sixth," said the Commodore.

The butler, whose name was John, came out with a big bowl. I thought it was peanuts or popcorn, but it turned out to be Goldwater buttons. The Commodore had John take the bowl out to the street, and offer buttons to the people in cars. A lot of people took them. Those people were disappointed. They were sore.

Some fifty-mile hikers, who'd actually hiked sixty-seven miles, all the way from Boston, asked if they could please lie down on the Rumfoord lawn for a while. They were burned up, too. They thought it was the duty of the President, or at least the Attorney General, to thank them for walking so far. The Commodore said they could not only lie down, but he would give them lemonade, if they would put on Goldwater buttons. They were glad to.

"Commodore," I said, "where's that nice boy of yours, the one who talked to us up in New Hampshire."

"The one who talked to you is the only one I've got," he said.

"He certainly poured it on," I said.

"Chip off the old block," he said.

Clarice gave that faraway freight-whistle sigh of hers again.

"The boy went swimming just before you got here," said the Commodore. "He should be back at any time, unless he's been decapitated by a member of the Irish Mafia on water skis."

We went around to the water side of the veranda to see if we could catch sight of young Robert Taft Rumfoord in swimming. There was a Coast Guard cutter out there, shooing tourists in motorboats away from the Kennedy beach. There was a sightseeing boat crammed with people gawking in our direction. The barker on the boat had a very loud loudspeaker, and we could hear practically everything he said.

"The white boat there is the Honey Fitz, *the President's personal yacht,"* said the barker. *"Next to it is the* Marlin, *which belongs to the President's father, Joseph C. Kennedy, former Ambassador to the Court of St. James."*

"The President's stinkpot, and the President's father's stinkpot," said the Commodore. He called all motorboats stinkpots. "This is a harbor that should be devoted exclusively to sail."

There was a chart of the harbor on the veranda wall. I studied it, and found a *Rumfoord Point,* a *Rumfoord Rock,* and a *Rumfoord Shoal.* The Commodore told me his family had been in Hyannis Port since 1884.

"There doesn't seem to be anything named after the Kennedys," I said.

"Why *should* there be?" he said. "They only got here day before yesterday."

"Day before yesterday?" I said.

And he asked me, "What would *you* call nineteen-twenty-one?"

"No sir," the barker said to one of his passengers, *"that is* not *the President's house. Everybody asks that. That great big ugly stucco house, folks, that's the Rumfoord Cottage. I agree with you, it's too big to be called cottage, but you know how rich people are."*

"Demoralized and bankrupt by confiscatory taxation," said the Commodore. "You know," he said, "it isn't as though Kennedy was the first President we ever had in Hyannis Port. Taft, Harding, Coolidge, and Hoover were all guests of my father in this very house. Kennedy is simply the first President who's seen fit to turn the place into an eastern enclave of *Disneyland."*

"No, mam," said the barker, *"I don't know where the Rumfoords get their money, but they don't have to work at all, I know that. They just sit on that porch there, and drink martinis, and let the old mazooma roll in."*

The Commodore blew up. He said he was going to sue the owners of the sight-seeing boat for a blue million. His wife tried to calm him down, but he made me come into his study with him while he called up his lawyers.

"You're a witness," he said.

But his telephone rang before he could call his lawyers. The person who was calling him was a Secret Service Agent named Raymond Boyle. I found out later that Boyle was known around the Kennedy household as the *Rumfoord Specialist* or the *Ambassador to Rumfoordiana*. Whenever anything came up that had to do with the Rumfoords, Boyle had to handle it.

The Commodore told me to go upstairs and listen in on the extension in the hall. "This will give you an idea of how arrogant civil servants have become these days," he said.

So I went upstairs.

"The Secret Service is one of the least secret services I've ever come in contact with," The Commodore was saying when I picked up the phone. "I've seen drum and bugle corps that were less obtrusive. Did I ever tell you about the time Calvin Coolidge, who was also a President, as it happened, went fishing for scup with my father and me off the end of the Yacht Club dock?"

"Yessir, you have, many times," said Boyle. "It's a good story, and I want to hear it again sometime. But right now I'm calling about your son."

The Commodore went right ahead with the story anyway. "President Coolidge," he said, "insisted on baiting his own hook, and the combined Atlantic and Pacific Fleets were not anchored offshore, and the sky was not black with airplanes, and brigades of Secret Service Agents were not trampling the neighbors' flowerbeds to purée."

"Sir—" said Boyle patiently, "your son Robert was apprehended in the act of boarding the President's father's boat, the *Marlin*."

"Back in the days of Coolidge, there *were* no stinkpots like that in this village, dribbling petroleum products, belching fumes, killing the fish, turning the beaches a gummy black."

"Commodore Rumfoord, sir," said Boyle, "did you hear what I just said about your son?"

"Of course," said the Commodore. "You said Robert, a member of the Hyannis Port Yacht Club, was caught touching a vessel belonging to another member of the club. This may seem a very terrible crime to a landlubber like yourself; but it has long been a custom of the sea, Mr. Boyle, that a swimmer, momentarily fatigued, may, upon coming to a vessel not his own, grasp that vessel and rest, without fear of being fired upon by the Coast Guard, or of having his fingers smashed by members of the Secret Service, or, as I prefer to call them, the *Kennedy Palace Dragoons*."

"There has been no shooting, and no smashing, sir," said Boyle. "There has also been no evidence of swimmer's fatigue. Your Robert went up the anchor line of the *Marlin* like a chimpanzee. He *swarmed* up that rope, Commodore. I believe that's the proper nautical term. And I remind you, as I tried to remind him, that persons moving, uninvited, unannounced, with such speed and purposefulness within the vicinity of a President are, as a matter of time-honored policy, to be turned back at all costs—to be turned back, if need be, *violently.*"

"Was it a Kennedy who gave the order that the boarder be repelled?" the Commodore wanted to know.

"There was no Kennedy on board, sir."

"The stinkpot was unoccupied?"

"Adlai Stevenson and Walter Reuther and one of my men were on board, sir," said Boyle. "They were all below, until they heard Robert's feet hit the deck."

"Stevenson and Reuther?" said the Commodore. "That's the last time I let my son go swimming without a dagger in his teeth. I hope he was opening the seacocks when beaten insensible by truncheons."

"Very funny, sir," said Boyle, his voice developing a slight cutting edge.

"You're sure it was my Robert?" said the Commodore.

"Who else but your Robert wears a Goldwater button on his swimming trunks?" asked Boyle.

"You object to his political views?" the Commodore demanded.

"I mention the button as a means of identification. Your son's politics do not interest the Secret Service. For your information, I spent seven years protecting the life of a Republican, and three protecting the life of a Democrat," said Boyle.

"For your information, Mr. Boyle," said the Commodore, "Dwight David Eisenhower was *not* a Republican."

"Whatever he was, I protected him," said Boyle. "He may have been a Zoroastrian, for all I know. And whatever the next President is going to be, I'll protect him, too. I also protect the lives of persons like your son from the consequences of excessive informality where the Presidential presence is concerned." Now Boyle's voice really started to cut. It sounded like a bandsaw working on galvanized tin. "I tell you, officially and absolutely unsmilingly now, your son is to cease and desist from using Kennedy boats as love nests."

That got through to the Commodore, bothered him. "Love nests?" he said.

"Your Robert has been meeting a girl on boats all over the harbor," said Boyle. "He arranged to meet her today on the *Marlin*. He was sure it would be vacant. Adlai Stevenson and Walter Reuther were a shock."

The Commodore was quiet for a few seconds, and then he said, "Mr. Boyle, I resent your implications. If I ever hear of your implying such a thing about my son to anyone else, you had better put your pistol and shoulder holster in your wife's name, because I'll sue you for everything you've got. My Robert has never gone with a girl he wasn't proud to introduce to his mother and me, and he never will."

"You're going to meet this one any minute now," said Boyle. "Robert is on his way home with her."

The Commodore wasn't tough at all now. He was uneasy and humble when he said, "Would you mind telling me her name?"

"Kennedy, sir," said Boyle, "*Sheila* Kennedy, fresh over from Ireland, a fourth cousin of the President of the United States."

Robert Taft Rumfoord came in with the girl right after that, and announced they were engaged to be married.

Supper that night in the Rumfoord cottage was sad and beautiful and happy and strange. There were Robert and his girl, and me, and the Commodore and his lady.

That girl was so intelligent, so warm, and so beautiful that she broke my heart every time I looked at her. That was why supper was so peculiar. The girl was so desirable, and the love between her and Robert was so sweet and clean, that nobody could think of anything but silly little things to say. We mainly ate in silence.

The Commodore brought up the subject of politics just once. He said to Robert, "Well—uh—will you still be making speeches around the country, or—uh—"

"I think I'll get out of politics entirely for a while," said Robert.

The Commodore said something that none of us could understand, because the words sort of choked him.

"Sir?" said Robert.

"I said," said the Commodore, " 'I would think you would.' "

I looked at the Commodore's lady, at Clarice. All the lines had gone out of her face. She looked young and beautiful, too. She was completely relaxed for the first time in God-knows-how-many years.

One of the things I said that supper was was *sad*. The sad part was how empty and quiet it left the Commodore.

The two lovers went for a moonlight sail. The Commodore and his lady and I had brandy on the veranda, on the water side. The sun was down. The tourist traffic had petered out. The fifty-mile hikers who had asked to rest on the lawn that afternoon were still all there, sound asleep, except for one boy who played a guitar. He played it slowly. Sometimes it seemed like a minute between the time he would pluck a string and the time he would pluck one again.

John, the butler, came out and asked the Commodore if it was time to turn on Senator Goldwater's floodlights yet.

"I think we'll just leave him off tonight, John," said the Commodore. "Yes, sir," said John.

"I'm still *for* him, John," said the Commodore. "Don't anybody misunderstand me. I just think we ought to give him a rest tonight."

"Yes, sir," said John, and he left.

It was dark on the veranda, so I couldn't see the Commodore's face very well. The darkness, and the brandy, and the slow guitar let him start telling the truth about himself without feeling much pain.

"Let's give the Senator from Arizona a rest," he said. "Everybody knows who *he* is. The question is: Who am I?"

"A lovable man," said Clarice in the dark.

"With Goldwater's floodlights turned off, and with my son engaged to marry a Kennedy, what am I but what the man on the sight-seeing boat said I was: A man who sits on this porch, drinking martinis, and letting the old mazooma roll in."

"You're an intelligent, charming, well-educated man, and you're still quite young," said Clarice.

"I've got to find some kind of work," he said.

"We'll both be so much happier," she said. "I would love you, no matter what. But I can tell you now, darling—it's awfully hard for a woman to *admire* a man who actually doesn't do anyhing."

We were dazzled by the headlights of two cars coming out of the Kennedys' driveway. The cars stopped right in front of the Rumfoord Cottage. Whoever was in them seemed to be giving the place a good looking-over.

The Commodore went to that side of the veranda, to find out what was going on. And I heard the voice of the President of the United States coming from the car in front.

"Commodore Rumfoord," said the President, "may I ask what is wrong with your Goldwater sign?"

"Nothing, Mr. President," said the Commodore respectfully.

"Then why isn't it on?" asked the President.

"I just didn't feel like turning it on tonight, sir," said the Commodore.

"I have Mr. Khrushchev's son-in-law with me," said the President, "He would very much enjoy seeing it."

"Yes, sir," said the Commodore. He was right by the switch. He turned it on. The whole neighborhood was bathed in flashing light.

"Thank you," said the President. "And *leave* it on, would you please?"

"Sir?" said the Commodore.

The cars started to pull away slowly. "That way," said the President, "I can find my way home."

—from *Welcome to the Monkey House*
(1970)

———

Edmund Wilson on the Beach

By Alfred Kazin

IN A STAINED old Panama hat, the long white dress shirt that he wore everywhere—"I have only one way of dressing"—brown Bermuda shorts that bulged with his capacious middle, and carrying a handsome straight gold-topped cane that had long been in his family, Edmund Wilson, having been driven there by his wife, Elena, now walked slowly, with some difficulty, along the edge of the great ocean beach at Wellfleet on Cape Cod. Finished with his long daily stint, he was now ready to look at Nature and have a talk.

The beach was full of interesting and notable people to talk to. There, on any August afternoon in the mid-1960s, could be seen Arthur and Marian Schlesinger, Gilbert Seldes, Allen Tate and Isabella Garder, Edwin and Veniette O'Connor, Richard and Beatrice Hofstadter, Robert and Betty Jean Lifton, Irving and Arien Howe, Harry and Elena Levin, Daniel and Janet Aaron. At times there could also be seen Stuart and Suzanne Hughes, Jason and Barbara Epstein, Philip and Maggie Roth, Marcel and Constance Breuer. Once there was a view of Svetlana, daughter of Stalin, accompanied by the Georgian writer Paul Chavchavadze, whose wife was a Romanoff and who herself often modestly made her way to the South Wellfleet post office to receive letters from her cousins in Buckingham Palace. It was said that Svetlana and Mrs. Chavchavadze had even compared notes on what it was like to live in the Kremlin.

On the beach sat television producers, government and U.N. advisers from the social scientists and psycho-historians, professors by the dozen—people all definitely "in." There was so much important, authoritative writing going on in Wellfleet that one professor's wife, trying to hush the neighborhood children, put her head out the window and said pleadingly to the children, "The professor is writing a book review. I'm sure all your fathers and mothers have reviews to write, too!" . . .

Wellfleet, just a few miles down from where Provincetown spreads over the tip of the Cape, was not as famous for writers and rebellions as Provincetown. It had no rebellions and no rebels. Its first notable summer folk were architects and designers from the Bauhaus; its next, psychoanalysts. By now it was distinctly, as the pretentious consort of a famous historian put it, *la plage des intellectuels*. It was indeed. By now there seemed to be a book for every day of American history. The universities and the mass media had joined in incessantly producing still more documentation of "just what makes us tick" and "our American heritage.' Nothing "American" was alien to the incessant cultural analysts and psycho-historians, many of them of recent immigrant stock, who each summer in Wellfleet held seminars and read papers at each other, endlessly fascinated by the wealth of material to which they felt happily related by their newfound status as academic authorities and advisers to government.

Edmund Wilson, who lived in Wellfleet the year round, hated it in summer and called it "the fucking Riviera." Oddly, Wilson was one of the few "old radicals" in Wellfleet, along with his friend Charlie Walker, the old Greek scholar and labor historian. I had first seen Wilson in Provincetown in 1940; he was carefully bicycling to the Portuguese bakery. He bought his crazily rambling house in Wellfleet before the main Cape highway, Route 6, had been laid out near his door. That was long before *la plage des intellectuels* in Wellfleet had become a continuation of Cambridge, New Haven, the Institute for Advanced Study, and the executive assistants' wing of the White House. When I had met Wilson in 1942, he was married to Mary McCarthy and already isolated from fashionable opinion by his obstinate isolationism. I had met him again, in London at the end of the war, at the great party given for him by the Ministry of Information when he was on his way to Italy and Greece as a roving correspondent for *The New Yorker*. He was still against the war, still bitterly suspicious of the English. True to his own British delight in being difficult, he turned a cold face to the many writers who had come to pay him homage and amazed me by his appeal: "We must stick together against these Limeys."

Wilson's arrival on the Wellfleet beach regularly caused a stir. A distinct mental avidity and nervous unrest fixed itself around his bulky antique figure. He was so definitely not of this time, of these younger people, this academic set. The sight of him in his Panama hat and well-filled Bermuda shorts, the cane propped up in the sand like a sword in declaration of war, instantly brought out in me the mingled anxiety and laughter that I used to feel watching Laurel and Hardy about to cross a precipice. There was so much mischief, disdain, and intellectual solemnity wrapped up behind that getup, that high painfully distinct voice, that lonely proud face. His immense authority for everyone on this beach—especially among the literary professors, who explained to their classes that Wilson was not "really a critic at all"—was clearly at odds with the too elegant cane, the stains so carefully preserved on the Panama hat, the absurdly formal long white shirt sometimes flopping over the bulky stomach in the Bermuda shorts. He was a "character." The improbably loud high voice—like no other voice you would ever hear, it seemed such a deliberate effort—launched into a "topic" before the man had even sat down. It amused and amazed as much as it intimidated. He asserted himself just by making his stage entrance onto what Thoreau, walking down here from Provincetown in all weathers, had in awe called "the great beach."

The ocean rolled and thundered. The sand shone. The cliffs of stark dunes overhead, green grass and tiny twisted shrub pine against the gold sand, gleamed with wild rosebushes. Our happiest times were here, at the edge of the land, the ocean, the dunes. The beach was a great body, and on this beach we were bodies again. Beyond "Joan's beach," where a wartime army hut had been moved as a summer cottage for a lady from New York and her painter boyfriend, still stretched the outermost Cape, forever beating in your ears from the ocean, the emptiness of that long wild ocean beach where you could still contentedly walk, make love, and skinny-dip.

But "Joan's beach" was a riot. The great beach was replaced every afternoon by the great society. Each year Joan's weathered old beach hut sank more abjectly into the sand while around it rose the mercilessly stylized avant-garde house of a wealthy Leninist from Philadelphia. A leathery old man with a shaven head and showing off a powerful chest, a man who looked just as photographically virile as the old Picasso, walked with emphatic strides to the "nudies' beach." In the great clown tradition of the good old American summertime, pliant young girls in striped tank suits and Huck Finn country straw hats sat in the lotus position practicing Yoga. The ocean gamboled, young men dived into rollers and then hopped up and down in the water waiting for a wave to carry them back to shore. Down the beach couples lay about open, free, and friendly as if they had just made the happiest love. Red Japanese kites with long tails bobbed up and down wheeled by the screams of the children on the cliffs.

In the midst of all this Edmund Wilson was hoarsely at the center of everyone's attention, sometimes forced against his will into the usual gossip and polemic. He sat without ease; he scooped up a handful of sand and let it drift slowly through his half-clenched fist as people running out of the water gathered around him only to run back into the water. So many staring, giggling, and deadly scrutinizers, guessing that he was "someone," made him nervous, but he unhappily sat on, unable to make his escape. So he talked. He talked as if he were reluctant to talk but too stubborn to stop. He talked as if talking were a physical difficulty forced upon him by a disagreeable world. But it was one he had learned to use for his own purposes, and even with cunning, in short, shy, killing observations. Then, looking as if he had just heard himself for the first time, he would throw his head back in a loud whinnying laugh.

—from *New York Jew* (1978)

———

"Literary Life on the Cape"

By E. J. Kahn, Jr.

IN ALFRED KAZIN's latest volume of memoirs, *New York Jew,* the eminent critic reveals that like other literary New Yorkers he has spent many a summer on the outer reaches of Cape Cod. The book is laced with reminiscences about men of letters who have frequented that seasonal haven, notable among them Edmund Wilson and Edwin O'Connor. There were a couple of Outer-Cape tidbits, though, that, conceivably for want of space, Mr. Kazin passed over. One he no doubt omitted out of modesty: an account of the time that Alfred K., occupying an old Cape Cod house with a steep staircase, heard the phone ring downstairs while taking a shower, rushed to answer it, tumbled down the steps, dislocated his shoulder and, when help arrived, was less worried about the considerable pain he was suffering than getting his nakedness veiled.

Another was the time that Ed O'Connor, expecting the editor of *The Atlantic Monthly* for lunch, remembered at the last minute that he was out of wine, leapt into his car, went roaring down his steep curved driveway, and crashed head-on into the car of his guest, Robert Manning, who, thinking he was late, was roaring up at full tilt. Still another was the time when a visiting reporter for a renowned newspaper, evidently desperate for summer copy, wrote a feature story from the Cape in which he described me as the Mayor of Truro and Edmund Wilson as one of my constituents. There were a few trifling inaccuracies in that account: Truro, where I have blissfully spent the last 30 or so summers, has no mayor; I have never held any office there; Edmund Wilson lived in Wellfleet, and he and I were unacquainted. Wilson, to the best of my knowledge, never tried to set that particular record straight, but I plan to do so when I get around to my own memoirs, which I have tentatively entitled *New York Too.*

People who are not especially familiar with the folkways of the Outer Cape—Truro, that is, along with its bracketing settlements of Wellfleet and Provincetown—sometimes describe it as a summer literary colony, but to those of us who more or less earn a living by writing and who happen to spend summers there, the characterization seems a mite high-toned. Most writers who gravitate to our region make a point of saying very little about their work, and pretend, insofar as possible, that they never do any writing after they cross the Cape Cod Canal. One would never suspect, for instance, from seeing Stanley Kunitz putter about his Provincetown garden, whip up soufflés in his kitchen, or prance around a tennis court, that a single line of poetry has ever crossed that protean man's mind. When my children were growing up, to cite a further example, I used to work seven days a week, all summer long (as I still affect to do), from 8 A.M. until lunchtime, except on mornings when the tide was right for sea-clamming. But inasmuch as the boys rarely got out of bed before noon, I succeeded fairly well in convincing them that the one thing no self-respecting Truro writer would ever be caught dead doing was writing. They thought that I was, like Robert Jay Lifton, William Gibson, B. H. Friedman, Mark Strand and other conscientious but reticent writers in our midst, just a tennis bum.

The low-keyed life that much of the writing crowd leads on the Cape (Edmund Wilson was, of course, sui generis, not being a tennis player) is probably quite dissimilar to what I gather is the situation on our neighboring islands, Nantucket and Martha's Vineyard. I have heard it said that being part of a Literary Colony over there is all-important, and that on the Vineyard writers frequently forgather to discuss their work in progress, with Art Buchwald holding forth eloquently on ideological trends and Lillian Hellman providing comic relief.

What sets Cape Cod writers apart from other summer residents in their communities is that the writers never really take vacations. Accordingly, we are rarely joined by publishers or editors, although, like Bob Manning, one of them may occasionally stop by for wine or tennis. The publishers and editors avoid us because they regularly go off on holidays—publishers go to tonier resorts than writers can afford (Chatham, say, where people wear neckties in August) and editors to grubbier ones, such as the Hamptons—and it would embarrass them to be obliged to perceive that writers do not.

It is just as well that these manipulators of our market keep their distance, because writers certainly do not wish to deceive *them* about their labors. Whenever anybody in either of those categories spends a night at our house, we put him in a bedroom where the clang of my manual typewriter is bound to abort his dreams. I imagine that some such alarm clock is also rigged up by, among other authors who have migrated to our neck of the dunes, the playwright Abe Burrows (we could once boast Eugene O'Neill), the fiction writers John Cheever, Anne Bernays and Ann Birstein, the historians Justin Kaplan and Doris Kearns, the art historians Katharine Kuh and Eleanor Munro, and such high-domed thinkers as Stanley Hoffmann, Richard Goodwin, Noam Chomsky and Betty Jean Lifton. Norman Mailer is a Provincetown monument of sorts (a tourist who thought I resembled him once threw a punch at me), and John McPhee slept there, too.

We have some writers who have nonliterary specialties. Joan Colebrook can open oysters at a beach picnic in the dark without either getting sand in them or drawing her own blood. The magazine writers Sarah and Nick Pileggi tool around Truro in a splendid ancient Daimler convertible that makes even the affluent psychiatrists who hang around the edges of our set drool with envy. (No Truro shrink has yet come up with anything more competitive than a run-of-the-mill Rolls-Royce.) Down the road from our house is an astonishing clan, the Watsons: There are about 10 of them, and they all turn out books—though they profess in the presence of nonwriters to care more about horses—as easily as other people bake cakes, which the Watsons also do in profusion.

As in most segments of society, we have anomalies. The political scientist Richard E. Neustadt is unarguably the main freak in our sideshow. He not only makes no secret of his industriousness but has a

"Man at Work" sign in his Wellfleet driveway with an appended warning that under no circumstances is he to be interrupted before 5 P.M. Inasmuch as no other writer has dared venture beyond this do-not-disturb barrier until teatime, there is no way of our ascertaining whether Dick is actually inside writing or is playing solitaire. Professor Neustadt aside, all the writers in our neighborhood simply assume that every other writer, no matter what his public posture may be, is privately plugging away at his trade. Last summer, for instance, Joan Lebold Cohen, who with her husband Jerome Alan Cohen forms one of the many writing couples of the Outer Cape (they only have a station wagon), came by our house one afternoon and asked if she could take my picture for a book jacket, I thanked her but said I wasn't working on a book. "You will be," she said. "Say cheese." I would hate to let Joan down, so I may start in on my memoirs this summer, if I can do it furtively enough. I wouldn't want to be the inadvertent cause of the Outer Cape's becoming known as a Working Writers' hangout.

—

"The S.S. *Longstreet:* 1964"

By Robert Finch

THE TARGET SHIP, we called it. The big ship, the target ship, the Liberty Ship. Before we knew its prosaic history, we imagined it a battleship hauled back from whatever unheralded glories it had known in World War II, not heroically sunk or even decently scrapped but ignominiously sat, plunked down in the Bay two miles off the Eastham flats, its belly resting on the sandy bottom twenty feet under at high tide.

For nearly two decades the fighters out of Otis Air Force Base had used it for target practice, pummeling it with target bombs and dummy rockets, not destroying it but, it seemed, mocking its enforced indestructibility with thousands of small gnat-holes ripped through its huge sides by the dull collision of dead metal on dead metal. Slowly, imperceptibly, its vast hulk rusted, rotted, fell in insignificant bits into the shallow water. There seemed something pathetic in its fate, that this piece of noble history should die, not in proud defiance of its attackers, but like some ancient show animal being slowly taunted to death.

For it was as a show you saw it then, from the shores of Eastham, Wellfleet, Orleans, and Brewster. It was imposing seen from the beach in the daytime, for at that distance it still retained its gun-gray appearance, the thickness of the atmosphere hiding the rust, looking sleek, indomitable, afloat. But it was best at night. Standing with the summer crowds on the docks at Rock Harbor or along the strands of Skaket, you watched the single, ominous red lights of the planes as they appeared, one by one, heading out across the Bay to the east, then circling slowly and steadily back across the dark water. Suddenly a huge cone of yellow light, emanating directly from before the red light, was thrown out across the black void, moving quickly, searching almost frantically, randomly, until the cone caught and instantly held its object: the vast, now-silvered hulk of the ship, half-lit and half-silhouetted in the glare, moon-like; or like some aboriginal sea beast finally tracked down in its watery lair by the furies of progress and marked for extinction.

The plane tilted down in a slow dive, the cone of light went suddenly out, and after two or three seconds of pure darkness (except for the small fierce moving red point of light) two to five bright soundless flashes burst well above the ship, while the spent shells fell uselessly and mockingly toward it, and you waited on shore again in darkness, silently and collectively counting the seconds somewhere between seven and eight until at last the deferred sound, burgeoning over the empty waters, fell in consummation on waiting ears: *Ka-thump. Ka-thump. Ka-thump. Ka-thump. Ka-thump.*

When it was over the crowds would casually depart, satisfied. It was often better than the drive-ins, and free to boot. It was all too naked to be a mystery, and yet among the residents it had come to assume the identity and the permanence of a monument, or at least that of a part of the local scheme of things, like the tide or the weather, with the latter's irregularity. Inland the target practice could be heard, day or night, clear to the ocean side, and people would stop momentarily, or turn in their sleep, and someone would say, or if alone, think, *It's the bombing.*

And on Skaket beach, where it could be seen clearly on sunny days, bright-colored bathers would saunter down to the water's edge and point their children to where the ship lay on the horizon in deceptively shallow water (so that it looked as if you could walk out and touch it) and tell uninformed myths about a history it never had and a future they could not imagine. It lay like a rainbow on the water, or a gray ghost—not so much a reminder as, by lying so heavily in the past, a duller to the memory of that man-spawned plague of war, lying only two miles and yet forever off the shores of this sun-drenched and inviolable American playground.

—from *The Cape Itself* (1991)

—

"Cod summer"

By Marge Piercy

June is the floodtide of green,
wet and lush and leafy, heavyladen.
In full summer the grass bleaches
to sand, hue of grasshoppers on the dunes.
The marsh begins to bronze.

Hot salty afternoons: the sun
stuns. Drops on our heads like a stone.
Among the pitch pines the sparse shade
simmers with resin.
Crickets shiver the air.
The path is white sand shimmering
leading down from the hill of scrub oak
crusty with lichens, reindeer moss,
ripe earth stars scattering their spores.

Nothing commands the eye
except the sea at the horizon.
We must actively look: textures
of ground cover, poverty grass, bearberry,
lowbush blueberry, wood lily, Virginia rose.
The dusty beach plums range on the gnarled branch
from soft dull green through blush and purple
like a tourist's sunset in miniature.

Sandy, dwarfed, particular
this landscape yields nothing from a car.
A salt marsh must be learned on foot, wading,
lumbering in the muck, hopping tussocks of salt meadow grass,
hay arising sideways from last year's fallen harvest.
The marsh clicks and rustles
with fiddler crabs scuttling to their holes.
The blue-eyed grass has bloomed.
Now we find fat joints of samphire
turning orange, the intricate sea lavender.
Under us the tide undulates
percolating through the layers, slithering
with its smell of life feeding and renewing
like my own flesh after sex.

We go in this landscape together learning it
barefoot and studious with our guides in a knapsack
catching Fowler's toads and letting them go.

The Boomhowers Eat Out

By Monica Dickens

SOME OF THE golden Cape Cod girls get jobs as waitresses at expensive restaurants, at a starvation wage, plus tips which they share, unwillingly, with the bus boys.

Sometimes they have to rush out after a slightly boozed customer and say, "Don't you realize I only get ninety-six cents an hour?"

Or a more subtle approach: "Was the food good?"

"Oh, sure, sure . . . what did we have? . . . Sure."

"Was the service good?"

"Oh, sure, honey. Just fine."

"Well"—the waitress shoves down a quick vision of her proud New England mother—"your tip didn't show it."

Tipsily he fishes out a crumpled dollar bill—"Keep the change"—and weaves out to his car to add to the hazards of the road.

Into such a restaurant one night come Eric and Eleanor Boomhower, a newly married couple from a small town in Iowa. They know it will cost them the earth, but what the hell. They aren't going to take any traveler's checks home.

The restaurant is famous. A Gourmet's Paradise. They keep hearing about it on the local radio station. Shall we? They're a bit sick of clam rolls and pizza. Why not? She puts on the aqua pants suit and he puts on the orange jacket that she still thinks may be a bit too loud, and they drive to the restaurant, where a merry boy in a striped fisherman's sweater drives their car away to the end of a vast, filled car park.

Inside the paradise there are candlelit bars, sophisticated drinkers, three boys and a guitar, waitresses whose uniforms reach the crotch, flickering lamps to tone down even the orange jacket. The Boomhowers join the end of a long line of men and women with hairpieces and wigs to cover sea-ruined hair. After about twenty minutes they arrive before a jolly young man in a Turkish blouse who gives them a number, like the draft, or the old days at the butcher's counter.

"Won't you enjoy one of our cocktail lounges until your table is ready?"

"My wife and I don't usually—"

An order is an order, however jolly. They go into the Olde Englyshe Tappe Roome and sit in chairs made out of half barrels, with a plate of crackers and cheese on the barrel top between them. Can you get a Coke in here? Would that be Englyshe enough? The waitress doesn't come anyway. Eric Boomhower eats an enormous amount of crackers and cheese to cover the fact that he is trying to get her eye, in case he never gets it.

He does. Her suntanned smile beams over him. Her huge thighs menace him at eye level.

"Two sweet Manhattans," he manages to say, and notices at that moment that everyone else in the Tappe Roome seems to be drinking martinis.

The Manhattans are so long in coming that they have eaten the rest of the cheese and crackers and don't really want any dinner. Can they creep out without the waitress or the jolly young man seeing them? What will the merry fellow in the car park think? Could they find their car without him?

He's got the key.

Just as they are getting up their nerve to run for it, the Manhattans arrive. As they are taking their first sip, an amplified voice calls something that sounds like "The Bloomflower party."

They jump and look around. Who on earth—? Oh, us. The waitress is there. "You may carry in your drinks." But she is there with a bill, and so Mr. Boomhower has to put down his glass and find his wallet and wait for the change and figure out the tip before he and his Manhattan can follow Mrs. Boomhower, who is following a hostess through room after room of people eating or staring over paper lobster bibs.

They come to port in the last room at the last table, in a dark corner by a window with a view of the car park. Perhaps they will see their car. They look at the menu. Eleanor couldn't get her contact lenses in after swimming, which is just as well since she cannot see the prices. What can they order that won't be much more than they want? They see other people's plates going by. The filet mignon looks like porterhouse, and the roast beef is cut as thick as a two-by-four.

They finish their Manhattans and drink three glasses of chlorinated water, which an obliging young man in a long stained apron tied twice around his coltish waist keeps filling up. They decide to order Fisherman's Platter, because people back home are going to want them to have had Cape Coddy things.

Their waitress, labeled Mary-Lu, is plump and harried, tendrils of damp hair on her hot face. But her smile is indomitable, and Mrs. Boomhower confides that she has a bird's appetite, and may she have a child's portion?

"I'm sorry. Baked, French fried, hashed brown, or Delmonico."

"No potatoes, thank you."

"Baked squash, green beans, cauliflower o grattin, Harvard beets."

"We don't care for any vegetables. Just the Fisherman's Platter and salad."

"Would you care for another cocktail?" She picks up the Manhattan glasses, only one of which has a cherry stem. Mr. Boomhower has eaten the other. After the *faux pas* of the child's plate, she won't be surprised to find them a one-drink couple.

She brings the salads an hour before anything else, and some sticky sweet rolls, with not enough butter. (*"Ask her for some more, Eric."*) But Mary-Lu looks so rushed and flustered, carrying enormous trays of food and getting her ample waist grabbed by a four-drink man at an aisle table, that they haven't the heart to bother her.

When their platters come, they are intimidatingly oval, to accommodate half a lobster, an ear of corn, a square chunk of breaded haddock, three codfish balls, two shrimps stuffed with bread, clams stuffed with God knows what, a paper cup of tartar sauce, a plastic dish of oily butter, and a mound of French fries.

"We didn't—" But Mary-Lu, inexorable as the Fates, dots the table with a half dozen dishes of cold vegetables *au jus* (in their own cooking water).

The butter makes a terrible mess on the Boomhowers and the table-cloth. There are no corn holders, or crackers or picks for the lobster, so they wash their fingers in the water glasses. Eric eats in silence. Eleanor casts around for things to talk about. She sees the mute couples all around them, and panics. Is this what marriage is?

At the next table misguided parents have brought two small boys who whine and make faces like apes and waste enormous amounts of Blue Ribbon Charbroil Steak and dash in and out to the men's room because there is a hot-air hand drier in there.

When the Boomhowers get their bill, it is about half what they usually spend on food in a week. If they give a two-dollar tip, that will be it, until they can cash another traveler's check. But poor Mary-Lu seems so harassed. They'd better. They leave the money on the table and walk out, so as not to inflict on her the embarrassment of thanks. As they reach the doorway, she runs after them with her brief apron and damp tendrils flying.

"Don't you know I only get ninety-six cents an hour?"

The next day Mrs. Boomhower goes to a hardware store and buys an electric coffeepot to heat soup in their motel room. Eric sends his mother a postcard with a picture of the famous restaurant.

We ate here last nite. Wow.

—from *Cape Cod* (1972)

———

Wellfleet in Summer

By Ira Wood

WELLFLEET.

A spoonful of honey. On a winter morning it is crystal sweetness and simplicity. On a morning in season it is thick with busy creatures, tourists, ants, scuttling, carrying, pushing, harder, faster, fighting for a better access to the sweet. The last unspoiled town on Cape Cod, Wellfleet is developing quickly. Local boys, plying the only trades that pay, build, cut sand roads far into their pitch pine forests to make way for summer villas of cedar and glass, homes that are used two months out of twelve and are washing down wind-tossed hillsides held in fragile place only by tenacious bearberry. I am not a citizen here, not even a washed-ashore, that grudgingly accepted non-native year-rounder, but a permanent through Labor Day guest, notching my status far above the overnight tourist and slightly below the summer home owner.

Wellfleet.

The summer town where a piece is not a nubile teenager or a triangle of boardwalk pizza but an essay in the *New Yorker*. The town where 1.4 members of every family has an agent, where psychiatrists block the narrow aisles of the local supermarket and sit cross-legged on the sawdust floor counseling their sullen children, "Do you *really* want to be sticking your fingers through the cellophane wrap on the ground chuck?"

Lawyers from New Jersey and their wives in unisex resort wear line the sidewalks rubbernecking network newsmen who jog into town for the *Times*. Ex–cabinet members and Presidential advisers have cocktails on the redwood decks of the colleagues they've left behind at Harvard and no one cares more for dressing than to throw a sports coat over what they've worn to pick blackberries. You'll see an occasional Mercedes on Main Street. On a cloudy day a Cadillac full of time-sharing condo owners from Harwichport might pull through on their way to Provincetown to show their house guests the fags. But the rule is a Ford station wagon, stored on blocks over the winter at a pondfront plot bought in 1954 at twelve hundred dollars—with the house—that is now worth a cool quarter of a million.

Wellfleet.

On any given summer morning Main Street turns into a drive-in movie parking lot, a frozen field of packed cars facing the post office from six directions. The lot has spaces for ten, and in winter, observing local tradition, people get their mail, peruse it quickly, say howdy to their neighbors, and leave. In summer, entire families park, run through the post office front door and disappear through the back. German tourists unload their bikes and coast to the beach. Retirees back in their Winnebago vans. The spry second wives of New York analysts, their children leaning on the horns of vehicles double parked in the middle of the street, cuss out grizzly local oystermen bottlenecked behind them proving that nothing hones rudeness and guile like shopping at Zabar's.

Everyone you have ever never wanted to see again shows up in Wellfleet . . .

August in Wellfleet.

When the razor edge of the dune grass crinkles brittle brown. When the sun burns a tired heat and the nights are long and cool. When the tomatoes ripen rich red, too much, all at once, and the beach plums color at their own sweet pace, so it takes two trips or three to collect enough to brew this winter's homemade brandy.

Paradise. Unique in all the world. I have snorkeled with a French baron and swapped my smoked bluefish for the eggplant of a two-time Oscar winner. Wellfleet in August. You come here if you possibly, possibly can. Unless. It is a rainy . . .

August in Wellfleet.

When the divorce rate for vacationing couples hovers at thirty-nine percent. When the bedsheets never dry and the dog smells like a compost pile. When the Sunday *Times* grows very, very boring by Wednesday. If you can get one.

Long, languorous breakfasts when you begin to notice that your husband chews his granola like a Clydesdale. Afternoons when the trees drip like bad pipes and you wear the humidity like a wet peacoat. Nights when you retire early only to bash your shins on the bicycles in the hall that will rust if they get wet. Neighbors on the right who scream until three a.m. and neighbors on the left who screw, grunting the passion of wild pigs.

—from *The Kitchen Man* (1985)

———

355

On Nauset Beach

By Adam Gopnik

A FRIEND WRITES:

I have just returned from a week of leisure. My wife and I decided to spend our vacation this year at a bed-and-breakfast near Nauset Beach, on Cape Cod—not the private, genteel Cape Cod of old shingle houses and secluded sailboats but the public, Patti Page Cape Cod of life-guards' chairs and Philbrick's snack shop ("On the Beach Since 1953") and enormous asphalt parking lots behind the dunes which fill up by eleven o'clock even on a weekday. Terrific place. We hadn't been on an American beach since a drizzly summer week on that same beach eight years ago, at a gloomy time in American life when just about every-thing—cars, vacations, the President—seemed to be running out of gas. So we were unprepared for the pleasures of an American beach—above all, for the sheer beauty and sensuality of American bodies. "Balanchine said that America is the land of the beautiful body," my wife announced on our first day (she was reading his biography), and this seemed over-whelmingly true—especially of those blondes who, by God only knows what genetic combination, still tan to a mahogany stain. As we fol-lowed the news about the mysterious waves of hypodermic needles and broken vials that were washing up on beaches only a little to the south, Cape Cod felt not just safer but, somehow, older.

On my first day of leisure, I decided to buy a copy of Thoreau's *Cape Cod* and find out more about the history of the place. I felt extremely complacent, up on my dune, as I began reading—Thoreau seemed to me a uniquely high-minded purchase—but as the week wore on I noticed a disconcerting number of similarly pallid types perched up on the dunes with *their* copies of *Cape Cod*. I suspect that a copy of Thoreau's *Cape Cod* serves the same essential purpose for a particular kind of vacationer that a scrap of bikini does for the sunbathers—it establishes the high-mindedness of the owner, despite any appearances to the contrary.

Thoreau's book, I discovered, is a fine, gloomy account of several long walking tours he took on the Cape about a hundred and forty years ago. In my ignorance, I had thought that *Cape Cod* was an early book about the nascent life of leisure in America; it is in fact the direct reverse. Thoreau's purpose in going to Cape Cod was to consider what New England must have been like in its original, austere state. The Cape, for Thoreau, produces the least comfortable (and the most typically and deeply "American") people, because it is the least comfortable of places, the most uninviting landscape on earth. The book begins with corpses from a shipwreck washing up onto the shore at Cohasset, passes through the drafty cabins of older Cape Codders, and proceeds to the remote seclusion of the Highland Light. Reading Thoreau on Nauset Beach while you are actually *on* Nauset Beach is an eerie experience. Over there, where a family is listening to old Jefferson Airplane cassettes, is doubtless the spot where Thoreau encountered the "wrecker"—a kind of ghoulish beachcomber who collected driftwood from recent shipwrecks—and meditated on mortality. There, where two girls in one-piece mock-snakeskin swimsuits are playing paddleball, is probably the spot where Thoreau saw an earlier beach beauty he described as "a Nauset woman, of a hardness and coarseness such as no man ever possesses or suggests," adding "It was enough to see the vertebrae and sinews of her neck, and her set jaws of iron, which would have bitten a boardnail in two." And yonder, where the line for Philbrick's begins, with its happy hungry children and whining hungry children, could well be the very spot where Thoreau decided that the sea-shore is "a wild rank place . . . strewn with crabs, horse-shoes, and razor-clams, and whatever the sea casts up,—a vast *morgue,* where famished dogs may range in packs, and crows come daily to glean the pittance which the tide leaves them." He went on to say, "The carcasses of men and beasts together lie stately up upon its shelf, rotting and bleaching in the sun and waves, and each tide turns them in their beds, and tucks fresh sand under them. There is naked Nature,—inhumanly sincere, wasting no thought on man, nibbling at the cliffy shore where gulls wheel amid the spray."

As always happens when you are reading a good book at leisure, the author became a companion, and I started to explain to Thoreau how *that* became *this*—how that Nauset woman became these Nauset women, and how that redoubt of Puritan austerity turned into this landscape of pleasure. But Thoreau answered that what interested him was not the mechanics of this transformation but the underlying transformation in the Spirit (a word he likes to capitalize) of the place and its people. And, as the week wore on, it came to seem to us—to me and my invented Thoreau—that in some respects, at least, the Spirit of the place and its people really hadn't changed much after all. To him Nauset Beach was a hostile place that demanded a determined life, and this is still so. The people of Nauset Beach may have entirely altered their determination of what they want to do, but they haven't much altered their determination to do it, and haven't at all altered their love of determination.

The leisure of an American beach is charged with a puritanical impulse—a love of labor. A beach—any beach—*is* a hostile place. A suntan is yielded up by a beach as unwillingly as was the paltry living the wreckers used to seek from it. Getting a tan requires patience, skill, and a feeling for wind and cloud and sun as subtle as a sea captain's. (First you put up the Bain de Soleil No. 15 sunblock; then, in the middle of the day, run it down and hoist up the No. 8; leave that up and cruise through the afternoon; then take it down and tack for home with the Coppertone No. 4.) There are bags and umbrellas and radios to lug and towels to shake out. There are lifeguards running races along the edge of the water all day long, back and forth, and attendants running ahead of them with bullhorns, asking everyone else to please get out of the runners' way.

This is not leisure as they know it in Europe; this is the old Pilgrim spirit finding new material to work on. What we were seeing on the beach, it seemed to us—to Thoreau and me—was not a replacement of the Puritans' vision of hostile nature and industrous man by a Mediterranean ideal of endless pleasure but something more interesting, and more authentically American: the marriage of a piety about accomplishment with the belief that the highest of all accomplishments is having a good time.

—from the "Notes and Comment" section of "The Talk of the Town" from *The New Yorker*, August 15, 1988

—

"Letter to My Summer House Guests"

By Mary-Lou Weisman

Another peaceful summer season has passed here in our cottage on the bay in Cape Cod, and I want to take this opportunity to thank you for being such perfect guests, and to reiterate the house rules so that your visit next summer may prove to be an even greater success.

The house gift. It is necessary to bring a small offering, preferably a large, cooked meal which can be eaten cold with the fingers. A hatch-back-full of zucchini from your garden is not welcome and is considered a hostile, provocative act. A new blender is an especially thoughtful idea. Last summer's blender, you will remember, burned itself out in a valiant five-speed attempt at pesto sauce. This is probably as good a time as any to let you know that I lied about the chewy little white chunks that clung to the linguini. They were not unosterized pignolia nuts. A white rubber spatula also makes a nice house gift.

What to bring. You will need a bathing suit, a toothbrush, dental floss in case of native corn, your own sun block, and proof of passage back to where you came from. Travel lightly. Steamer trunks will be confiscated. Yours is not to be a visit of nineteenth-century duration. I am not Jane Austen.

Meals. After the traditional welcoming corn on the cob and lobster dinner, further meals will not be provided. Do not be fooled by the splendor of this meal or the graciousness of your hostess. You are on hospitality death row. Make the most of it. Let me butter your corn. Let me crack your claws. I will even light your last cigarette. Do not offer to help me clear the table. Defy my martyrdom by the merest hint of rising from your place, and I will slam you back into your chair. By Saturday breakfast, before your zinnias (which I have picked for you and placed on your night table in happy anticipation of your Friday night arrival) have begun to wilt, you will find yourself on your culinary own. You may have been coddled on Friday night, but by Saturday morning you are underdone. The coffee is in the refrigerator and the filter papers are on the pantry shelf. I like mine black, with half a teaspoon of sugar.

If coffee nerves give way to an appetite for lunch, you are expected to help yourself from the refrigerator. Now it is my turn to feign trying to rise from my chaise lounge, and your turn to insist that you will not be waited upon. Make your choice quickly. Do not open the door and stare. Whenever the refrigerator door is opened, a light goes on in me. Although as a hostess I am certifiably brain dead, the 25-watt glow reflected off the white interior enamel produces the same effect upon me, splayed out on my chaise, as an electrode applied to the nerves of a formaldehyde frog on a laboratory table. I twitch with phantom, hostess guilt. If you do not conclude within seconds that there is nothing to eat except baking soda, I will feel compelled to assist you to that conclusion by reciting the contents of the refrigerator, starting and ending with a bottle of mossy capers and a can of Bon Vivant vichyssoise left over from the botulism recall of the '60s. If you can think of nothing to make with capers and a convex can of soup, but continue to starve, I will switch my compulsive attention to the contents of the pantry shelves and begin to recite the dusty inventory of seasons of ambitious but unexecuted festive Saturday lunches—a tiny bottle of anise extract, the forerunner of a dandy bouillabaisse; a gauze bag of bouquet garni, destined for soupe de moules; and a tin coffin of anchovy fillets, with key, which, so far, has failed to metamorphose into salade Niçoise. Unless you are prepared to wait in line at the A&P reading in the *National Enquirer* about Princess Di and your horoscope (which will tell you that this is the perfect weekend for you to stay home and take stock) I recommend that you spare us both this hopeless, ritual game of no-win bingo, and eat out.

Laundry. There is no laundry. There are no towels. In the event that wetness occurs after swimming or showering, guests are requested to jump up and down on the deck until the condition clears up. The beds are made fresh at the beginning of every season. In order that subsequent guests may also enjoy clean sheets, please sleep on top of the bedspread.

Conversation. I will not ask you if you had a good night's sleep if you will not ask me. Do not tell me your dreams. Since I am not responsible for the weather, but only feel as if I am, statements like, "I love a rainy day at the beach" are regarded as insincere and passive-aggressive. So are the questions, "Is there anything I can do?" and "Where do you keep the ice cubes?" Unwelcome topics of conversation include periodic reports that you are "unwinding" (you are not unwinding, you are feeling the first heady symptoms of malnutrition), and estimates of the height of the stack of mail that awaits you on your desk. Be especially careful not to tell me how lucky I am to be able to be on vacation all summer. I am not on vacation. I am entertaining you. Permissible subjects of conversation include my dreams, my tan, and your stretch marks.

Weather. After two consecutive days of rain, the impulse to go home is a healthy one and should be acted upon.

Your departure. Do not strip the bed. (See "laundry" above.) Do not leave anything behind. If you do, you may purchase it next summer at bargain prices any Wednesday between 11 A.M. and 4 P.M. from the Sisters of the Immaculate Visitation at St. Mary's by the Harbor thrift shop. Should you finish a book while you are here, remember—this is a literate household. Sidney Sheldon novels are not a welcome addition to our bookshelves.

Off-season communications. If I should, in the course of speaking with you during the winter months, prove to be suffering from short-term memory loss and invite you once again for a visit next summer, please be good enough not to remind me of it next spring.

The New
Cape Codders

❦❦❦❦❦

T HE CHRONIC CHANGES that have taken place on Cape Cod since the end of World War II are hinted at by certain basic statistics. From 1940 to 1990 the Cape's year-round population increased from about 30,000 to over 175,000. Each summer those numbers swell to 500,000 or more. (It is said that in August Truro has a higher number of psychiatrists per capita than any other town in the United States.) In 1940 the entire value of the local retail trade was $20 million a year; today the tourist trade alone brings in an estimated $700 million annually. Since 1945 over 90 percent of the Cape's pastureland has disappeared, and with it have gone most of its open-field bird species, such as blue-birds, bobolinks, and meadowlarks. From 1950 to 1970, urban devel-opment increased 150 percent, and from 1970 to 1990, an average of 5,000 acres *annually* (roughly the size of Provincetown) was developed for residential and commercial uses.

Such numbers can suggest the dimension of some of the physical, sociological, and economic changes this peninsula has undergone in the past half century, but the reality of that transformation and what it means to the human and natural experience of Cape Cod are more dif-ficult to apprehend and express. Yet change, and an accompanying sense of loss, form perhaps the dominant strain in contemporary Cape Cod literature.

Recognition of the changes that have overtaken this peninsula was delayed by denial—denial on the part of town officials and developers who maintained that one could have one's Cape and eat it, too, and denial on the part of both natives, tourists, and washashores that the old Cape that they had known and loved was being transformed into something strange and not necessarily richer. The myth of "old Cape

Cod" (and the blindness to the new Cape Cod it was becoming) was strengthened by an enormously popular 1950s hit song of that name by Patti Page, by local chamber of commerce propaganda, by an unending flow of romanticized photographs and books, and by a fearful nostalgia in the country at large—which was undergoing its own unprecedented transformations.

It was not until 1968, when most of the major changes had already taken place or had been made inevitable through local zoning or the lack of it, that John Hay, in his "Post-Epilogue" to a new edition of Kittredge's *Cape Cod,* finally stated bluntly what had been true for some time, that "[t]he old historical peninsula, with its woodlots, its sandy roads and semi-isolation, is no more." It terms of self-recognition for the Cape this was a landmark statement, and it seemed to mark a turning point in the way that serious writers viewed the Cape.

The sense of change and loss is not something new in the Cape's literature, as shown by Kittredge's earlier "Epilogue" to his own book. Taking the long view, in fact, one could say that the entire history of Cape Cod has been one of displacement and replacement: of the Indians, the original forest and the marshes, wolves and heath hens, the original Pilgrim settlers, the old village life, the beaches, dunes and glacial bluffs, the land itself.

But the changes of the past half century have been so profound, rapid, and widespread that they represent a different *kind* of change. Hay calls it "A Change in History"—a discontinuity and rootlessness that in fact amounts to a *loss* of history and a compelling need "to face in new directions." He suggests that the future fate of Cape Cod is now linked to and reflects the changes in the nation at large far more than its own history or local influences.

One landmark book that recognized the Cape's new reality was Monica Dickens's *Cape Cod,* published in 1972. With its handsome photographs, it looks, at first glance, like another conventional celebration of local color. The text, however, is a hardheaded, and often scathing, look at the sociological as well as the physical changes that had taken place in the author's beloved adopted land. Perhaps because of her work with the Samaritans, the suicide-prevention organization she founded, Dickens was exceptionally aware of the need to publicly recognize the social consequences and costs of the Cape's uncontrolled growth and urbanization: divorce, poverty, homelessness, drug use, prostitution, etc. It is a tribute to her strength as a writer that in spite of the book's predominantly critical tone, her deep and abiding affection for the Cape comes through.

There has been an elegiac tone in much Cape writing of the past few decades. Much of it has reflected a sense of loss of the traditional Cape culture and the figures that represented it, as in Brendan Galvin's "Lost Countrymen." By the same token, the Cape Codders of E. S. Goldman's stories are not the sea captains and fishermen of Joe Lincoln's books, nor the remnant local characters in some later fiction, nor the bronzed soap-opera characters in the totally imaginary summer playgrounds of contemporary pulp fiction set on the Cape. Instead, Goldman chronicles the ordinary, often bleak, and sometimes violent lives of the retirees, new residents and their children, city commuters, itinerants, and dispossessed natives that now make up the major components of the Cape's permanent population.

Not all the changes have been lamented, however, and the New Cape has its celebrants as well. A writer like Walter Teller, for instance, can sardonically observe that shopping plazas form the new "village centers," yet also point out that the new Mid-Cape Highway,as much as Thoreau's Great Beach, can provide an exhilarating and novel perspective from which to view this land. Lewis Thomas, on the other hand, celebrates the "collective intelligence" that he observes in the gathering each summer of scientists from all over the world on the beaches of Woods Hole.

More important, many contemporary writers have exhibited a newly formulated understanding of the place they have chosen to live. Poets like Brendan Galvin and Marge Piercy have drawn new, and more hopeful, figures of the Cape Codder, figures willing to learn to live with the seasonal cycles of the land, to rediscover the essential nature of and to work in harmony with "this small and intimate place." Finally, Nosapocket's powerful modern vision of the long-dead giant-spirit Maushop suggests not only the continuing cultural vitality of the Wampanoag people, but also that there are older powers still at work upon this land than we may acknowledge. The shape of the new Cape Codders may after all incorporate that of the oldest ones of all.

It is from such writers—those who acknowledge what the Cape has lost and the overwhelming problems it faces today, yet who find new ways to celebrate and rededicate themselves to the special quality and spirit of the life that endures here—that I hear the most promising voices for the Cape's future and its future literature.

The ultimate future of Cape Cod, of course, is, as it has always been, in the hands of the sea that shaped and surrounds it. Geologists now estimate that at present rates of sea level rise, the ocean will finally claim this peninsula in about six thousand years, and old Cotton Mather's prediction will at last come true, that "shoales of codde-fishe bee seene swimming on its highest hills."

"Epilogue"

By Henry C. Kittredge

To-day the tide of old affairs has ebbed from the Cape shores and left them high and dry. Not even sentiment can blow the breath of life into the sails of the vanished fishing fleet nor call back the dead glory of the clippers. No analysis of the sandy soil—however cheering—can lure the young Cape-Codder back to the abandoned farms. Time will not turn backward in its flight, nor can imagination swell the meager gleanings of boat fishermen or the barrels of whiting in the freezers to the bulk of the full fares of cod and mackerel that two hundred schooners piled on the wharves of Wellfleet and Provincetown in the forties. Land and Sea have failed the Cape-Codder; and the best of the rising generation have moved away.

But what of the others—those whose years are ripe enough to recall the salt works and the packets? Has the passing of the old and busy days left them bitter and resentful, or, what is just as bad, are they content to live on the flimsy basis of a prosperous past? They have been saved from both fates by a whimsical sense of humor, half revealed, yet ever present, which guides their sayings and doings through the lean years. Where did they get it? asks the psychologist. Certainly not from the stern brethren of Plymouth nor from the bitter malcontents who left England after the Acts of Conformity. It did not come to them unbidden from their early struggles with a sandy soil. Rather it followed as the result of a true perspective—that great prerequisite for a humorous point of view—and this perspective they learned from sea-going fathers and grandfathers who had picked it up in the far corners of the world: from Shanghai bartenders and San Francisco crimps; from the sultry banks of the Ganges and from matching wits with British captains in the Master Mariners' Club at Calcutta; they pulled perspective along with codfish from the rugged waters of the Grand Banks and pursued it from Hatteras to Nova Scotia with the mackerel. And though their sons and grandsons inherited no ships and sailed on no far voyages, yet they caught the perspective that enables them to-day to distinguish great matters from small, and so to look at life with a humorous slant. The picture of the Ringleader, or the Belle Creole, or the Leading

Wind, which hangs over the stove in the sitting-room, is the symbol of this saving and instinctive point of view.

So the Cape-Codder feels no qualms about nailing up roadside apple stands for the automobilists, or about filling his spare rooms with transients for the night. Some have built shore-dinner restaurants or converted the old barn into an antique shop for the summer visitors. Others have set up a garage or a filling station. If whales no longer visit their shores, rich city folk do, and with easy adaptability, Cape men and women take the goods the gods provide them. What, they argue, is the use of a proud history if it does not make them independent? Why claim descent from the Pilgrims if they cannot serve tables without losing their pride? And the twinkle in their eyes, which Grandfather Howes brought from the ends of the world and handed down to them with the teakwood blanket-chest—that twinkle appears for a moment as they put the tourists' money in the till, and they chuckle quietly at the ways of the world.

—from *Cape Cod, Its People and Their History* (1930)

——

"A Change in History"

By John Hay

THE HISTORY OF Cape Cod is fairly well known. I say fairly well because I do not see how it is possible to recapture the deep complexities of what was present and now is past, although there is enough past left in us to provide great confusion about the times we have to face. Many tourists run after "charm" or what is "quaint," terms which are slight enough to admit that they have very little to do with the dark realities of three centuries. Now we come and go in great bounds, from great distances. Motion and change make our constancies. We are in no need of staying put. We are attracted by the starlight in the heavens we have created for ourselves. We look on the earth's great flowing beauties with an inclined eye. For all its "conquest of nature," perhaps because of it, our civilization has a tenuous hold on the waters and lands it occupies. We are in danger of being overlords, not obligated to what we rule.

We do not "visit" in the old sense of the word, stopping in for fish chowder, or rum or a cup of tea, nor are we customarily invited in because we are tired and out of our way. There is no time for that, and besides there are too many of us.

The new human plantings do not fit the old outlines. Cape Cod is now subject to a population spreading out as a result of the tremendous growth of cities and towns. It is predicted that the number of winter residents will increase by forty or fifty thousand in the next twenty years, and the summer visitors to the Great Beach may pass all bounds eventually. As the speed of transition has been increased between one era and another so has our individual speed, in arriving and departing. When you buy a piece of land on the Cape you do it as an investment, as a kind of fluid security, not for its own sake or something too priceless to let go. There are always other places to move to. Each man used to be his own nomad, now nomadism is supplied to all of us by the mechanics and riches of society. During the tourist season the average length of visit per person has been estimated at three days, enough time to sense the breadth of things if not the circumstances.

If we are all to be itinerants, wasting and leaving, or suburbanites, Cape Cod will have a hard time keeping what open beauties it still displays, even with the National Park, which has saved a great deal of it from the seemingly unalterable army of bulldozers in the nick of time.

The record, written all over the Cape in the form of cut-over woodland and wasted topsoil, does not say much for human foresight at any time, with or without the bulldozers. In that respect we have not changed, though we are not as dependent on the locality we live in as we used to be. Food and resources come from afar. Still, all places, regardless of the human adventure, have their underlying tides, their own measured and perhaps measureless pace, and they shade their inhabitants in subtle ways. We continue to be affected by what we can neither transform nor avoid. No amount of dry ice stops the hurricane. We have no barriers to keep off the arctic air. So those of us who live here still complain helplessly about each other or the weather, while ghosts of penury and puritanism still haunt the local houses. . . .

Our age may give the lie to all those who are interested in antiques, even if there any old ones left. Perhaps there is no alternative if we have to get to the moon or bust. Will there ever be such a thing as an antique rocket? But there is still a flow of age, a distant sense of things that it is possible to find, hanging like mist over an inlet, booming like the sea over the far side of a hill.

You can still walk the Old King's Highway in some areas, a single-track road where it is easy to imagine a horse and wagon or a stage, during the years when it took two days to get to Boston and the sea route was the preferred one. Even with the jet planes droning overhead and the cars grinding gears in the distance and the about-to-break sound of the future in the sky somewhere ahead, it is as ancient and distinct as the outline of an oak tree. Just its narrowness is enough. I spent half one afternoon trying to find it in one part of its extent, and at last there it was, quite clearly, just the right size for the eighteenth century, with narrow ruts in sandy ground, lowered, indented, washed out in some places, grown over in others, but a ghost with definition.

In the Wellfleet and Truro areas you can still see how the houses were located here and there along the old highway, or dotted around in sheltered hollows back of the beach. In the wintertime you are very likely to meet no one, since there are comparatively few year-round residents. Once the place was full of local need, local talk, or tragedy. What wrecks now occur along the treacherous offshore bars can usually be taken care of by men of the Coast Guard who can get to the area quickly in a jeep and sound the alarm by phone. When there was no radar for ships, hardly any means for wide and quick communication with authorities on land, localities were responsible for the wrecks that might occur off their own shore. There were volunteer lifeboat crews composed of men from neighboring houses, with a boat kept ready in a hollow above the beach, ready to be launched out to the rescue, in terrible seas that were a common part of existence.

In the early part of the nineteenth century Cape Cod towns had between three and four hundred sailing ships between them and a majority of their men went out to sea. . . .

Many of the lights that welcomed sailors, or warned them off, are now gone from the headlands and from houses along the shore that no longer have to worry about their men any more than they have to worry about themselves. The mackerel fleets are no longer thick on the horizon. The wharves are gone that used to take in the mackerel at Wellfleet on the Bay side. No one eats salt mackerel any more that I know of. I have a friend who spent his boyhood in New York State who was given salt mackerel to eat on Sunday mornings. It had been soaked in milk overnight, having been taken out of a "kentle," which was a small wooden keg, the top wider than the base, about a quarter of a barrel in size. His observation was that it was much too salty a dish for his taste.

The talkers at the livery stable, the central store, or the barbershop are also gone, as well as the sea captains who retired at the age of forty-five or fifty to become big men in their communities. The horses, truck gardens, fish heads, rum and rum runners are gone too, and what old men still whittle boats for the tourists on the beach? The ancient marvels who used to gather Cape Cod moss on their backs, telling hilarious stories about chicken stealing, cow "dressing" (manure), boundary disputes, occasional romantic murders, and hard days at sea no longer seem to be available for reference. What a lot of solid objects seem to have gone from the world!

Perhaps I have left history behind too soon, saying, in effect: "Choose what age you like. You may find yourself in another." Perhaps it is no fault of mine.

During my autumn and winter walks I did find a lasting pleasure in recognizing old things, reconstructing neighborliness, even from a distance, learning to see the silence—the growth and shape of things, the riches of "slow time." The ponds especially, in the Wellfleet and South Truro regions, protected by the woods around them and the land leading up to the cliffs above the beach, were clear and deep and seemed to reflect quiet habitation over a long time. The water lapped on sandy shores in the sweet, airy winter stillness, broken by the loud, bright braying of blue jays. Coon tracks were sharply etched on the shallow margins where they had gone fishing for freshwater mussels that left meandering traces on the pond bottom. On the far ends in the shadows there were occasional ducks, like blue-winged teal, mallards, or scaups.

At Gull Pond in Wellfleet one January day there were scarfs of ice along the shore, and out in the center herring gulls flew up and settled down on open water where a light cold wind broke across the surface. Wavelets were continually pushing and jostling broken ice so that it made a high singing, almost bell-like sound.

Around these ponds were crows, evidence of owls, wintergreen leaves to taste, and wind whisking through the pines, or oaks still carrying dead leaves. I heard the odd little hornlike note of a nuthatch as it was rounding the scaly plated trunk of a pitch pine. Pale light moved through the woods and across the hollows. Silvery trees bordered gentle mossy roads, their tracks loaded with fallen leaves. It was all in a special Cape proportion, colored silver and gray, like the Atlantic, or the herring gulls, the clouds and the sky, or an old house that suddenly showed up in true style and balance, not to be imitated by any century but its own.

Then I walked out to see the great green breakers roaming in, and to hear their thunderous bone and gut fall across the length of the beach.

The sound held and it took away, a monumental assurance of power past all the roughness and directness of the old life, its quiet suspension in the present, and the wrenching of the not-yet born.

What you have to face after all, in this low wooded land, in the continual dip and rise of its contours, is consummate change, the way the beach itself, or the dunes are changing, keeping a general state for a minute, or even a lifetime, but quite beyond catching. Its history is water.

Water created it in the first place. When the last enormous glacier melted back leaving its indiscriminate load of rubble out in the sea, it had also created a profusion of holes, basins, gullies, the "kettles" which are now dry or semidry hollows, bogs, or still holding water as ponds and lakes, and valleys, broad and narrow runs with outlets to the sea. At one time Cape Cod must have been streaming with water like a whale's back when it rises to the surface. Now many of the original streams, rivers, and ponds are wholly or in part dried out, but without too much imagination you can fill the landscape with water all over again. Scientific exactitude, geologic reconstruction, make it possible to confirm your sense of the place as full of remnant and abiding fluidity. There is hardly a piece of land on the entire peninsula that does not suggest this.

It is water thousands of years behind, water inseparable from the motions of the future, a power roaring in and destroying, pushing, grinding, ebbing back. It is water in the rain; water in the deep, still ponds; water in the underground darkness; in the gentle seaward running streams; in the tidal estuaries and marshes lowering or flooding over; as sleet; or snow; in icy gales full of the howling emptiness of the winter sea, when the cold metal of the wind pounds on your back and cuts at your face, as it sweeps down the semifrozen sands of the beach where the green and white surf fumes in, rolling and churning with impersonal passion.

Even now the history of Cape Cod is a history of enduring weather, of the same exposures. Only our terms are not the same. Some years ago I stood on the high hills of North Truro late one afternoon, watching the sun's red path shining and moving across the wide waters of the bay, thinking of sea surfaces moving over the round earth to its poles, and the poverty of the winter world around me, stripped to ultimates, everywhere exposed, and exposed to everything. The round hills were so bare that the little separate houses in the distance, down in hollows or perched on the long slopes, seemed to shiver. They glittered like so many frost flakes in the air. I had just come from Provincetown and seen a dragger unloading its fish, and the fishermen cutting them up with red, raw-meat hands. The wind was shipping up the water. The gulls were crying over the racing, lathered shore.

It came to me that what had brought me here had not so much to do with a feeling for the old Cape, with its churches in their simple New England grace, or clam-digging, beachcombing, old wrecks, driftwood, or fish weirs, real as it was in me, but a great new outwardness, a universal human event. Each man undergoes a series of changes during his lifetime in a sequence of experience that corresponds to that of the world. He has in him the revolutions, the escapes from holocaust, the interspaces of peace, the fact of war, the anxieties, the cry that his being be fulfilled, the never-ending human examination and measuring of things. So I found myself to be "way out," a Cape Cod term anteceding the Beat Generation, and meaning far from your home base, with very few old promises behind to sustain me. I had to come to terms with an age without age, a locality without location, perhaps a divinity in fires of no precedent or name. Above all I was required to change, to face in new directions.

The gulls floated in the cold air with customary ease. On my way home I saw a great blue heron flying over a marsh and inlet, its broad wings spread out like a cloak, long legs stretched straight behind it, with feet curled up stiffly, head and neck crooked back. Then it landed in shallow water. Its wings folded and it stood straight up, with a surprising, statuesque height and gaze, the long neck and head above a flock of ducks that were swimming and feeding near by, assuming the kind of composure special to a race of herons that would serve indefinitely. The wind ruffled the water, swept over reeds and curving grasses, sending the last light of day roving in splendid colors over the entire marsh.

All the measured lights and shadows of day and night, the tides of the sea and the tides of the season, the response and joint association of all life's components in that place stayed much the same as they had ever been, in spite of the way we hurled in our roads and relocated ourselves without rest. Its natural order was still there for old expectation to seize upon; though in terms of accumulated knowledge and wants it was more complex than it had ever been, and would have to endure a human association that was itself on the waters of change, holding hard to the mechanics of its coming. Cape Cod had suddenly lost a slow, accumulative history, perhaps in a matter of twenty years, and would be treated like the rest of the world—as it happened, as it would come about under human auspices. Our problem, one of many,

might be this: how could we reconcile universal commitment with the
inviolable nature of a single place?

—from *The Great Beach* (1963)

———

"Lost Countrymen"

By Brendan Galvin

When I stood in the glass drugstore
with the clerk who couldn't find anything
but the cash register,
the two of us caught in the air
inside a goblet ringing to shatter,
I remembered those men
who seemed to have climbed
out of the skysails
and short bunks of Whalers
after New Bedford shut down.
They came from houses behind
the little ponds, and walked
their grandfathers' trails
to gas pumps like old-movie robots,
and stores that sold everything.
While the boss wore a tie
and died fat, Norwell Fisher
climbed for fly swatters
and rum-soaked cigars, and knew
which tool would do what.
Asberry Paine's beagles,
who seemed to travel the town
under haloes, visited where he dug
a foundation hole in a single day.
They were men in shirt-sleeves
and bib overalls and high-topped

sneakers. They got on with it,
they did till the last day, and were
up to the irony of posing with tourists
who thought them rickety, back-country
Charlie Chaplins.
But those wiry getters and sweepers
are all gone now, and that clerk
is only a clerk, and can't help it.

———

from *Cape Cod and the Offshore Islands*

By Walter Teller

IF CAPE COD's old roads are beautiful, the new, in their way, are more so. Broad and unspoiled, they slice through where no trail existed before. They show remarkable morainal profiles; they reveal grand ice-molded contours. They pass through terrain you could hardly otherwise see. If you walked through it Indian fashion, you would not sense the surface, nor become aware of the bulk; you could not see the forest because of the trees.

The more I traveled the great Mid-Cape U.S. 6 Highway, the more commanding I found it. Limited access, generous right of way. Wide, open-armed, running high or cutting deep, this uncluttered new route unveils panoramas and sparsely settled pine-covered miles. . . .

In Orleans I reached the Lower Cape, that is, the part that runs north and south. The Lower Cape differs from the Upper Cape in having more wind, less traffic, and a greater feeling of space—buildings lower and smaller and main streets wider.

The old part of Orleans village looks 19th century, pleasantly frontier, unplanned and easy-going, yet it is studded with banks in new buildings, red brick and white clapboard—bankers' colonial. Red bricks and white clapboard for the Cape Cod Five Cents Savings Bank—six words that tell about Cape Cod values, life, happiness, and the pursuit of wealth.

The old center contains a little graveyard. Fenced with granite posts and galvanized pipe, it lies in a corner of Main Street and Route 6A, next to the movie house. Here rest a smother of Smiths. Also, Susanna, consort of Heman Doane; infant sons of Heman and Pamela Doane; Mrs. Mariad, wife of Leonard Young; Pauline Snow, wife of Josiah P. Young; John and Thankful Jarvis. A bunch of names—they bring to mind the everyday life of the past.

The old center you might say, resembles an old apple tree, its heart-wood gone, its heart-hollow expanding, yet continuing to grow at the circumference. Orleans has four shopping plazas built in chain-store colonial style. The most distant plaza includes a cheese store and calls itself the Village Center. Perhaps it is the new center, or will be in time. Parking areas become the new style of village square.

———

The Poor on Cape Cod

By Monica Dickens

ONE OF THE difficulties about living and working on the Cape all year is that leisured visitors, both the invited ones and those who drive three thousand miles and surprise you with a call from the corner store, expect you to be at leisure too, permanently, from guest to guest.

They see the whole Cape as a perpetual vacation place, carefree, prosperous, smiling as it greets them with raised prices.

They don't see the backside of Cape Cod. The backside used to mean Nauset Beach. Now it means the poor.

There are several schools of thought about the poor who are scattered all over Cape Cod.

One is that it is better to be poor here, because you are surrounded by free amenities, like the weather and the beaches.

Another is that it is worse, because you are surrounded by people who have more money and nicer houses than you.

There is another which thinks that poverty is a permanent state, like the color of your skin. Labeled Poor, you will always need help, and there will always be jobs for those who help you.

Another, while agreeing that in any society there will always be some people who can't ever cope, believes that most poverty need only be a stage on the way up to something better. You should be helped to get off the backside, not to stay there.

Another sees the Cape's poor like drug addicts and discharged mental patients: sure, they need help and housing, but not next door to me.

For years and years the pattern of life on the backside of Cape Cod has been to pay a cheap winter rent and move in with Grandma or Aunt Rose when the rents double or triple in June and the summer tenants trot willingly to the fleecing.

Some displaced people had to camp out. Some families had to live in trucks and old cars, and wash their hair in ponds and kneel on the car floor to dry it by the heater. They could not leave the Cape, since they had no money and nowhere to go. They could not find a cheap place here to settle in and look for work.

They could not find work anyway, because there were no unskilled winter jobs, except after snowstorms, and even the lowliest summer jobs were snapped up by eager young college boys and girls who were bright and attractive. And white.

Gradually the backside people, even those who had got used to moving in with Grandma and Aunt Rose, thirteen people in half a house, began to see that all this was unfair.

But it is the pattern of life, said the Cape Codders (which used to mean anyone who was monosyllabically surly enough to be a quaint native, and now means anyone who has been here long enough to root a wisteria). We all live that way.

How about split families, they said, with the husband sweltering in New York and the family on the Cape? How about the children who for generations have summered with the salty browned sailing grandmothers? And the sons of scientists who move out of cheap Woods Hole housing to spend the summer with a girl on a derelict boat in the harbor? Is all that unfair?

Grandma and Aunt Rose didn't say much. They were pretty busy. The frontside grandparents complained at cocktail parties on oceanside lawns that the only people the summer pattern was unfair to was them.

"I can't do a thing next week. I've got my grandchildren coming." (Eyes to heaven.)

"Last year you were disappointed because they all went to Colorado. I thought that was why you retired to the Cape—so that your married children could come back with *their* children."

"I didn't know they'd come back with children like that. They never go to bed. They eat all the peanuts when people come for drinks."

Meanwhile, some of the poor were waking from their long nomadic apathy. They dug into cottages and motel rooms. They learned how to bully civil servants. They read leaflets that advised "disruption, harassment, and increased militancy."

Advertisements appeared in city newspapers warning tourists not to come to Cape Cod and drive the natives into the street. This made anyone who had looked forward to renting a summer cottage very nervous, especially if they had paid a deposit.

Before Memorial Day, other advertisements invited sympathizers to "Come on down and do anything you like on the bridges."

This did not mean chucking yourself off, but joining an amiable march of displaced tenants across the Canal, carrying babies and slogans, while motorists yelled out of the window, "Get yourself a job!" and the marchers made rude signs at them with their fingers.

Policemen from all over the Cape turned up in crowd control regalia of helmet and shield and gas mask. In case of car blockades, garage owners were paid to park their tow trucks all day by the bridges. Everyone had quite a good time. The Governor of Massachusetts took note.

While he was taking it, several homeless families took over the National Guard Armory in Hyannis. The noise of babies wailing and children shrieking was like the echoes of hell under the vaulted gymnasium roof. Bored and bitter teen-agers, with nothing to do and no heart or will to find anything, lay out the heat of noon on army cots. Mothers took turns making soups and stews. A woman with rollers in her hair ate a steak without putting in her teeth, and embarrassed a boyish local reporter by accusing him of trying to make money out of the poor.

One delicate young mother, very near to giving birth, worried about what would happen to her six other small children when she went to the hospital.

And wept out of big eyes like plums because the pattern of the Cape was changing again, more violently, and there would be fewer cheap places to rent next winter.

"I'm not risking another sit-in."

Over at Dunroamin' by a lake in the woods, the Portuguese owner, who had built the cabins and the pool himself, wept with rage as he

377

tried to repair the winter's damage in time to get his summer customers in. Shrubs torn out. Rocks in the swimming pool. Holes kicked in the cabin walls. Human and animal excrement ground into the carpets.

"This Cape is changing. The kids look at a landlord the way they look at a cop. The women yell four-letter words at me when I tell them their lease is up. For a Portugee, that's hard to take, from a woman. I'm shutting up next winter. Getting off the Cape. It does not enthuse me."

A black father of three got sick of looking for work and spent some of his welfare allowance on booze. Thus proving to the delight of his neighbor that what he had been saying in the bars was right. Welfare recipients spend the money on booze and are unemployed only because they don't want to work.

Later the black man was arrested for falling down in the street, and locked up with some youths who were caught sleeping on the beach. Thus proving that to be poor on Cape Cod can be a crime. Shove it under the rug, as the Pilgrims in that first year at Plimoth shoved their sick onto an island and forgot them.

As chickens will peck a diseased hen to death. As horses will kick a feeble old mare in the head, so she can't hold back the herd.

The neighbor, who was also the landlord, managed to get rid of the nuisance of the black family, with their broken tricycles and unattractive laundry lines. That summer, he took in a Fresh Air kid, who had been dragged to the Cape to make up the quota, and spent the two weeks complaining that the ocean was not as much fun as the neighborhood pool in the Bronx.

In a lopsided gray cottage near a bog ripening with tiny young cranberries, a slightly senile old lady was quietly starving to death, because she had been warned by an aggressive woman who saw her exchanging food stamps in the supermarket, that if she stayed on Welfare, she must come to protest meetings and learn to hate the people who doled out the money.

On the shores of a wide bay, a city family was sanding the bottom of their boat and dusting out a house full of last summer's shells and unfinished jigsaws.

As she swept the porch and looked out at the sea beyond the humpy dunes, and the familiar shapes of green marsh in the river, the mother's eyes were calm with relief at the unchanging safety of Cape Cod.

—from *Cape Cod* (1972)

———

"The MBL"

By Lewis Thomas

ONCE YOU HAVE become permanently startled, as I am, by the realization that we are a social species, you tend to keep an eye out for pieces of evidence that this is, by and large, a good thing for us. You look around for the enterprises that we engage in collectively and unconsciously, the things we build like wasp nests, individually unaware of what we are doing. Most of the time, these days, it is a depressing exercise. The joint building activity that consumes most of our energy and binds us together is, of course, language, but this is so overwhelming a structure and grows so slowly that none of us can feel a personal sense of participating in the work.

The less immense, more finite items, of a size allowing the mind to get a handhold, like nations, or space technology, or New York, are hard to think about without drifting toward heartsink.

It is in our very small enterprises that we can find encouragement, here and there. The Marine Biological Laboratory in Woods Hole is a paradigm, a human institution possessed of a life of its own, self-regenerating, touched all around by human meddle but constantly improved, embellished by it. The place was put together, given life, sustained into today's version of its maturity and prepared for further elaboration and changes in its complexity, by what can only be described as a bunch of people. Neither the spectacularly eminent men who have served as directors down through the century nor the numberless committees by which it is seasonally raddled, nor the six-hundred-man corporation that nominally owns and operates it, nor even the trustees, have ever been able to do more than hold the lightest reins over this institution; it seems to have a mind of its own, which it makes up in its own way.

Successive generations of people in bunches, never seeming very well organized, have been building the MBL since it was chartered in 1888. It actually started earlier, in 1871, when Woods Hole, Massachusetts, was selected for a Bureau of Fisheries Station and the news got around that all sorts of marine and estuarine life could be found here in the collisions between the Gulf Stream and northern currents offshore, plus birds to watch. Academic types drifted down from Boston, looked around, began explaining things to each other, and the place was off and running.

The MBL has grown slowly but steadily from the outset, sprouting new buildings from time to time, taking on new functions, expanding, drawing to itself by a sort of tropism greater numbers of biological scientists each summer, attracting students from all parts of the world. Today, it stands as the uniquely national center for biology in this country; it is the National Biological Laboratory without being officially designated (or yet funded) as such. Its influence on the growth and development of biologic science has been equivalent to that of many of the country's universities combined, for it has had its pick of the world's scientific talent for each summer's research and teaching. If you ask around, you will find that any number of today's leading figures in biology and medicine were informally ushered into their careers by the summer course in physiology; a still greater number picked up this or that idea for their key experiments while spending time as summer visitors in the laboratories, and others simply came for a holiday and got enough good notions to keep their laboratories back home busy for a full year. Someone has counted thirty Nobel Laureates who have worked at the MBL at one time or another.

It is amazing that such an institution, exerting so much influence on academic science, has been able to remain so absolutely autonomous. It has, to be sure, linkages of various kinds, arrangements with outside universities for certain graduate programs, and it adheres delicately, somewhat ambiguously, to the Woods Hole Oceanographic Institute just up the street. But it has never come under the domination of any outside institution or governmental agency, nor has it ever been told what to do by any outside group. Internally, the important institutional decisions seem to have been made by a process of accommodation and adaptation, with resistible forces always meeting movable objects.

The invertebrate eye was invented into an optical instrument at the MBL, opening the way to modern visual physiology. The giant axon of the Woods Hole squid became the apparatus for the creation of today's astonishing neurobiology. Developmental and reproductive biology were recognized and defined as sciences here, beginning with sea-urchin eggs and working up. Marine models were essential in the early days of research on muscle structure and function, and research on muscle has become a major preoccupation at the MBL. Ecology was a sober, industrious science here long ago, decades before the rest of us discovered the term. In recent years there have been expansion and strengthening in new fields; biologic membranes, immunology, genetics, and cell regulatory mechanisms are currently booming.

You can never tell when new things may be starting up from improbable lines of work. The amebocytes of starfish were recently found to contain a material that immobilizes the macrophages of mammals, resembling a product of immune lymphocytes in higher forms. Aplysia, a sea slug that looks as though it couldn't be good for anything, has been found by neurophysiologists to be filled with truth. Limulus, one of the world's conservative beasts, has recently been in the newspapers; it was discovered to contain a reagent for the detection of vanishingly small quantities of endotoxin from gram-negative bacteria, and the pharmaceutical industry has already sniffed commercial possibilities for the monitoring of pyrogen-free materials; horseshoe crabs may soon be as marketable as lobsters.

There is no way of predicting what the future will be like for an institution such as the MBL. One way or another, it will evolve. It may shift soon into a new phase, with a year-round program for teaching and research and a year-round staff, but it will have to accomplish this without jeopardizing the immense power of its summer programs, or all institutional hell will break loose. It will have to find new ways for relating to the universities, if its graduate programs are to expand as they should. It will have to develop new symbiotic relations with the Oceanographic Institute, since both places have so much at stake. And it will have to find more money, much more—the kind of money that only federal governments possess—without losing any of its own initiative.

It will be an interesting place to watch, in the years ahead. In a rational world, things ought to go as well for the MBL as they have in the past, and it should become an even larger and more agile collective intelligence. If you can think of good questions to ask about the life of the earth, it should be as good a place as any to go for answers.

It is now, in fact. You might begin at the local beach, which functions as a sort of ganglion. It is called Stony Beach, because it used to be covered, painfully, by small stones. Long ago, somehow, some committee of scientists, prodded by footsore wives, found enough money to cover it with a layer of sand. It is the most minor of beaches, hardly big enough for a committee, but close enough to the laboratories so that the investigators can walk down for a sandwich lunch with their children on sunny weekdays. From time to time, pure physicists turn up, with only a few minutes to spare from a meeting at the National Academy summer headquarters, tired from making forecasts on classifiedly obscure matters, wearing the look of doom. The physicists are another species, whiter-skinned, towel-draped against the sun, unearthly, the soles of their feet so sensitive that they limp on sand.

A small boy, five-ish, with myopia and glasses, emerges from the water; characteristically, although his hair is dripping his glasses are bone dry; he has already begun to master technique. As he picks his way between the conversations, heading for his mother, who is explaining homology between DNA in chloroplasts and bacteria, he is shaking his head slowly in wonderment, looking at something brown and gelatinous held in his hand, saying, "That is very interesting water." At Stony Beach the water is regarded as primarily interesting, even by small boys.

On weekends, in hot midsummer, you can see how the governing mechanisms work. It is so crowded that one must pick one's way on tiptoe to find a hunching place, but there is always a lot of standing up anyway; biologists seem to prefer standing on beaches, talking at each other, gesturing to indicate the way things are assembled, bending down to draw diagrams in the sand. By the end of the day, the sand is crisscrossed with a mesh of ordinates, abscissas, curves to account for everything in nature.

You can hear the sound from the beach at a distance, before you see the people. It is that most extraordinary noise, half-shout, half-song, made by confluent, simultaneously raised human voices, explaining things to each other.

You hear a similar sound at the close of the Friday Evening Lecture, the MBL's weekly grand occasion, when the guest lecturers from around the world turn up to present their most stunning pieces of science. As the audience flows out of the auditorium, there is the same jubilant descant, the great sound of crowded people explaining things to each other as fast as their minds will work. You cannot make out individual words in the mass, except that the recurrent phrase, "But look—" keeps bobbing above the surf of language.

Not many institutions can produce this spontaneous music at will, summer after summer, year after year. It takes a special gift, and the MBL appears to have been born with it. Perhaps this is an aspect of the way we build language after all. The scale is very small, and it is not at all clear how it works, but it makes a nice thought for a time when we can't seem to get anything straight or do anything right.

—from *The Lives of a Cell* (1974)

"Ship in a Bottle"

By Annie Dillard

ON THE BAY side of Cape Cod, my husband and I own half of a summer cottage and a seventeen-foot Thistle. A Thistle is an old class boat, a racing sloop; it is open, so you can pile in families for picnics.

A year ago July we were embarked upon such a picnic when I found the extraordinary ship in the bottle. We had sailed into fog. The pale bluffs of Wellfleet's Great Island—our destination—seemed lower as we approached them. Then we saw the bluffs blur in fog and vanish. When the fog covered our boat, the wind died back and the children began to gripe. "Look—," my husband started to say to distract them, but there was nothing to see. Beyond the boat the air in every direction glowed. We could see each other in sharp focus—this friend scrambling for a jacket, that friend with a white strip of zinc oxide on his nose. And we could see a circle of waves, dark and crisp around our hull. We heard the boat move through the water.

We sailed in a moat of clarity, a floating island like a flat galaxy of matter in a void. When a corked bottle floated by, I reached over the side and let it slide into my palm. It seemed something was in it, something hanging in shreds like torn cloth. It was a ship in a bottle; we all could see when I brought it aboard. The children, predictably, were not interested.

The bottle was sixteen inches long, blown of glass green at its base. It could have held thirty-six ounces of rum, say, or molasses. Its cork was tight. Someone had cunningly fashioned a ship inside it: a three-master, classic ship-rigged, beamy and round-hulled, and heavy-decked. The ship's intricate ratlines looked to be varnished black carpet thread. Her maker had so brilliantly miniaturized the rest of her hull, deck, and rigging, and each glowing canvas sail, that no one could guess its origin; you could see the ship only in its whole perfection and imagine a real ship shrunk. Every detail of her rail was carved walnut, it looked like, and her masts were spruces the size of matchsticks. Even the weave of the billowing canvas sails was in scale, so those furled on the yards did not bulge; even the grain of wood on the decks was in scale, as if lumbered from bonsai trees. On the transom, brass letters spelled *FRAM*.

This perfect ship floated, as it were, in a crude blob of plaster painted blue.

I trust you have seen ships in bottles. I mention this one and its provenance only because it proved itself unusual six months later, long after I had forgotten about it.

Our summer cottage has no insulation; we close it every fall and flee. We draw the curtains and drain the pipes. The cottage abuts Blackfish Creek, an estuary that empties into Wellfleet Bay. The mean tide range is ten feet; twice a day our moored Thistle careens itself on a mud flat, and twice a day it floats in the basin of water the tide brings. We have often heard that ice piles up on the tide line in winter—we have seen snapshots of muddy, spongy ice lining the beach below our cottage—but neither of us had ever seen it until last winter.

Last winter, my travels took me to the Cape in January. It was only a short jog to visit our empty cottage. I was alone. Daylight was fading when I got there. On the windy beach I saw the shore ice heaped in broken slopes. The tide was out, but the yard smelled like ice, not mud flat. I entered the cottage and stumbled into the porch furniture heaped inside. Because the house was no warmer than the yard, it seemed colder. The familiar paintings on the walls, the red end tables, the frozen couch, the junky lamps—all of these things looked haunted and dear, like beloved objects people put in graves with corpses, to accompany them.

I opened the front curtains. My eyes fell on the ship in the bottle, which lay mounted on the windowsill. My husband had carved for the bottle a wooden stand. We had bored guests all that August with the bottle's small story, what we knew of it: We found it floating in the bay, in a fog.

Now, standing at the windowsill, I saw something I will not forget or ever explain. The bottle's blue water had frozen to white ice. On the ice were many men and dogs; they lived and moved. I could make them out in the bottle's dim blue light. The yellowish Samoyeds fought on their tethers; men dressed in fur parkas stroked the dogs and faced each other, gesturing, with lively expressions and open mouths as if talking on an ordinary occasion. Wooden cartons—on the ship's intricately small scale—lay strewn about the ice, as did sledges, a potbellied iron stove, and debris too small to recognize. The ship listed on the ice, undamaged. All her rigging was bare; no canvas was in sight. A rough gangplank bridged her deck and the ice.

The men alone interested me. I smiled at them and hazarded a wave. They stood in twilight, unseeing. I resisted, barely, the impulse to knock on their bottle—only because I remembered chastening public aquarium signs to the effect that it drives the animals and fish mad if you knock on their glass, which is so precisely what I want to do that it seems almost worth it. Down on the white ice in the bottle, one man beat his gray mittens together. He was talking, apparently, with two bareheaded men, both brown-haired, with iced-up beards. I could see their breaths. I could see my own breath, too; it was an effort to keep it from fogging on the bottle. The men, ship, and spars cast no shadows; it was too dark.

Two men—glistening fur parkas, dark leggings, high fur boots—stood at one edge of the ice and simultaneously tore off running to the other edge. When they reached it, they both fell on their backs and laughed. I could see the startling cuts of white that their teeth made in their opened beards. A cloud of white vapor appeared over each tiny face. The two men stood and made their way up the gangplank and into the ship; one of them opened a hatch on deck and walked into it. The other man followed, and so did everyone else; the men were clearing the ice. They climbed the gangplank, ducked into the ship, and vanished; I watched the last fur boot step over the hatchway, and watched the hatch close. The ship did not twitch. The ice held it fast.

Now it was dark, inside and out. The chunks of shore ice on our familiar Cape Cod beach held the last light like clouds. In the cottage, behind me I could see only a black heap I knew was porch furniture. My hands were cold. I looked from the window again and saw Jupiter north of Orion's bare shoulder.

Inside the dark bottle, over the ship, in the bottle's sky, dimly, a fabric of dark colors hung and moved. I could see stars through its spread. The lights waved and billowed across the sky; their low edge curved like a hem.

A little snow was blowing across the wooden ship; it blew across the wood cartons and iron stove on the ice. The dogs lay fanned out at the end of their traces, each curled, each facing the wind, each with its nose under its tail. A stovepipe on the ship's deck let out a thread of white smoke, and the wind took it.

Last week—in mid-May—when my husband, daughter, and I opened the summer cottage together, I walked in first and spread the living room curtains. On the windowsill the ship in the bottle looked just as it had when we first found it, just as it had last August: a wooden ship bearing many bright square sails. Its round hull rested on a blob of plaster painted blue.

We settled into our summer routines. Last night I was reading on the couch beside the windowsill, as is my habit. My husband was out, my daughter asleep. I finished a book (*Great Heart,* the story of a Labrador canoe expedition) I enjoyed so much that when it ended in my hands and I looked back through it and studied the maps and read the beginning again, I put it down in sorrow, and, rather than rise and find another book so betrayingly soon, I picked up the ship in a bottle.

As I had so often during this past week, I turned the bottle over in my hands. I searched the ship's wooden deck for a sign of the hatch that led belowdecks. Again I sought in the rigging for men, and tried at the wheel, and the rail, and the peak. I searched the blue plaster sea. I looked under the sea, even—between the plaster and the glass, as if for bodies. But it was on the surface of the sea that I saw something new, a cylinder the size of a splinter. It was too regular for a splinter, however; both ends were flat. The cylinder tumbled when I turned the bottle.

It was with pliers, finally, that I uncorked the bottle. The cylinder slid into my palm. It was a log of cork; age or water had blackened it. A seam circumscribed it. With care I pulled both ends; the cork parted at the seam and revealed a wooden cylinder within. This inner cylinder was the size of a chocolate jimmie, the sort children sprinkle on ice cream. In the scale of the ship in the bottle, the cork log was the size of a hand telescope and the inner cylinder the size of a cigar case. I saw with something akin to disgust that this small cylinder was itself a case; a seam disclosed its wooden cap. I have no patience with small things and, frankly, no interest in them. Close views of forest moss or leaves bore me to exasperation, sewing frightens me, tiny dolls appall me—I like volleyball, I like to slam the ball.

Still, having come this far, I had to open the wooden case. Two pairs of tweezers did the trick. Inside the case I found two sheets of yellowed paper curled lengthwise. Written on the papers was a small text.

I have just spent the morning reading this wretched text under a microscope, with my husband, and transcribing it. I keep my only microscope at the Cape Cod cottage; in recent years I have looked through it only at sand. I laid the papers side by side on a glass slide and covered them with another glass slide. My husband and daughter stood by my study desk interested and eager to the point of hopping, both of them. I noted that their hopping shook the floor. When my neck wearied of this sore work, however, and my husband took it over, I hopped too; the words came out so slowly. The words did not explain in any way what the ship called the *Fram* was doing in the bottle, or in the ice. In fact, there is no clear inference—given the peculiar nature of this bottle—that the cork case came from the ship. The cork case and its broken text could have floated into the vicinity of the *Fram* on the surface of the great intermingled sea all ships share. (Except, of course, that the bottle's sea is a pouring of plaster corked off on a windowsill. Every theory has problems.)

Under the microscope I saw a clear, smooth script—brown ink on yellowed paper. I expected a broken grain to the magnified handwriting, because magnified ordinary writing or print shatters under magnification and reveals flaws. But in this case magnification merely restored the document's original scale. I could make out eleven or twelve lines of script at the same time, before I had to nudge the slide.

12th. There was so much visibility last week on the 8th [it began] that we bottled some in flasks and stored the flasks, tightly stoppered, in one of the forward holds. Today, our first day of no visibility, a day of blinding fog, we made our experiment. The captain signaled me, and I signaled the mate: He walked forward into the bows, uncorked the first flask, held it in an outstretched arm, and released its contents into the air.

At once blue sky streaked from the flask and ripped across the fog. It was a banner of clarity, and it floated. In it, I could see a petrel dashing along the top of the water, and I could see calm seas to the horizon. I sat on the rail and looked down. Through the banner of clarity I could see several inches into the water, which was green and filled with jellyfish.

The banner-shaped patch of visibility was ten feet long and as narrow as the flask's neck. As our ship drew along slowly (for there is rarely great wind in a fog), all aboard realized that we should soon lose the visibility over our stern. The captain gave an order, and a man, Larsen, on the afterdeck reached out with a belaying pin and snagged it. He moved it with care, rolling the pin until the center of the clear patch wrapped around it. He lowered it from the air, gingerly pinched it at a corner, and, trailing it from his fingers like a Chinaman's kite, carried it to the captain.

We were hard-pressed to keep the men from feeling of it, for we suspected, and rightly, that touching it would smear the visibility with finger smudges, or, worse, tear it. Accordingly, the captain held it by the same corner Larsen had used, and waved the men away. Slowly he brought a shred of it before his eyes. He looked through it thoughtfully, out to sea. He passed the flowing thing, as if it were an angel, to the sailmaker, who sat and brought his curved needles to bear on its corners. He fashioned delicate grommets there, and whipped their edges with cod line. Then the mate lashed the visibility to the lee bow between forestay and shroud. There it cut a slash of clear and colored vision in the fog. It revealed the sea and the sky, far and near in their proper colors. The pale fog lay all around the slash like a limed wall.

We sent a man forward for another flask. The ship possessed altogether two dozen flasks of visibility. The captain will decide how many we might use now, and where he will hang them. We hope to sight Spitsbergen after dawn.

The pages ended here, at one paper's lower edge. My tale ends here, too, as my story converges on the present and finds me at my desk. I have stored the small papers in the slide case between two glass slides lashed together, so the papers do not blow away. This cottage is old and loosely made. Even here at my desk I smell mud at low tide; the west wind carries it.

———

"Earthly Justice"

By E. S. Goldman

I

AT FIRST THE words were in the wrong sequence to be heard, for death is slight news until a familiar name is in it. "Killed . . . Pittsburgh . . . *Sherroder!*"

Try it yourself. How much do you really care about people starving in Africa or sleeping on the sidewalks of Boston or being shot in their garages in Pittsburgh? You care, yes. You're human, and nothing is alien et cetera. But as if they were your own flesh and blood? No aunt of yours is in any of those fixes; not that you know of. Nothing happens that you care all that much about until you hear a name.

I was reading *The Black Arrow* and half-listening to KDKA on the shortwave. I didn't hear anything until I heard the name of my father's sister.

Killed . . . Pittsburgh . . . Sherroder! *Aunt Leora!*

I held onto the book as to a brother in a scary place while the news-caster put it in order again for late-arriving minds. (The way they used to before jobs were filled by people with no memory of how things should be done. Now they write for radio as if you were tuned from the first word, as if you had nothing to do but sit there and hear them tell the story from A to Z. If you miss the name of the country where the airplane went down in the first sentence, they never tell you again.)

"The dead woman's husband, Dr. Myron Sherroder, a well-known Pitts-burgh physician, was at home at the time—"

The young don't often play a part as large as being the first to know. I burst out of my room and went down the stairs shouting, "Aunt Leora's been killed! She was shot!"

Leora was very close to us. She and Mother had been best friends since middle school. She often came down from Dedham to stay with us at the shore, and after she married and moved to Pittsburgh, the visiting went on as before. Uncle Myron was part of it. The only regret about Myron was that he was a golfer and not a fisherman as we were in our family; but he was accommodating and could be jollied into wading in for smallmouth on a gray day.

Mother was choked and bewildered and kept saying in an unearthly groaning voice I had never heard before, "What do you mean? Leora? What do you mean? What do you mean? Leora?"

It seemed to me that she was angry with me, which was unreasonable. I had interrupted her kind of sewing that is done on a small linen drumhead. She thrust the tambourine, her fingers extended as if to take me by the shoulder to shake out the nonsense as she had when I was younger. I wasn't sure she would remember the needle. I flinched and looked to Dad.

When my father clenches his jaw, the muscles become bone, his lips bulge as if they have under them the pads a dentist slips in to take up saliva. He has never been a slack man in mind or body and does not appreciate it in others. He assessed the possibility of error in a twelve-year-old boy.

He held a finger up toward Mother to ask her to hold back and asked me to say again what I had heard. He went to the phone.

Instead of calling Uncle Myron as I expected, he asked for Pittsburgh information, and then the number of the police station nearest the Sherroder address.

The questions he asked the police desk and the way he hung up said enough. Separating the more-or-less-known from the said-to-be-known, the police were able to say that they had received a report by telephone at 9:47 P.M. from a man stating that he was the husband of the deceased. The witness at the scene stated that he had found Mrs. Sherroder on the floor of the garage, apparently dead, apparently as a consequence of multiple wounds, apparently from shotgun fire. It had happened a little more than an hour ago and the investigation was just beginning. Dad made this report piecemeal in a halting voice while he held Mother.

"I'd better call Myron," he said, gently letting her go.

Myron hadn't realized it was already on the radio. The detectives were there taking pictures and asking questions, and he had been waiting for an opportunity to break away and make the call. After they spoke awhile Dad said, "Life is long, Myron. Take every day one at a time. I'll be there on an early plane," and hung up.

Mother had her voice under control. "What did he say?"

"He doesn't know much more than we do. Leora went to an evening meeting of the Handicapped Services board. He had the television on to a wildlife documentary and didn't hear a thing. When it was past the time Leora usually got home he walked out and saw the garage door open. She was lying beside the car. She was shot. They haven't found a gun."

While Mother made the family phone calls, Dad went to the window and stood fully ten minutes with his hands behind his back, staring through the dark at the few stars of houses on the far side of the bay. Mother left Grandma Dewaine for him. He could have waited until morning and seen Grandma on his way to the airport, but it would have been awful if she heard it first from a reporter calling to ask if she had a photograph of her daughter. He told her that Leora had died in an accident without suffering and that he would stop by in the morning. Being prepared in this way she could be relied on to get through the night. Dewaines managed. She was a Dewaine by assimilation.

Mother was also that much a Dewaine, but only that much. She took the phone and asked Grandma if she would like somebody to spend the night with her. She would be glad to come up herself. Would she like Dad to be with her. Would she like her good friend Betty Morse to be called. Mother listened to the timbre of Grandma saying No, that was unnecessary, she would be all right; and was satisfied. It was left as before that her son would stop there early on his way to the airport.

Although Dad had anyhow decided to take the Pittsburgh flight in order to be with Myron on the first difficult day, our family assumed that burial would be in the Dewaine plot in Brewster. When he called to give Myron his flight number, he learned that the service and burial would be in Pittsburgh.

"I don't understand such a decision," Mother said. "Leora has no family in Pittsburgh. They have been married so few years. Myron's family is out West. Your mother is only a two-hour ride from Brewster. It is inconsiderate to bury Leora in Pittsburgh. She ought to be in your family plot. Did you say that to him?"

"I made the case. It's Myron's decision to make. I can understand that he would want her nearby."

"There are others to think about."

"They have many friends in Pittsburgh."

"Friends are not family. Friends do not come to visit your grave site. It is a strange decision."

"It may be arbitrary but it isn't strange. It's his decision to make. It isn't easy to argue at a time like this."

"When is a good time? After the burial?" I seldom heard Mother that sharp with Dad.

"He and Leora chose the site with care. In his view, he is accommodating her wishes."

"In his view."

We all went to Pittsburgh for the funeral.

When people have lived their years it is possible to take satisfaction in memory, and even for levity to soften grief, and after long illness it is possible to speak of relief, but this was a day of harsh, unrelieved mourning, the most solemn day of my life. In the chapel, Uncle Myron sat between his brother Andrew and my father, and beside Father was Grandma Dewaine. Then Uncle Tom Dewaine, then Mother. They sat by bloodline. Except around a dinner table I had never before, at an occasion, seen Father not sit beside Mother. Because of the nature of the wound the casket was closed.

Very little was said among us. When Grandma shook with hidden sobs, Dad took her hand. I did the same to my sister, at first awkwardly; then, when she clutched it to show how glad she was to have it, with (I suppose the right word is) pride.

After the cemetery Mother took Marnie and me directly to the plane. She did not want to stay over. She said tomorrow was a school day and we should be back. My father spent the rest of the day in Pittsburgh with Myron, talking to the police and the district attorney. They posted a reward.

II

You may have forgotten the story by now or may have it confused with the celebrated case of the Cleveland doctor's wife. The death of Leora Dewaine Sherroder was much less a story than the Cleveland story but it was closely followed in Pittsburgh and on Cape Cod where there are three columns of Dewaines in the phone book. You call a Dewaine to put on a roof, survey your land, pick up your rubbish, send you a nurse. To fish out of Rock Harbor, you sign on the *Cape Corsair,* Cap'n Pres Dewaine. You bank with Leo at Samoset 5¢ Savings. To cater a wedding you call Carolyn.

Dewaines hidden by marriage under other names must be many columns more. The only big rich Dewaines I know of are Ananders, through Cousin Peg. Delbert Anander knew what land to buy and how long to hold it, and how to run a bank and when to sell it. My father was the fourth Dewaine with the hardware and heating store, the first with the oil trucks.

The story in the newspaper about the will gave me an uncomfortable insight that others might not see Aunt Leora's death as I did. It didn't say anything that wasn't already known in the family: except for named bequests, everything was left to Uncle Myron as remainderman. They had no children. Simply stating in the newspaper that Myron was Leora Dewaine's heir seemed to imply something.

In follow-up stories, Leora became the heiress of the Dewaine fortune, the Dewaines became *Mayflower* descendants. The family had oil interests. A reporter discovered that a brother of Leora's great-grandfather had been a governor of Massachusetts; the family became politically influential. Myron was a kidney specialist; he had been consulted by a Mellon; he was a member of a country club; he became a socialite doctor. They had no children. The socialite doctor was the sole heir.

With such people, in such an environment, all things are possible. You don't have to go beyond your own mind.

Uncle Myron was my friend who took me to the zoo; and to the museum to see the dinosaurus xylophony stretching down the hall ("From *zonnng* on his nose"—Myron had impressive range—"to *tinnngggg*"); and to Three Rivers Stadium to see a big-league baseball game.

We sat in a box behind first base. A high foul went up and I saw that if it did not go up forever it would come down sometime later that day right where I was. Everybody around me stood up. I thought if I could get my hands on that ball I could hold it.

The day was chilly, and the men wore gloves, but I was a boy and of course hadn't thought I needed gloves. While my head followed the nearly vertical rise of the ball Uncle Myron grasped my left hand. "Here's a glove to take the sting out." He raised his voice to the crowd around us. "Give the kid a shot at it."

They cleared a space. I don't think any crowd today would stand back to give a kid a shot. I followed the ball higher than I had ever seen a ball go, while I worked the bunching out of the palm of the glove and displayed the floppy fingers as a target.

I was sure I was under it, but misjudged the angle of the fall, backed into the men and finally fell backward into the seats; and the ball, ignoring the chance to make a stylish landing in a gray suede glove, dropped beyond my farthest reach. My failure that day—despite the cooperation of the entire world to help me succeed—is not yet forgotten. It enhances the memory of Myron Sherroder, my friend, who the newspaper said without saying it might have been the one who killed Aunt Leora.

I began then to understand how words say things that aren't in them. Words reach for meanings that are already inside the hearer. In a card trick the magician fans out the cards and says, "Pick one." Psych the cards as hard as you want, you can't psych a ten of diamonds out of a tarot deck. You have to take a card that's there. I wanted it another way, but the statement that the husband of the murdered woman was the beneficiary of her will picked up the card from my standard human deck.

I began then to read about the case as others would. One day at school I took a question from a friend—"How is your uncle coming with that murder case?" It said to me that when they spoke of Leora Sherroder's murder in their home, they assumed that her husband, the socialite doctor who had inherited her money, was probably complicit in some way. And I could not help but think it too.

I was troubled. I didn't tell my father how I felt, but I put a question in a form that betrayed me. "What if—?"

Before responding, my father laid his narrow eyes on me. "That's the way people are. In this house we do not think like that. My sister was a good judge of character. She chose your Uncle Myron. As far as we know they had a good marriage."

Why "As far as we know . . . ?"

I remembered too that when Dad called Myron that first night he hadn't said to him that he thought he was innocent. I wondered if Myron had noticed that.

I never heard my father say anything about innocence. What I understood him to say was that we had to wait respectfully, withholding judgment, as long as the process took; forever, if necessary. We had a stake in the values of organized society.

We were right to wait. In a few weeks the Pittsburgh police let it out that they were looking for a white man about forty years old with a butch haircut driving a late Plymouth white two-door who had been seen several times in the neighborhood in the week of the murder and nobody knew who he was. They found what they believed was the gun in the Allegheny River about five miles from the house and began to trace it. The gun was a Winchester twelve. There are a lot of them around. We have one in our house.

That got the newspapers going again.

Dad went to Pittsburgh. He saw Uncle Myron. He talked to the district attorney and to Detective Gertner, who had the case from the beginning. Gertner said privately they weren't getting anywhere looking for the man in the Plymouth. There weren't any fingerprints on the gun; they hadn't been able to trace it.

The detective told Dad something else. He did not look at Mother as he reported it.

"They are talking to a woman they say Myron had been seeing be-fore—" It's not easy to say *Before my sister was murdered.* "I have to say that bothers me."

"What did Myron say to that?" Mother asked.

"He's where he was. He knows they're looking into a lot of things."

"Did he say he knew what they were looking into?"

"He mentioned the gun and the man who had been seen in the neighborhood."

"That's all been in the papers. He didn't say anything about the woman?"

"He said 'and the usual gossip you can expect.' "

"Did he say what that was?"

"No, and I didn't ask him. He is a smart man. He can guess what comes to me."

It reinforced my impression that Myron was guilty. I was not so convinced that I would have been unable to be a fair juror; but I thought it probable, and I was sure I was not alone in our house to think it—not since Father's "as far as we know . . ."—not since Mother's refusal to stay in Pittsburgh after the funeral, and the clipped severity of her manner when Myron's name came up. I was in a conspiracy not to acknowledge that a guest had made a bad smell and there was no dog to look at.

III

Uncle Myron was indicted for first-degree homicide—I don't know why the language needs another word for murder.

"That must mean he's pretty guilty," I said.

Expressing judgment in an important matter made me feel impor-tant. I didn't know that before the law you are either guilty or not, there is no pretty to it.

My father stiffened his lips. "I don't want that said again in my hear-ing. A trial is to find that out. We have the adversarial system in this country as the best way to get at the truth. There is nothing like two sides putting up the best argument they know how. You may think you know Uncle Myron's defense, but you don't till you hear it argued. I don't want you to forget that."

Dad went to the trial to hear the woman for himself for the two days she was a witness. She testified that she had carried the gun from the garage when Uncle Myron told her to and had thrown it in the river.

Uncle Myron's lawyer brought out that she was seeking revenge because Myron had started to see other women. He brought out that she was an alcoholic. She and a former boyfriend were involved in a larceny, and the district attorney had made a deal to let her off a perjury charge in exchange for her testimony in the Sherroder case. She could even have been the one who committed the murder. Myron's lawyer brought all that out.

"She didn't make a very good witness," my father said. "Myron's lawyer doesn't think she will be convincing to the jury."

But there wasn't any doubt that Myron had something going with her—she knew too much about his life for it to be otherwise.

Myron said she only knew enough to make up the rest in order to get the reward. "I'm sorry all this comes out in this way that must seem sordid to you," he said. "I can't blame you for what you must think."

"Of course he can't blame you," Mother said. "What are you supposed to think? Leora was your sister. Did he still pretend he hadn't been going out with other women?"

"He said he had done what a lot of men do and he apologized for it. He said Leora would have understood why he saw other women had she known, even if she might not necessarily have condoned it."

"Not necessarily. I should think."

Myron had said, "I am not asking you to tell me what you now think about this. I only want you to hear me when I say I had nothing to do with it. I am entirely innocent."

"What *do* you think?" Mother asked.

My father's jaw muscles became bone. "I wasn't hired to be God," he said.

The afternoon the case went to the jury it was expected that deliberations probably wouldn't start until the next day. I was in bed with the lights out and the radio button in my ear when a bulletin came on that the jurors had decided to convene to test their sentiment. They found they had a verdict right away. The judge was coming in to hear it.

I got up and told Mother and Dad. We sat in the library and waited.

None of us made a guess what the verdict would be. It wasn't a ball game or somebody's else's family or anything that doesn't count and you can show how smart or how dumb you are. When something is close to you, you don't look at it the same way as if you're separated from it. In traffic the car ahead of you can be in the middle and won't get out of the way and you get mad. When you're in position to go around, you see it's somebody you know well and you cool off. You wave. Anything that is close to you is different.

The verdict was "Not Guilty."

To tell the truth, I didn't feel the relief you would expect from knowing that my uncle wouldn't have to spend the rest of his life in jail or be electrocuted. I certainly wouldn't have taken any joy from a guilty verdict, but it would have been more fitting and satisfying to human nature.

I suppose I am saying that my Aunt Leora, of my father's blood and therefore of mine, had been murdered, and that the way we are made requires that somebody be accountable. Almost any somebody rather than nobody. I'm the first to agree that for the sake of civilization we must respect the verdict of a court; still it isn't necessarily satisfactory to our natural sense of what is just.

I sensed that my mother felt the same, and for a moment that my father did too, but he said abruptly, "That's the verdict. The reward stands. We are going to look that much harder."

He called Uncle Myron and told him he knew the experience had been hard but he hoped he could get on with his life. He invited him to do some fishing. They arranged a weekend. Mother said, "You invited him *here?* I would just as soon you hadn't."

"I don't want to lose touch."

"I will never be comfortable with Myron. But it's up to you. I suppose men understand these things better." I supposed that wasn't what she thought.

IV

Uncle Myron was grateful that we made him one of us. The truth is that without Leora he was a foreign substance. He could not attach himself by shaking my hand and telling me I grew an inch a week; by swinging my sister in the air; by trying to find a place to kiss on Mother's averted cheek. Dad hurried him through the greetings and got him to the stairs of the tower room overlooking the bay. He and Leora always had that room.

Next day was raw and drizzly, an ordinary April day. A good breeze came across from the northeast and the tide went out all morning. The open bay wouldn't be very comfortable. I thought they would fish Drum Pond, but Dad said, "Myron, have you ever fished Shelf Lake with me?" Uncle Myron couldn't remember that they had.

I don't think Myron ever fished before he married Leora. As often as not when they visited, he would go over and play Great Dune while the rest of us went to a bass pond. Dad certainly wasn't going to play golf and he didn't offer any choices.

"We'll go over there. We'll get some shelter from the wind. I have a new suit of Red Ball waders you can break in for me. I'll wear my old one."

They loaded rods, boots, waders, parkas, slickers, boxes of lures, leaders, spare lines and tools, and a lunch. They were ready for bass or trout all day in any weather. They dropped me at Everbloom Nursery where I had a Saturday-morning job.

Bob Everbloom and I were moving azaleas from the back field to front beds, beginning in a drizzle we knew would get heavier, and when it did Bob decided we had enough of outside work. I could have worked under glass but I didn't come to do that. I liked to be outside on week-ends. I said I would skip it, they didn't need me in the greenhouse. I borrowed Bob's bike and headed for Shelf Lake. They were carrying enough extra tackle to outfit me.

All this country around here, all of Cape Cod, is the tailings left after the great glacier thawed and backed off to Canada. It's all rock brought down by the ice and melted out, pockets of sandy soil from old oceans washing over, and a skin of topsoil from decay. Those big stands of trees are in sand not too far down, then rock. The only clay is wherever you happen to dig your foundation; you can't get drainage, I never saw it fail.

After the margin sand Shelf Lake is a basin of underwater boulders and tables of rock fed by springs and the runoff from Spark's Hill. The surrounding land is in conservation. What falls they let lie. The bones of old downed trees lie around the rim. Those spines of big fish stuck in the ground are dead cedars. A couple of paths lead in through heavy woods.

It was too raw a day for people to come for wilderness walks, and most of the fishermen around here are either commercial and need the quantities they get in saltwater or they want the fast action of bay fish-ing. Our Jeep was the only vehicle parked at NO VEHICLES PERMITTED BEYOND THIS SIGN. On a busy day there might be two. I locked the bike to the Jeep's bumper and went down the woods path.

Nearing the bottom I heard my father call, "Left, farther left, toward the cove."

Through the trees I glimpsed that they were both in hip-deep, Uncle Myron a hundred or so yards west and working farther. Rain dimpled the water. Away from the lea of the hill, fans of wind patterned the surface like shoaling fish. I was troubled by something but didn't con-centrate my attention on what it might be as I was busy picking through catbrier that snatched into the path.

"Another ten yards. They're in there," my father called out.

Then I realized what troubled me. Myron was on the edge of the shelf that gave the lake its name. It fell off without any warning into a deep hole. I took a running step and opened my mouth to shout but it hardly got out when he let out a bellow and pitched down.

My mind churned with what could be done and what I had to do. I could get around to the shoreline nearer to him, and dive in and help him out of his gear. I could—

But I didn't move because more dumbfounding to me than the accident itself was that my father acted as though it wasn't happening. He heard Myron and saw him flail to stay afloat and go under in seconds. He knew as I did that Myron, under the roiled water, fought to get out of his parka and sweater, then out of the waders that were filling and turning into anchors; and my father turned away and cast.

I was locked on dead center. Dad began to reel in. His rod bent. He had a bass fighting and flopping like a sand-filled stocking. Working light tackle, he had to give and take carefully not to lose it. The ripples settled out of the water where Myron had been—it was erased!—and my father was unslipping the net with his free hand and playing the bass with the other.

I was terrified—not frightened, terrified—as much for my father as for myself. He had deliberately led my uncle to be drowned. I tried to make it happen differently in my mind, but I could not doubt what I had seen and heard.

When at last I found the will to move, it was not toward him but back up the trail, to be away and alone long enough to get my bearings before I had to face him.

I rode the bike in the rain to the nursery and put it in the toolshed. Nobody was around. I didn't have to talk to anybody.

Behind the mall down the road from Everbloom's the receiving platforms stood on iron legs, backed against the cement block, the cheap side of the stores. Weather swept over the blacktop, pooling where the graders hadn't got it right. On raw bulldozed ground beyond the blacktop, weeds and a few stringy locusts tried to start a forest again. A tree line the bulldozers wouldn't get to for a few years failed into the mist at the end of this world. Nobody ever came back there unless a truck was unloading. I hunched under a dock.

As the evidence against Uncle Myron had become stronger and weaker and stronger again in the year that had passed since Aunt Leora's death, I had felt in myself many times the sufficient certainty that he had killed her so that I could imagine myself doing to him as my father had.

I had imagined aiming the gun—the same gun, the twelve-gauge, to make the justice more shapely—and firing. I could do that, I had told myself.

Under the shelter of the platform, I knew I had only been telling myself a story. I could have put my finger on the trigger but not pulled. I might have led him to step off the shelf, but duty as I understood it, as I had learned it from my father, would have compelled me to save a drowning man even if I had been the one who put him in peril.

I had had the chance and not used it. I had not burst out of the trees shouting. I had not waded in. I had watched; then run to get the bike.

My father had pulled the trigger and turned away as if it were nothing.

I drowned in questions. Why had I done nothing? Was it because I was young and not much was expected of me? Was it because it had happened in the presence of my father, and it was not my place to put myself forward where he did not? Was I bound to silence forever? What would happen if he were suspected? And stories were in the paper?

And he went on trial?

Would I come forward to witness for him to say that his account of the event was whatever he said it was? Would I be able to stick with a lie like that—for my father, who had made lying a hard thing for me to do?

What if somebody in one of the cars that had passed on the road recognized me? What if it was reported and I was taken to the police station and asked what I knew and why I had not volunteered it before?

What was expected of me? I had nobody to ask.

The rain drew off. I would have to go home. I took with me the simplest of stories to account for myself. I had biked to Nickerson Park, in the direction of Shelf Lake, and when the rain began had got under the cover of a firewood shed.

A diver found Uncle Myron bundled at the foot of the shelf in forty feet of water. It was never discussed after my father explained that Myron had been warned, that he must have lost track of where he was while my father had been inattentive. Anybody who knew that water and how you could become engrossed working a five-pound bass on a three-pound line understood how easily it happened.

Myron's brother came to the Cape to make arrangements to ship the body to Pittsburgh for burial alongside Aunt Leora. He was Uncle Andrew to me, although we never knew that family very well. They were westerners, we were easterners, we met only at anniversary parties, weddings, funerals.

He said Myron had been a good brother and he would miss him. I suppose in some way he felt that my father had a degree of responsibility as the accident had happened in our territory, so to speak, but he didn't indicate it.

The circumstances were such that the card of suspicion never turned over in anybody's head. Nobody who knew Ben Dewaine would have thought it for an instant.

V

I lived difficult years with my father after that, although all the difficulties were within me. On the surface our close relationship was undisturbed. We fished and hunted together as before, and I took many problems to him for a viewpoint.

As I had declared against going into the family business it was thought that I might become a lawyer. I have an orderly mind and some ability to express myself and therefore thought it too. I was well along in college before I decided to do other work. In those early years, the years in which we allow ourselves to think abstractly, I often reflected about justice, but I never allowed myself to discuss it with my father, fearing that one word would take me to another until I reached one that I would regret.

I came to have considerable respect for Pilate. I thought how much more difficult Pilate's problem may have been than the press reported. I would want to know more about what kind of man Pilate was before I concluded that he had a worn-out conscience or that he had settled for an epigram.

Nine years later the man with the brush haircut turned himself in.

He couldn't live with it. It happens all the time. They see the victim's face at night and think of what a life is and what it is to destroy one, and they get disgusted with themselves. They begin to think there may be Eternal Judgment after all and they will be accountable. They show up at police stations and have to convince desk officers that they aren't nuts. They call up reporters and meet them in diners. They ask priests to be go-betweens. They hire lawyers to get them the best deal.

The man's name was Rome Hurdicke.

Again it was a story in the papers. He had parked, looking for opportunity as he had on other nights, and this night a dark place beside the lane beyond the Sherroder house had been the cover that attracted him. He had followed Aunt Leora into the garage intending to bluff her with the gun. She had been slow to respond. He thought she was about to call for help. He panicked and shot her and then thought only about getting away. The most singular event in two lives, and it was from beginning to end so ordinary that it could have been set in type like a slogan to be called up with a keystroke.

The newspapers rehashed it and added the strange fate that befell so many people associated with the crime. Four of the jurors were dead. The judge had been killed in a private plane accident. The woman who claimed to be the well-known socialite doctor's mistress committed suicide. The husband of the murdered heiress drowned in a fishing accident on Cape Cod.

There could be no doubt Hurdicke was the man. He told them where and when he had bought the gun, and they verified the numbers. They found the Plymouth still in service, three owners forward and a coat of white paint two coats down. It was an old case, and as he had turned himself in he got twenty years and was eligible for parole in twelve.

And so, Uncle Myron's life had been taken without cause.

I think somebody—perhaps his brother Andrew—may care for Myron as we cared for Aunt Leora, and if he knew the circumstances of his death would yearn for human justice as my father did. I don't know. I can't deal with how Uncle Andrew might feel. My father is my flesh and blood and he is a good man.

I can't deal with my own guilt. If I had responded on the instant that I saw Uncle Myron pitch into the water could I have saved him?

I don't know. I will never get over not making the attempt, but confession offers me no way out, for it would be to witness against my father. I am tribal enough to say that my duty is to him, to keep the secret. In some matters it is true that what is not known does not exist. It exists for us who know it.

After Hurdicke confessed I watched my father closely. I trembled that he might turn himself in or even take his own life in remorse. I didn't know if he would be more likely to do it if he knew that I knew his secret, or if he thought he alone knew what had happened at Shelf Lake. As a son who had become also a father I knew that some fragment of his life he intended to be an object lesson for me, but I couldn't know how much.

His manner, naturally reserved, became wintry. He gave up his places on church and hospital boards, and reduced his responsibilities at the company. Time passing without incident did not lull me to suppose that he had made his peace with Uncle Myron's ghost, any more than Hurdicke had made his with Aunt Leora's. Nevertheless, he went on with his life in a normal way, at a lowered tone, into his retirement years.

He entered then a remission in which he seems to have regained his appetite for a more active life. Mother said the other day, "He had a new garden turned over. He is talking about going west in the fall to hunt ram. He rejoined his skeet club. I think he is coming into good years."

That may be, but I have marked my calendar.

I don't know how Father accepts that the sentence of the man who killed his sister has been commuted to time served. Hurdicke will be released next week. I can hope only that my father has had enough of dealing out justice on earth.

—from *Earthly Justice* (1990)

"Place Keepers"

By Brendan Galvin

Gray day, slow November hours.
The sea must be smoking
all the way out to the Banks.

Two cars in the beach lot.
In patched waders,
in water to her hips, the widow
who fishes with sand eels
she scratches up for herself,

and half a mile down the flats,
a man like a god
walking among a tranced flock, laying hands
upon each Canada goose without one
lifting off, the tide shrinking from him
beyond the final tumble of the jetty.

No miracle because, closer,
the birds are black-and-white effigies

staked in mud; at jetty-side,
in a stone blind under a stone-colored
blanket, his thermos and dog.

His breath is laced with rye.
His hat mimics fallen leaves; the loops
on his sand-colored vest are charged
for birds. Now he comes back for the jug,
his rosy Hello to the dog
visible in the hanging droplets.

The widow's beach fire
struggles through broken fish boxes
she watches her pole
for the deep flex of winter flounder.

———

"Winter Oysters"

By Brendan Galvin

February: water and sky a gape
hinged at Great Island,
mudflats and cottages scoured
of summer, but a few car trunks
open to wire buckets and rakes
with serious teeth, and a few
aficionados of wind
sliding thick socks into waders
and hooking up, ready under hoods
and watch caps to break through
the tideline's rime, later
to break with short, upturned blades
into shells parted from rocks

and "dead man's fingers."* This
is how we like them, not summer-thin
and weepy tourist fare, but hale
as innkeepers, their liquor clear,
fat with plankton that thrives
under a glaze drifting just below
green water, and without any
lemon sundrip or condiment
but a dash of bourbon to punctuate
each salty imperative.

Ellen's poem

"This small and intimate place"

By Marge Piercy

I

The moor land, the dry land ripples
bronzed with blueberry. The precise
small hills sculpted with glittering
kinnikinnick broil under the sharp
tack of the red-tailed hawk cruising
in middle air. A vesper sparrow
gives its repetitive shrill sad cry
and the air shimmers with drought.

The sea is always painting itself
on the sky, which dips low here.
Light floods the eyes tight and dry.
Light scours out the skull

Codium fragile, a gelatinous seaweed with finger-like projections that attaches to
oysters and other shellfish.

like an old kitchen sink made clean.
We are cured in sunlight like salt cod.

II

We are cured in sunlight like salt cod
stiffened and rot repellent and long
lived, long lasting. The year-rounders
are poor. All summer they wait tables
for the tourists, clean the houses
of the summer people, sell them jam, fish,
paintings, build their dwellings, wait
for the land to be clean and still again.

Yet blueberries, black- and elderberries,
beach plum grow where vacation homes
for psychiatrists are not yet built.
We gather oysters, dig clams. We burn
oak, locust, pitch pine and eat much fish
as do the other scavengers, the gulls.

III

As do the other scavengers, the gulls,
we suffer, prey on the tides' rise and ebb
of plenty and disaster, the slick that chokes
the fisheries, the restaurant sewage
poisoning mussels, the dump leaching lead
into the water table; the lucky winter
storm that tosses up surf clams or squid
in heaps for food, fertilizer, future plenty.

This land is a tablet on which each pair
of heels writes itself, the raw scar
where the dirt bike crossed, the crushed
tern chicks where the ORV roared through,
the dune loosed over trodden grasses.
We are intimate with wind and water here.

IV

We are intimate with wind. Once
this was a land of windmills flapping
sails like a stationary race of yachts.
We learn the winds on face and shingles,
the warm wind off the Gulf Stream in winter,
the nor'easter piling up snow and wrecks,
the west wind that hustles the rain clouds
over and out to sea, the cold northwest.

We are intimate with water, lapped around,
the sea tearing at the land, castling it up,
damp salty days with grey underworld light
when sneakers mold like Roquefort, paper wilts.
On moors webbed in fog we wander, or wade
in the salt marsh as the wet lands ripple.

———

Encounters with a Maushop

By Nosapocket

I'VE HAD THREE encounters with this being and it lives in Asher's Pass, what we call this wooded area.* And there I heard, the first time I heard it it was walking in the river and the stones underneath his feet was crumbling and crushing, popping, and it was kind of frightening. And I was with a friend who was Pima Indian from the Southwest. She got frightened. I said, "Well, let's get in the car. Just keep your finger on the keys but don't start it until we get a glimpse of this and see what it is." It came closer and closer and at the very second it seemed that it was going to pop out, it got up out of the river and went up the pass and you couldn't see it. We drove off, anyway, not knowing how big a

---

* South of Mashpee Center.

stride it had or anything, but it was not interested in seeing us. But I took it as an honor and a message, an omen of some sort, that this thing allowed me to be near it. My second encounter with that [was] a year later. My family homestead is right along the Mashpee River, and we're off about a quarter of a mile from it, and this same being, heavy footed enough to shake the ground as it walked, came up to my window and I'd estimate that this had to be—it itself had to stand about as high as that owl I was telling you about. It leaned on my windowsill and just breathed. And its chest I would say had to be about five feet wide. Its lungs were bigger than my body, and it just breathed. I was paralyzed with fear. I just laid there and listened, and it stood there and didn't do anything. Its nasal passages made a growling sound . . . maybe I was listening, trying to figure out what it was doing there and find out if it was hostile or what was the case. But it just came and stood there for maybe a half an hour or so, and then it left. The following morning I went out to see the footprints. I figured they had to be at least two feet long, and I got out there and there was no footprints near the house or in the direction that I listened to it going—no footprints whatsoever. And that's when I began to think of it more as a medicine being, a Big-foot or a Sasquatch, or a Maushop-type being, and I was not very frightened, but excited that such beings still lived amongst the Mashpee Wampanoag people [which] was very special knowledge to me; so I sought out, I looked for it, and of course they couldn't find it. But my next encounter with it I was camping in Asher's Pass on the other side of the river, and I was doing an arts and crafts program with the young Indian children. They went to the bay to collect shellfish for our meal, and I stayed at the camp making a sweat lodge. And I heard the footprints again, and wanting to see it this time for sure, I decided to hide in a hole that had a dead tree laying on top of it. So I got underneath there and waited and listened, and when I was certain that it was in the open I took a peek, and there was nothing there that I expected to see. There was a small bird, and it was only like three inches off the ground itself, and very small and a green bird. And the color green is the calm color, one that will bring you that. So I watched it, and the bird walked the entire perimeter in a perfect circle around the camp. It took a long time for it to walk it, but it walked with the footsteps of a Maushop. That bird I have seen, but it made no sense to me at all, for how this whole thing came about. The people that I've heard that have seen this being down at Asher's Pass were frightened and they didn't stop to really look good enough to find out what it was. It was just a towering human being that had a lot of hair, and it just decided that a glimpse frightened them. . . . So I haven't really found any accurate descriptions or something that people have said. . . . Other people have heard the same footsteps. . . . The green bird has another symbol and . . . the power of a medicine being such as a Maushop. . . . The green bird is, first its size and yet its intensity. Its size [is] a subtle reminder to us, as a small tribe in itself, that our medicine needn't be regarded as weak because we're small in numbers. But we have the intensity of medicine beings, so a reassurance, in those years of my life, studying very hard and looking very deep in our culture and our woods for ways to reassure and strengthen our tribal self-concept and to help balance the intrusion of newcoming people into our territory—something that was very, very hard for everyone to deal with. And I looked to the woods and to the Creator for assistance, and this is one of the ways that many different experiences, vision quests, and things, looking for this kind of story to tell my own people, and it worked. The green bird is symbolic of our tribe, and calm is being our power for this time rather than rage or demonstrations. . . . A calm state of clear mindedness is what the bird was symbolic of.

—from *Spirit of the New England Tribes* (1986) by William S. Simmons

Epilogue

"Cape Cod"

By George Santayana

The low sandy beach and the thin scrub pine,
The wide reach of bay and the long sky line,—
    O, I am far from home!

The salt, salt smell of the thick sea air,
And the smooth round stones that the ebbtides wear,—
    When will the good ship come?

The wretched stumps all charred and burned,
And the deep soft rut where the cartwheel turned,—
    Why is the world so old?

The lapping wave, and the broad gray sky
Where the cawing crows and the slow gulls fly,—
    Where are the dead untold?

The thin, slant willows by the flooded bog,
The huge stranded hulk and the floating log,—
    Sorrow with life began!

And among the dark pines, and along the flat shore,
O the wind, and the wind, for evermore!
    What will become of man?

Biographical Sketches

CONRAD AIKEN (1889–1973), poet, novelist, playwright, essayist, and short-story writer, was born in Savannah, Georgia, and raised in Massachusetts, where his mother had Quaker ancestors from Bass River in Yarmouth. He attended Harvard, where one of his professors was **George Santayana.** For many years he lived in England, Europe, and Boston. In 1940 he and his third wife, the artist Mary Hoover Aiken, moved into 41 Doors, a beautiful old eighteenth-century saltbox farmhouse on Stony Brook Road in Brewster. "Mayflower" and several other of his later lyrics draw their imagery from this setting. *Selected Letters of Conrad Aiken* (1978) contains some wonderfully vivid and humorous accounts of his life here on the Cape, including his friendship with poet and nature writer **John Hay.**

TIMOTHY ALDEN (1771–18??), was born in Yarmouth, Massachusetts, and educated at Harvard. He was the author of *Memorabilia of Yarmouth* (1797) and *Collection of American Epitaphs* (1815). About 1817 he moved to Meadville, Pennsylvania, where he was president of Allegheny College.

EVERETT S. ALLEN (b. 1916), journalist, lecturer, and author, was born in New Bedford, Massachusetts, and in 1938 began working as a reporter for the *New Bedford Standard-Times,* which in those days covered Cape Cod. His works include *Arctic Odyssey: The Life of Rear Admiral Donald MacMillan,* on the Arctic explorer from Provincetown (1962); *This Quiet Place: A Cape Cod Chronicle* (1971); *Children of the Light: The Rise and Fall of New Bedford and the Death of the Arctic Fleet* (1973); and *Martha's Vineyard: An Elegy* (1982).

GABRIEL ARCHER (d. 1609 or 1610) was a "gentleman" aboard the *Concord* on Bartholomew Gosnold's 1602 expedition to New England. His *Relation of Captain Gosnold's Voyage to the North Part of Virginia* has been reprinted many times, but its original date of publication is uncertain.

JOSEF BERGER (1903–1971) was born in Denver, Colorado, and was a newspaper reporter for nearly a decade in Kansas City and New York. Unable to make a living in the city after the Crash of 1929, he and his wife, the designer and editor Dorothy Gay Thomas, moved to Provincetown in 1934. There, under the pseudonym Jeremiah Digges, he wrote *Cape Cod Pilot* (1937) as part of the Federal Writers' Project American Guide Series. In 1938 he received a Guggenheim Fellowship and moved to Gloucester, where he researched and wrote what is probably his best book, *In Great Waters: The Story of the Portuguese Fishermen* (1941).

HENRY BESTON (1888–1968) was born Henry Beston Sheahan in Quincy, Massachusetts, attended Harvard College, and served as a French volunteer in World War I. In 1926 he came to live in the Fo'castle, a dune cottage of his own design, on Coast Guard Beach in Eastham. He left the beach the following summer and published the classic account of his stay there, *The Outermost House,* in 1928. That same year he married the writer Elizabeth Coatsworth. They moved to a farm in Nobleboro, Maine, where he spent the rest of his life. In 1964 the Fo'castle was designated a National Literary Landmark. It was carried out to sea in the Great Storm of February 1978.

JOHN PEALE BISHOP (1892–1944), poet and essayist, was born in Charles Town, West Virginia. He attended Princeton, where he was friends with **Edmund Wilson** and F. Scott Fitzgerald. After serving in France in World War I, he worked with Wilson on the editorial staff of *Vanity Fair,* where the two men were close friends of **Edna St. Vincent Millay,** then lived in Paris during the late 1920s. He summered in Wellfleet in the 1930s and in 1938 built a house, Sea Change, in South Chatham, where he lived until his death.

WILLIAM BRADFORD (1590–1657), *Mayflower* passenger, governor and historian of the old Plymouth Colony, was born in Yorkshire, England. As a boy he joined the Separatist congregation of William Brewster, and in 1609 he removed with them to Holland. In 1620 he sailed with the rest of the *Mayflower* company to "Northern Virginia," where they made a landfall on November 11 in Provincetown Harbor before permanently settling at Plymouth. Bradford served as governor of the colony for thirty years. He wrote his monumental *History of Plimoth Plantation* during the years 1630–1651, though it was not published until 1856. It is generally regarded as the first significant English literary work written in this country. In addition, he is thought to have been one of the contributors to *Mourt's Relation* (1622).

JOHN BRERETON OR BRIERTON (1572?–1619), an English rector,

sailed with Bartholomew Gosnold on his 1602 expedition to the New England coast. *A Brief and True Relation of the North Part of Virginia* (1602) is the earliest-known description in English of the Cape Cod landscape and its inhabitants.

THORNTON W. BURGESS (1874–1965), a native of Sandwich, was a prolific author and a pioneering conservationist. He is best known for his once immensely popular children's nature books, especially the "Old Mother West Wind" series and *The Adventures of Peter Cottontail* (1914). He wrote more than 15,000 stories and published 170 books during his life. Many of the locales in his stories are drawn from the woods and ponds around the Green Briar Nature Center in East Sandwich, established in 1976 to honor Burgess's accomplishments and carry on his work in environmental education.

DOUGLAS CARLSON (b. 1943) was born in Oneonta, New York, and graduated from the State University College at Fredonia, New York. He is Associate Professor of English at the Jamestown Community College in Jamestown, New York, and is the author of *At the Edge* (1989) a collection of essays. He has summered on the Lower Cape since the early 1960s.

SCOTT CORBETT (b. 1913) was born in Kansas City, Missouri, and graduated from the University of Missouri in 1934. After serving in World War II, he moved with his wife to East Dennis. He was one of the founders of the Cape Cod Museum of Natural History in Brewster and wrote several books about the Cape, including *We Chose Cape Cod* (1953), *Cape Cod's Way* (1955), and (with Captain Manuel Zora) *The Sea Fox: The Adventures of Cape Cod's Most Colorful Rumrunner* (1956). After moving to Providence, Rhode Island, he embarked on a highly successful career as a writer of juvenile books, including the best-selling *The Lemonade Trick* (1960).

MONICA DICKENS (1915–1993), the great-granddaughter of Charles Dickens, was born in London, England. In 1951 she married Roy O. Stratton, an author and retired U.S. Navy officer, and moved to Falmouth, Massachusetts. She wrote, in addition to *Cape Cod* (1972), several dozen novels, autobiographies, and other works of nonfiction. She was the founder of Samaritans, U.S.A., a suicide-prevention organization with centers in Boston, Providence, and Falmouth.

JEREMIAH DIGGES See **Joseph Berger.**

ANNIE DILLARD (b. 1947), winner of the Pulitzer Prize for *Pilgrim at Tinker Creek* (1974), was born in Pittsburgh and attended Hollins College in Roanoke, Virginia. For several years she lived in Puget Sound, Washington, the setting for her novel *The Living* (1992). Since 1978 she has summered in "Off Plumb," a cottage in South Wellfleet, and in the winter she lives with her family in Middletown, Connecticut, where she has taught at Wesleyan College.

MARK DOTY (b. 1953), a resident of Provincetown since 1990, grew up as an army brat and spent his adolescence in Tucson, Arizona. He graduated from Drake University and received an MFA from Goddard. In 1990 he moved to Provincetown, where, he says, "I imagine myself living forever." Doty has published three books of poetry, the most recent of which, *My Alexandria* (University of Illinois Press, 1993), was chosen by Philip Levine for the National Poetry Series. He teaches at Sarah Lawrence College and in the MFA Writing Program at Vermont College.

ALAN DUGAN (b. 1923), twice awarded the Pulitzer Prize for poetry, was born in Brooklyn and graduated from Mexico City College. He taught at Sarah Lawrence College from 1967 to 1971 and has been associated with the Fine Arts Work Center in Provincetown since 1971. He lives in Truro with his wife, the artist Judith Shahn.

TIMOTHY DWIGHT (1752–1817), the grandson of the famous theologian and philosopher Jonathan Edwards, was born in North Adams, Massachusetts. A precocious learner, he entered Yale College at the age of thirteen and graduated with highest honors in 1769. In 1783 he was ordained as a Congregational minister, and he served as president of Yale from 1805 to 1817. Dwight was a man of enormous talents and energy and published numerous volumes of epic poems, sermons, and discourses. The five-volume *Travels in New England and New York* was published in 1821–22.

RALPH WALDO EMERSON (1803–1882), the most influential American essayist, was born in Boston and graduated from Harvard in 1821. He moved to Concord in 1835 and became a major figure in the American Transcendentalism movement and the foremost member of the Concord literary community, which included the young **Henry David Thoreau.** His essays on nature, self-reliance, intellectual independence, the spiritual nature of reality, and a unifying "Over-Soul" strongly shaped American thought in the nineteenth century. His muscular prose, highly metaphoric style, and provocative thought have had a profound influence on such later writers as Thoreau, Walt Whitman, Emily Dickinson, Robert Frost, and **Annie Dillard.**

ROBERT FINCH (b. 1943), a native of New Jersey, grew up in West Virginia and graduated from Harvard College in 1967. He has lived in Brewster since 1971 and has published four books of essays about Cape Cod, including *The Primal Place* (1983) and *The Cape Itself* (1991) with photographer Ralph MacKenzie.

BENJAMIN FRANKLIN (1650–1730), uncle of Benjamin Franklin, the inventor, author, and statesman. In 1715 he moved from London and lived with the Franklins in Boston for several years. It was here, presumably, he recorded his account of the Provincetown sea monster.

BRENDAN GALVIN (b. 1938) was born in Everett, Massachusetts, and has summered in the Wellfleet area since 1939. He was educated at Boston College, Northwestern University, and the University of Massachusetts, from which he received his Ph.D. in 1970. Galvin is Professor of English at Central Connecticut State College and founder and director of the Connecticut Writers Conference. A recipient of a Guggenheim Fellowship for Poetry in 1988 and the first O. B. Hardison Jr. Poetry Prize from the Folger Shakespeare Library in 1991, he has published a dozen volumes of poetry, most recently *Saints in Their Ox-Hide Boat* (1992).

E. S. GOLDMAN (b. 1913) grew up in Pittsburgh and attended the Experimental College of the University of Wisconsin and the University of Pittsburgh, where he majored in philosophy. For many years he ran Tree's Place, a tile and ceramic store in Orleans. He began writing fiction in his seventies, and in 1988 published *Big Chocolate Cookies,* a novel. A collection of short stories, *Earthly Justice* (TriQuarterly Books, 1990), most of which are set on Cape Cod, won the first annual William Goyen Prize for Fiction.

ADAM GOPNIK (b. 1956) was born in Philadelphia, Pennsylvania, and moved to Canada when he was twelve. He graduated from McGill University and later won a fellowship to the Institute of Art in New York City. In 1983 he edited fashion copy at *GQ Magazine,* where he later became the magazine's first fiction editor. After working as an editor at Alfred A. Knopf, Gopnik joined the staff of *The New Yorker* in 1987, as an editor and writer, and since then has contributed more than a hundred pieces.

JOHN HAY (b. 1915), a native of Ipswich, Massachusetts, grew up in New York City and Lake Sunapee, New Hampshire. He attended St. Paul's School in Concord, New Hampshire, under Master **Henry Kittredge** and graduated from Harvard College in 1937. He studied with poet **Conrad Aiken** in Brewster, served a stint in the army in World War II, and moved permanently to the Cape in 1947. Hay has published a dozen books of nature writing; *The Great Beach* (1964) won the John Burroughs Medal. A founder of the Cape Cod Museum of Natural History in Brewster, he served as its president for a quarter of a century. He has also taught writing at Dartmouth College.

CYNTHIA HUNTINGTON (b. 1951) was born in Meadville, Pennsylvania, graduated from Michigan State University, and received her M.A.

from the Bread Loaf School of English at Middlebury, Vermont. In 1978 she came to Provincetown as a Fine Arts Work Center Fellow and stayed for seven years. She has received two NEA fellowships, has taught at the University of California at Irvine, and is currently Associate Professor of English at Dartmouth College in Hanover, New Hampshire, where she lives with her family. She is the author of *The Fish-Wife* (1986), a collection of poems, and a forthcoming prose work, *A Foot on the Earth,* based on several summers spent at the Provincetown dune shack *Euphoria.*

HENRY JAMES (1843–1916), one of America's greatest novelists, was born in New York City, was educated privately and in Europe, and graduated from Harvard Law School in 1862. Though he spent most of his adult life in England and Europe, his novels frequently contrast American and European cultures and mores. Some, such as *The Bostonians* (1886), have a New England setting. *The American Scene* (1907), a book of essays based on a tour of the United States after an absence of twenty-five years, contains a vivid description of the village of Cotuit.

HERMAN A. JENNINGS (fl. 1890), author of *Provincetown, or Odds and Ends from the Tip End* (1890). What little is known about Jennings is found in Josef Berger's *Cape Cod Pilot:* "In addition to writing his 'history,' which somehow gets the pirate Sam Bellamy aboard the British warship *Somerset* and does a number of other marvelous things, Jennings was an undertaker, wreck master, real estate dealer and auctioneer sans pareil." He once made $10 auctioning off an ironing board as an antique bundling board.

E. J. KAHN, JR. (b. 1916) was born in New York City and graduated from Harvard College in 1937. He has been a staff writer for *The New Yorker* since 1937 and has summered in Truro for over forty years. In addition to numerous magazine articles he has published nearly twenty books, including *The Separated People: A Look at Contemporary South Africa* (1968) and (with his son Joseph P. Kahn) *The Boston Underground Gourmet* (1972).

ALFRED KAZIN (b. 1915), one of America's foremost literary critics, was born in Brooklyn and educated at the College of the City of New York and Columbia University. He is best known for *On Native Grounds* (1942), a "moral" study of modern American prose literature, and several autobiographical volumes, including *A Walker in the City* (1951) and *New York Jew* (1978).

HELEN KELLER (1880–1968) was born in Tuscumbia, Alabama. At the age of nineteen months she suffered a fever which left her blind and deaf for life. The story of her education and intellectual liberation by Anne Sullivan, a young teacher from the Perkins Institute for the Blind in Boston, has been recounted and dramatized many times, most notably in her autobiography, *The Story of My Life* (1903), and the motion picture *The Miracle Worker* (1962). During her long life she wrote a dozen books, worked tirelessly for social reform for the disabled, and was the recipient of numerous national and international awards and honorary degrees.

EDWARD AUGUSTUS KENDELL (1776?–1842) was an English author of miscellaneous works and a social reformer who sought to improve the lot of colonial peoples and to provide inexpensive, quality literature for the masses. During 1807–1808 he traveled throughout the Northeast, chronicling his wanderings in the three-volume *Travels Through Part of the United States* (1809). He is best known today for his various books for children, such as *Burford Cottage and Its Robin Red Breast* (1835).

HENRY C. KITTREDGE (1890–1967) was born in Cambridge, Massachusetts, and graduated from Harvard College in 1912. For many years he was a teacher, master, and rector at St. Paul's School in Concord, New Hampshire, where **John Hay** was one of his students. From early childhood he spent most of his summers at his family's house in Barnstable, where his three Cape Cod books—*Cape Cod: Its People and Their History* (1930), *Shipmasters of Cape Cod* (1935), and *Mooncussers of Cape Cod* (1937)—were written.

STANLEY KUNITZ (b. 1905), one of America's most prominent living poets, was born in Worcester, Massachusetts, and graduated from Harvard College in 1926. His ten books of poetry have garnered numerous honors, including the Pulitzer Prize in 1959 for *Selected Poems, 1928–1958*. He has edited a number of standard literary reference works and has held teaching positions at many institutions, including Bennington College, the New School for Social Research, and Columbia University. In 1968 Kunitz was one of the founders of the Fine Arts Work Center in Provincetown, where he has summered for many years.

JAMES LAZELL (b. 1939), field biologist, ecologist, and herpetologist, was born in New York City. He received his M.A. from Harvard in 1966 and a Ph.D. from the University of Rhode Island in 1970. For many years he was on the scientific staff of the Massachusetts Audubon Society. Since 1980 he has been president of the Conservation Agency, a non-profit conservation / wildlife research organization headquartered in Jamestown, Rhode Island. His works include *Reptiles and Amphibians in Massachusetts* (1972); *This Broken Archipelago: Cape Cod and the Islands, Amphibians and Reptiles* (1976); and *Ribbon of Sand* (1992).

CLARE LEIGHTON (1899–1989) was born in London and came to the United States in 1939. Known primarily for her illustrations and woodcuts, she became one of the foremost wood engravers of her generation. In addition to writing fifteen self-illustrated books, Leighton illustrated numerous classics of American and English literature. She summered in Wellfleet for many years, where she was commissioned to do the stained-glass windows for the Wellfleet Methodist Church.

JOSEPH (1825–1870) and EMILY CROSBY (1831–1897) LINCOLN, parents of Cape Cod author **Joseph C. Lincoln,** were both natives of Brewster. Joseph Sr. was a sea captain who commanded many merchant vessels to ports as far as Surinam and Russia. His wife, Mary, accompanied him on several voyages. Their extensive personal and business correspondence, covering the period 1852–1873, is housed in the Sturgis Library in Barnstable Village, Massachusetts.

JOSEPH C. LINCOLN (1870–1944), Cape Cod's most successful native author, was born in Brewster, the only child of Captain **Joseph** and **Emily Crosby Lincoln.** He grew up in Boston, summering in Brewster, where he spent many hours in the local blacksmith shop, listening to local stories which he later put into his novels. In 1899 he moved to New York and in 1902 published his first book, *Cape Cod Ballads*. In 1904 his first novel, *Cap'n Eri,* containing the homespun humor and keen characterizations that were his trademark, was an instant best-seller. Over forty more Cape Cod books followed, making him one of the most popular authors of his time. In his later years he again became a legal resident of Cape Cod, spending his summers in a large house in Chatham overlooking Pleasant Bay.

WILLIAM MARTIN (b. 1950) was born in Cambridge, Massachusetts, and educated at Harvard and the University of Southern California. He is the author of several screenplays and four novels, including *Back Bay* (1980) and *Cape Cod* (1991). He has spent more than thirty summers on the shores of the Cape and lives with his family in Weston, Massachusetts.

HERMAN MELVILLE (1819–1891) was born in New York City. In 1839 he went to sea for five years, traveling on whalers and other ships in the South Seas. These adventures provided him with the basis for his popular early romances, *Typee* (1846) and *Omoo* (1847), and his masterpiece, *Moby-Dick* (1851). Subsequently his popularity waned; he published no prose after 1857 and died in relative obscurity. His novella *Billy Budd,* completed just before his death, was published in 1924.

THOMAS MERTON (1915–1968) was born in France and attended Columbia University. In 1941 he became a Trappist monk at the Gethsemani Abbey in Bardstown, Kentucky. Though the Trappists observe strict vows of silence, Merton became a leading writer and intellectual influence of his generation, publishing numerous volumes of poetry, essays, plays, meditations, and novels, as well as his well-known auto-biography, *The Seven Story Mountain* (1948).

EDNA ST. VINCENT MILLAY (1892–1950) was born in Rockland, Maine, and gained early notoriety with the publication of her poem "Renascence" when she was nineteen. She graduated from Vassar in 1917 and lived in Greenwich Village, where she was associated with the Provincetown Players, for whom she wrote several plays, including *Aria del Capo* (1921). In 1920 she summered with her family in Truro, where she was courted by **Edmund Wilson.** During the 1920s her popular lyrics expressed the cynical gaiety of the age and she was often described as "the female Byron."

SUSAN MITCHELL (b. 1944) was born in New York City and edu-cated at Wellesley College and Georgetown University. She has pub-lished two books of poetry, *The Water Inside the Water* (1983) and *Rapture* (1992). She was a Fellow at the Fine Arts Work Center in Provincetown in 1977 and 1978, and a Guggenheim Fellow in Poetry in 1992. Currently she lives in Boca Raton, Florida, where she is the Mary Blossom Lee Professor in Creative Writing at Florida Atlantic University.

"G. MOURT," the signature on the first edition of *A Relation or Jour-nall of the Beginning and Proceedings of the English Plantation Setled at Plimoth in New England,* published in England in 1622, was most likely an alias of George Morton (1585–1624), who served as the chief agent of the Pilgrims in London. Commonly known as *Mourt's Relation,* the book was the first account of the Plymouth settlement. A vivid and remarkably candid narrative, the *Relation* is generally thought to be the work of Edward Winslow (1595–1655), **William Bradford** (1590–1657), and possibly other colonists, compiled by Morton.

HOWARD NEMEROV (1920–1991) was born in New York City, graduated from Harvard College in 1941, and served as a pilot in World War II. He spent summers on the Cape in Brewster and Wellfleet. Best known as a poet, Nemerov received the Pulitzer Prize, the National Book Award, and the Bollingen Prize for his verse. During his long career he taught at many colleges and universities, including Benning-ton, Brandeis, and Washington University, St. Louis. In 1988 he served as U.S. Poet Laureate.

NOSAPOCKET (Ramona Peters) was born in Hyannis, Massachusetts, in 1952, and educated at Bacone Junior College in Bacone, Oklahoma, and the University of Arizona, from which she received a B.A. in Ele-mentary Education. A member of the Mashpee Wampanoag tribe, she has worked in Indian education programs in Cape Cod schools, as cul-tural arts instructor and spiritual specialist at the Wampanoag Nation

House in West Barnstable, and as Wampanoag Indian interpreter at Plimoth Plantation. She has been Indian cultural specialist for the University of Arizona, the Ford Foundation, and the John Muir Institute in Napa, California, and has served as a delegate to numerous Native American societies. She recently illustrated a children's book, *Strawberry Thanksgiving,* by Paula Jennings.

MARY OLIVER (b. 1935) was born in Cleveland, Ohio, and attended Ohio State University and Vassar College. She worked at Steepletop, the estate of **Edna St. Vincent Millay,** as secretary for the poet's sister. Since 1964 she has lived in Provincetown, where she has served as chairman of the writing department of the Fine Arts Work Center. Oliver is the author of seven books of poetry. *American Primitive* won the Pulitzer Prize for poetry in 1984, and *New and Selected Poems* (1992) received the National Book Award. She has been a visiting faculty member at Case Western Reserve University and Sweet Briar College.

AMOS OTIS (1801–1875), a native of Barnstable, spent his early years on his father's farm, taught in local schools as a young man, and spent most of his life as a bank cashier in Yarmouth. He was a prolific and popular columnist in local Cape Cod newspapers. His uncompleted *Genealogical Notes on Barnstable Families* appeared as a series of articles in *The Yarmouth Register* in the 1870s and was published posthumously in 1888.

JACQUELYN HOLT PARK (b. 1937) was born in Bath, New York, and educated at the University of North Carolina, Columbia University, and the University of the Pacific. She was guidance counselor at the Truro and Provincetown Elementary Schools in the 1970s and principal of the Provincetown Elementary School for three years. Currently she teaches writing at Western Connecticut State University. *A Stone Gone Mad* (1991) was her first book.

CHARLES H. PHILBRICK (1922–1971) was born in Providence, Rhode Island, and graduated from Brown University, where he taught English from 1947 to 1971. He summered with his family in Wellfleet for many years and was a friend of **Conrad Aiken, John Hay,** and other poets living on the Cape. In addition to *Wonderstrand Revisited: A Cape Cod Sequence* (1960), he published several other volumes of verse and poetry anthologies.

MARGE PIERCY (b. 1936) was born in Detroit, Michigan, and graduated from the University of Michigan. During the 1960s she was a political organizer for radical antiwar groups, an experience which was used in her novel *Vida* (1980). Most of her novels and much of her poetry explore the relationship between personal and political issues, particularly political self-awareness in women's lives. Since 1971 she has lived in Wellfleet, where she and her husband, the novelist **Ira Wood,** are prolific gardeners. Many of her poems have been inspired by the Cape Cod landscape, and her novel *Summer People* (1989) is set in Wellfleet.

ELIZABETH REYNARD (1896–1962) was born in Boston and graduated from Barnard College. She was for many years Associate Professor of Literature at Barnard and an outstanding scholar in eighteenth-century English literature and American literature. During World War II she served in the WAVES and attained the rank of lieutenant commander. For many years she shared a home in Chatham with her friend Virginia Gildersleeve, Dean of Barnard. It was during her time on the Cape she unearthed and collected, often from oral sources, the material for her "individual renderings" of the legends, tales, and folk chronicles in *The Narrow Land* (1934). In addition, she is the author of *The Mutinous Wind,* a novel based on the legend of the pirate Black Sam Bellamy, captain of the *Whydah,* and Goody Hallett, the "Witch of Eastham."

SHEBNAH RICH (1824–1907) was born in Truro, the son of Shebna Rich, a master mariner. (He is said to have added the "h" to his name to distinguish himself from his father.) He lived most of his life in Boston, where he was a commission merchant, but summered at the family homestead on Long Nook Road. In addition to *Truro—Cape Cod,* he published a pamphlet titled "New England Mackerel Fisheries." According to a Truro Historic Resources Survey, his daughter Evelyn, a meticulous student of Rich family history, did not consider her father very accurate and was not pleased to have the Rich genealogy included in his book; her copy of the history is said to contain numerous penciled corrections in her hand.

WYMAN RICHARDSON (1890–1948) was born in Boston and graduated from Harvard Medical School. He learned ornithology as a boy by studying birds in the Boston Public Gardens and hunting them in the ponds and marshes of Eastham. He practiced medicine in Milton, Massachusetts, and "escaped at every opportunity" to his beloved Farmhouse, a two-hundred-year-old Cape half-house overlooking Salt Pond in Eastham. The essays in *The House on Nauset Marsh* appeared originally in the *Atlantic* and were published posthumously in 1955.

GEORGE SANTAYANA (1863–1952), philosopher and writer, was born in Spain, reared in Boston, and graduated from Harvard. From 1889 to 1912 he taught literature and philosophy at Harvard, where one of his students was the poet **Conrad Aiken.** During this period he made many trips to the Cape, including a summer picnic excursion at Wareham which inspired the lyric "Cape Cod." After 1914 he lived in Europe. Among his best-known works are *The Life of Reason* (1905–6), a five-volume treatise on the role of reason in human experience, and *The Last Puritan: A Memoir in the Form of a Novel* (1936).

THOMAS SHEPARD (1609–1649) was a Cambridge-educated preacher in England. In 1635 he was banned for his Puritanism and emigrated to New England. There he was a prominent clergyman in Cambridge, Massachusetts, a prolific writer, and one of the founders of Harvard College. He preached extensively to the region's Indians and one of his works, *The Sincere Convert* (1941) was translated into the Algonquin language.

ROGER SKILLINGS (b. 1937) was born in Bath, Maine, and attended Bowdoin College. He was a Fellow at the Provincetown Fine Arts Work Center from 1969 to 1971. His other works include *Alternative Lives* (1974) and *In a Murderous Time* (1982). He currently lives in Provincetown.

WALTER TELLER (b. 1910), journalist and writer, was born in New Orleans and graduated from Haverford College. He was cofounder and copublisher of the *Bucks County* (Pennsylvania) *Gazette* and has taught writing at the New School for Social Research and the Bread Loaf Writers' Conference. In addition to *Cape Cod and the Offshore Islands* (1970) he is the author and editor of more than a dozen books, including several volumes on the life and voyages of Captain Joshua Slocum.

LEWIS THOMAS (b. 1913), physician and writer, was born in Flushing, New York. He has had a long and distinguished medical career, including presidency of the Memorial Sloane-Kettering Cancer Center. His first collection of essays, *The Lives of a Cell* (1974), won the National Book Award. His most recent book is *The Fragile Species* (1992).

HENRY DAVID THOREAU (1817–1862), native of Concord, graduated from Harvard College in 1837 and became a friend **Ralph Waldo Emerson** and other Concord writers. He called himself "a mystic, a transcendentalist, and a natural philosopher to boot." His best-known works are *Walden: or, Life in the Woods* (1854), "Civil Disobedience" (1849), and his fourteen-volume *Journal* (1906). *Cape Cod,* published posthumously in 1865, was based on visits he made there in 1849, 1850, and 1855; some chapters originally appeared in *Putnam's Magazine* and *Atlantic Monthly.*

KURT VONNEGUT, JR. (b. 1922), was born in Indianapolis, studied biochemistry at Cornell University, and was drafted into the infantry during World War II, where he was captured by the Germans and survived the fire-bombing of Dresden by Allied bombers. During the 1950s and 1960s he lived in Barnstable and taught at the Hopefield School in Sandwich. His many novels include *Player Piano* (1952), *Cat's Cradle* (1963), and *Slaughterhouse Five* (1969). His first play, *Happy Birthday,*

Wanda June, was first produced on Cape Cod in 1960. *Welcome to the Monkey House* (1968), a short-story collection, contains several stories set on the Cape and an introductory essay, "Where I Live," on Barnstable Village.

MARY HEATON VORSE (1874–1966) was born in New York and raised in Amherst, Massachusetts. She lived in Greenwich Village in the early 1900s and in 1907 came to Provincetown, which remained her residence for the rest of her life. Widowed twice, she wrote magazine stories to support her children and was one of the founding sponsors of the Provincetown Players. During her lifetime she was best known as the foremost pioneer of labor journalism in the United States in such works as *Men and Steel* and *Labor's Millions,* and as an activist for socialism, women's rights, and world peace. "Kibbe Cook's house," the full Cape in which she lived for nearly sixty years on Provincetown's Commercial Street, is described in detail in her memoir *Of Time and the Town* (1942), and is marked with a plaque in her honor.

MARY-LOU WEISMAN (b. 1937) was born in New Haven, Connecticut, and graduated from Brandeis University. She has been a reporter and humor columnist and was the author of the *New York Times* syndicated column "One Woman's Voice" from 1978 to 1980. In 1982 she published *Intensive Care: A Family Love Story,* a chronicle of her son's death from muscular dystrophy.

RICHARD WILBUR (b. 1921), one of America's foremost living poets, was born in New York City and graduated from Amherst College. He has spent summers in Brewster and Wellfleet. Wilbur has published more than a dozen volumes of poetry (including *Things of This World,* which won both the Pulitzer Prize and the National Book Award in 1957) and is well known as a translator of the plays of Molière and other dramatists. He has taught English at Harvard, Wellesley, and Wesleyan College and since 1977 has been writer-in-residence at Smith College in Northampton, Massachusetts. In 1987 he served as this country's second Poet Laureate.

ALEC WILKINSON (b. 1952) was born in Mount Kisco, New York, and graduated from Bennington College. He worked as a police officer in Wellfleet, an experience related in *Midnights* (1982). *The Riverkeeper* (1991) contains a section on the Provincetown fishing fleet.

EDMUND WILSON (1895–1972) was born in Red Bank, New Jersey, and graduated from Princeton in 1916. Primarily known as one of this country's foremost literary critics (*Axel's Castle,* 1931; *The Shores of Light,* 1952; *Patriotic Gore,* 1962; etc.), he was also the author of novels, travel books, essay collections, volumes of poetry, histories, social criticism, and plays, as well as editor of several posthumous works by his lifelong friend F. Scott Fitzgerald. Wilson first came to Cape Cod in 1920 and courted **Edna St. Vincent Millay.** During the 1920s and 1930s he was an active member of Provincetown's summer art and literary community. In 1941 he and his second wife, the writer Mary McCarthy, bought a house in Wellfleet, where he lived for the rest of his life. His extensive observations and reflections on his life on Cape Cod are found primarily in a series of volumes of collected notebook and diary entries—*The Twenties* (1975), *The Thirties* (1980), *The Forties* (1983), and *The Fifties* (1986)—edited by Leon Edel.

DAVID WOJAHN (b. 1953) was born in St. Paul, Minnesota, and educated at the University of Minnesota and the University of Arizona. A Fellow at the Fine Arts Work Center in Provincetown in 1980 and 1983, he has published three books of poetry: *Icehouse Lights* (1982), which won the Yale Younger Poets Prize; *Glassworks* (1987); and *Mystery Train* (1990). He now lives in Chicago and teaches at Indiana University, where he is Lilly Professor of Poetry.

IRA WOOD (b. 1950) was born in New York City and graduated from the State University of New York at Albany in 1971. He is the author of two novels, *Kitchen Man* (1986) and *Going Public* (1991), and several works of interactive fiction for children and young adults. In 1976 he came to Cape Cod and married the author **Marge Piercy,** with whom he co-authored a play, *The Last White Class* (1980). They now live, write and garden in Wellfleet. "As a city person," he writes, I found the adjustment to the Cape difficult, some evenings driving fifty miles to the mall to try on work boots for diversion. Eventually tiring of seeing the same movie three nights running, I turned in desperation to reading. (I had actually mastered the mechanics before entering grade school but had not had the occasion to use them until moving to a town where the TV reception was pure snow on all three channels and the last store closed at six.) One of the first things I noticed about the Cape was that everyday working people did not think it odd to see me at all hours of the day, not at work, but just walking around town thinking. Of course, this could have been due to the staggering rate of off-season unemployment but I chose to see it as an example of their long history of toleration for artists."

Permissions

Copyright © renewed 1988 by Thornton W. Burgess. By permission of Little, Brown and Company.

Carlson, Douglas: "Eastham" from *At the Edge* by Douglas Carlson. Reprinted by permission of White Pine Press.

Corbett, Scott: "The Reverend Horatio Alger, Jr." from *Cape Cod's Way*. Copyright © 1955 by Scott Corbett. Copyright renewed 1983. Reprinted by permission of Curtis Brown, Ltd. Copyright by Devin-Adair Publishers, Inc., Old Greenwich, Connecticut, 06870. Permission granted to reprint "Sears Village" from *We Chose Cape Cod* by Scott Corbett. All rights reserved.

Dickens, Monica: Excerpts from *Cape Cod* by William B. Berchen Monica Dickens. Copyright © 1972 by William B. Berchen. Text copyright © 1972 by Monica Dickens. Used by permission of Viking Penguin, a division of Penguin Books USA Inc.

Dillard, Annie: "Ship in a Bottle" by Annie Dillard originally published in *Harper's Magazine* September, 1989. Copyright © 1989 by Annie Dillard. Reprinted by permission of the author and Blanche C. Gregory, Inc.

Doty, Mark: "Difference" from *My Alexandria* (Champaign: University of Illinois Press, 1993) © Mark Doty. "Rope" and "A Letter from the Coast" © 1993 Mark Doty. Reprinted by permission of Mark Doty.

Dugan, Alan: "Note: The Sea Grinds Things Up" © 1961, 1962, 1968, 1972, 1973, 1974, 1983 by Alan Dugan. From *New and Collected Poems 1961–1983*, first published by The Ecco Press in 1983. Reprinted by permission.

Finch, Robert: Excerpt reprinted from *The Cape Itself,* Text by Robert Finch, Photographs by Ralph MacKenzie, by permission of W. W. Norton & Company, Inc. Text copyright © 1991 by Robert Finch. Photographs copyright © 1991 by Ralph MacKenzie. "The Legend of Screaming Island" copyright © 1992 by Robert Finch. Reprinted by permission of the author.

Galvin, Brendan: "Place Keepers," "Pitch Pines," "An Old Map of Barnstable County" from *Atlantic Flyaway* by Brendan Galvin. Copyright © 1980 by Brendan Galvin. Reprinted by permission of the author. "Lost Countrymen," "Winter Oysters" from *Winter Oysters* by Brendan Galvin. Copyright © 1983 by Brendan Galvin. Reprinted by permission of the author.

Goldman, E. S.: "Earthly Justice" from *Earthly Justice*. Originally published by Another Chicago Press / TriQuarterly Books. Used by permission.

Index

Released Back into the Sea"
(Oliver), 232
Huntington, Cynthia, 167, 234
"Hyannis Port Story, The" (Vonnegut), 331

"In Blackwater Woods" (Oliver),
230
In Great Waters (Berger), 162

James, Henry, 305
Jennings, Herman A., 198
Joe Crocker and the Sabbath Whales
(Berger), 127
Journal of Henry David Thoreau, The
(Thoreau), 261
Journals (Emerson), 63

Kahn, E. J., Jr., 344
"Katy Dos Passos" (Wilson), 279
Kazin, Alfred, 341
Keller, Helen, 310
**Kendell, Edward Augustus, 59,
123**
Kitchen Man, The (Wood), 354
**Kittredge, Henry C., 54, 72, 78,
116, 146, 147, 152, 168,
170, 173, 255, 366**
Kunitz, Stanley, 128, 308

Lazell, James, 248
Legend of Maushop, The (Nosapocket), 9
"Legend of Screaming Island, The"
(Finch), 101
Leighton, Clare, 316
"Letter from the Coast, A" (Doty),
297
"Letter to My Summer House
Guests" (Weisman), 359
Lincoln, Captain Joseph, 157
Lincoln, Emily, 157
Lincoln, Joseph C., 85, 145
"Literary Life on the Cape" (Kahn),
344
Lives of a Cell, The (Thomas), 379
"Lost Countrymen" (Galvin), 373

Martin, William, 108
Maushop's Smoke (Alden), 6
"Mayflower," from (Aiken), 14, 96
"MBL, The" (Thomas), 379
Melville, Herman, 76, 112
Memorabilia of Yarmouth (Alden), 6
"Memory of Cape Cod" (Millay),
314
Merton, Thomas, 307
Methodist Ministers (Kittredge), 54
Millay, Edna St. Vincent, 314
Millennium Grove (Thoreau), 304
Ministers and Whales (Thoreau),
110
"Mirage on the Dunes" (Reynard), 6
Mitchell, Susan, 285
Moby-Dick (Melville), 76, 112
Mooncussers and the Wreck of the
Whydah (Kittredge), 147
Mooncussers of Cape Cod (Kittredge),
170, 173
Mourt, G., 17
Mourt's Relation, from (Mourt), 17
Moving In (Aiken), 315
"Mussels" (Oliver), 228

Narrow Land, The (Reynard), 6, 8,
30, 44, 52
Nature's Year (Hay), 89
Nauset Indian's Dream of the Black
Man, A (Shepard), 13
"Nauset Sands" (Bishop), 197
Nemerov, Howard, 223
New York Jew (Kazin), 341
Night at the Pilgrim House, A (Thoreau), 261
Nosapocket, 9, 56, 406
"Not Any's" Representatives (Thoreau), 29
"Note: The Sea Grinds Things Up"
(Dugan), 224
Now I Remember (Burgess), 120

Of Plymouth Plantation, from (Bradford), 14